Shading, Lighting, and Rendering with Blender EEVEE

Create amazing concept art 12 times faster using a real-time rendering engine

Sammie Crowder

BIRMINGHAM—MUMBAI

Shading, Lighting, and Rendering with Blender EEVEE

Group Product Manager: Rohit Rajkumar
Publishing Product Manager: Kaustubh Manglurkar
Senior Editor: Keagan Carneiro
Content Development Editor: Adrija Mitra
Technical Editor: Saurabh Kadave
Copy Editor: Safis Editing
Project Coordinator: Rashika Ba
Proofreader: Safis Editing
Indexer: Subalakshmi Govindhan
Production Designer: Ponraj Dhandapani
Marketing Coordinator: Elizabeth Varghese

First published: April 2022

Production reference: 2240622

Published by Packt Publishing Ltd.
Livery Place
35 Livery Street
Birmingham
B3 2PB, UK.

978-1-80323-096-2

`www.packt.com`

To my mom, dad, and brother, who have always made life exciting. To Bremen and Paige, who didn't mind me playing with Blender for 4 hours a night during the graveyard shift. Without you both I would never have gotten this far. And to Jen, who inspires me every day and stuck with me through every chapter of this book.

Contributors

About the author

Sammie Crowder first discovered Blender 8 years ago, and she has been using it to create ever since. After self-teaching while working at a library for several years, she started using Blender as an educator, creating short - and long-form animations that explain complex scientific concepts for the University of Colorado. Following several years of developing that program, she transitioned to using Blender 3D to create synthetic data for machine learning applications. Her current focus is on education, using Blender and other tools to get underserved groups into technology and art-based industries. She lives in beautiful Colorado with a dog, two cats, a lizard, and her partner. When she's not working in Blender she likes to read, hike, and garden.

I would like to thank the generous developers at the Blender Foundation for creating such a wonderful software package and providing it to people for free. I would also like to thank the Blender community, who provide awesome content to learn this software and create amazing works of art that never cease to inspire me.

About the reviewers

Volodymyr Borovkov is an experienced freelance 3D artist who is currently working in the automotive industry and has used Blender since 2014. He also has expertise as a Blender teacher, UE5 real-time rendering artist, game designer, RaceSim modder, and 2D designer.

Stephan Seeliger is a 3D artist with over 10 years of experience in Blender. He is a full-time system operator and has been running his own 3D company (CG-Mechanics) for over 2 years, which deals with 3D reconstructions. At the same time, he regularly publishes German Blender tutorials on his YouTube channel *Geblendert*, helping Blender beginners get started. His technical background consists not only of many years of experience in Blender, but also of a degree in technical computer science. He tries to carry technical workflows with Blender and other programs into the industry and expand the 3D area there.

Table of Contents

3
Lights, Camera...

4
Non-Physical Rendering

Section 2: Real-Time Rendering – Mini-Project 2 – Creating a Realistic Environment Concept

5
Setting Up an Environment with Geometry Nodes

6

Screen Space Reflections – Adding Reflection to the Water

7

Faking Camera Effects for Better Renders

8

Using Alphas for Details

Section 3: Advanced Features – Mini-Project 3 – Creating a Sci-Fi Concept

9

Lighting an Interior Scene

10
Working with Irradiance Volumes and Cubemaps for More Accurate Rendering

11
Kitbashing – Adding Details Fast

12
Special Effects with EEVEE – Fire and Smoke

13
Exploring the Wide World of Blender

Preface

3D animation has always been a difficult art to master. First, there's the complicated software, the artistic sensibility required, and the need for expensive computer equipment. However, as the discipline has evolved, more and more people have been able to clear these necessary hurdles to learn 3D and advance the overall complexity and ability of animation and design. Nothing else has quite brought the art form to the masses like Blender 3D. Officially created in 1994, Blender 3D has evolved over the past years to slowly become the only open source 3D application available for free to any user who cares to download it. The open source aspect facilitates a truly amazing and supportive Blender community. I myself started using Blender as a hobbyist and, thanks to the superb support of the Blender community, managed to learn and grow enough to transition to using it for work and have been working as a 3D professional ever since.

Over the years, Blender has gone through a great many iterations, adding a truly crazy feature set: not only can you animate, but you can also rig, texture, simulate, video edit, and much, much more. The most groundbreaking release of the last few years was the 2.8 release, which changed fundamental aspects of the UI, but also added some amazing features that we, as artists, can leverage to create work faster and with improved control.

Who this book is for

This book represents an intermediate-to-advanced look at a specific part of Blender: The EEVEE rendering engine. This rendering engine is a specific and unique part of Blender, but also interacts with every other aspect of Blender on every level, which is why we'll still be covering Materials, Lighting, Cameras, and every other aspect you may have learned about before in 3D, but from another angle. We'll also cover some brand-new aspects of Blender, including Geometry Nodes, the Asset Browser, and more, so there's something for everyone. I want this book to show you how to do things faster and with more direction. This book will provide practical tips that will guide someone already familiar with Blender to make huge strides with EEVEE in a small amount of time. It doesn't matter whether you're a hobbyist, a 3D artist, or a developer looking to expand your horizons, I know firsthand the frustration of having something not turn out how you want it and having to start your 748-hour render all over again, along with the annoyance of having a bad computer and not being able to make the things you want owing to that limitation. I want this book to help you overcome those problems and make cool art and design work that you can put in a portfolio or show your friends, with them not believing how easy it actually is to use EEVEE.

A lot of the principles we're going to cover also have applications in game design. Game Engines are real-time renderers by necessity. Most things inside EEVEE have a direct crossover to Unreal Engine or Unity. If you want to start creating your own games, it's a great idea to learn EEVEE so that you can understand how Game Engines work as well as use Blender to make assets.

Whatever your reasoning, Blender's EEVEE real-time rendering engine is one of the best innovations to come out of the Blender Foundation in years.

What this book covers

Chapter 1, *Introducing EEVEE – A Real-Time Rendering Engine*, talks about what makes EEVEE important to an artist, and why they should consider using EEVEE for their art, while also introducing the mini-project format.

Chapter 2, *Creating Materials Fast with EEVEE*, explains how to quickly create materials that can be used in enabling you to come up with different ideas quickly. This will include making procedural and non-procedural textures, as well as using Blender 3.0's Asset Manager. They will then apply those materials to the first part of the mini-project.

Chapter 3, *Lights, Camera...*, describes the basic settings of lighting and how to use a camera to render a scene in EEVEE, This way, you will have a base-level knowledge of why it is different from a ray-tracing engine and become familiar with the quirks of a real-time engine.

Chapter 4, Non-Physical Rendering, demonstrates how to finish off our non-realistic scene by using different techniques to what will be looked over in the later chapters dealing with realistic renders. We'll configure rendering settings, show how to integrate other aspects of Blender (compositing, grease pencil, and the like), and finish off our mini-project.

Chapter 5, Setting Up an Environment with Geometry Nodes, heralds the start of a new mini-project. This time, we'll work on some more realistic subject matter by undertaking an outdoor environment scene. This chapter will be about prepping our environment (ground plane, lights, and camera) and then using Geometry Nodes to scatter a number of props around the scene.

Chapter 6, Screen Space Reflections – Adding Reflection to the Water, provides information about Screen Space Reflection functionality, while also explaining how to use Reflection Planes and Reflection Cubemaps. This will allow us to enhance the realistic rendering of water in the scene and provide a much better output.

Chapter 7, Faking Camera Effects for Better Renders, discusses the render panel at length and talks about the various ways to fake realistic effects that EEVEE offers. This will cover ambient occlusion, bloom, depth of field, shadows, indirect lighting, and other aspects that can help to fine-tune a render.

Chapter 8, Using Alphas for Details, includes a lot of miscellaneous tips and tricks for getting EEVEE to work a lot better with an environmental scene by using Alphas to fake birds in the scene, fake volumetrics, and more. We will then walk through the render settings for a realistic scene.

Chapter 9, Lighting an Interior Scene, covers how, in this chapter, we'll look at ways to make lighting faster in EEVEE, how to troubleshoot some common lighting problems, and how to create some cool effects with the lights.

Chapter 10, Working with Irradiance Volumes and Cubemaps for Accurate Rendering, demonstrates how to make Irradiance Volumes and Reflection Cubemaps, how to position them, how to work with the lighting to get the correct result through baking, and why these tools are needed to achieve close-to-realistic lighting.

Chapter 11, KitBashing – Adding Details Fast, in this chapter, by using simple assets pre-prepared for the user, we will work through the idea of using smaller pieces that can be duplicated to create intricate sci-fi designs. We will also introduce the concept of trim sheets and talk about shortcuts to use in creating materials for sci-fi scenes.

Chapter 12, Special Effects with EEVEE – Fire and Smoke, includes a brief workflow for simulating fire and smoke inside of EEVEE. Because there aren't any great ways to do this as easily as in Cycles, this will also include some tips to create a better shader in volumetrics, how to utilize the quick smoke function for faster results, and how to cache the simulation to keep working on the scene better. A brief overview of how to use Cycles and EEVEE together will also be provided.

Chapter 13, Exploring the Wide World of Blender, endeavors to provide you with a jumping-off point, along with suggestions on how to further the knowledge that has been acquired in this book, including personal projects to tackle, further books to read, and other resources to get more information on this topic and others related to it.

To get the most out of this book

From a basic technical perspective, it's important to have a working internet connection, some storage space on your computer, a three-button mouse, and hardware that is compatible with Blender (learn more at `https://www.blender.org/download/requirements/`).

This book is an intermediate to advanced level overview, so it assumes that you have some basic knowledge of Blender and have worked with the program before. That's not to say you should know every single thing about Blender (which might be impossible!), but you should at least know basic modeling, how to add objects, how to add materials, lights, cameras, and how to render (generally). There will be portions of the methodology that I will skip over to get to the meat of the topic quickly, so if you don't have some of this basic knowledge, you might struggle to use some of the more complicated tools. If you don't have all the knowledge suggested, I suggest looking into other *Packt* publications (*Blender 3D by Example*, by *Oscar Baechler and Xury Greer*, is highly recommended) to learn some of these base skills because we will be building on top of them. Or, if you're a fast learner, feel free to work through these mini-projects and then do outside research on any aspect you feel isn't covered to your satisfaction. The great thing, as I've said, is that Blender is very community-focused and someone on *StackExchange* (`https://blender.stackexchange.com/`) or *BlenderArtist* (`https://blenderartists.org/`) will be more than willing to answer your question. All the information is out in the open, ready for you to assimilate and deploy it. If you're not quite sure you have enough background information to start the book, I would recommend working through Andrew Price's *Beginner Series* to give yourself a better foundation for the mini-projects we'll be completing. That beginner's series is available on Youtube at `https://www.youtube.com/user/AndrewPPrice`.

Software/hardware covered in the book	Operating system requirements
Blender 3.0	Windows, macOS, or Linux
PureRef (optional)	Windows, macOS, or Linux
Krita (optional)	Windows, macOS, or Linux

PureRef and Krita are optional (free) downloads, but I find they are useful in planning and editing images.

Download the example code files

You can download the supporting files for this book from GitHub at `https://github.com/PacktPublishing/Shading-Lighting-and-Rendering-with-Blenders-EEVEE`. If there's an update to any file, it will be updated in the GitHub repository.

Download the color images

We also provide a PDF file that has color images of the screenshots and diagrams used in this book. You can download it here: `https://static.packt-cdn.com/downloads/9781803230962_ColorImages.pdf`.

Conventions used

There are a number of text conventions used throughout this book.

`Code in text`: Indicates code words in the text, database table names, folder names, filenames, file extensions, pathnames, dummy URLs, user input, and Twitter handles. Here is an example: "In the `Chapter 12-Start.blend` file, I have hidden our Hangar from view so that we can create the fire without Blender having to render the entire scene plus the fire at once."

Bold: Indicates a new term, an important word, or words that you see on screen. For instance, words in menus or dialog boxes appear in **bold**. Here is an example: "Next, go to the **Object** menu located in the top-left corner (next to the **Add** menu) and click on it."

> **Tips or Important Notes**
> Appear like this.

Get in touch

Feedback from our readers is always welcome.

General feedback: If you have questions about any aspect of this book, email us at customercare@packtpub.com and mention the book title in the subject of your message.

Errata: Although we have taken every care to ensure the accuracy of our content, mistakes do happen. If you have found a mistake in this book, we would be grateful if you would report this to us. Please visit www.packtpub.com/support/errata and fill in the form.

Piracy: If you come across any illegal copies of our works in any form on the internet, we would be grateful if you would provide us with the location address or website name. Please contact us at copyright@packt.com with a link to the material.

If you are interested in becoming an author: If there is a topic that you have expertise in and you are interested in either writing or contributing to a book, please visit authors.packtpub.com.

Share Your Thoughts

Once you've read *Shading, Lighting, and Rendering with Blender's EEVEE*, we'd love to hear your thoughts! Scan the QR code below to go straight to the Amazon review page for this book and share your feedback.

https://packt.link/r/1803230967

Your review is important to us and the tech community and will help us make sure we're delivering excellent quality content.

Section 1: Configuring in EEVEE – Mini-Project 1 – Stylized Scene

Let's jump right into creating a scene. In this section, we're going to learn how to optimize materials for EEVEE, create lights and cameras, and render the final scene. After finishing this section of the book, you should have the confidence to create your own stylized scene.

In this section, we will cover the following chapters:

- *Chapter 1, Introducing EEVEE – A Real-Time Rendering Engine*
- *Chapter 2, Creating Materials Fast with EEVEE*
- *Chapter 3, Lights, Camera...*
- *Chapter 4, Non-Physical Rendering*

1
Introducing EEVEE – A Real-Time Rendering Engine

With the 2.8 release, Blender has added another rendering engine to its already impressive software: EEVEE. EEVEE is a real-time rendering engine that allows artists to preview their work quickly and accurately, as well as cutting down render times and a need for top-of-the-line GPUs or expert experience. This book will be an intermediate/advanced look at EEVEE, detailing the many ways you can use EEVEE to create awesome, fast concept art and get to your final render faster, with more ability to iterate on style, content, and direction. This book will go through three different mini-projects that will introduce various styles and content that will be immediately applicable to any project, for any user from professionals to hobbyists.

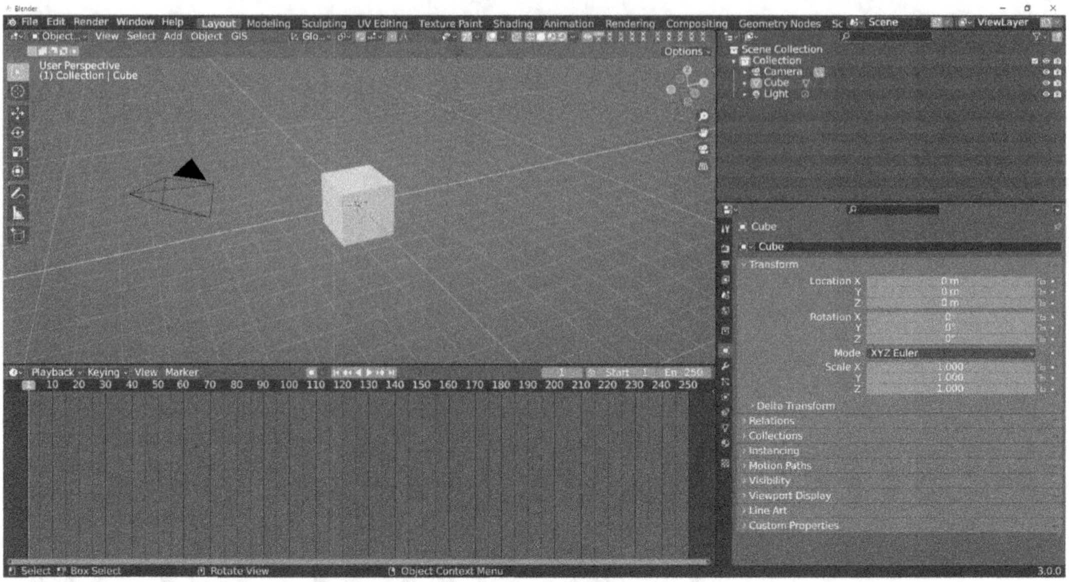

Figure 1.1: The Blender UI

We'll be using the Blender 3.0 release, which has some completely new and fantastic features that even industry pros will want to know more about. EEVEE has been updated in this version to be faster and expand the array of features already available. As more and more studios make use of real-time rendering and other ray-tracing shortcuts, the tips and tricks in this book will become more and more essential to animation as an industry, setting you up to be ahead of the curve when it comes to creating fast, interesting, and flexible art.

In this chapter, we'll learn what EEVEE is and configure Blender for our upcoming mini-projects.

The main topics we'll be covering are as follows:

- What is EEVEE? EEVEE as a rendering engine
- Why use EEVEE and what are the advantages of using EEVEE?
- Configuring the start of mini-projects

Technical requirements

This chapter is mostly an introduction to the technology, but having the latest version of Blender downloaded from `https://www.blender.org/` is recommended to be able to start exploring the world of EEVEE, and can provide a useful point of reference as we talk about limitations. Another great point of reference is Blender's docs: `https://docs.blender.org/manual/en/latest/render/eevee/index.html`.

We'll go over many of the things covered inside the EEVEE official docs, but reading through and being familiar with the various terms will help you to pick up some of these concepts faster as we encounter them in our mini-projects.

What is EEVEE? EEVEE as a rendering engine

Before we dive headfirst into the absolutely astounding feature set that EEVEE provides, let's cover a little bit of what makes it so great, but also touch on some of the limitations.

EEVEE is an acronym that stands for **Extra Easy Virtual Environment Engine**, though originally it was named after the evolution Pokémon, Eevee. EEVEE is a *real-time* rendering engine. By real-time, we mean that we can preview our animations and designs in real time (or as close to it as physically possible). We can make changes to materials and instantly get an idea of what exactly is happening with those materials. We can move lights and cameras freely to understand what we're framing and how we're framing it. As you can imagine, this ability to see things in real time is a game-changer. But EEVEE isn't the only real-time engine being implemented in state-of-the-art graphics programs. Other real-time rendering engines that work similarly to EEVEE are Unreal Engine and Unity. As you may know, both of these are game engines, and as such are primarily used to create video games. As it utilizes the same rendering system as a game engine, it's very easy to see how EEVEE can be much faster than a render engine of a different style.

Most 3D artists are very familiar with ray-tracing. This is the most common method of scene calculation, where light rays are shot from lights then bounced off surfaces a specific number of times, providing illumination, material properties, and camera initialization. Being a real-time rendering engine, EEVEE does not perform light calculations like a ray-tracing engine such as Cycles would. EEVEE performs its scene calculation through a method called rasterization. Rasterization is a scene *estimation* model. This estimation model takes the scene information and provides a visual of what the scene *should* look like, not what it actually looks like. With this scene estimation technique, we can fake effects such as reflections, volume, and global illumination, but it is just that, a fake. We'll go over the optimum ways to fake some of the more advanced results that EEVEE can provide in our three mini-projects, because after all, 3D is all about how to make something look real, while in reality, it's all just pixels on a screen.

While EEVEE differs a lot from Cycles, it is also similar in some ways. EEVEE uses the same shading type as Cycles, which allows an easy transition from Cycles to EEVEE and back again. Most other render engines use this same type of shading, the Physically based shading model that has been the industry standard for many years now. **Physically based shading or physically based rendering** (shortened to **PBR** usually) is a way of calculating how light reflects off objects. It assumes that all objects will reflect light, some more than others, and their reflection values will make them shinier or more diffused. This allows light to be bounced off the objects in a scene. Because EEVEE uses PBR, we can use material shaders to determine how the light will bounce off something, or how the light will pass through something. These principles directly transfer from Cycles or another ray-tracing engine, so having some familiarity with those principles is recommended if you want to get the most out of this book.

> **Side Note**
>
> The Blender Foundation hosts a variety of demo files on their website, `https://www.blender.org/download/demo-files/`.
>
> A fantastic way to understand the speed and utility of EEVEE is to take any of the labeled EEVEE files for a test run. Taking inspiration from the way other people have used EEVEE for different kinds of projects and in different production environments can really open your mind to the possibilities of the engine.

Why use EEVEE and what are the advantages of using EEVEE?

EEVEE is an absolutely fantastic set of tools when put in the right artist's hands. This book is a crash course on how to use the tools provided by Blender and EEVEE to create stellar artwork, and one of the first things to learn about a tool is when to use it and when not to.

There are four main ways we can use EEVEE when we're going about creating a 3D scene:

- The first is to use EEVEE to preview our scene, and when we're ready for the final render, switch to Cycles for a more realistic final result. This can save a 3D artist a lot of time by sacrificing some accuracy in the development stage. This is something that we will only cover briefly in this book.
- The second way of creating with EEVEE is to preview and render inside EEVEE. The pros of this are increased speed in previewing and in the final render, but because EEVEE is not a ray-tracing engine, the final render inside EEVEE will potentially be less realistic. This is the type of work we'll be doing in all of the projects that we create in this book.

- The third is the ability to see volumetrics in real time. We'll be exploring volumetrics in great detail in this book, and you'll use them in all the projects we'll work on.
- The last big advantage that we have in EEVEE is the ability to see emissions accurately in the viewport. We can use this as a shortcut to see the results of our light shaders without needing to add them to the compositor later. We'll use this in the third project we work on.

So, for extreme realism, we're always going to want to use a ray-tracing engine. But for speed? The ability to update and preview a scene in real time in the viewport is immensely helpful, particularly for more complicated scenes. It means that you can update, view, and make changes in seconds or minutes, rather than the slower workflow of updating, taking 20 minutes to render for a preview, make changes, and repeat. As artists, we can gain a better understanding of what exactly is happening in our scene, we can apply design and color theory more accurately, and provide the changes our art director wants, faster.

Limitations of EEVEE

In terms of the limitations of EEVEE, we'll cover specific points as we come to them, but when getting yourself set up to start our mini-projects, you should be aware of a few things:

- Firstly, EEVEE works with your GPU to render. While having a beefy GPU isn't exactly necessary, it should be noted that an older or less powerful GPU will slow down your render times a little bit.
- Secondly, because of how EEVEE evaluates lights and materials, there may be points that it fails, situations where you're using too many lights, too many refracted materials, or your GPU gets overloaded and crashes. This won't come up in the mini-projects we're working on in this book, but it's important information to know when you're working beyond this book on your own projects, or in a studio utilizing EEVEE in its pipeline.
- Shading is also a little different in EEVEE. Because we're using the GPU in EEVEE you'll probably run out of memory in EEVEE sooner than Cycles. In shaders, running out of memory will probably look like a texture that turns up pink. Don't worry about this for our projects though, we aren't creating complicated enough textures for this to happen to us. EEVEE also isn't able to utilize Particle Info nodes or bevels, but it does have added nodes such as Shader to RGB that we will explore.

> **Side Note**
>
> A great resource to read through for more information on where EEVEE is weak is the limitations page in the Blender documentation: `https://docs.blender.org/manual/en/latest/render/eevee/limitations.html`.

At its current development stage, EEVEE is not going to be the cure-all for every single problem you face when using a ray-tracing engine. The decision to use EEVEE should always be made with the following in mind:

- Do I need extremely realistic lighting or materials?
- Do I need to work on my CPU exclusively?
- Am I creating effects that need extensive volumetric rendering or similar?
- Do I need extremely complicated materials or utility nodes such as Bevel, Particle Info, or IES Texture?

If you answered yes to any of those questions, use Cycles for your final render, but consider using EEVEE to preview your work. If none of those features are a concern, EEVEE is the way to get results quickly. An alternate third approach is to combine rendered aspects from Cycles and EEVEE, rendering the aspects best done realistically in Cycles and everything else in EEVEE.

As stated previously, many game engines use very similar techniques to EEVEE, so if you're interested in creating game art inside of Unity or Unreal, you'll have a much easier time transferring that knowledge from the concepts we'll cover in this book to your engine of choice.

Before we start implementing the mini-projects, we need to set up and customize Blender.

Setting up – configuring the start of mini-projects

If for some reason you don't have Blender already set up on your computer, let's walk through the steps to install it and talk a little bit about general settings to make your life easier.

Download and install the latest version at `blender.org`. We'll be using the 3.0 release in this book, but if you have computer compatibility problems with that version, feel free to use 2.93, being aware that some aspects covered herein are not available in version 2.93.

After downloading and setting up, we should be ready to roll! Blender is a highly customizable program, though, so if you also want to take time to set up a different color palette or change your viewports, feel free to do that. Some important add-ons to activate in Blender that we will get a lot of use out of are good to set up too.

Navigate to **Edit** in the toolbar, then select **Preferences**.

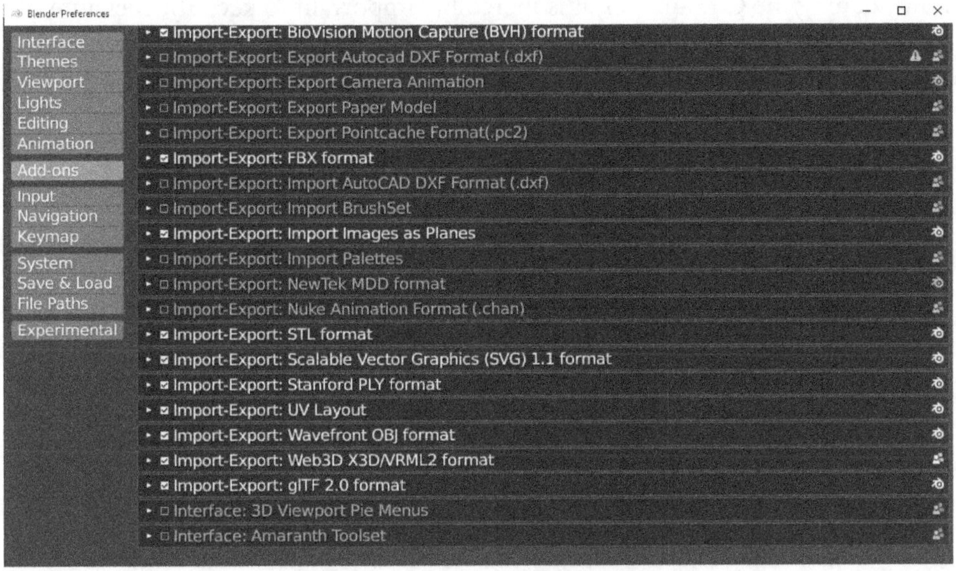

Figure 1.2: The Preferences window

Let's add **Import Images as Planes** and **Node Wrangler** to start with, as we'll get a lot of use out of them. In the search bar, start typing the title of the add-on and it should appear in the window. These add-ons are pre-installed, so we don't have to import a package to activate them; we just have to activate them in the Blender **Preferences** window.

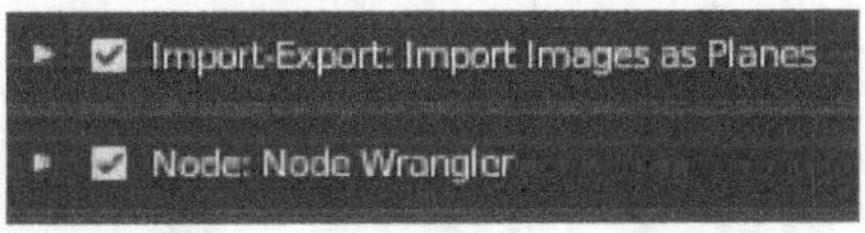

Figure 1.3: Customizing your Blender preferences

File structure

When downloading the GitHub files, it is incredibly important to keep the filenames the same. Blender references texture files, which means that it looks at a file path that you determine to add the textures files to our main Blender file. If Blender loses the file path, it will show up as bright pink in the Rendered and Material views.

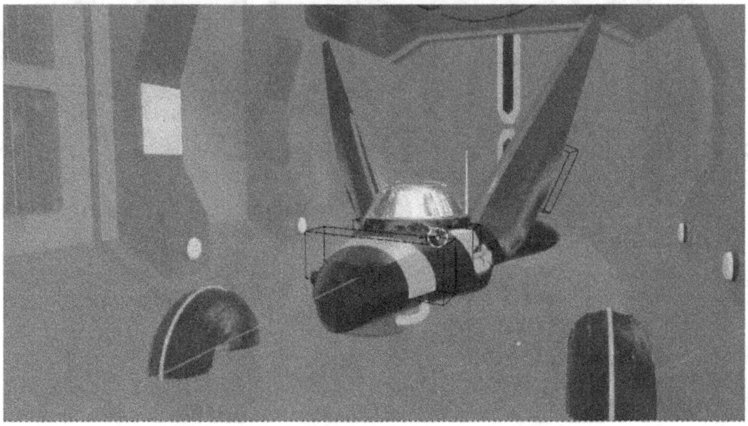

Figure 1.4: The pink textures of death

If you find this happening to you, there's an easy fix. All you need to do is tell Blender the new place to find the textures:

1. Select **File | External Data | Find Missing Files**.

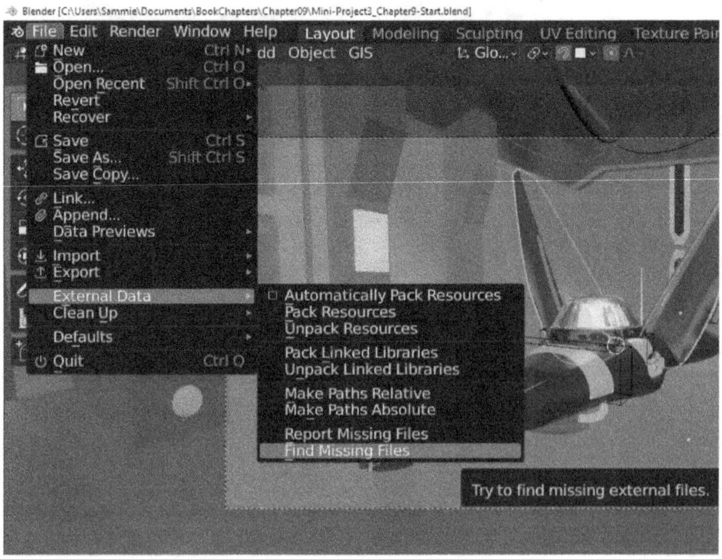

Figure 1.5: Find Missing Files menu

2. Toggle on the **Settings** menu on the right side.

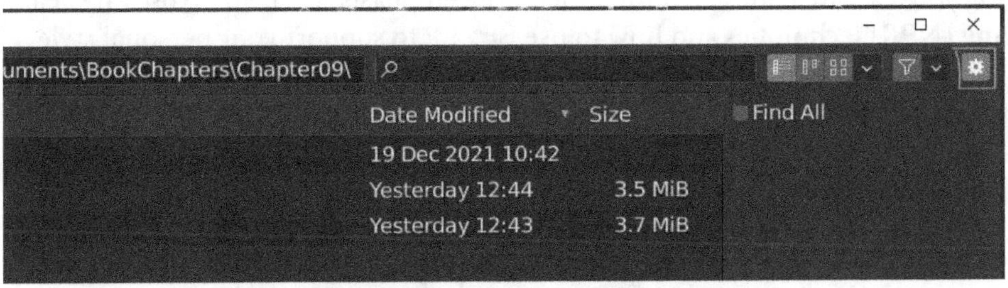

Figure 1.6: Settings menu in Find Missing Files

3. Check the box that says **Find All**.

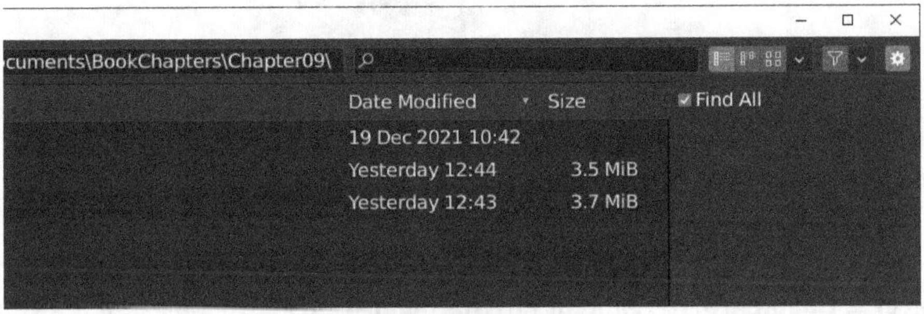

Figure 1.7: Find All

4. Navigate to the file location that contains all the textures for the Blender file.
5. Press *Enter*.

Blender will have found all the texture files, matched them to the original texture names, and refreshed them. Your Material and Rendered views should now be normal, with no bright pink textures.

An overview of the mini-projects

In order to feel like you're able to apply EEVEE to projects, we're going to be working through three different mini-projects so you can understand different applications, different techniques, and even how to blend EEVEE with other ways of rendering. I want you to have fun and look back after finishing this book knowing that you made something tangible and feel confident that you can apply the techniques to your own work.

Mini-project 1: Chapters 2, 3, and 4: Stylized render: We'll look at how to make something you'd see in a Studio Ghibli movie. The emphasis will be on **Non-Physical Rendering** (**NPR**) techniques and how to use EEVEE to support your personal style.

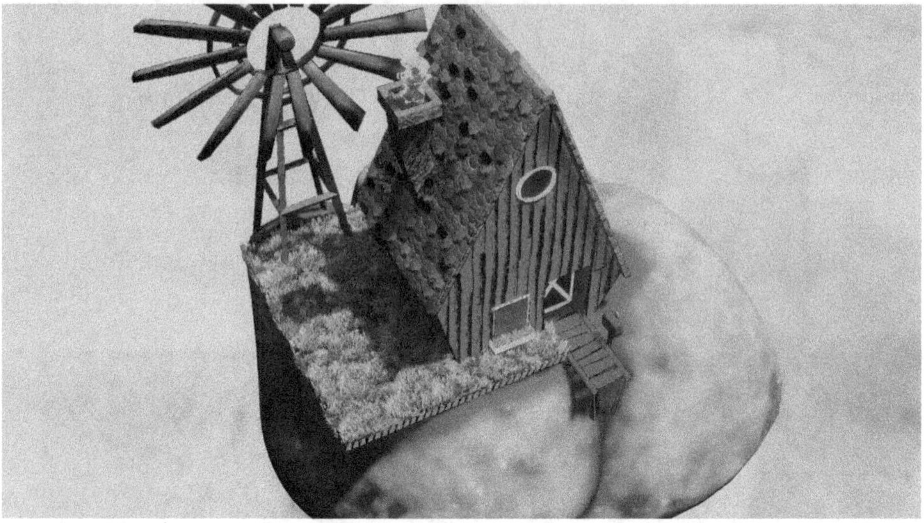

Figure 1.8: The final image from mini-project 1

Mini-project 2: Chapters 5, 6, 7, and 8: Environment scene: We'll look at new features such as Geometry Nodes and how to create more realistic style renders in EEVEE, including shortcuts and tips for faster rendering.

Mini-project 3: Chapters 9, 10, 11, and 12: Sci-fi scene: Kitbashing, rendering effects, and some extremely advanced aspects will be covered to create an out-of-this-world sci-fi scene.

Summary

We talked about the *what* and *why* of EEVEE in this chapter and outlined the contents of the book and what you'll be learning.

In the next chapter, we'll jump headfirst into the *how* of EEVEE, starting with our first mini-project.

2
Creating Materials Fast with EEVEE

This chapter will cover the magic of materials in EEVEE. After modeling, materials can define the look of the scene and give the person who is viewing your art a feel for the texture of the world you're creating. Want to show that an abandoned mansion you're working on is old and falling down? Mix dirt into your materials. Want the nice shiny architectural render you're working on to look sleek and modern? Use reflectivity and shiny materials with little to no dust. There are so many ways to use materials to really bring life to your scene, and we'll cover a couple of them in depth in this chapter.

The focus of this chapter will be stylized materials in EEVEE, but much of this lesson can be applied to any other scene you care to make in Blender. I like to break materials up into two categories, image-based materials and procedural materials. Texture materials are ones that involve using images to create a shader. As an example, using this methodology, we'd download a picture of a lizard's scales and apply it as the diffuse in our shader, and as a result, create a lizard scale material.

Conversely, when working with procedural materials, we're working with Blender's mathematically computed images to create materials. So we can take the **Noise Texture** (an inbuilt texture in our material space) and play around with the values until it looks like a lizard's scales, and then apply it to our shader to create the same material. There are pros and cons to both approaches, but to distill the arguments, image-based materials are easy to create and faster to render but can be hard to scale or edit flexibly. Procedural materials are hard to create but easy to scale and edit flexibly.

In this chapter, we're going to be using both approaches to create two different materials, one being the wooden plank material for our house (an image-based material); the other, the smoke material for the smoke coming out of our chimney of the house (a procedural material). So, while we're working on both examples, feel free to experiment. Try playing with values and color so you feel comfortable making tweaks to your own shaders.

In this chapter, we're going to cover the following main topics:

- Materials in EEVEE
- Creating our first image-based material
- Creating our first procedural material

Technical requirements

Make sure Blender is up to date and download the packet from `https://github.com/PacktPublishing/Shading-Lighting-and-Rendering-with-Blenders-EEVEE/tree/main/Chapter02` to start this chapter. I've provided both a `.blend` file, which should open directly in Blender if double-clicked.

We'll be attaching nodes to the material output of the node tree inside our material editor to create interesting and varied materials that depict our environment. As an intermediate user, I assume you're already aware of how to switch into the material editor and add different types of nodes and attach them. You should also have a basic understanding of texture coordinates and UVs. As long as you've worked with materials a little bit, it should be easy to follow along with me, but if you're feeling overwhelmed or don't understand something, I'll provide some external resources for each section that you can choose to watch or read to get you more up to speed.

Materials in EEVEE

Materials in EEVEE are not that different from materials in Cycles. Of course, there are many ways to get better materials in EEVEE that don't even exist in Cycles (and vice versa), but the main concept of materials is exactly the same as you are aware of with Cycles. The Blender developers have been really great at adding to the functionality of EEVEE so that materials that work with Cycles should mostly work with EEVEE (there are some exceptions, but for the most part this is true). If we look closely at the material output node in any material node tree, we can see that the default option is **All**, which means materials will work, regardless of whether you switch to **Cycles** or **EEVEE** in the render panel. We can focus our output by choosing a target engine. I find that to be extraneous, but it's good to know in case you want to hyper-focus your material development on one engine.

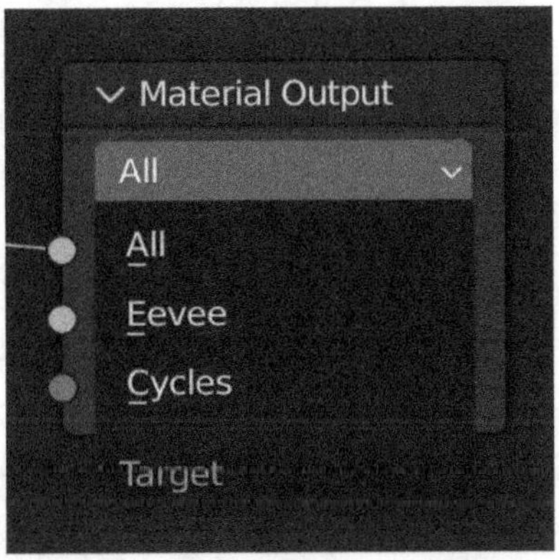

Figure 2.1: Material Output node

When creating art fast (which is one of the main reasons for using EEVEE – speed), it's often not worth spending hours or days tweaking values and images to create materials that are perfect. Sometimes, good is good enough to get our ideas across. Of course, feel free to spend as much or as little time on materials as you want, but in this chapter, we'll be creating a non-photorealistic scene that will only require simple shaders and rely more on stylization and embellishment.

> **Side Note**
>
> Non-photorealistic is a term we're going to use a lot in this chapter. It can most easily be described as "cartoon" style. Instead of trying to make a scene that involves creating a realistic or "photo-real" look, we're instead using stylized shaders and creating exaggerated geometry to make something less real and more *representative* of reality. **Non-photorealistic rendering** is often shortened to NPR.

Why materials are a little different in EEVEE

Materials are a little different in EEVEE due to the fact that we're approximating light bounces. There are a number of features that work instantly inside of Cycles that will have to be set up in order to work with EEVEE. Fortunately, these aspects are easy to configure and will give us results that we can see directly in the viewport. Be prepared to not immediately see the result you want from a material in EEVEE. Tweaking and experiment will become part of our workflow, so you're comfortable with working with the shader until it's tuned to perfection.

At this point, we're almost ready to jump headfirst into our image-based material, but first, we have to deal with the fact that we have no lighting set up. Let's fix that with a little tip for quickly previewing lighting so we can get on with the materials faster.

Quickly previewing lighting ideas for fast iteration

I want to get up and running on a project as fast as possible. Some people would advocate setting up your lighting and camera first in this situation, but I think it's a lot better to just throw yourself into materials and worry about lights later. But, as a practiced Blender user, you'll be screaming, *How can I see my materials accurately without lighting?!*

There's a simple fix here that I think allows us to get to the fun design work quickly. This little hack will use Blender's inbuilt HDRIs, so we don't have to source our own right now:

1. First set our newly opened scene to the **Shading** scene configuration. The tabs at the top of the window have specific workflow steps on them that allow us to open the specific tools that are relevant quickly, instead of trying to flip between different context windows.

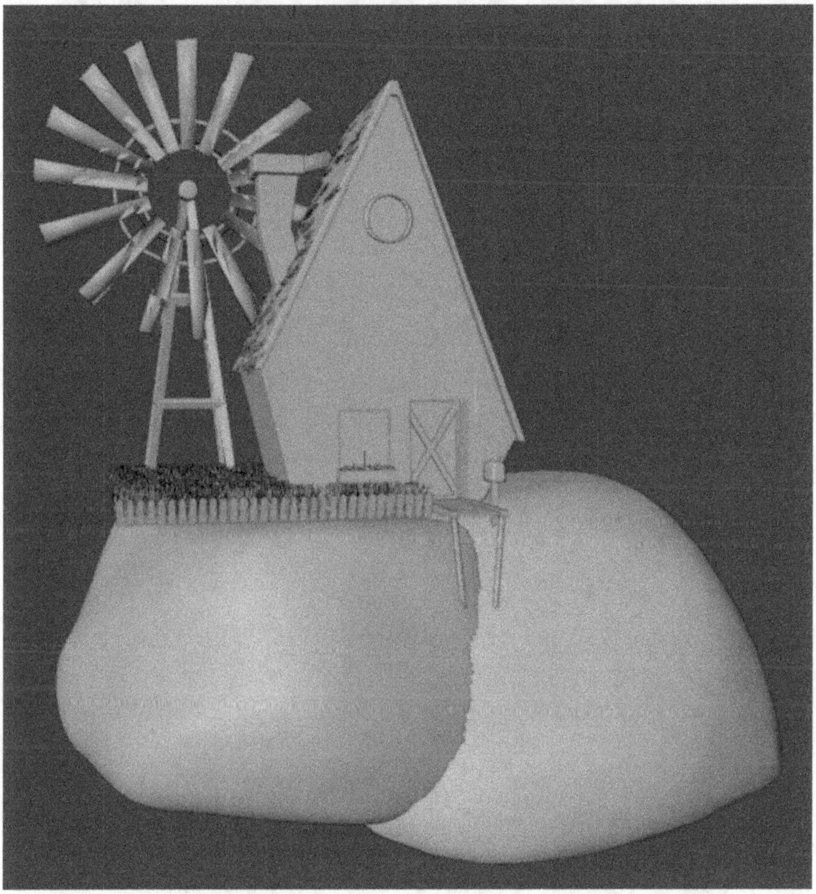

Figure 2.2: Solid viewport preview

2. Next, we want to make sure we're set to work in EEVEE. The Render menu is on the right toolbar and looks like a little camera or TV. As we can see, the choice of render engine is given to us on a drop-down menu. Make sure that is set to **EEVEE** for now so we can see accurate results in our viewport.

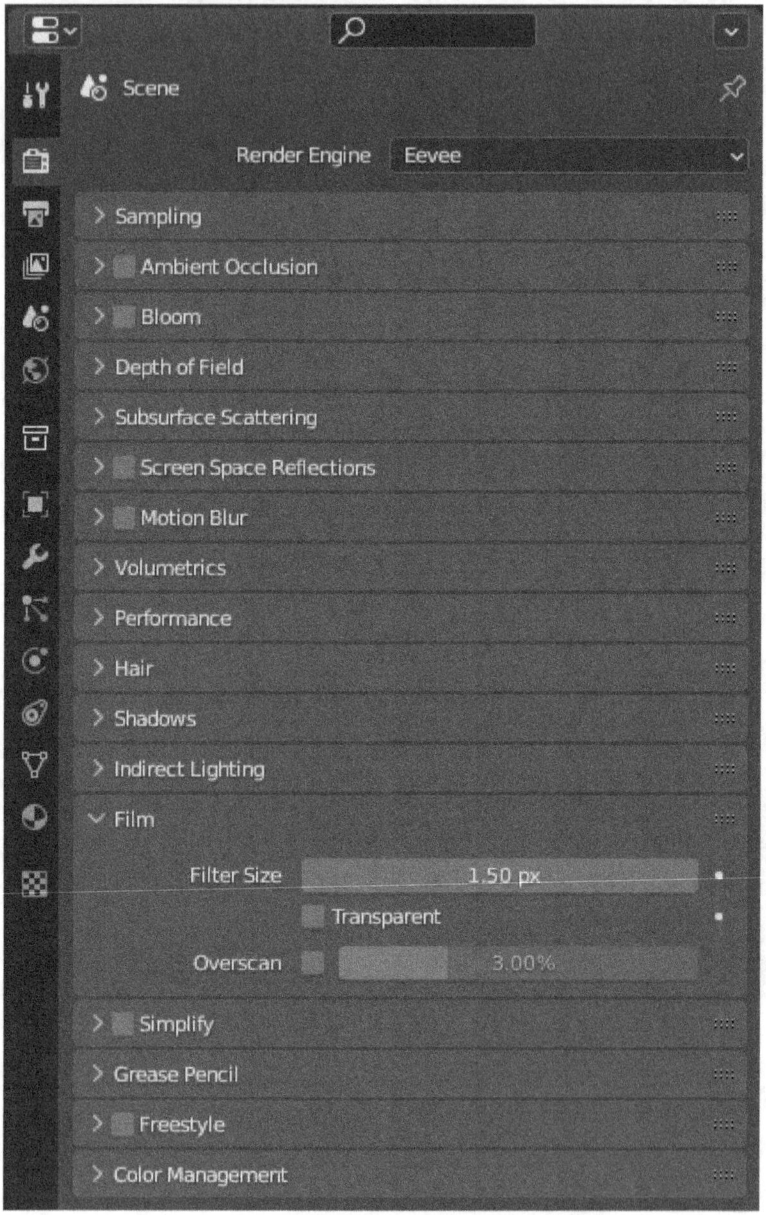

Figure 2.3: The Render panel

Blender comes complete with a few HDRIs we can use by default. Starting in Blender 2.8, it is possible to set our scene to be lit with a really simple click and start to conceptualize our materials without needing to spend time on lighting or rendering yet (those will come later).

> **Side Note**
> HDRIs are awesomely powerful when working in 3D to light a scene. We'll look at them in more detail in subsequent mini-projects, but right now, it is a great idea to go to `https://polyhaven.com/` and check out some of their CC0 HDRIs. They're completely free and great quality, useful for any project.

3. By clicking into the rendered viewport shading mode (or using the shortcut to the Pie menu – *Z* on the keyboard), we can see our scene as it will be rendered.

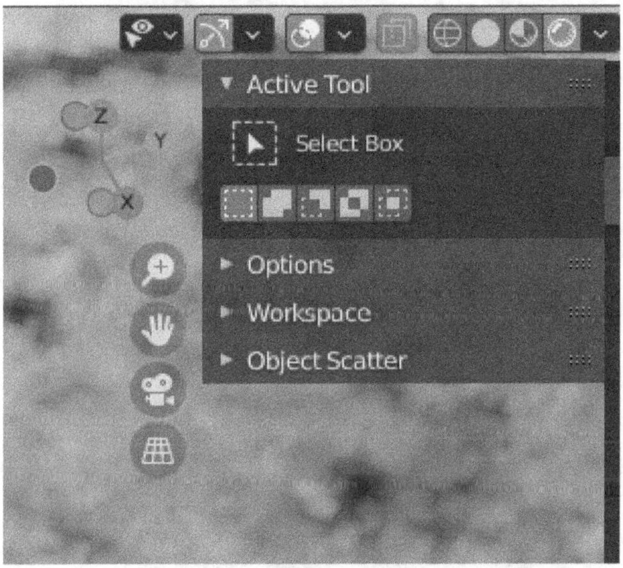

Figure 2.4: The render shading menu

4. Then, click the down arrow next to the **Viewport Shading** menu. This will give us the **Viewport Shading** option.

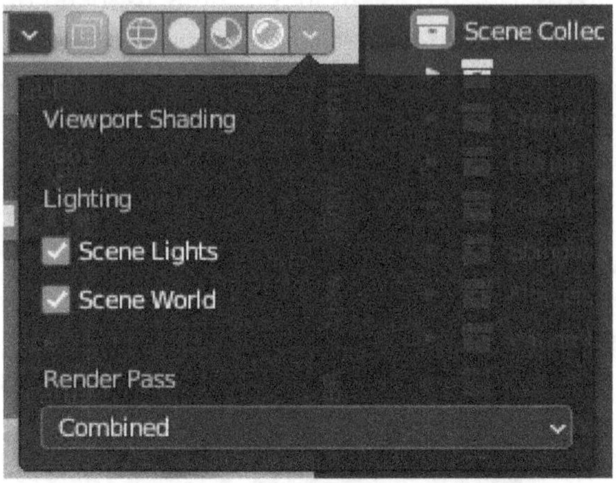

Figure 2.5: Viewport Shading options

5. From here, if you turn off **Scene Lights** and **Scene World** by unchecking them, the menu will change to something a little more like this:

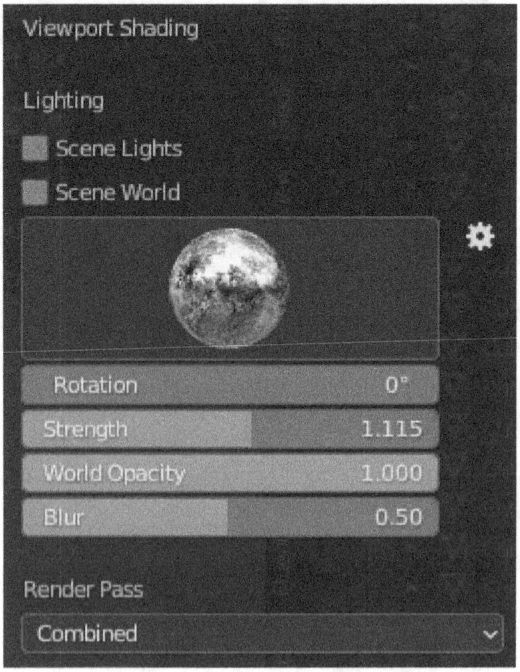

Figure 2.6: HDRI panel options

This menu gives us the ability to change the overall strength, rotation, and opacity of the HDRI that Blender has loaded automatically for us.

6. It is even possible to change to another HDRI so you can preview some different looks by clicking directly on the silver ball and selecting another HDRI icon.

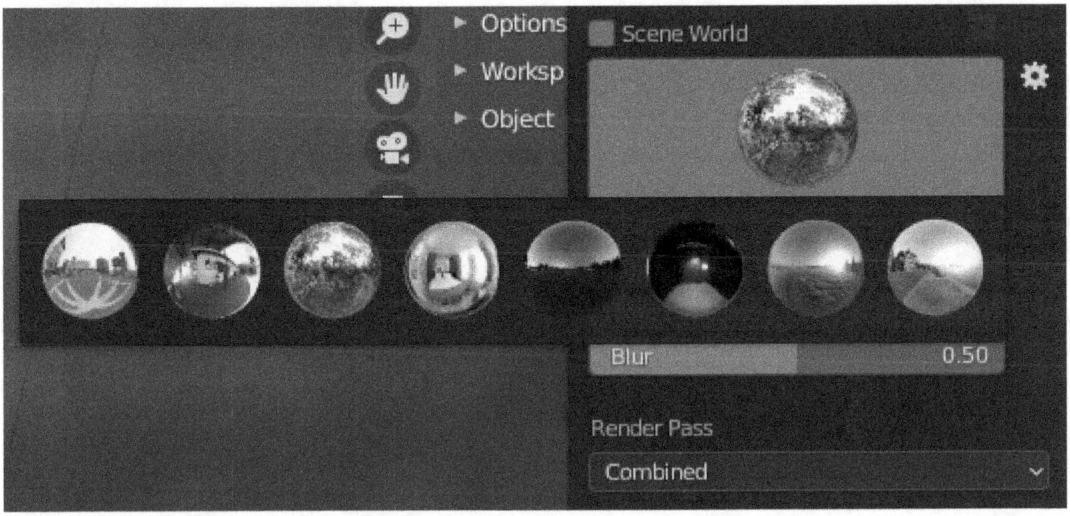

Figure 2.7: Options for different HDRIs

> **Side Note**
> Keyboard shortcuts are the backbone of any 3D artist's workflow – we all have different ones we've grown to like over time, so reading the documentation and even making your own keyboard shortcuts is encouraged. I'll be doing my best to call out some of the more useful keyboard shortcuts in these side notes. *One of my favorite time-saving shortcuts is Z* for opening the shading Pie menu.

Cool! Now we have an awesome, well-lit scene so that we can preview different lighting styles and colors without really doing much. We will have to tune our lighting eventually, but this is great to get right to something more useful like materials. This allows us to be flexible in how we create materials. If the director tells you to light something like it's night time then changes their mind later on, you may need to rework your materials completely. By using the default HDRIs in Blender, it's easy to switch between the eight options, see how light will affect the materials you're working on, and be open to iteration and change as the project progresses.

Next, we'll tackle the meat of this chapter and start adding some life to our mini-project by creating an image-based texture for the wooden exterior of our House-In-The-Sky.

Creating our first image-based material

Time to make our first texture for the project. I'm going to be working on the plank texture for the front and sides of the house, but feel free to select another object you want to add and follow along. The steps should be the same, and I've added some other textures to the GitHub repository that should do the trick, or feel free to find your own. This section of the texturing stage will be exceptionally simple but hopefully will give us a cool, stylized look as well as teaching you how to set up a really quick image-based texture. Here's the main gist of the process:

1. Add two-click Principled Setup.
2. Add the **Shader to RGB** shader for a stylized look.
3. Tweak the values if needed.

> **Side Note**
>
> There are a lot of free CC0 (free to use with minimal copyright protections) sites that have popped up in the last couple of years that are really easy to grab textures from.
>
> These are three highly recommended websites with a good array of materials, usually with the full range of diffuse to normal maps that can be plugged into a **Principled** shader:
>
> `https://ambientcg.com/`, `https://www.sharetextures.com/`, and `polyhaven.com`

Two-click Principled Setup

This step abstracts away the tedious workflow of importing images, organizing them, and connecting them to sockets. With the Node Wrangler add-on, we can make materials so easily that it's almost too good to be true:

1. Create a material and select the **Principled** shader node that comes by default with the material.

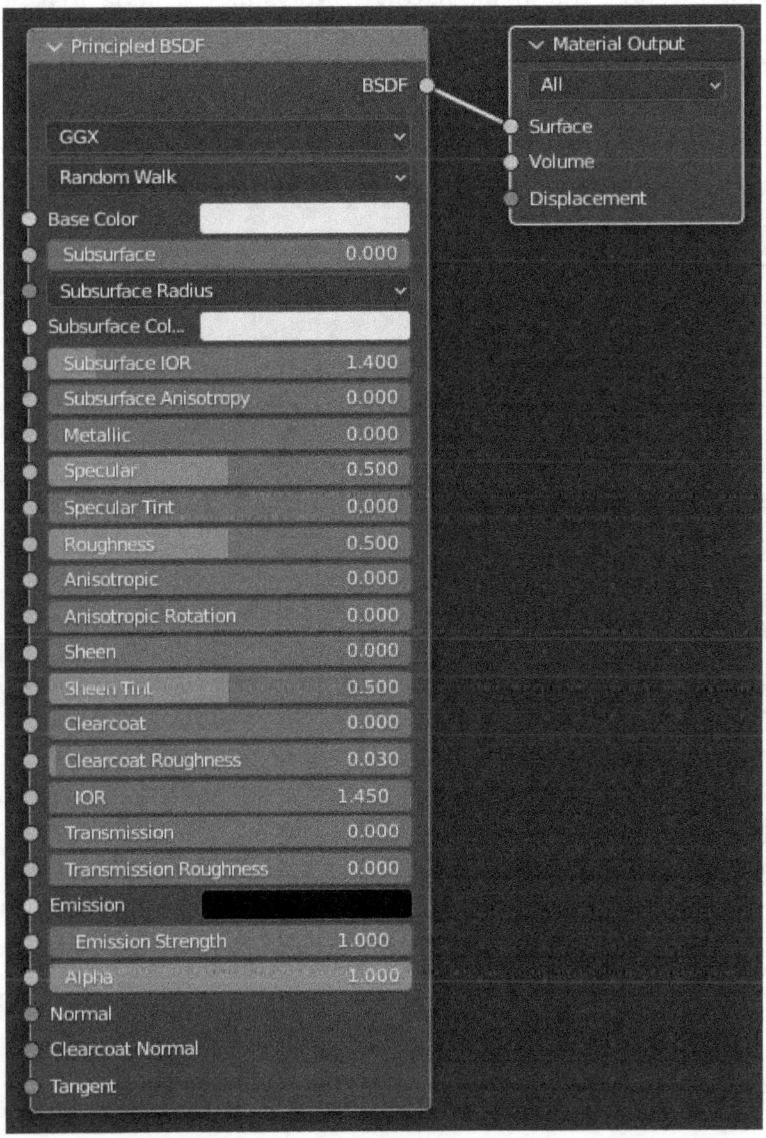

Figure 2.8: Principled node shader

2. Use the keyboard shortcut *Ctrl* + *Alt* + *T* to open a file browser window.
3. Select all the textures (the **BaseColor**, **Metallic**, **Roughness**, and **Normal** images provided in `textures` folder in the `Chapter 2` folder on GitHub; I chose the `Planks` material in this example) that belong to the material. This shortcut relies on your textures being labeled correctly, so make sure the **Normal map** has **Normal Map** in the name, and so on.
4. Confirm the selection. You should have a well-organized material to base our further tweaking on. You'll notice the **Normal** map that is required between the **Normal map** and **Principled** shader. This node takes the colors from the **Normal** image and translates them to displacement, so we need to make sure the **Normal** map node is added between the **Normal** image and the **Principled** shader.

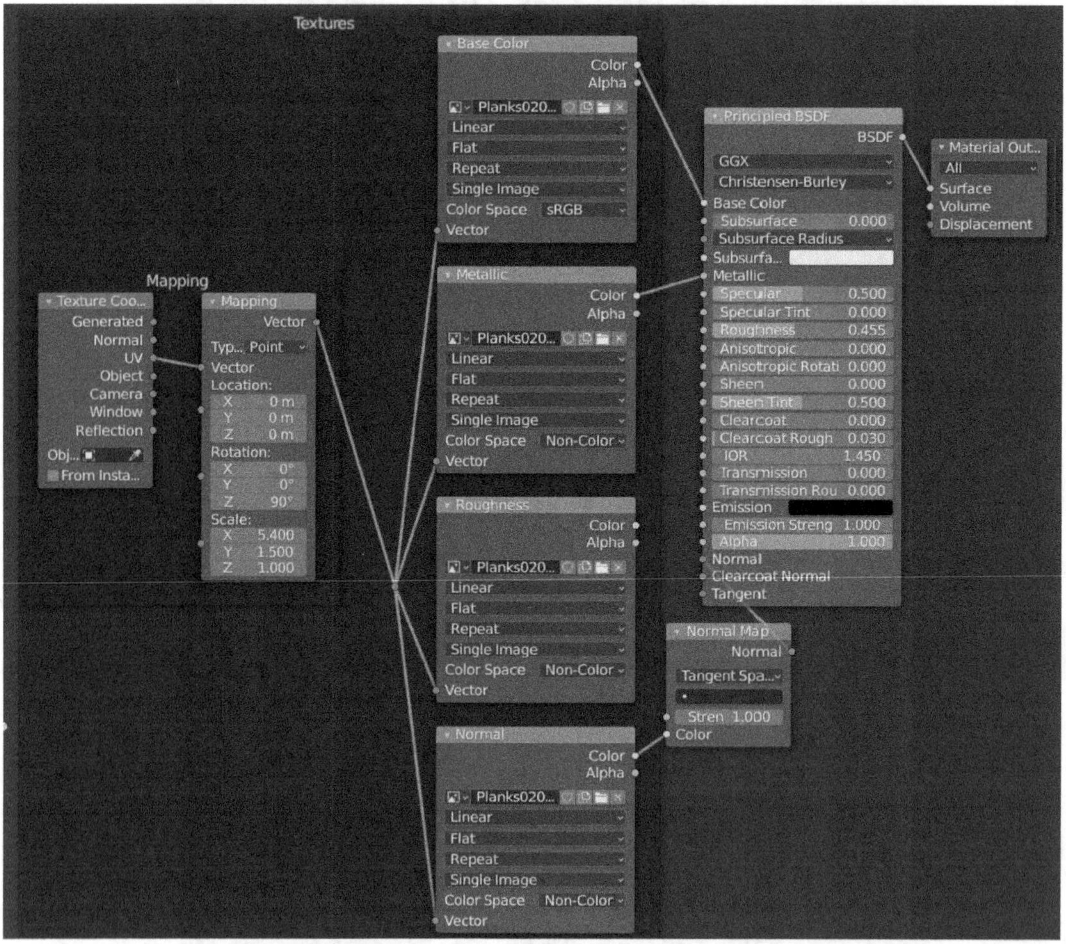

Figure 2.9: Full material setup

As you can see, this is an awesome way to set up a material really quickly. Try changing some of the values to see how they affect the material in the viewport. You should get lightning-fast updates to the scene – no having to wait for Cycles to recompile the viewport or noise in the image. Almost too good to be true, right?

I wanted the wood planks of my material to run up and down instead of side to side, so setting my rotation in the **Mapping** node easily fixed that. Then I increased the scale values, making the **X Scale** value equal to **5.4** and the Y **Scale** value equal to **1.5**. The **Z** value isn't being used in this case – since we only have a 2D texture, we only need to tweak two dimensions. I also changed the **Z Rotation** to 90 degrees. The overall idea here is to tweak the values on the **Mapping** node to get the planks to have the right aspect ratio. I find it's easier to tweak these **Mapping** nodes rather than try to re-UV unwrap things to get them to fit properly. It's just a matter of texturing inside of one Blender workspace rather than jumping back and forth between the UV and the material workspaces.

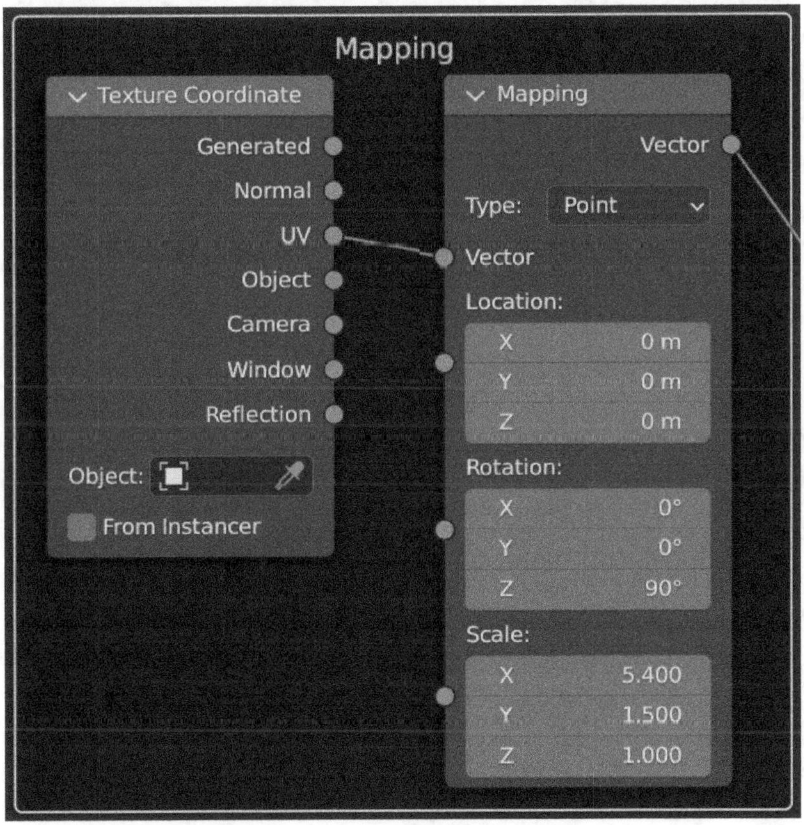

Figure 2.10: Mapping nodes

Side Note

You may notice that the connectors between different nodes have different colors. This is an update in Blender 3.0 and allows us to visualize the type of information that is being transferred between nodes.

Shaders in EEVEE and Cycles are bright green.

Vectors are dark blue/purple.

Colors are yellow.

I ended up with something like this in the viewport.

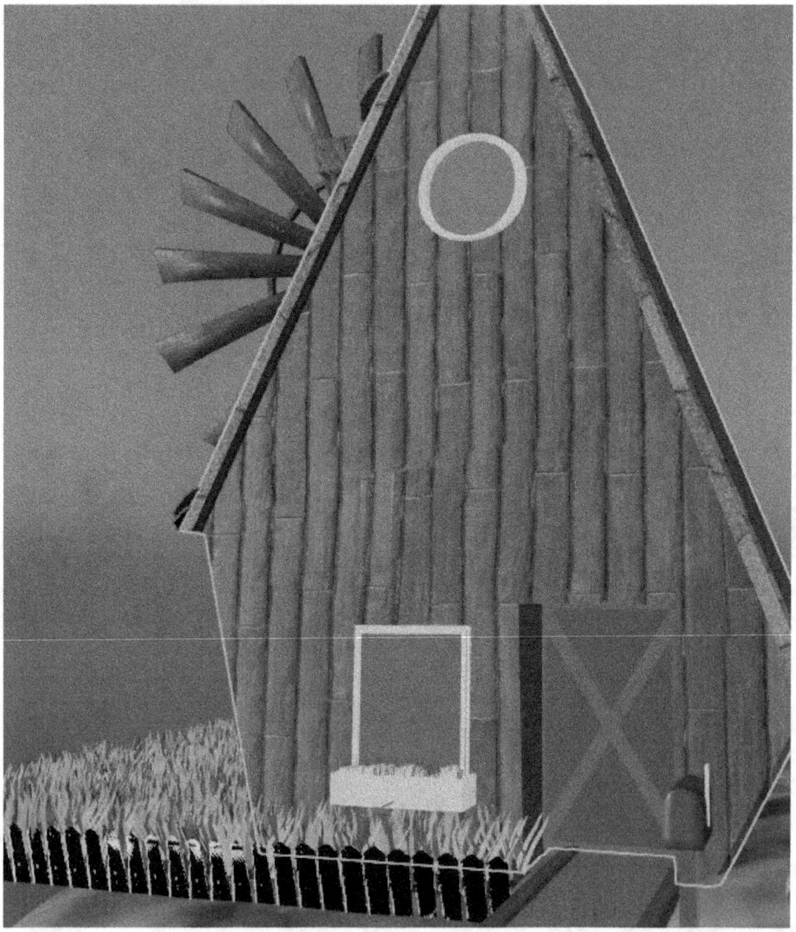

Figure 2.11: Initial material

Of course, wood is not the only material we can create using a **Principled** shader. Refer to the Blender manual if you would like more information on using the **Principled** shader and how the shader works: `https://docs.blender.org/manual/en/latest/render/shader_nodes/shader/principled.html`.

Shader to RGB

The look that we just created with our **Principled** Setup isn't exactly stylized – it's more realistic than the overall feel we're going for here. Inside of EEVEE, we can use the **Shader to RGB** node to convert our realistic material into a flatter, shaded-cell material that can easily be tweaked for our needs:

1. Connect the **Shader to RGB** node between the Principled shader output and the **Material Output** node.

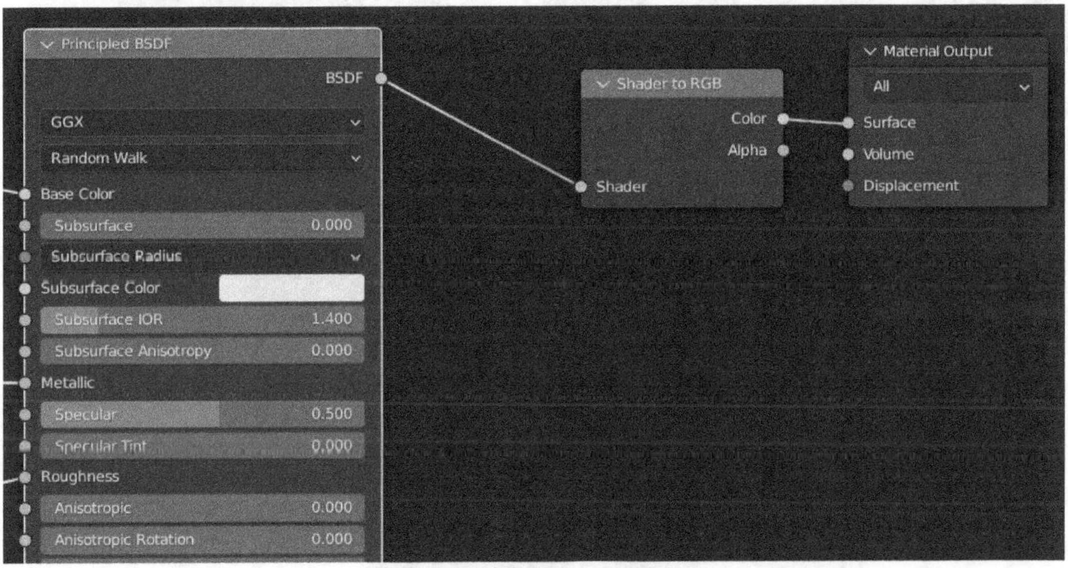

Figure 2.12: Shader to RGB node

You won't see much of a change to your material at this point. The magic is in the next step.

2. Add a **ColorRamp** in between the **Shader to RGB** node and **Material Output**.
3. Set the **ColorRamp** interpolation to **Constant**, which means the colors will change at a constant rate, without mixing between colors at the markers.

4. Add a few extra colors to the **ColorRamp** by clicking the plus icon on the left side of the node and add some arbitrary colors.

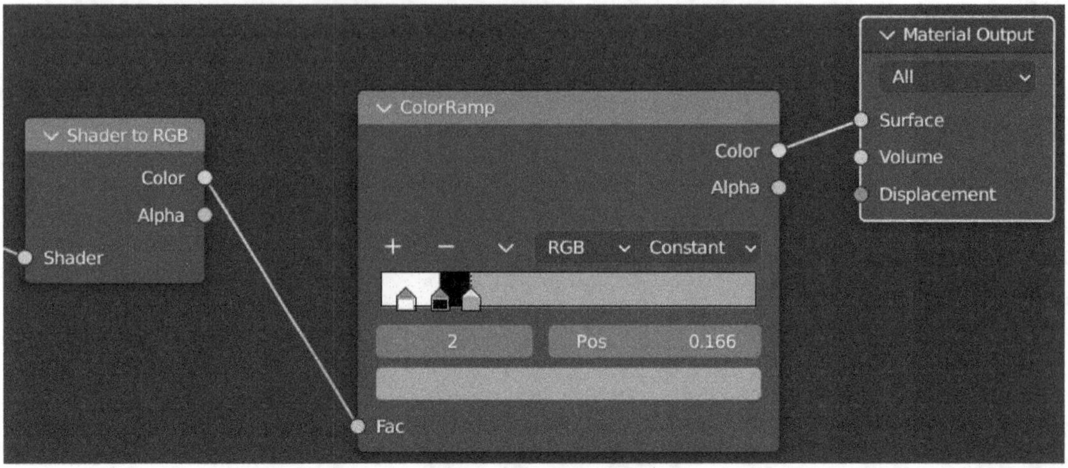

Figure 2.13: ColorRamp added to shader

I ended up with something like this:

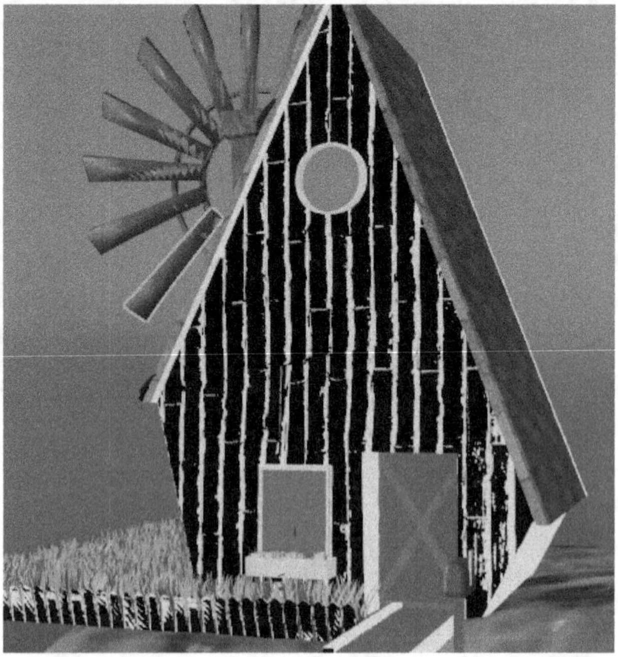

Figure 2.14: Result of ColorRamp

The overall viewport looks like something out of a comic book now.

5. To see the full effect, using the **Viewport Shading** drop-down menu that we discussed before, change the rotation of the HDRI and see how it affects the overall color of the material. The material will now react to light by changing the color of the texture.

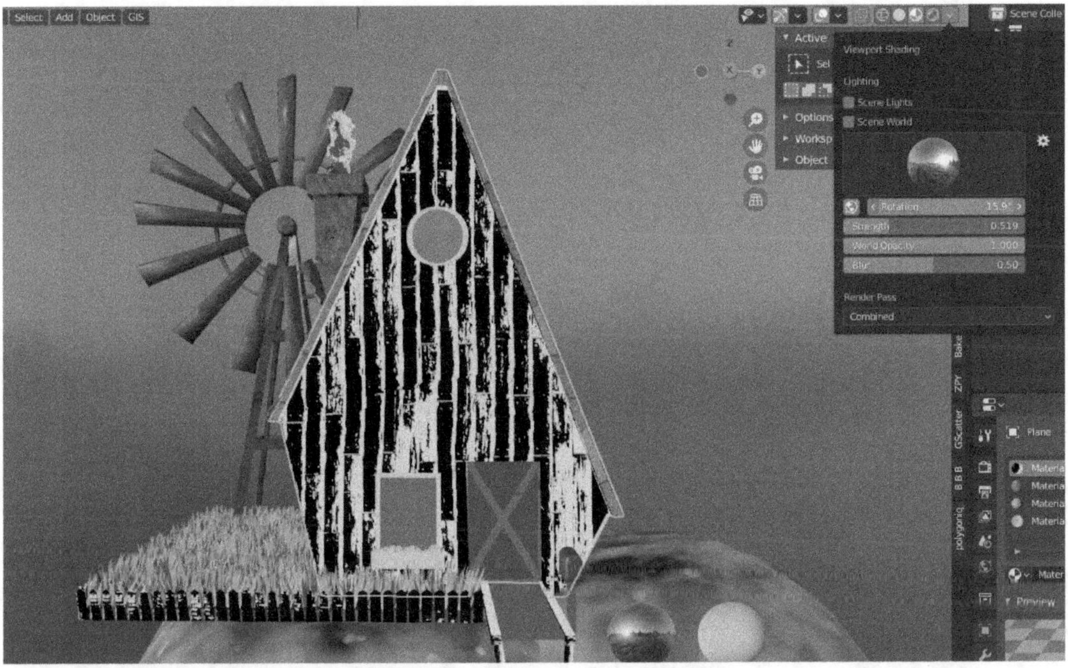

Figure 2.15: Changing light to affect the material

Places that are shadowed become black (as the leftmost color on my **ColorRamp**) and lit areas are yellow (as the rightmost color on my **ColorRamp**).

6. The last node to add is a **Math** node between the **ColorRamp** and the **Shader to RGB** node. Set the drop-down **Math** method to **Power** and set that to somewhere around 0.5. This gives you more leverage with the **ColorRamp** to experiment with different values.

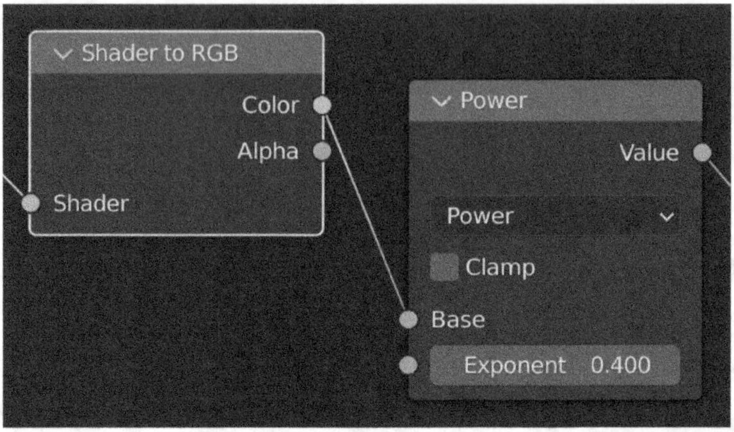

Figure 2.16: Power node added

Play around with the values. There's really no "right" number; it's what looks good to you.

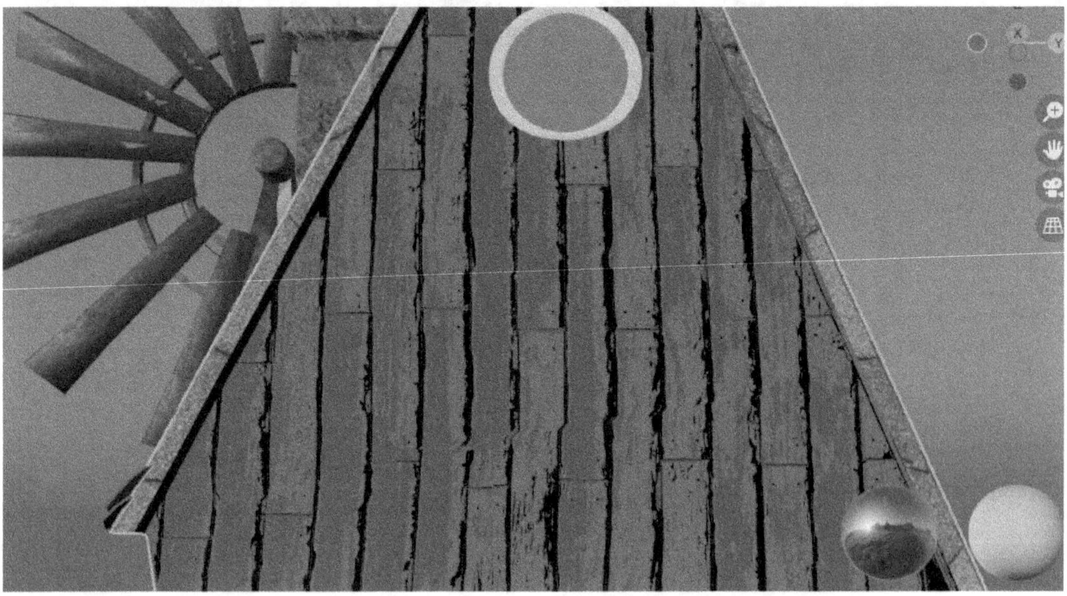

Figure 2.17: Material shader after adding the Power node

This is what I ended up with. I picked some colors from the original texture, to still give it a wooden look. From a close-up of the material, it's easy to see that we've maintained most of the detail from the original texture, but now we have a much more abstract, stylized version of it, with very little effort.

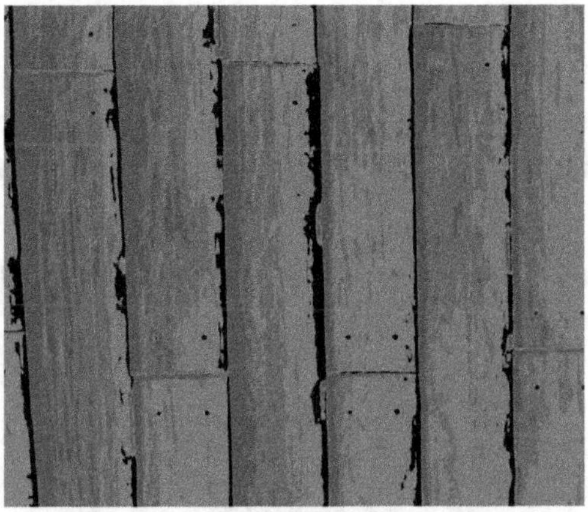

Figure 2.18: Close-up of the material

That concludes a little bit on how to manipulate and integrate principled textures into an EEVEE workflow. We'll be utilizing Node Wrangler in later chapters to create quick textures, but I won't really go over the process in detail beyond what we've already covered, so make sure you have that under control before moving on to the next section of this chapter.

Creating our first procedural texture

Procedural textures are textures that don't involve using images. Because we're using inputs into the shader that are scalable and manipulatable, we ultimately have more flexibility over what the final output of our shader looks like. We also don't need to go looking for textures online when we create them procedurally. The procedural texture that I want to create today is going to be a huge time saver for us. While sometimes it's appropriate to simulate smoke for your scene, it can also be very heavy on the computer and requires some knowledge of how physics works inside of Blender. But there is another way of creating smoke or other VFX in EEVEE so that we can continue to work in real time – by faking it with a procedural shader! Most video games also take this route, creating shaders that fake the look of smoke, fire, or plasma guns. Creating real-time effects is a great skill to have both in EEVEE and for game design, so let's jump into designing that shader for our stylized scene.

The base mesh

The first thing we want to do is create some geometry that will form the basis of our simulation. I started with a cube and extruded a couple of times, scaling to create a kind of zig-zag pattern, and came up with something like this. It's supposed to represent a really, really simple smoke column that tapers at the top. Stick to simplicity at this point, as we'll layer details on top of this base.

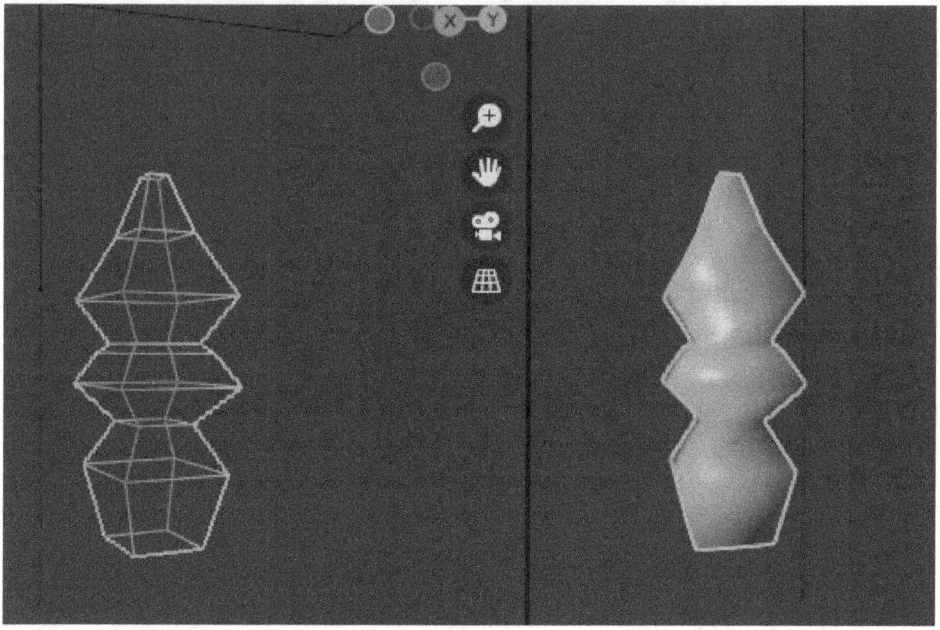

Figure 2.19: The smoke mesh

Next, let's add a couple of modifiers to our mesh:

1. First, a **Subdivision Surface** modifier, set to the **Simple** subdivision style. Change the levels in the viewport and **Render** to **2**.
2. Then add a **Displace** modifier, set **Coordinates** to **Object**, and leave **Direction** as **Normal**. As you can see in our modifier, we still need an object for our coordinates to work with.
3. Add an **Empty** object (**Plain Axis** is just fine) to the scene. Set the **Displace** modifier to work with the **Empty** object we just placed.
4. We still have a little more work to do on our **Displace** modifier, namely adding a texture. If you click the icon on the far right in line with the texture name on the **Displace** modifier, you'll be taken to the **Texture** menu.

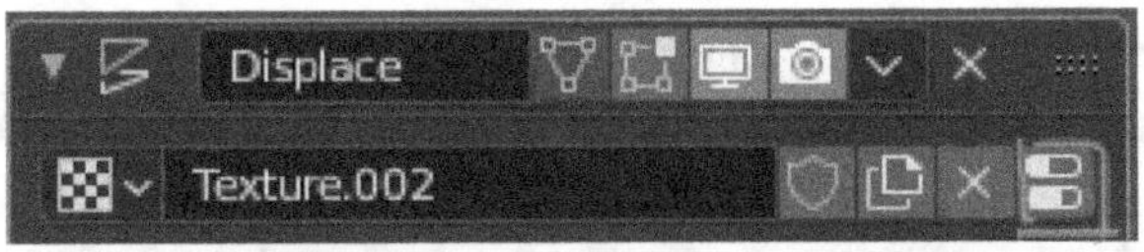

Figure 2.20: Go to the Texture menu

5. Click the **New** button to create a new texture, then set the drop-down menu labeled **Type** to **Clouds**. You can play with the values of the **Displace** texture, but I left mine at the defaults for simplicity. My **Displace** texture looks something like this.

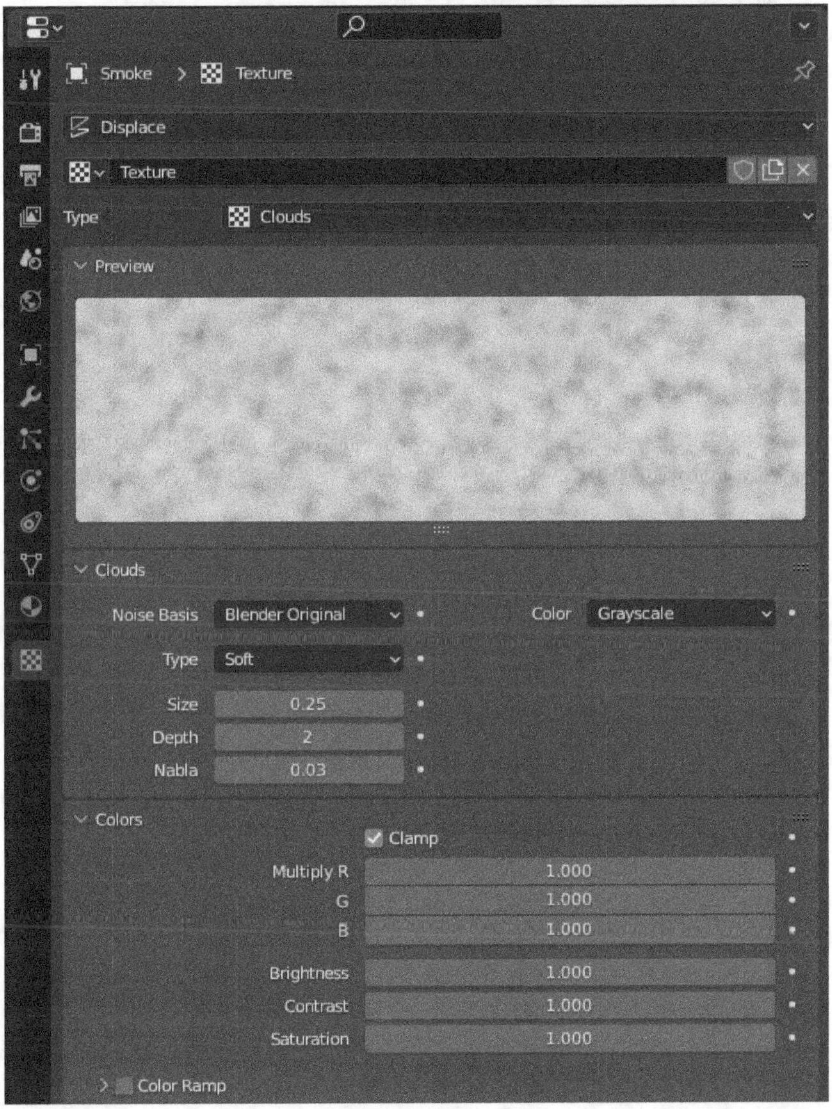

Figure 2.21: Cloud texture

And my modifier stack now looks like this. I decided to tone down the strength of my **Displace** modifier to get a more subtle look, but whatever looks good to you is the value you should choose.

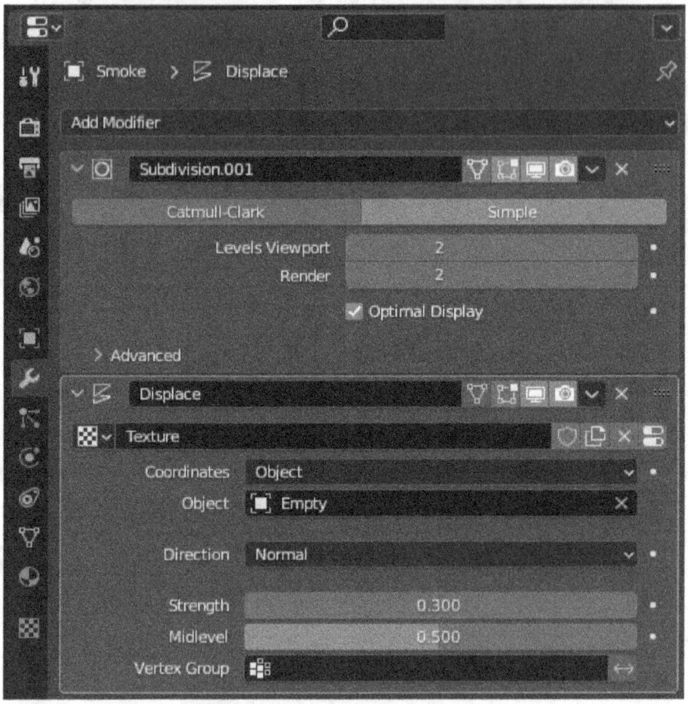

Figure 2.22: Displace modifier

6. If you try moving your **Empty** object on the Z axis, you should see it now causes your smoke object to displace randomly, kind of like smoke does.

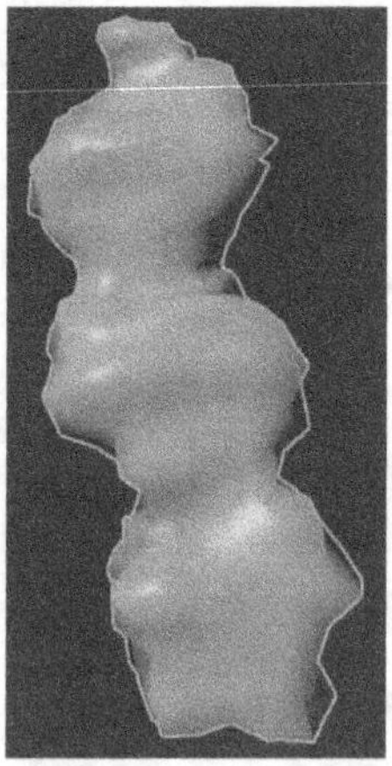

Figure 2.23: Mesh result

Texture creation with procedural nodes

Next, we need to create a new material to set up our shader to add even more detail:

1. After adding that new material, open up the material editor and we'll get into the shading of our smoke.
2. First, let's add a **Texture Coordinate** node and a **Mapping** node, connecting the **Object** output on the **Texture Coordinate** node to the input on **Vector** on the **Mapping** node.
3. Next, create a **Normal** node (not a **Normal** map) and connect the **Mapping** node to the **Normal** input on the **Normal** node.

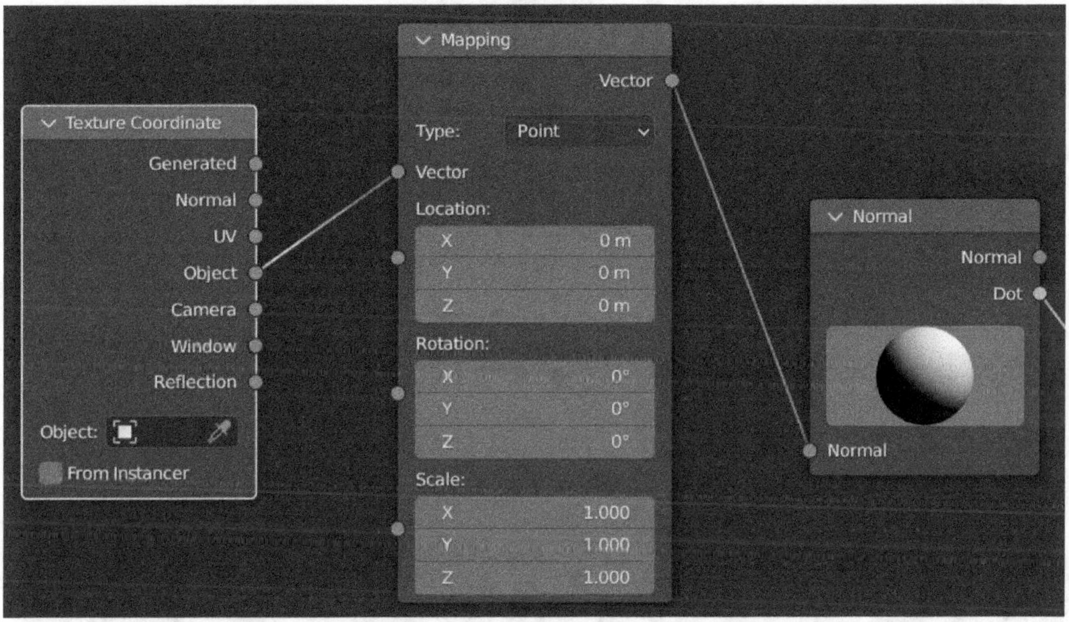

Figure 2.24: Normal and Mapping nodes

The **Normal** node manipulates the direction of the normals on the object shader level.

4. If you click on the white dot in the **Normal** node and drag it, you can see how it affects the color of our smoke material. Try that out, but the overall effect this has on our material won't be apparent until later, so don't try to get it perfect right now.

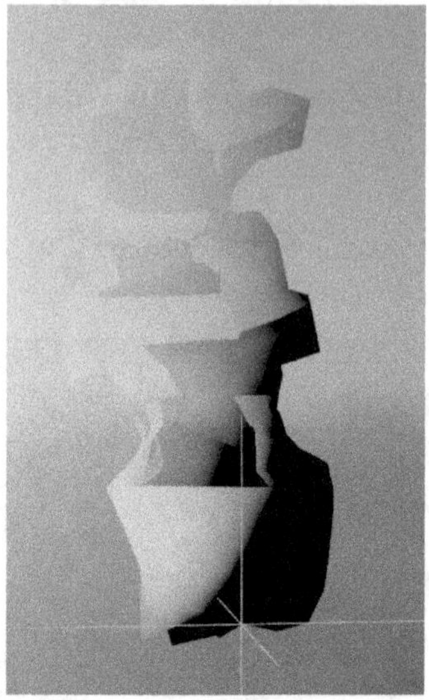

Figure 2.25: The smoke after playing with the Normal node

5. Next, let's add a **ColorRamp** to the **Dot** output of **Normal** (Color Ramps are great utilities to control the output of a node – I use them liberally).
6. Then, let's add a **Mix** color node and plug the output from the **ColorRamp** into the bottom socket of the **Mix** node. This **Mix** color is going to let us add some more noise into the shader so we get more detail on the smoke.

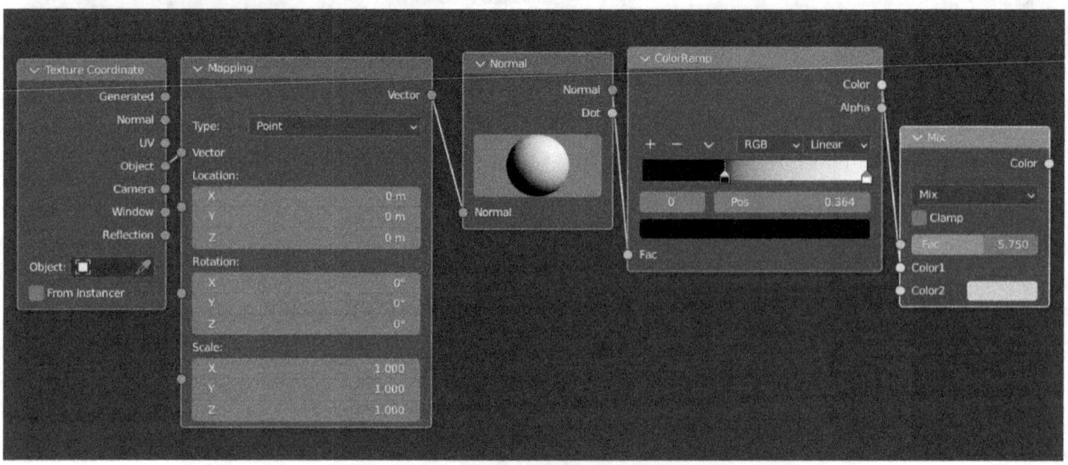

Figure 2.26: Adding the color Mix node

7. Now let's add that noise, by adding – you guessed it – a **Noise Texture** node. We'll add a **Mix** color node and a **Voronoi Texture** node to round out this noise section of the texturing. Set the **Voronoi Texture** node to **Smooth F1** with **Smoothness** of **1** and **Scale** of **7.5**.
8. Combine the **Noise Texture** node and the **Voronoi Texture** node together with the **Mix** node, and then attach that **Mix** color node to the top input of our other **Mix** color node, which I set to a factor of 0.575. This combines our **Normal** node and **Noise Texture** node together.

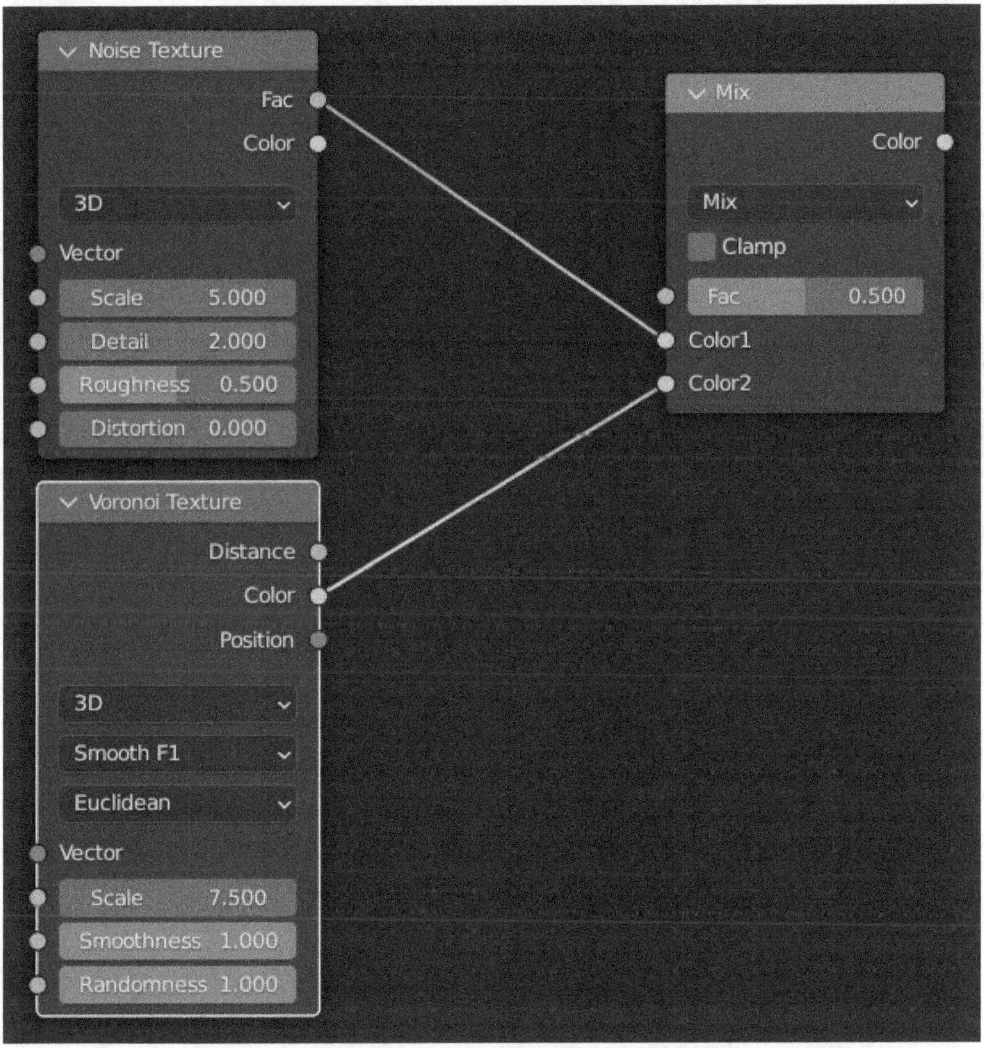

Figure 2.27: Mixing in the Noise Texture and Voronoi Texture

9. It's also important we give the **Voronoi Texture** mapping coordinates. You can do this with Node Wrangler by selecting the **Voronoi Texture** and using the shortcut *Ctrl* + *T*.

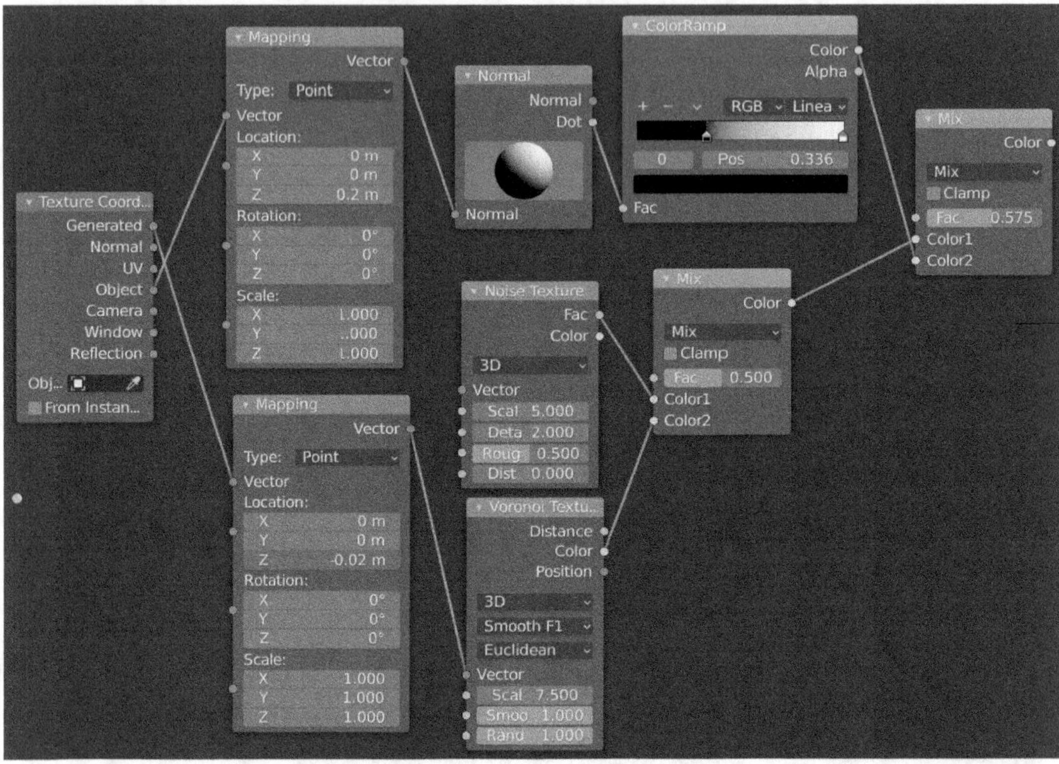

Figure 2.28: Adding it all together

Okay, our texture is looking interesting, but not necessarily smoke-like yet. So, let's add some Color Ramps to get the colors we're looking for.

10. Add two Color Ramps, each set to **Constant** interpolation.

11. Attach the result of the **Mix** color node to both Color Ramps. The top ramp is going to be our alpha, describing the transparency of our image. The second ramp is going to give the smoke its coloration. This is something you can play around with and reference some pictures or videos of smoke to refine the numbers you are using. Reference *Figure 2.35* for a zoomed-out view of the shader if you are having problems assembling the nodes correctly.

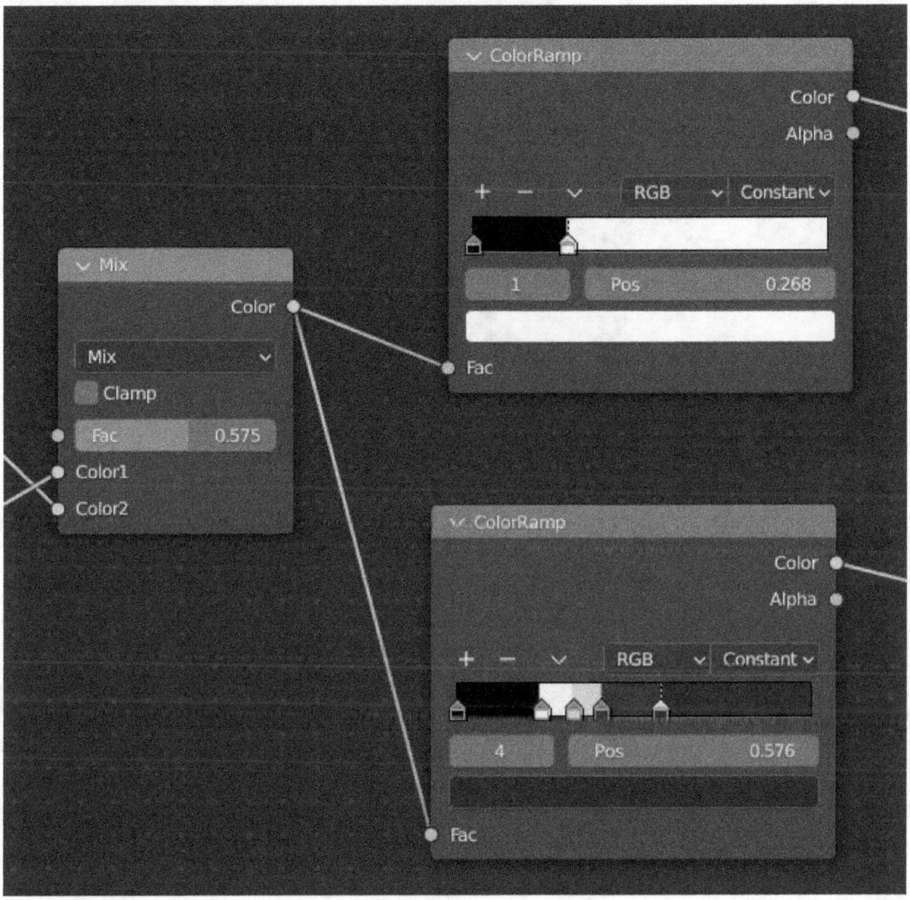

Figure 2.29: The two Color Ramps

That's it for the texture creation process.

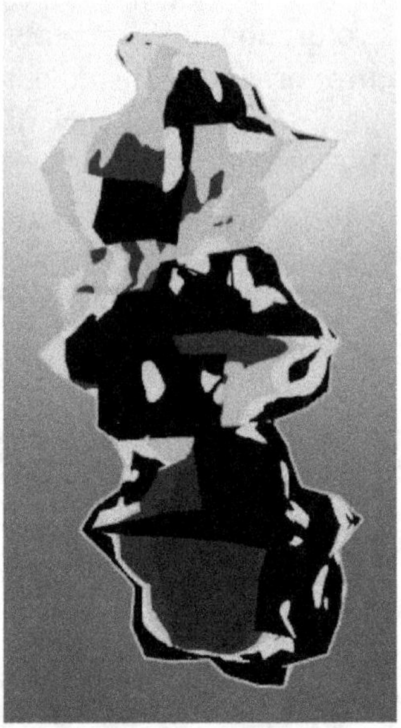

Figure 2.30: Result from the lower Color Ramp

Adding shading to the material

Now we're going to use the outputs from our two Color Ramps to add shading to the material:

1. Add an **Emission** shader, **Mix Shader**, and a **Transparent** shader.
2. Plug the top Color Ramp into the factor of the **Mix Shader**.
3. Plug the bottom Color Ramp into the **Emission** shader.
4. Then plug the **Emission** shader output into the bottom input of the **Mix Shader**, and stick the **Transparent** shader into the top input of the **Mix Shader**.

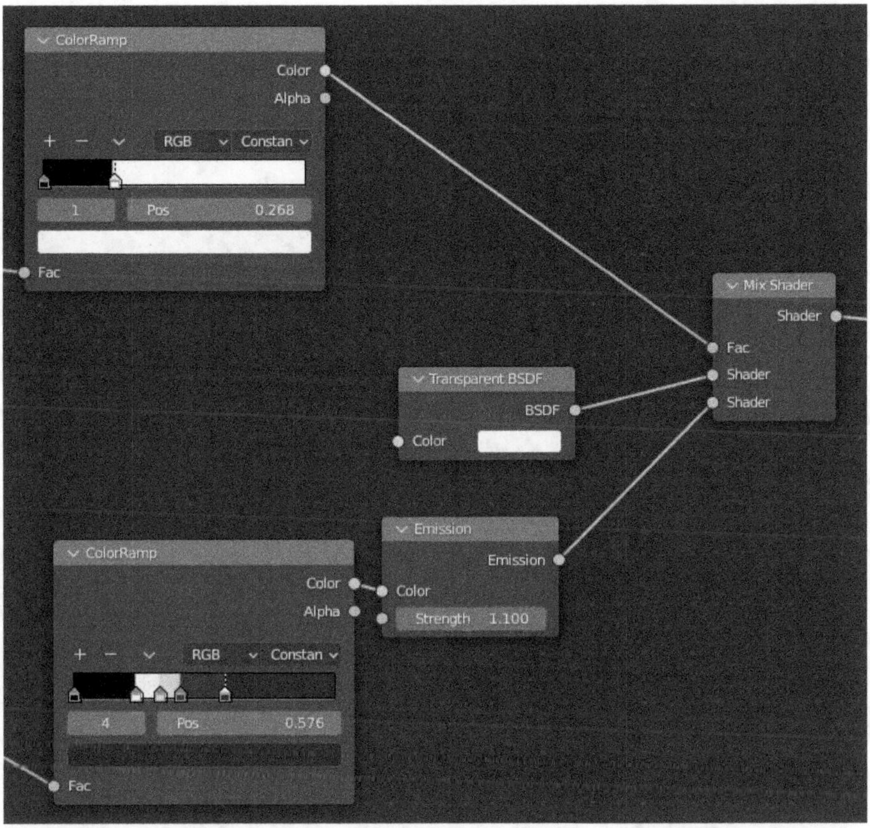

Figure 2.31: Adding Emission and Transparent shaders

If you've been following along with my exact values, you should have something like this:

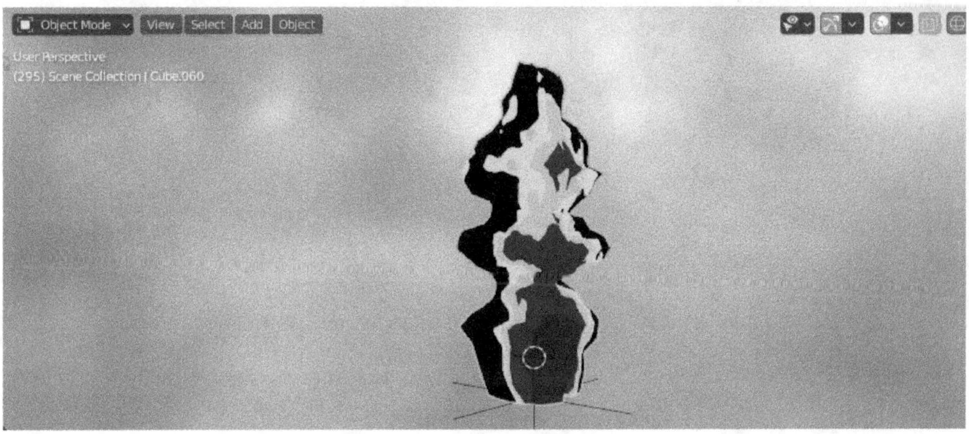

Figure 2.32: The material after adding shaders

We have a kind of cool smoke shader here – but we're not getting the transparency from our shader that we should be getting. This is because EEVEE defaults materials to be opaque regardless of what actual shaders you're using. Let's fix this.

5. Select the material, scroll down to the material settings in the Properties panel and change **Blend Mode** from **Opaque** to **Alpha Blend**.

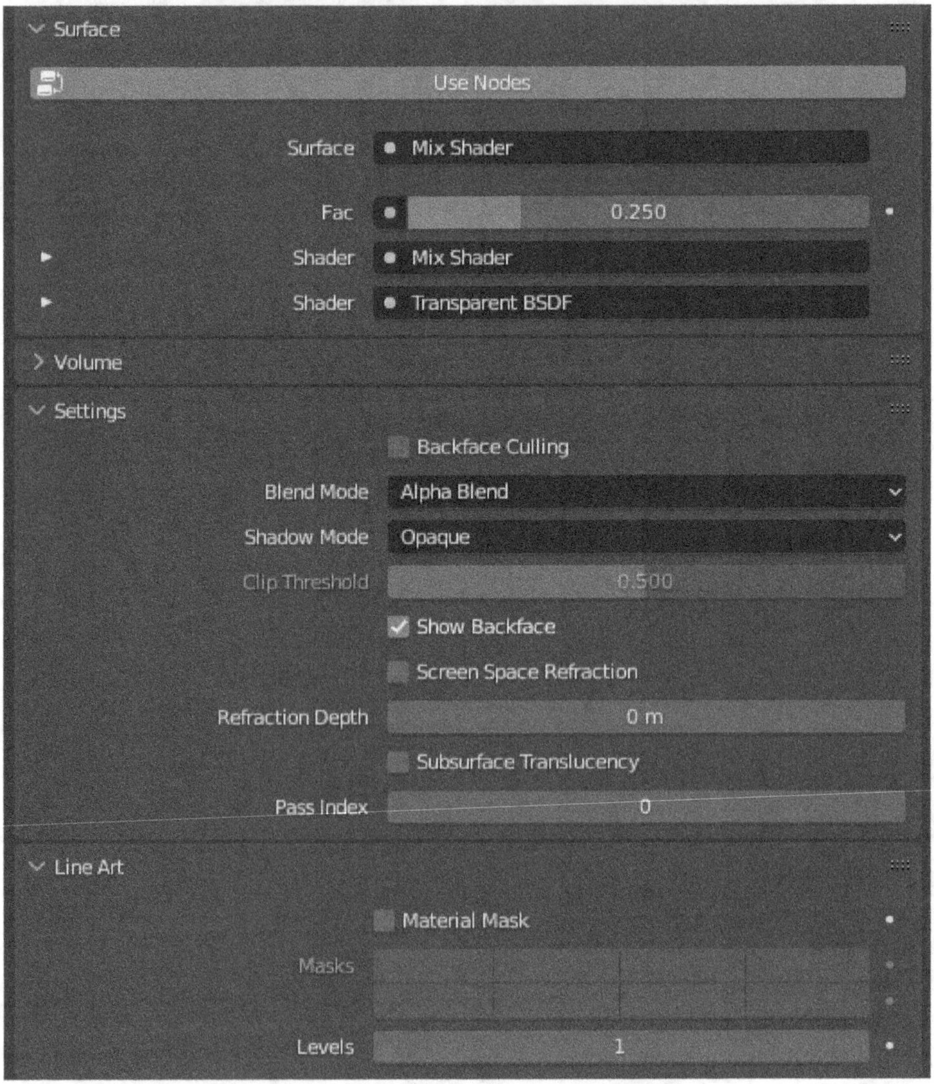

Figure 2.33: The Smoke material settings

So now our transparency is showing up and we get some wispy trails out from the main center of the shader that give us a smoky feeling:

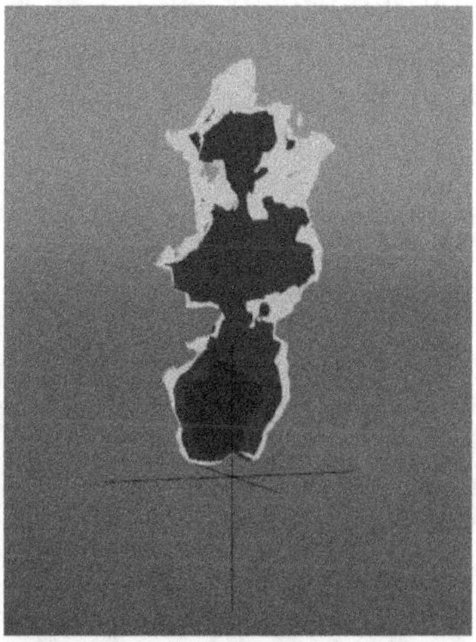

Figure 2.34: The smoke

The last thing we need to do is give the "smoke" a little more translucency because smoke isn't entirely opaque.

6. Add another **Mix Shader**, take the output from the previous **Mix Shader**, and plug it into the first socket of the new **Mix Shader**. Then add another **Transparent** shader and plug it into the second socket. I set my **Mix** factor to .35, but play around with what looks good to you.

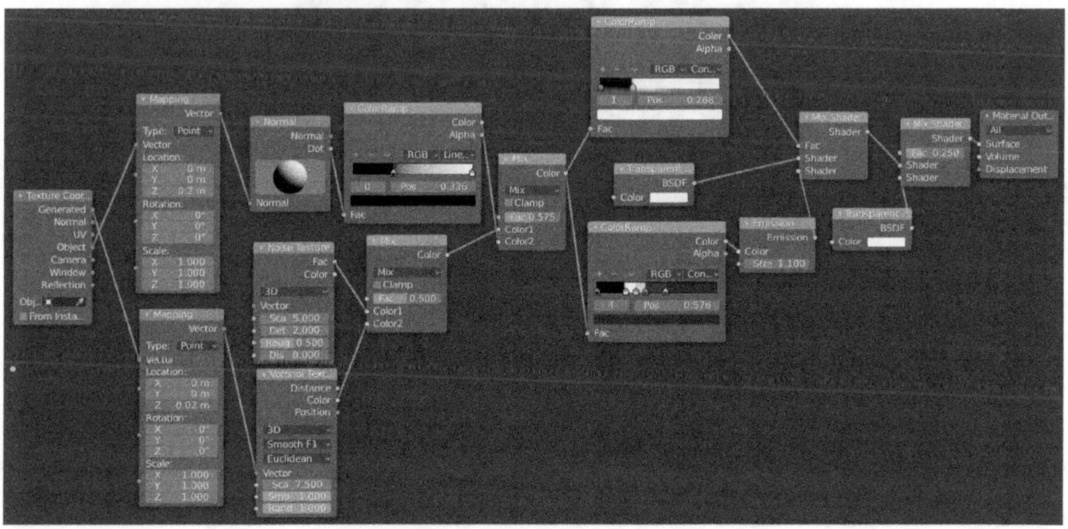

Figure 2.35: Final node shader setup

The final node setup is inside `Smoke_Shader.blend` in the GitHub repository, in case you need to look it over in more detail. The very last step in this shader setup is only required if you want to animate the smoke. Of course, you can move the **Empty** object on the Z axis and the smoke will move based on that, but it's not very convincing. We can add an animation to the Z location of our **Voronoi Texture** that will give the smoke a little more of an upward movement.

7. Right-click on the **Voronoi Texture's** node's **Z Location** value and select **Add Driver**.

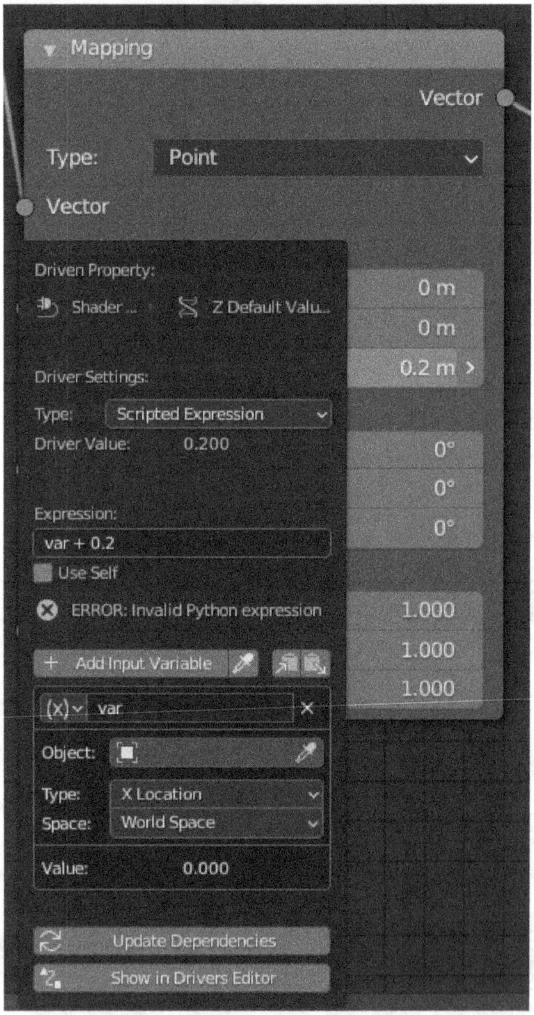

Figure 2.36: The driver settings

Drivers are mathematical expressions that we can use to automatically animate something.

8. In this instance, we'll take the negative frame number provided by Blender and divide it by 50, so the texture will move over time. That expression gets typed in as `-frame/50` in the **Expression** box in the driver properties.

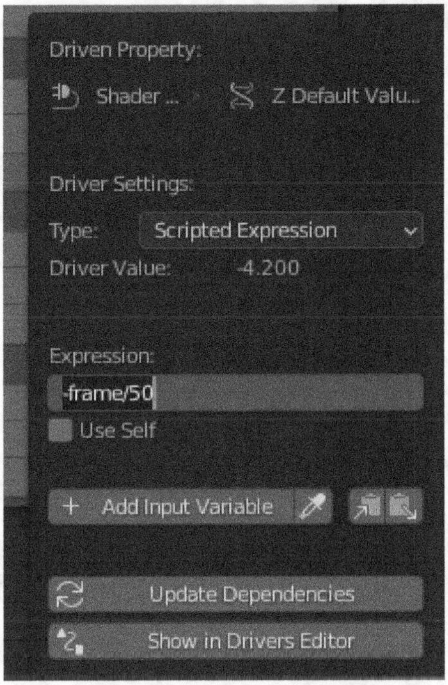

Figure 2.37: Expression creation

9. You'll notice Blender shows that this expression is invalid. All you have to do to fix this is delete the **var** input variable that comes by default with every driver by clicking the **X** in the right corner of the variable box and then **Update Dependencies**.

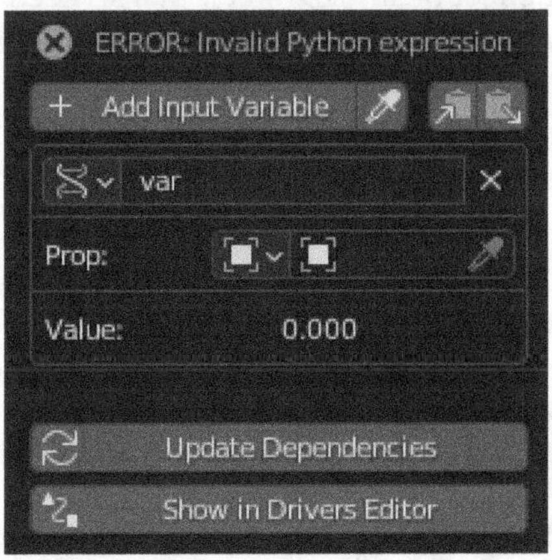

Figure 2.38: Deleting the variable

Here's what I ended up with!

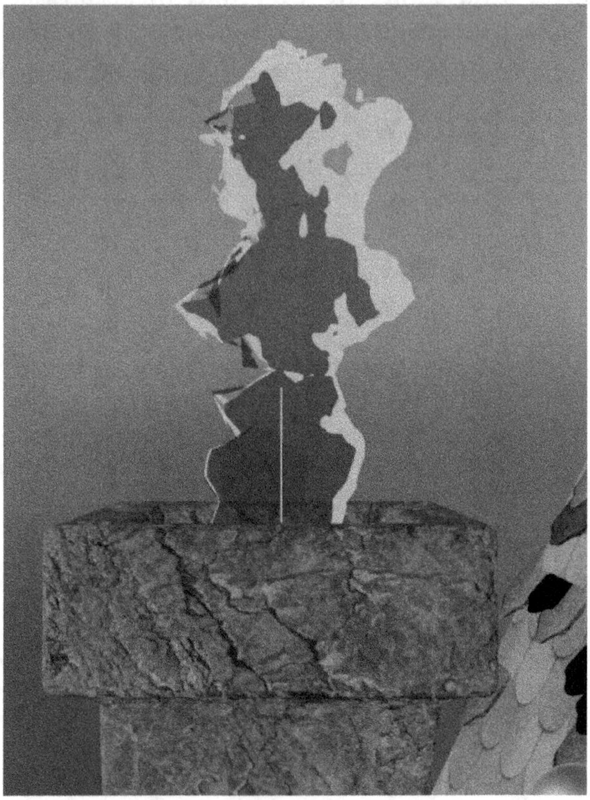

Figure 2.39: NPR smoke shader

You can move the **Empty** object up and down and see how the warping from the **Displace** modifier causes the flickering effect of smoke (albeit in a stylized manner). This is a really simplified version of this effect, and you could spend a lot more time and energy working this into something with a huge amount of detail, but this is a good starting place to work through some of the processes of creating stylized real-time VFX.

Summary

In this chapter, we covered two really useful ways of creating materials, one that involved using textures and one that involved using the inbuilt tools that come with Blender. Both are useful processes to know so that we can create textures fast and with style and composition in mind.

In the next chapter, we'll work on setting up the cameras and lights in the scene to showcase the work we've already done.

3
Lights, Camera...

From the last chapter, you should understand some of the very specific EEVEE material techniques that you can employ in your art and design. Practicing the creation of materials will only make your art better. But there's another topic that contributes to the look of your concept as much as, if not more than, materials, and that topic is lighting. Lights influence how we see things and how we understand their interaction with other objects; our materials aren't going to even be visible if we don't add lights to our scene.

In this chapter, we're going to walk through lighting an outdoor scene with EEVEE. Cycles has multiple additions to its rendering engine that make rendering things outside a lot easier, including Global Illumination and the Nishita Sky shader. But lighting a scene in EEVEE is possible too, especially if we use the render panel to add some effects and are smart about how we use the tools that we do have.

In this chapter, we will cover the following:

- Adding lighting to our mini-project
- Creating and configuring cameras
- Learning about the Line Art modifier

Technical requirements

In the last chapter, we left off at creating two materials, but we didn't delve into creating materials for every single piece of the mini-project. If we were to do that, this book would be thousands of pages long, and you wouldn't want to read it. So, from this point, there are two options: you can download `Mini-Project-Chapter 3` from GitHub and start with a file that has materials I've created for you, so you can jump straight into lighting.

The other option is to take the file from the last chapter that you worked on and use it to practice creating materials using the methods we went over so that when you get to this point, you won't need to download the aforementioned file. Do whatever you're most comfortable with. Regardless of your choice, make sure to download the resources for this chapter as well, so you have access to the HDRI I'll be using: `https://github.com/PacktPublishing/Shading-Lighting-and-Rendering-with-Blenders-EEVEE/tree/main/Chapter03`.

> **Material Creation Resources**
>
> Obviously, there are hundreds of approaches to creating materials, and YouTube is a great resource to get tutorials from. One channel that I would recommend is CG Cookie; their small videos are great bite-sized pieces of really useful information. Do a YouTube search for topics that you may want to know more about to get more information about the truly expansive topic of material creation. For more information on material creation, check out: *Top 6 Blender Nodes To Make Any Material in Blender* `https://www.youtube.com/watch?v=yffWd4kI51Q`.

Adding lighting to our mini-project

Lighting is the cornerstone of any good render, and in this chapter, we're going to work through the process of adding lights, tuning them to suit our overall environment, and then making sure they work properly inside of EEVEE. I'll cover both the artistic and technical aspects of what we're doing. We'll add a world lighting system and a few simple lights and then consider some of the ways EEVEE can be used for better lighting, especially in the compositing stage.

World lighting system

If you've been following along (or downloaded `Mini-Project 1-Chapter 3`), you should have something resembling what I have here, a scene with a lot of materials but not a lot of lighting:

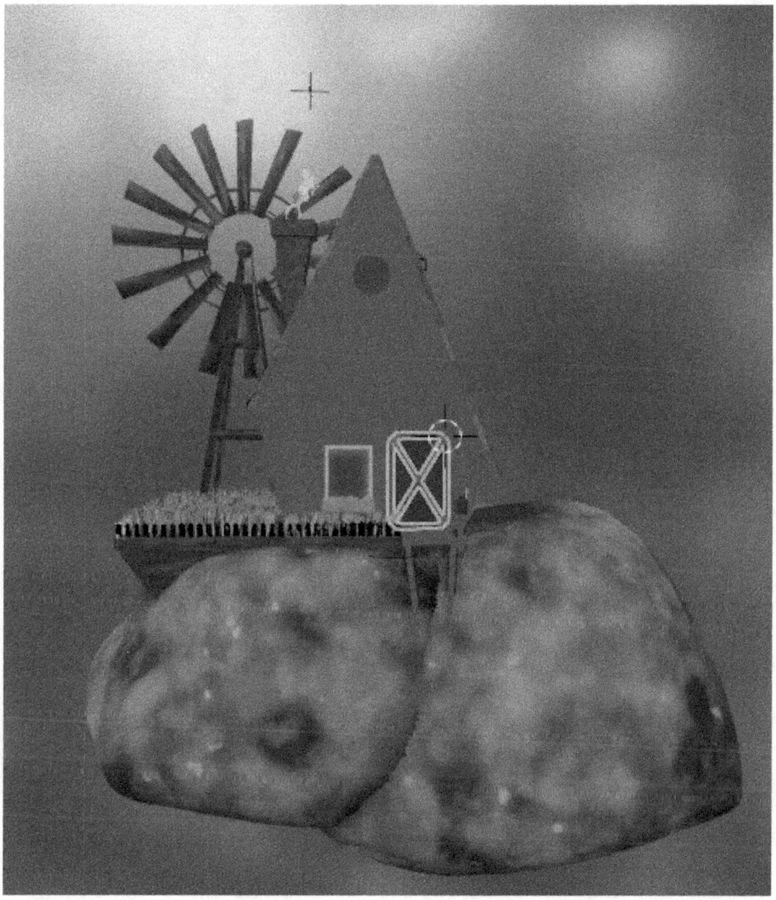

Figure 3.1: Scene with minimal lighting

Let's start to fix up our lighting by adding a world lighting system and tweaking it so we still get some good shadows inside the scene:

1. The first step is to disable the previous changes we made to the viewport shading. Now that we are working on lighting, we want to be able to see that lighting in the viewport so that we can make changes in real time.

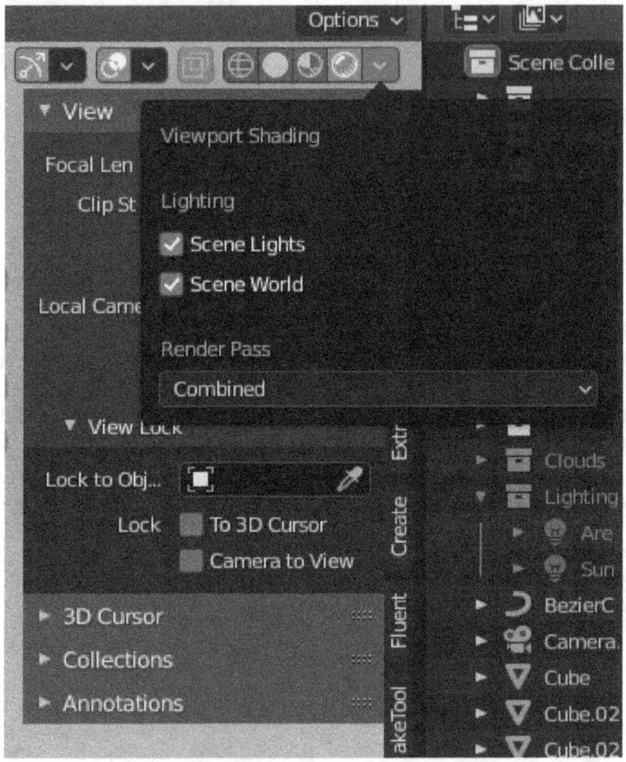

Figure 3.2: The Viewport Shading menu

2. Now, we can create a world lighting system. Do that by navigating to the **World** tab on the right-hand toolbar.

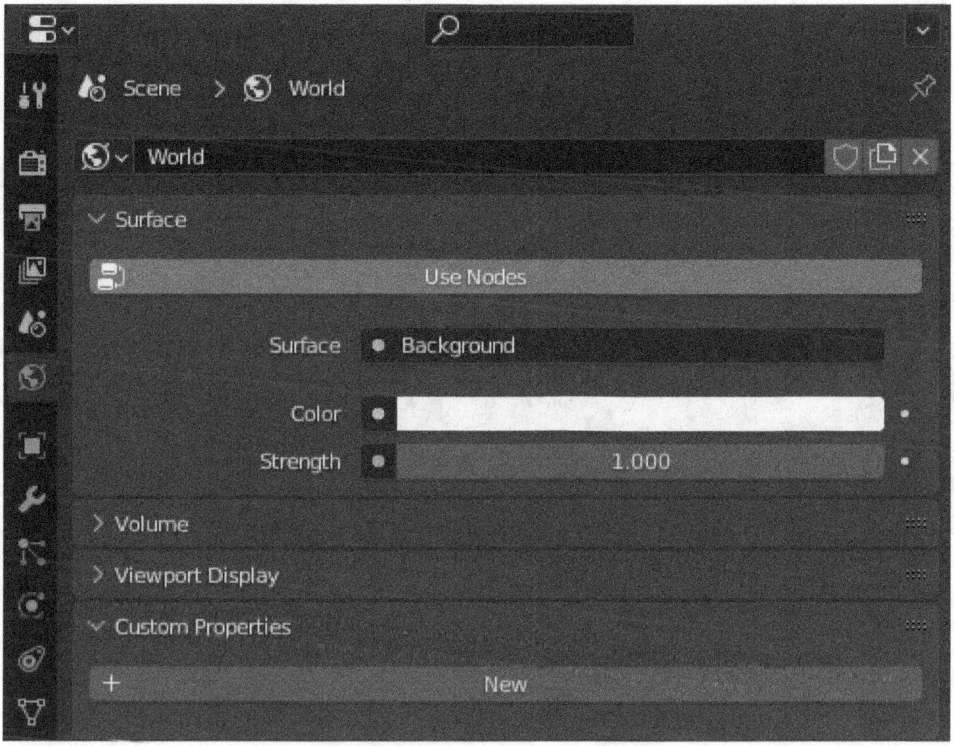

Figure 3.3: The World tab in the properties menu

3. Click the yellow dot to the right of the **Color** option. You should get a fly-out menu that will let you change the **Color** node directly in the toolbar.

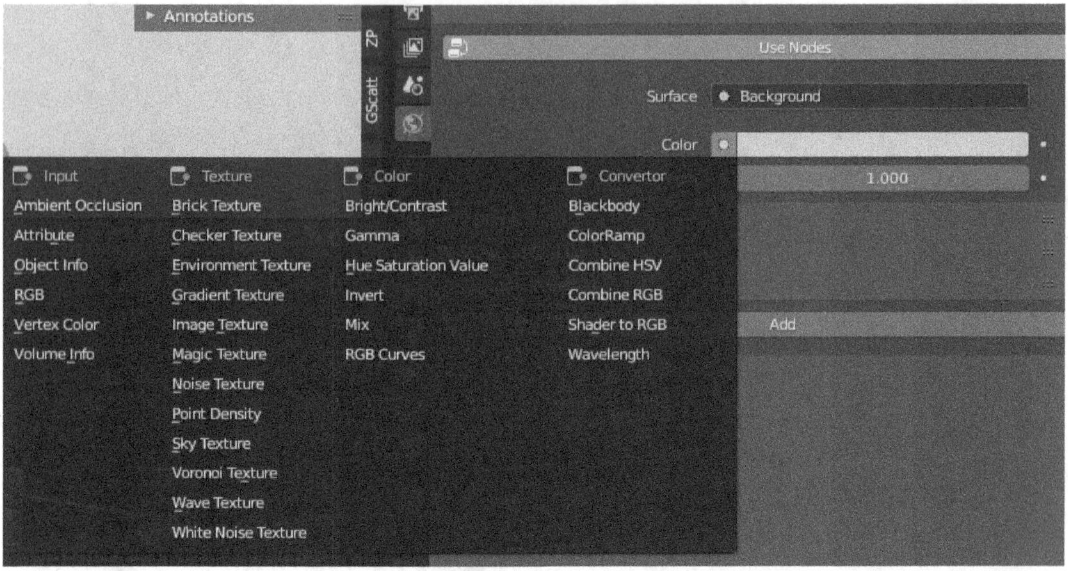

Figure 3.4: Adding an environment texture

4. Select **Environment Texture** in the **Texture** column. Now the toolbar should give you the option to open an environment texture from your hard drive.

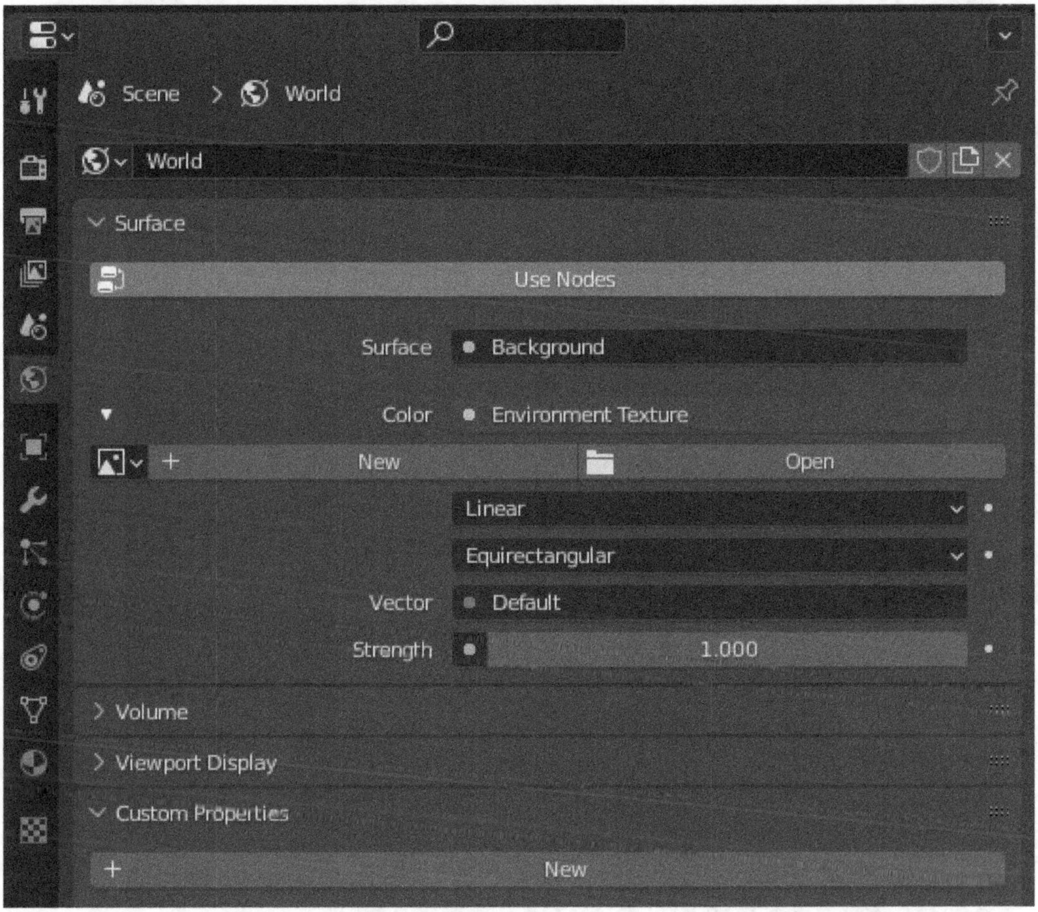

Figure 3.5: Adding an HDRI file

5. Select the **Open** button and open where you've stored the HDRI; you could have downloaded it from GitHub, or use any other HDRI you like instead.

You should now be able to see the world lighting system we just added in the viewport.

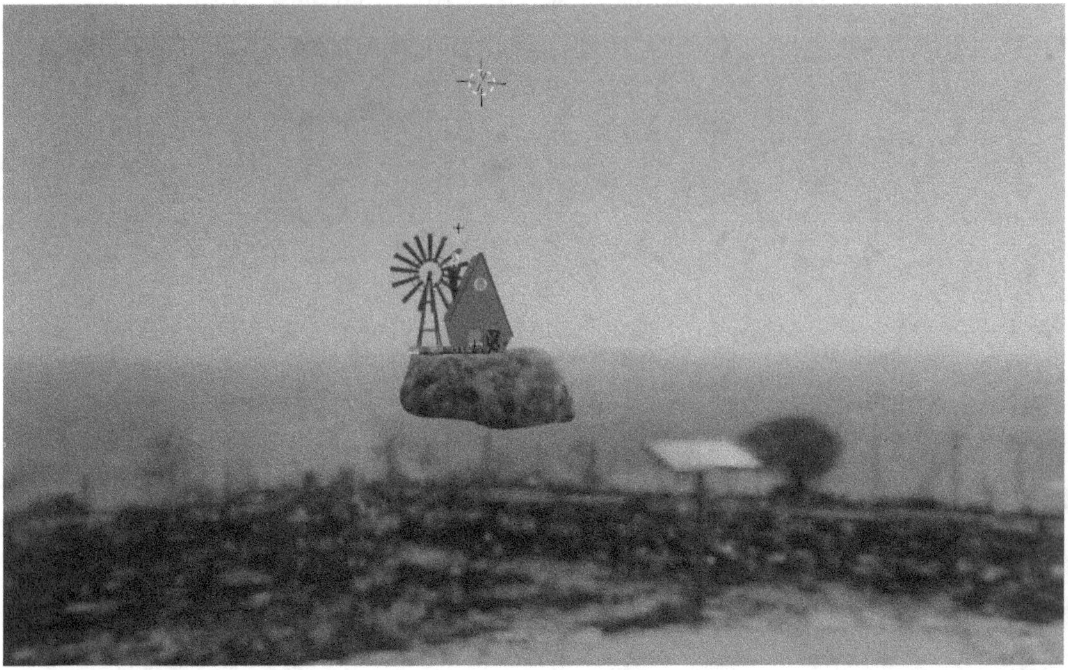

Figure 3.6: The viewport after adding the environment texture

Cool! But if you look at the render viewport, you might notice something is wrong with the lighting we just added... There aren't any shadows! In the next section, we'll figure out how to manipulate our HDRI so it gives us a background but allows us to substitute other aspects for the shadow-casting light.

Changing to the world shader editor

In order to better manipulate our environment texture, let's flip over to the world shader material space:

1. Go to the **Shader Editor** pane we set up for editing materials. Or, select the change editor button at the top left of any individual pane and select **Shader Editor**.

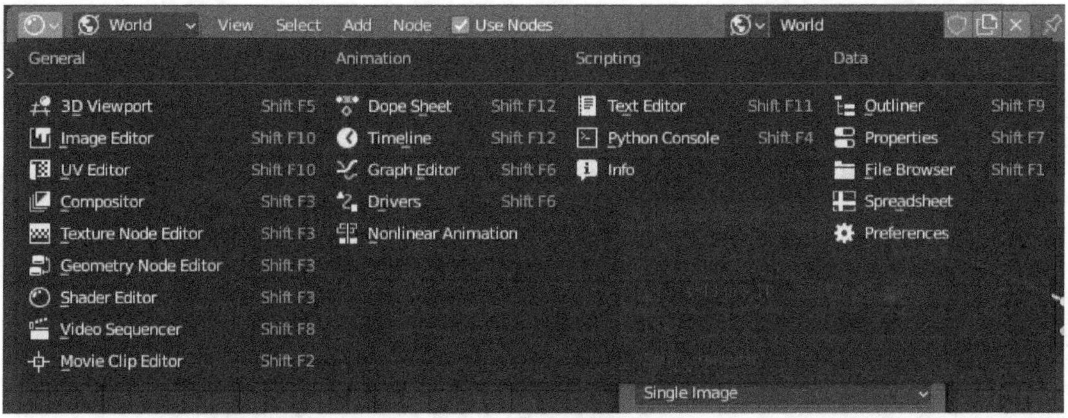

Figure 3.7: Opening the Shader Editor pane

2. Then, right next to that button is the **Shader Type** selection. Select the **World** option.

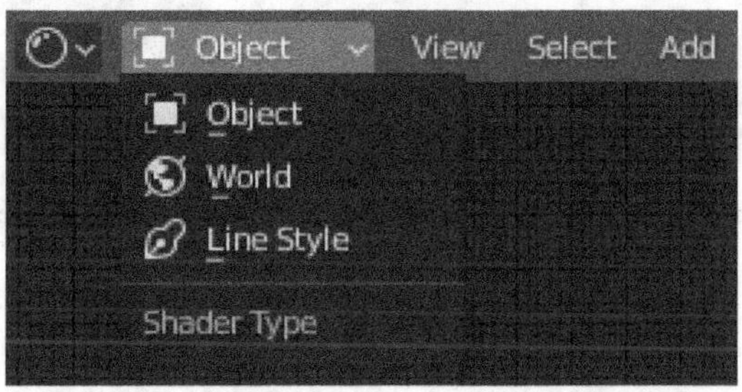

Figure 3.8: Shader Type selection options

3. We can see the HDRI we just added as a node graph.

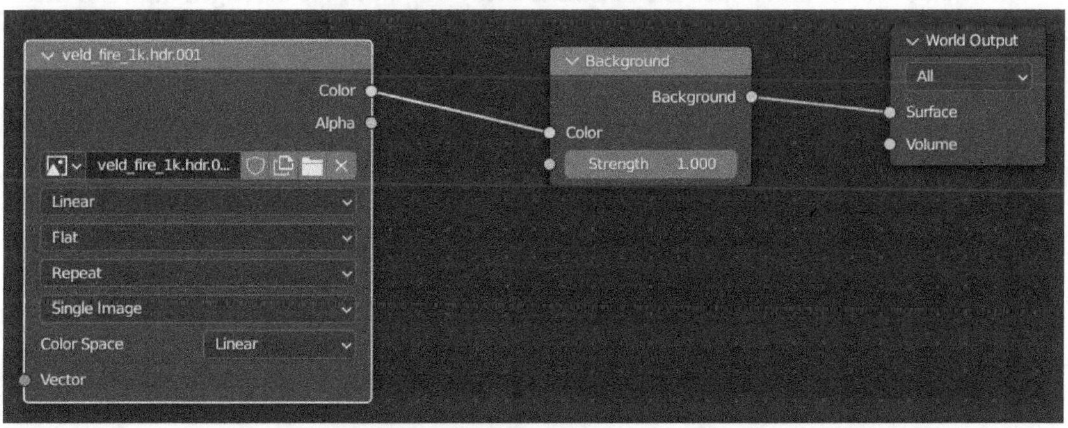

Figure 3.9: The HDRI in the node editor

Changing the HDRI to fit our scene

Now that we have the node graph open, we can start to change what is happening in the scene:

1. Select the environment texture and use the node wrangler shortcut we previously went over, *Ctrl* + *T*, to add a **Texture Coordinate** and **Mapping** node. Tweaking the **Z** rotation value will spin the HDRI so you can decide what is going to be in the background of your scene.

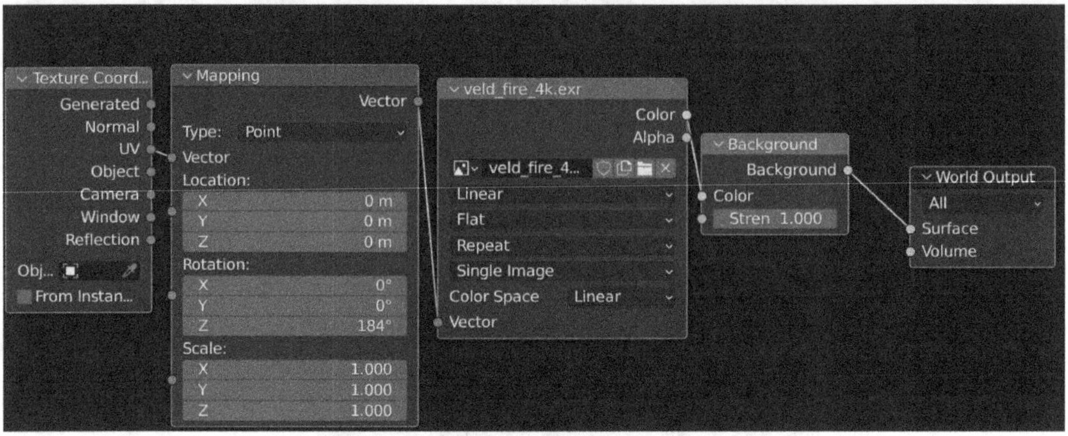

Figure 3.10: Mapping the HDRI texture

2. Now, let's limit the lighting so it only lights the background, not our objects. We're using this technique because EEVEE does not accurately calculate shadows using an HDRI light. So, we want the HDRI as a background for our lighting, but we want to use a sun light to add shadowing to the house. Add a **Light Path** node to the shader editor and attach the **Is Camera Ray** output to the **Strength** input on the **Background** node. **Is Camera Ray** tells the **Background** node to have **0** strength for areas that don't have camera rays and **1** for areas that do.

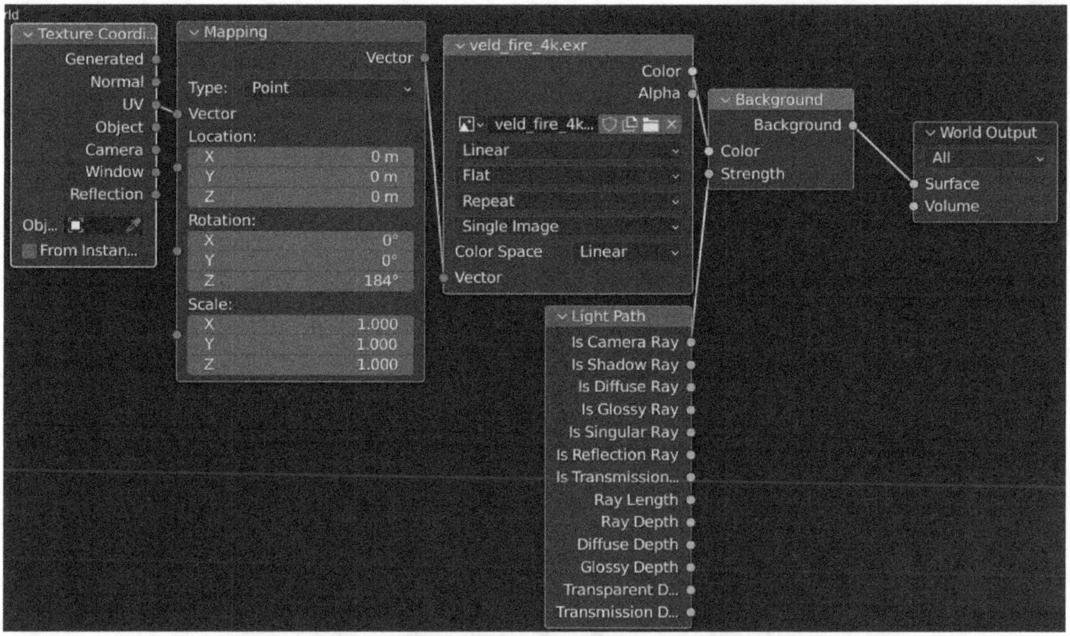

Figure 3.11: The Light Path node and Is Camera Ray set up

3. The final touch to make is adding an **RGB Curves** node between the HDRI output and the **Background** input and tweaking the background to your lighting. I decided I wanted the sky to be much bluer, so I increased the blue channel and the overall **Color** channel.

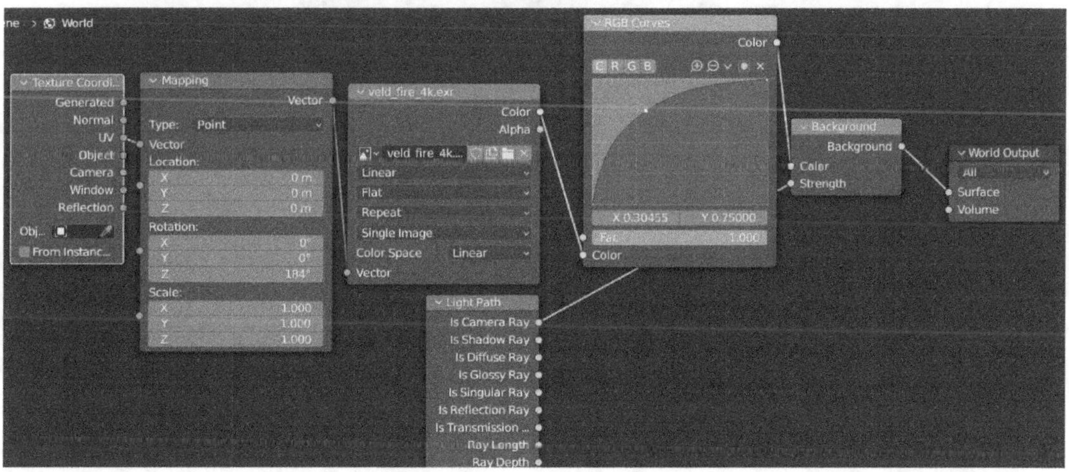

Figure 3.12: The RGB Curves node

4. The final look that we just created should show the HDRI in the background of the scene, but we should see minimal light hitting our mesh objects. This allows us to add a sun light in the next section to light the mesh objects with shadows and variations in lights.

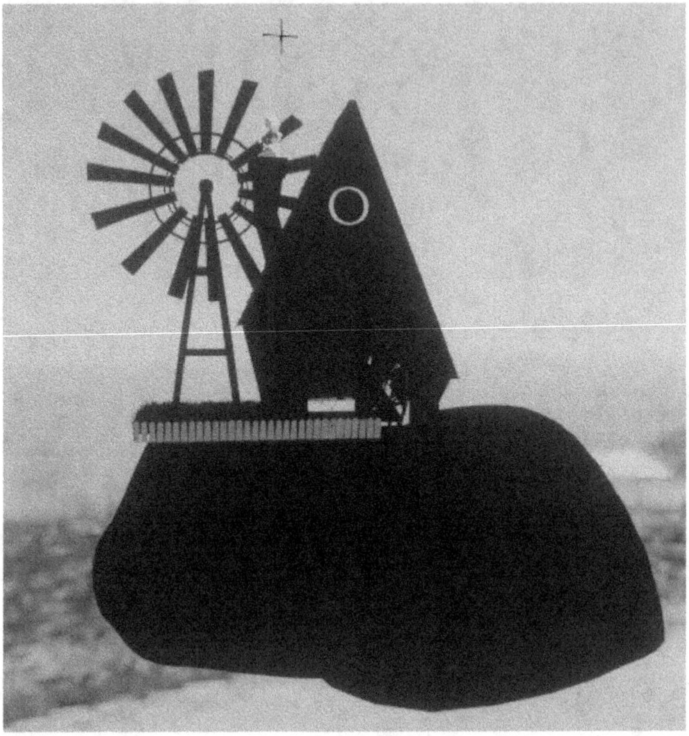

Figure 3.13: The HDRI lighting

Why are we using an HDRI just as our background without using the light from the HDIR? Well, as we discussed before, EEVEE doesn't have Global Illumination (yet), so the HDRI light won't actually bounce around our scene and produce shadows. As you can imagine, having no shadows makes everything look very strange and completely unnatural, which is not the look we're going for here. So, we limit the HDRI to the background of the scene and now we can work on creating shadows and highlights with the tools given to us in EEVEE, building on the basis of the HDRI. In the next section, we'll add some light objects and configure them to work with what we just created.

> **HDRI Resources**
>
> HDRIs are amazing resources, but for your average 3D artist, it can be hard to make your own. Luckily, there are a couple of sites that provide free HDRIs for a variety of environments. HDRLabs is one that I personally use for most of my projects. Poly Haven also has a great collection:
>
> `http://www.hdrlabs.com/sibl/archive.html`
>
> `https://polyhaven.com/hdris`

Adding lights to our scene

Now the HDRI is set up with EEVEE, we have an idea of how to light the scene, based on what our HDRI already has. We have an HDRI that has a lot of ambient blue light and a sun ray that comes from the right to the left on our screen. So, let's create some lights to mimic that setup, but since these lights are objects, EEVEE will be able to calculate their shadows. The first light we'll create is the area light.

Adding an area light

Area lights can be added through the standard **Add** menu, which can be accessed by hitting *Shift* + *A* and then navigating to **Lights** and clicking on the **Area** option. You should now be able to see the Light options menu in the right toolbar by clicking on the Light options button while the area light is the active object in your scene:

1. Let's change the color of the light to a light blue, which we can actually color pick using the eyedropper tool from the HDRI.
2. Increase the power of the light to `20000` (or more – decide what looks good to you!).
3. Then, increase the size to `50 m`.
4. Make sure the **Shadow** option is checked under the next subheading.
5. Raise the area light so it's about `50 m` on the positive *z* axis.

My area light properties look something like this:

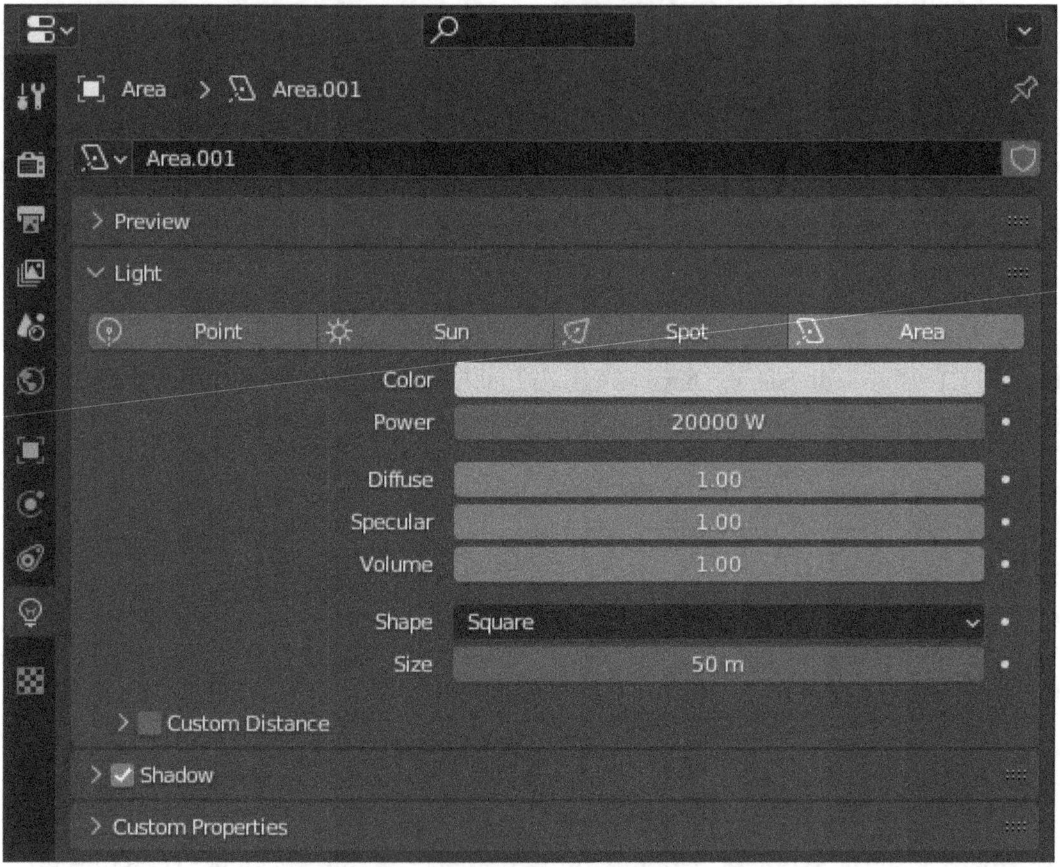

Figure 3.14: Configuring the area light

At this point in time, the light we have probably won't be all that impressive. The area light is only meant to simulate an ambient light that is diffusely reflected from the sky, so our house should be illuminated a little bit, but not much. Let's add a sun light, which does exactly as advertised... simulates the sun!

Adding a sun light

Sun lights can be found in the same menu as the area light, so go ahead and add one and navigate to the Light Options tab for our sun light object:

1. Change the color of the sun light to a very light yellow/orange.
2. Increase the strength to `10`.
3. Change the angle to `0.525`. The angle of the sun represents the size of the sun and therefore the overall hardness of the shadows. I also selected the sun and rotated it with the *R* key, so it was angled roughly from where the sun was in the HDRI we used.
4. Make sure **Shadow** is checked.

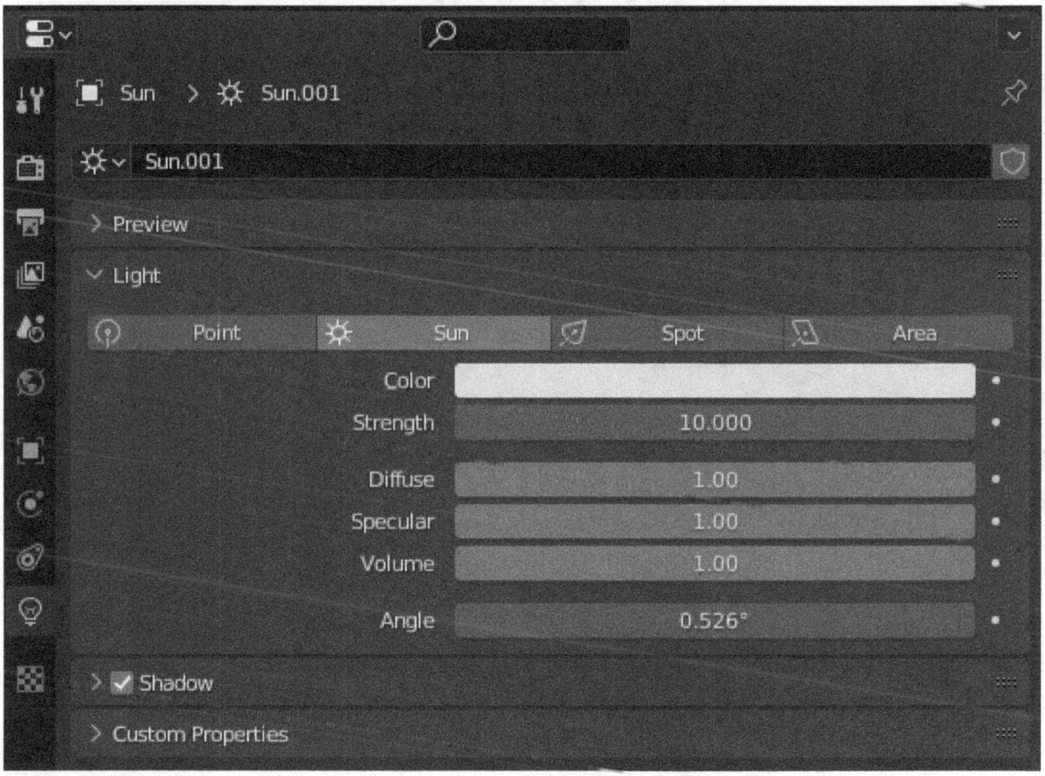

Figure 3.15: Configuring the sun light

Right now, the light in our scene should be pretty close to what we would have achieved with the HDRI, but with shadows. The materials we created in the last chapter react to the lighting that we have in the scene, so now is the time to look over them again and tweak them if necessary.

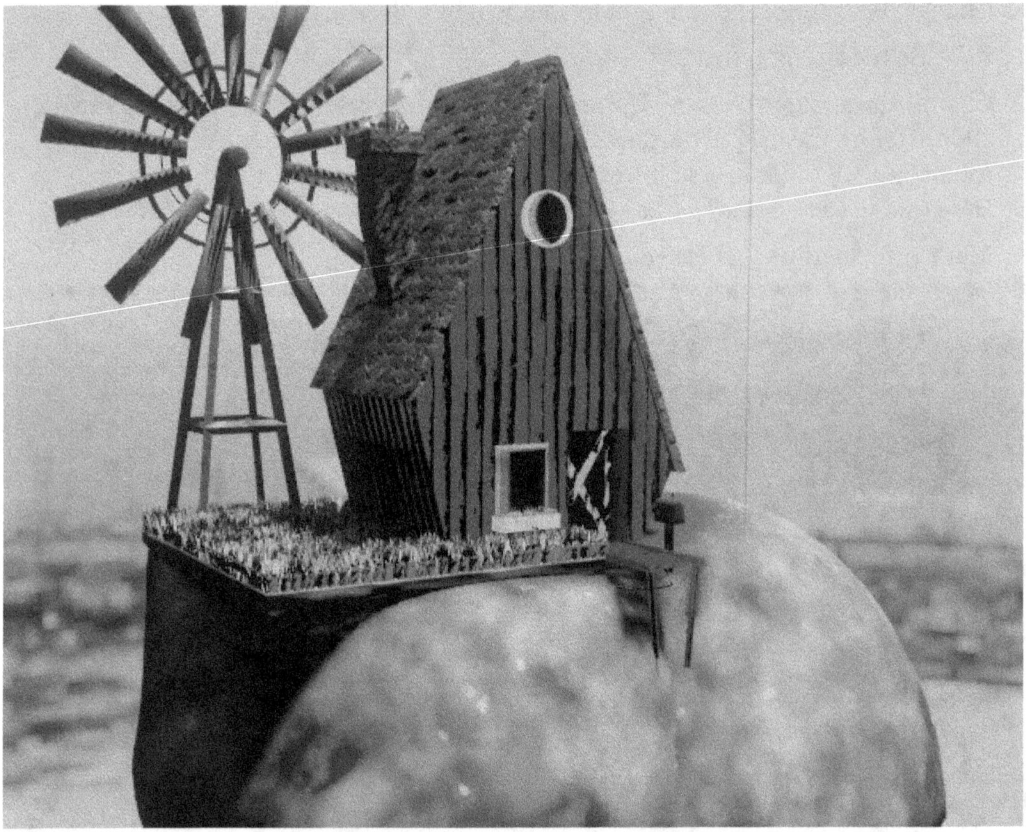

Figure 3.16: My lighting result

EEVEE can sometimes pose problems to a normal workflow, such as shadows not working with an HDRI, but with some quick and clever thinking, it's pretty easy to overcome the setback. In later chapters, we'll learn more about complex lights that need to be baked for EEVEE, but for now, let's leave this simple outdoor lighting setup as is.

In this subsection, we've worked on adding a lighting system that works with EEVEE and you understand a little more of the eccentricities of working with a real-time renderer. In the next section, we'll work on adding a camera and setting up the composition.

Creating and configuring cameras

The camera is maybe one of the most important parts of creating a 3D scene, because if you don't have a camera, you won't be able to render the scene and save it. But it's often very difficult for Blender users to use the camera intuitively and frame a shot with a composition that makes sense. In this section, we'll create a camera and go over some useful ways of using that camera, for both a general workflow and an EEVEE workflow.

Adding a camera

Let's add a simple camera to our scene. We'll use the typical workflow of *Shift* + *A* and then select the camera. This adds a camera to wherever our cursor is in the scene. Working with the camera like you would any other object, by selecting it, using the transform, and moving it, is very difficult. You can't see what the camera is seeing and it's hard to narrow in on a shot. So, we'll use two very cool tools here to position our camera the way we want:

1. Inside the 3D viewport, use your mouse to position your view to what you generally would want to camera view to look like. I decided I wanted to look down on the house from an acute angle.

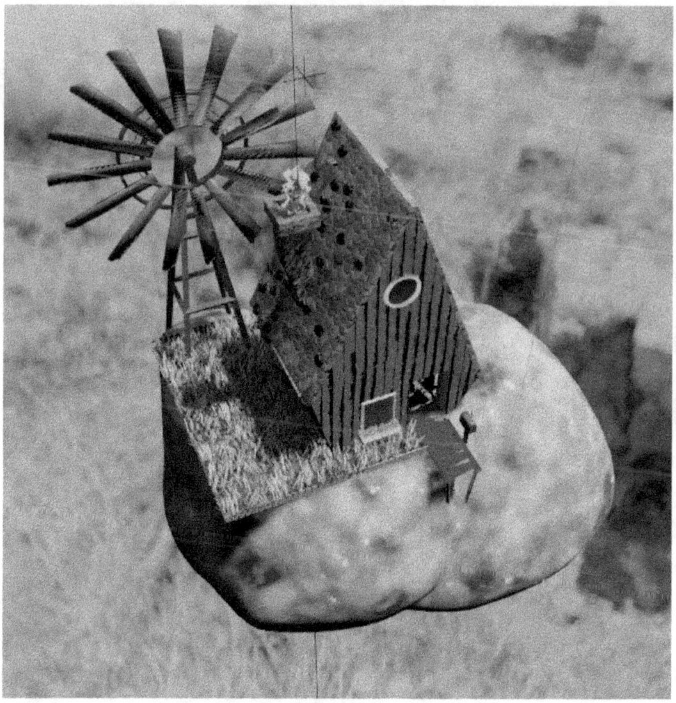

Figure 3.17: My view in the viewport

2. Once you have the view you want, press *Ctrl* + *Shift* + *0* on the Numpad.
3. The camera view should now match your viewport view. You can test this by pressing *0* on the Numpad to toggle your camera view on and off.

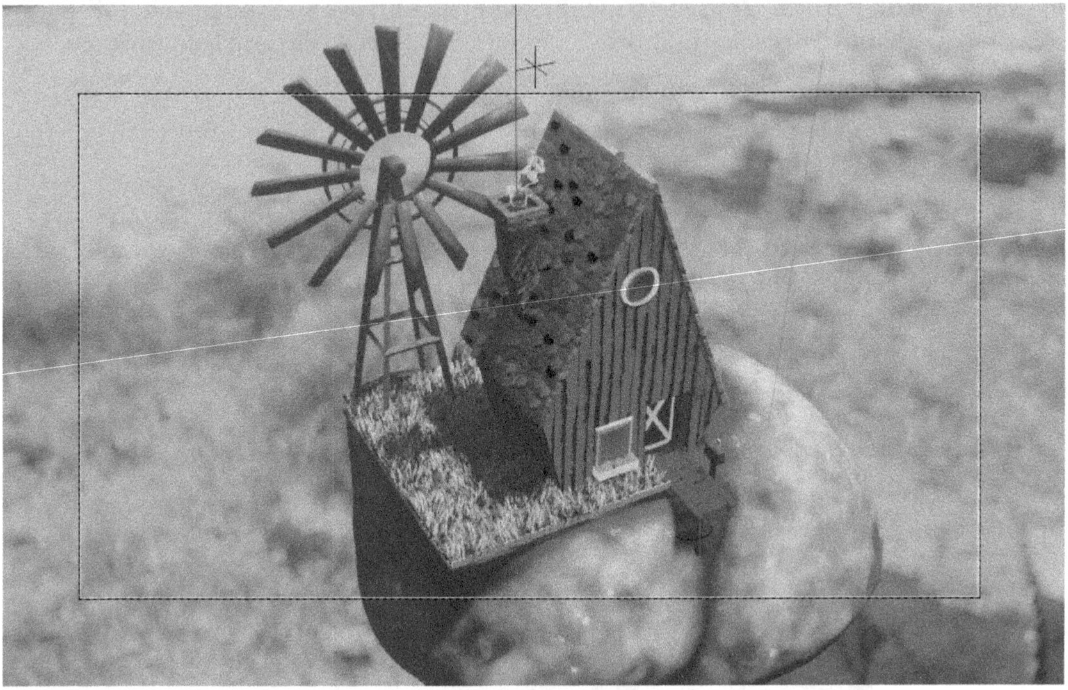

Figure 3.18: My camera view after pressing Ctrl + Shift + Numpad 0

4. We can now tweak our view directly in the viewport. Make sure you're already in **Camera View** mode. Press *N* while in the 3D viewport to open the right-hand side menu, if you don't already have it open. Select the **View** tab and check the box next to **Camera To View**, which is underneath the **To 3D Cursor** box. You can now use your mouse to move your viewport as usual, but now the camera will be locked to your viewport.

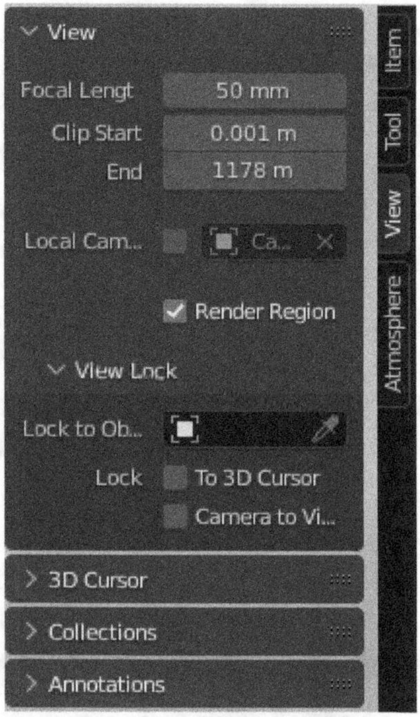

Figure 3.19: Checking the Lock Camera to View box

5. Simply uncheck the **Camera to View** box when you are happy with your camera view.

We've successfully added a camera and used two distinct methods to edit the camera view, therefore providing us with a better way to compose our render. Next up, we'll explore some camera properties that can help you create a better render.

Camera properties

You might be aware that in Cycles, there's a way to create a render border, so you don't render anything that's outside of the camera view in preview. This functionality doesn't exist in the same way inside of EEVEE; we have to use the camera properties to mimic this function:

1. Select the camera in the outliner.
2. Using the right-side properties menu, navigate to the 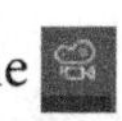 tab.
3. Scroll down to **Viewport Display** and select the **Viewport Display** area drop-down to see more options.

4. Check the box next to **Passepartout** and turn the value up to `1.000`.

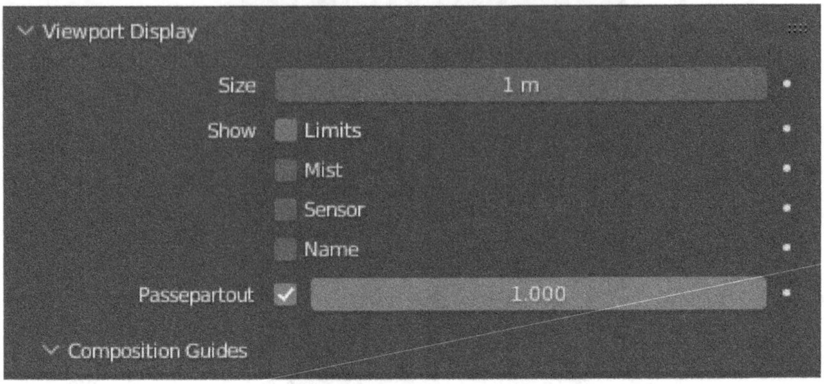

Figure 3.20: Selecting the Passepartout option

5. You should now only see what the camera will render, with the rest blacked out. I find this really helps me to fine-tune the image that I want without being distracted by things that won't ever appear in the final render.

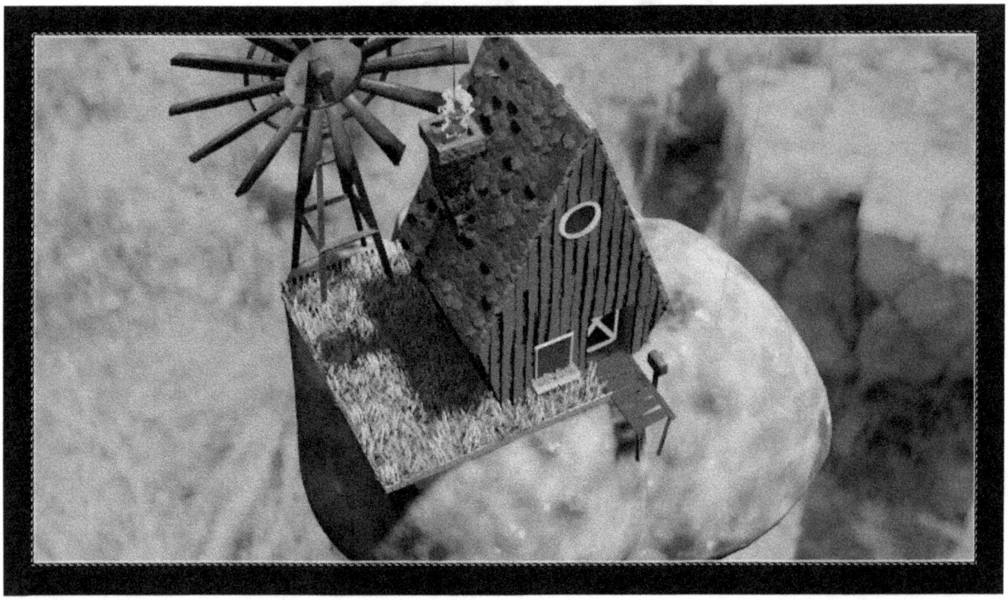

Figure 3.21: The viewport with Passepartout

Another really interesting setting is a submenu of the **Viewport Display** menu, the **Composition Guides**. These guides provide different overlays to assist with composition. I like to use the **Thirds** option (which can be activated by checking the box) to line up the features of interest on where the lines intersect. This is called the rule of thirds and is a very traditional way of composing an image.

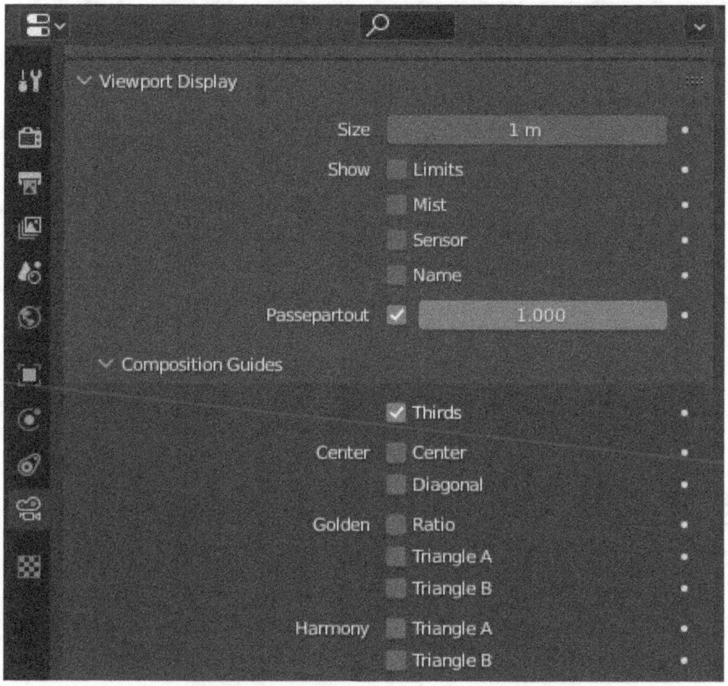

Figure 3.22: Checking the Thirds option

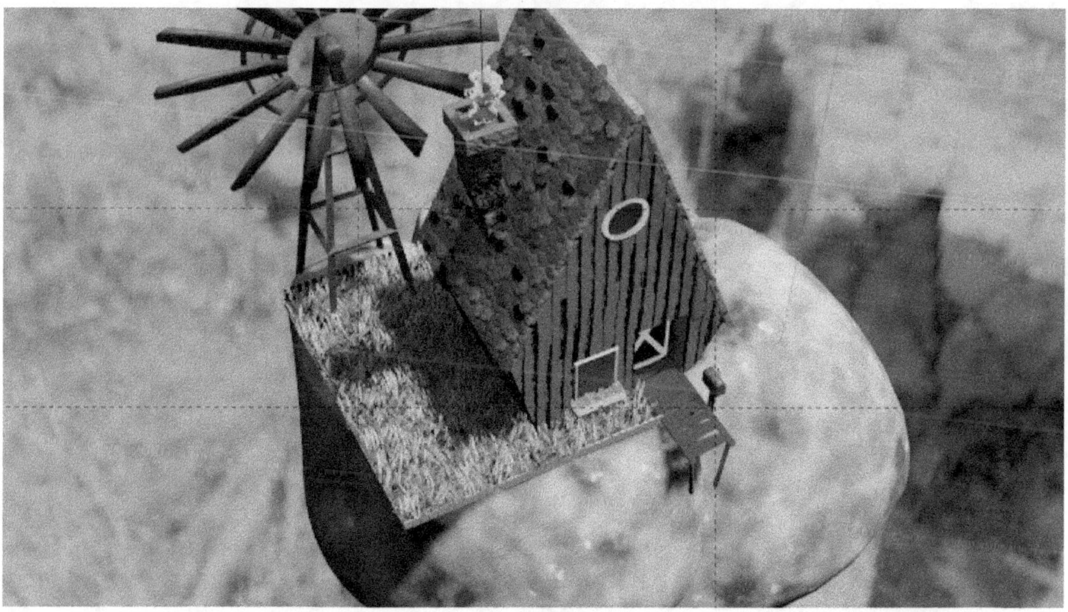

Figure 3.23: Thirds superimposed over the viewport for help in composition

> **Learning More about Composition**
> Composition and design are infinite topics that you could spend a lifetime studying and still not know everything about. I would suggest learning some basic photography concepts as you advance in your career in Blender. Online resources are very useful to get an overview of composing and also understand more about lighting and design in general. Check out this site if you want to start learning about the Rule of Thirds and other Composition concepts: `https://digital-photography-school.com/rule-of-thirds/`.

Now that we've learned about composition and some materials, we'll briefly discuss a new aspect of Blender 3.0 that streamlines the process of creating cartoon-style line art.

Learning about the Line Art modifier

A quick, cool effect to add further interest to the house in the sky we're building is the Line Art modifier. This is a brand-new modifier that was added with the past release of 2.93. Previously, there was a postprocessing ability to add lines to the geometry of your objects, but now we can actually see that in the viewport; so, let's give it a try and see whether we can push this house we're working on to be a little more stylized. The Line Art modifier only works if you already have a camera in the scene, so that's why we're adding the Line Art modifier now.

The Line Art modifier only works with a **Grease Pencil** object, so let's add a **Collection Line Art** object to the scene.

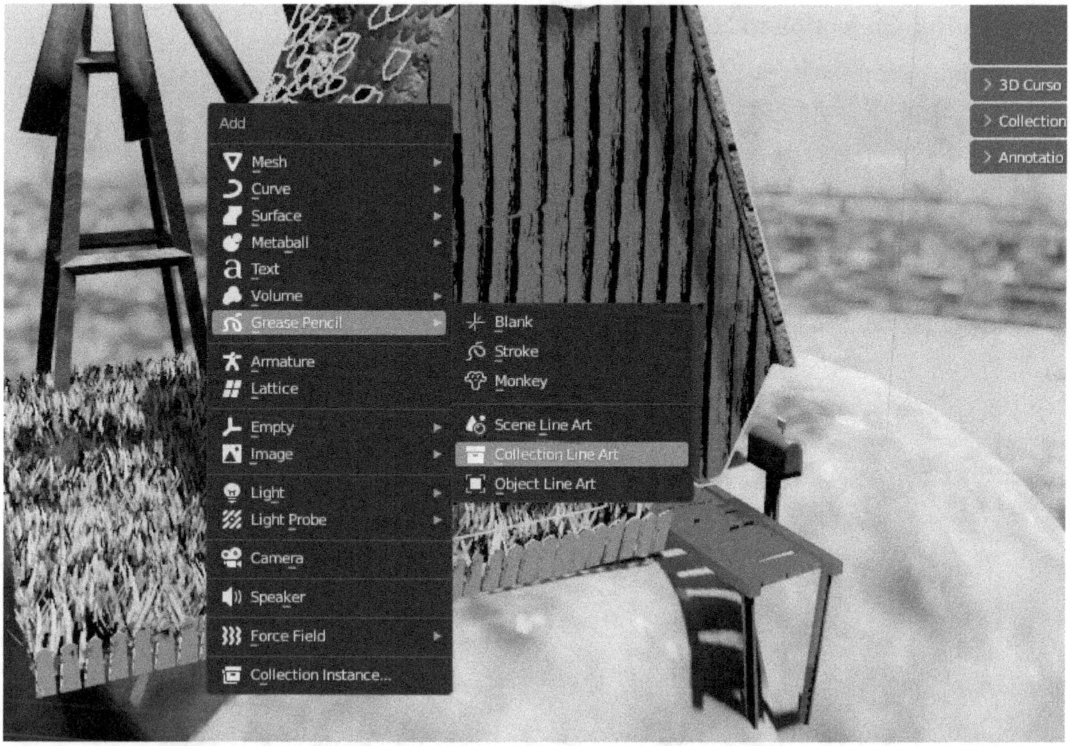

Figure 3.24: Collection Line Art modifier

Side Note

Shift + *A* is the shortcut for the **Add** menu, something that I recommend you use instead of the more laborious **Add** button on the menu bar.

Change **Source Collection** to **House** and **Target Layer** to **Lines**.

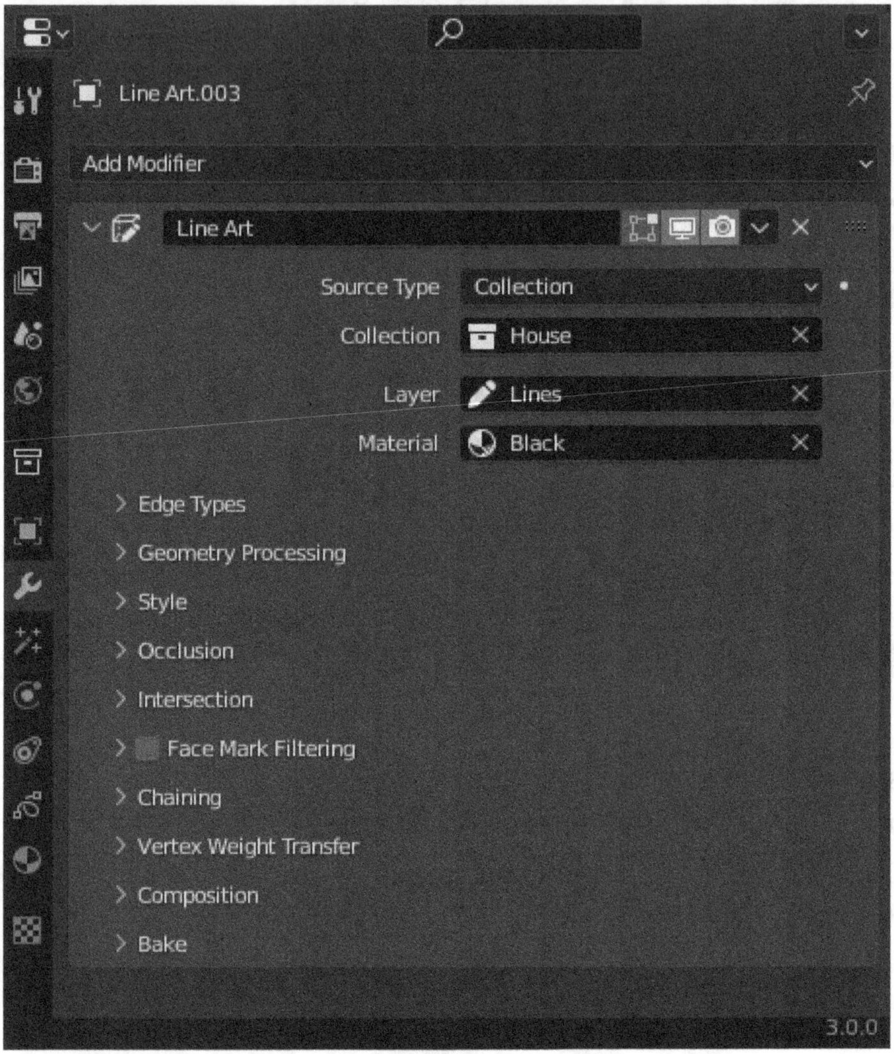

Figure 3.25: Line Art modifier options

Target Material only takes **Grease Pencil** materials. I have mine set to just a simple black color, but you can go into the **Grease Pencil** material toolbar and add any number of line colors to try out. Materials in **Grease Pencil** work similarly to other materials, but in this menu, you have the option to fill or just render a stroke. Try out some of these options and see whether you can come up with something you like.

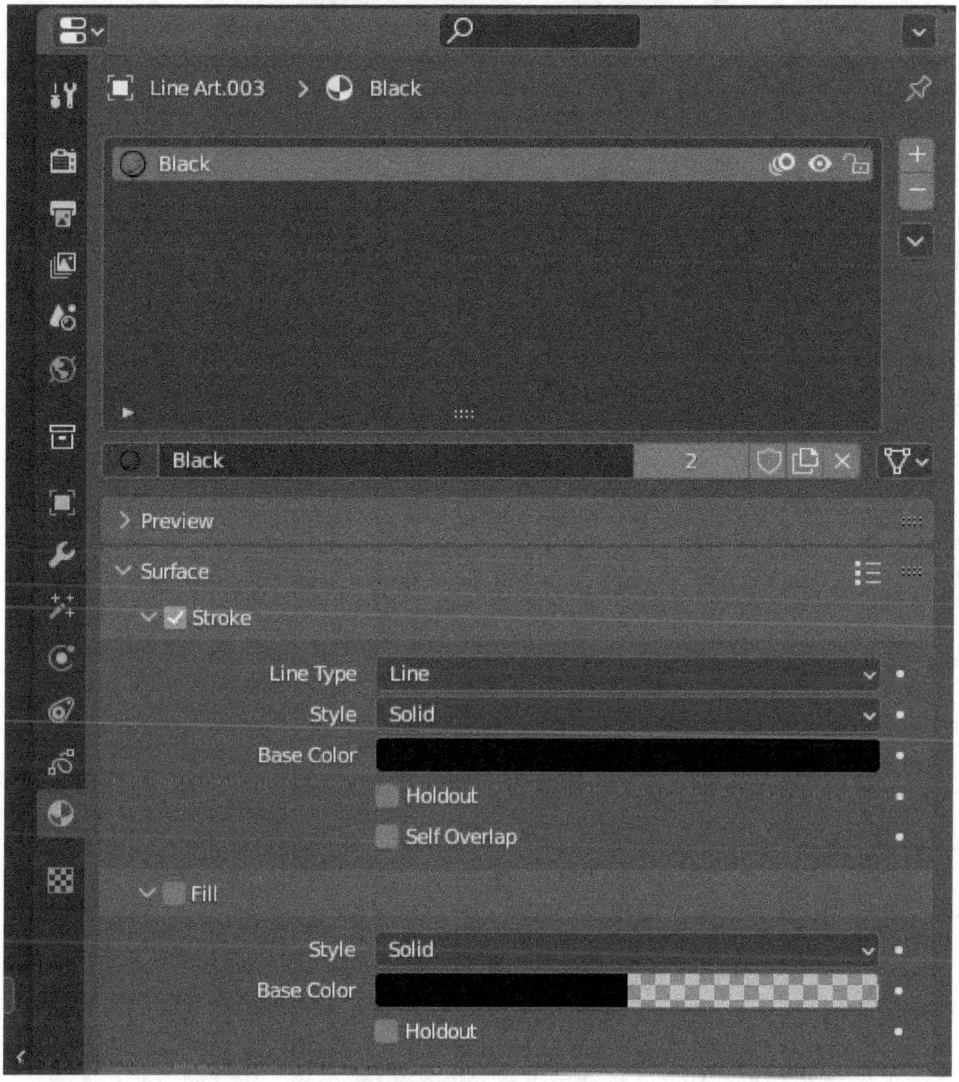

Figure 3.26: Grease Pencil material

My final Line Art modifier renders lines onto my object inside of the 3D viewport. It's also an awesome feature if you just want to render lines for a "blueprint" effect.

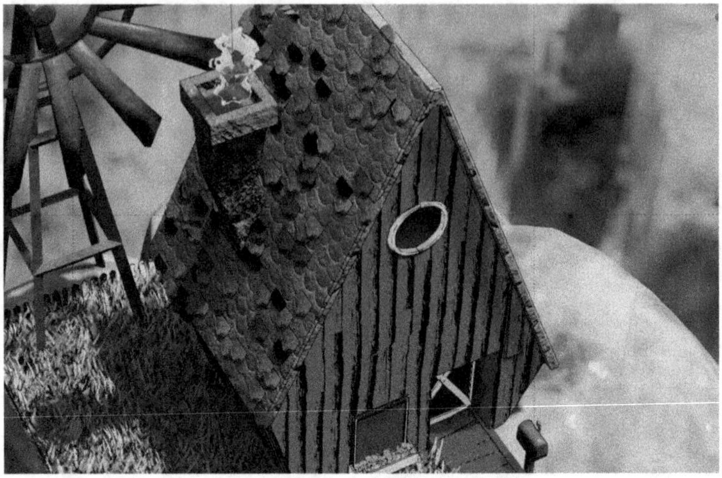

Figure 3.27: Line art applied to the house

> **Side Note**
>
> You may notice a slowdown in your processing ability with the Line Art modifier when you try to go into edit mode. I recommend adding the Line Art modifier when you're done with a piece of the scene and are ready to render, or hide it from the viewport while you work on other things to save yourself some lag and possible crashes. It's still a feature very much in development, so bear that in mind when using it.

The Line Art modifier is a work in progress I hope you can now see the power of such a feature and the ways to use it in your future art.

Summary

In this chapter, we looked at lighting cameras and the Line Art modifier, covering some of the peculiarities of working inside of EEVEE. We're already seeing that EEVEE can sometimes provide roadblocks that can be annoying to navigate around, but overall, being able to see our render in real time far outweighs those pain points. The Line Art modifier in particular is something to keep an eye on, as more features for this tool are added in future versions of Blender. This is just the beginning of this powerful feature.

I hope that you are starting to grasp the awesome power of EEVEE and are ready to take the work we've done, add some simple volumetrics, and then render it out as a full scene in the next chapter.

4
Non-Physical Rendering

The last chapter ended with us applying some of the finishing touches to our materials, modeling, effects, lighting, camera, and design. But in 3D animation, and especially with EEVEE, that isn't enough to consider a piece of art "finished." As you know, we have to render! And rendering can sometimes be the trickiest part of the equation that is a scene. If you've worked with EEVEE before inside of Blender, you know how frustrating it can be to make EEVEE do what you want. There's so much to know and understand about how EEVEE works that when it comes to rendering, it can seem overwhelming. That's why we're starting with a non-physically rendered scene so that we can start to understand how to use some of the tools the Blender developers have given us and start to feel more comfortable setting up EEVEE for success. In *Sections 2 and 3* of this book, we'll go over more techniques in the rendering stage, so don't feel too bad if you still have questions after this part; we'll get to them, I promise! For now, we'll look at a few things:

- Adding clouds to our composition
- Configuring Render settings
- Using layers to combine elements in the compositor

Technical requirements

In this chapter you again have two options – download my prepared and completed file with all my assets, materials, lights, and cameras, or use your own that you created. We'll be finishing off the scene and then rendering it out, so make sure you're working on a computer with a GPU with the best specs that you can muster. Rendering is the most time-intensive and computationally expensive part of the animation process, so plan accordingly. Even if you don't have an amazing computer, EEVEE is obviously a lot less intensive than Cycles, so don't worry if you're trying to work on a laptop or an old computer. It's just better to work with the best you have for this chapter. The other file you might want for this chapter is named `MiniProject1_Compositing.blend`, and will be used in the final compositing section.

The sample files used in this chapter are available here:

`https://github.com/PacktPublishing/Shading-Lighting-and-Rendering-with-Blenders-EEVEE/tree/main/Chapter04`

Adding clouds to our composition

We've created a cool house with some fun features, but, we can still see the empty space around the house, which doesn't really lend itself to a good composition. Let's fix this right now. The reason we've waited until the very end to add the clouds to our scene is that the volumetric shader we'll be using requires tweaking the Render settings, so it doesn't make much sense to create clouds until we're ready to render. We're starting from the file I have set up, which looks something like this at the start:

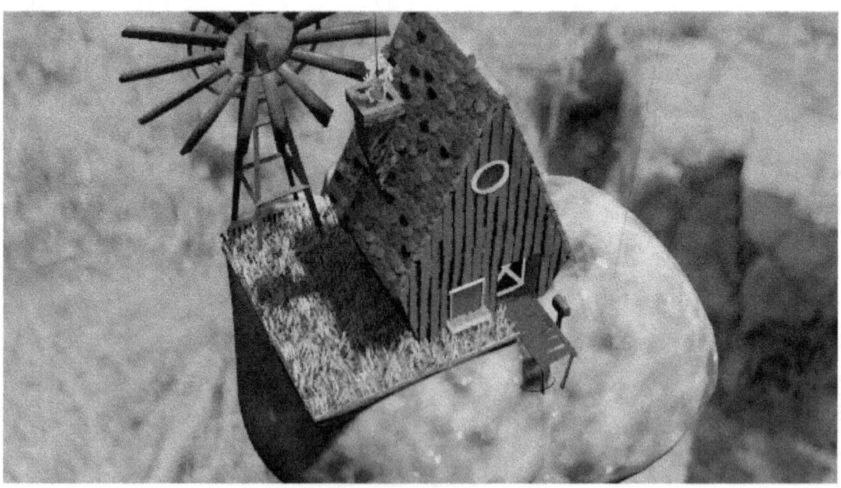

Figure 4.1: Starting image

I'm looking from the camera view and all my lights, materials, and background are set up. The house looks good, but we probably don't want that blue surrounding space; it doesn't look good! Let's add some clouds to fix it:

1. Add a cube to the scene, using *Shift* + *A*, and select the Cube object.
2. Give it a new material and delete the **Principled** shader that comes by default.
3. Add a **Principled Volume** node and plug it into the **Volume** input under **Material Output**.

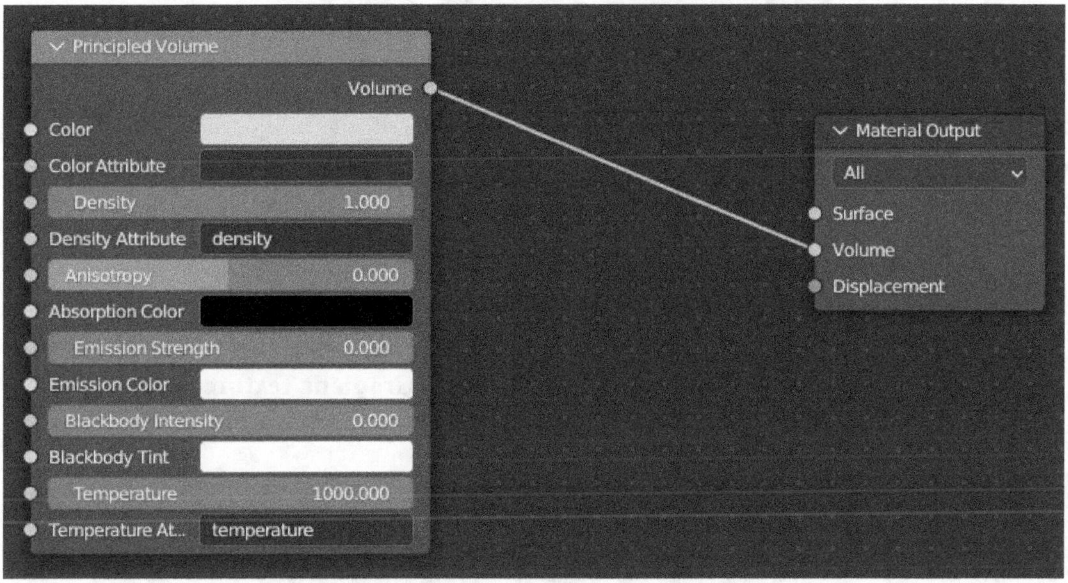

Figure 4.2: Principled Volume shader

4. Let's try an experiment to show how **Principled Volume** works inside EEVEE because it doesn't work as expected. If we go to the cube we added the **Principled Volume** shader to and edit it, you can see that the **Principled Volume** shader doesn't actually change with the geometry shape. The **Principled Volume** shader in EEVEE can only be rendered in a cube shape! So we can't model some cloud geometry and just have clouds work; we need to apply some shader magic.

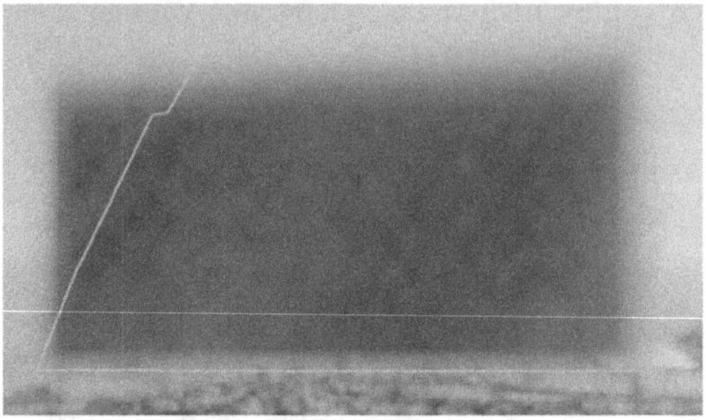

Figure 4.3: Volume shader only rendering in cubic form

5. Undo the previous edit (*Ctrl* + *Z*) and come back into the shading workspace. Add a **Texture Coordinate** node, a **Mapping** node, and a **Gradient Texture** node, with the dropdown changed to **Spherical**. Set them up as in the following screenshot:

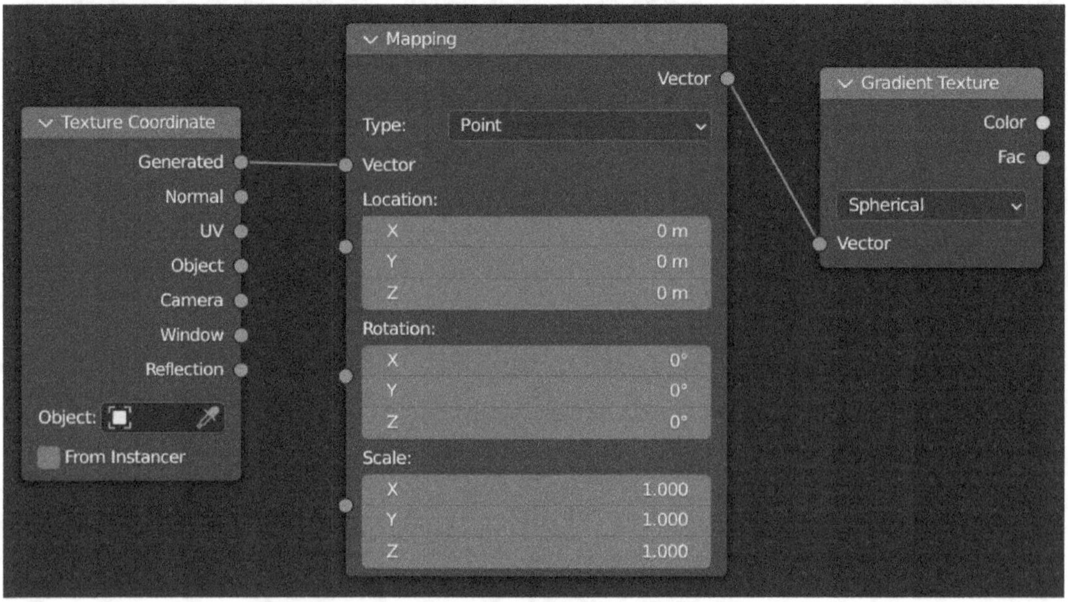

Figure 4.4: Mapping node

6. Then, use the *Ctrl* + *Shift* shortcut and click on the **Gradient** node to preview the **Gradient Texture** node in the viewport. You might not see the result instantly (I have to rotate my cube around to see the **Gradient Texture** node being projected on it).

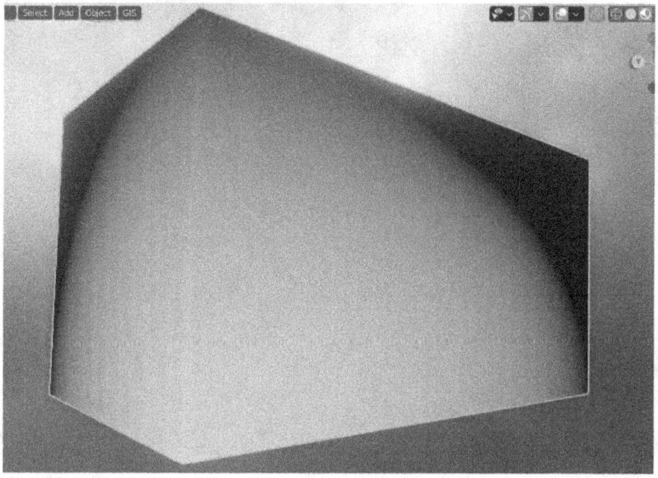

Figure 4.5: Gradient Texture default

7. I tweaked a lot of my values in the **Mapping** node to make **Gradient** cover my cube how I wanted. These are the values I ended up with, but experiment and see what you prefer:

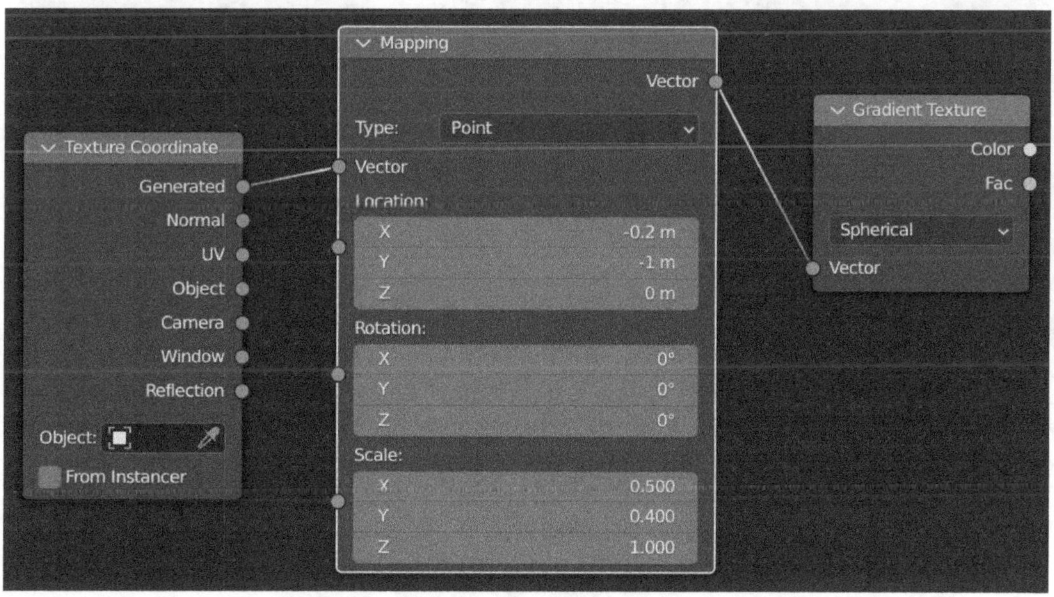

Figure 4.6: Mapping node with changes

When we preview **Gradient Texture** with the new mapping, you should have something like this on your cube:

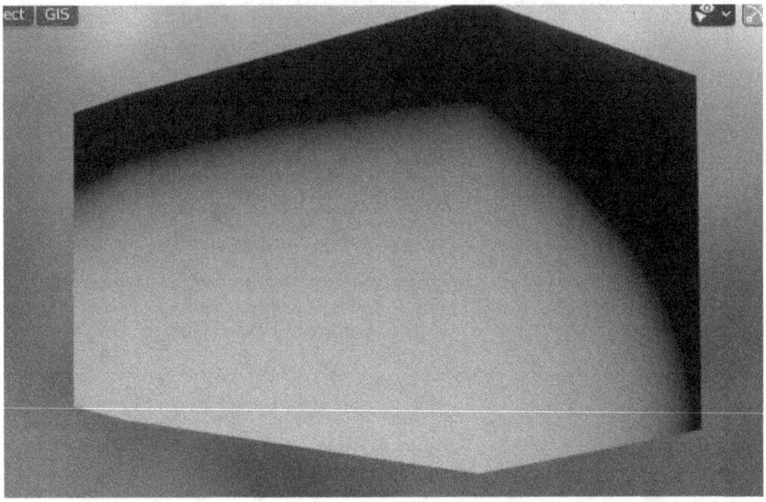

Figure 4.7: Gradient with mapping changes

8. Next, we'll add **Noise Texture** and a **MixRGB** node.

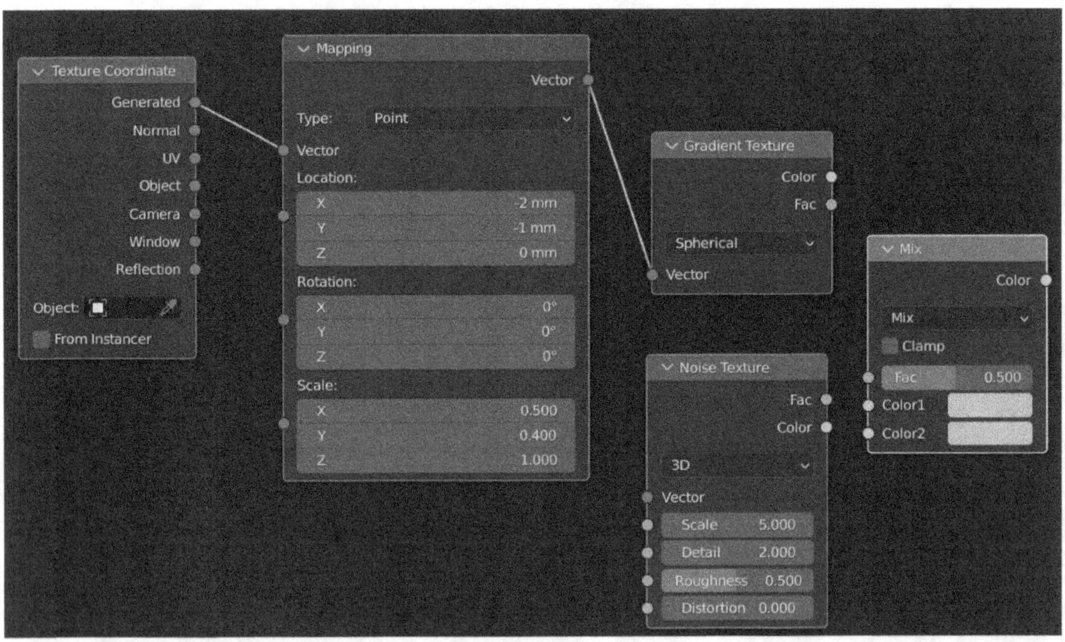

Figure 4.8: Adding MixRGB and Noise Texture

9. Put the output of **Gradient Texture** into the top **Color** input of the **Mix** node and the **Fac** output of **Noise Texture** into the input of the bottom **Color** socket of the **Mix** node. Change the **Blending** mode of the **Mix** node to **Multiply**, change **Fac** to **1**, and then use our shortcut of *Ctrl* + *Shift* + *Click* on the **Mix** node to preview it.

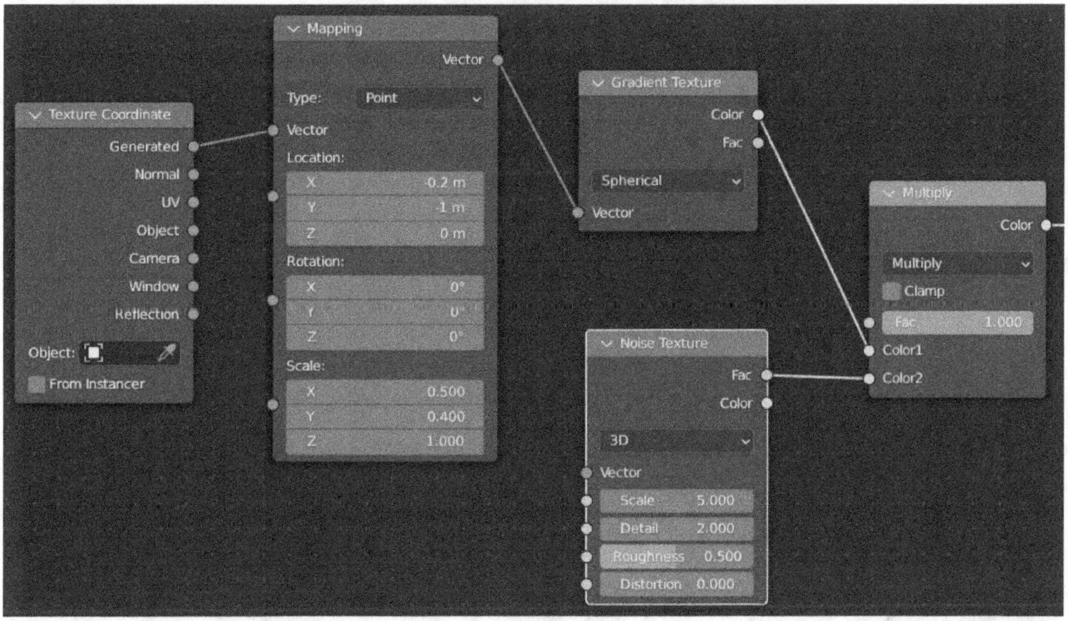

Figure 4.9: Mixing with Noise Texture

> **Node Wrangler Preview**
>
> Node Wrangler is an amazing add-on (especially since it's free!), and one of its most amazing pieces of functionality is the ability to preview any node in the viewport by just pressing *Ctrl* + *Shift* and clicking on the node you want to preview. Try it out. It's very useful to be able to preview a specific part of your shader without having to wonder whether you're tweaking the right value.

10. Next, we'll add a color ramp to the output of the **Mix** node. This creates a gradient of color that we can change by moving the color sliders on the left and right.

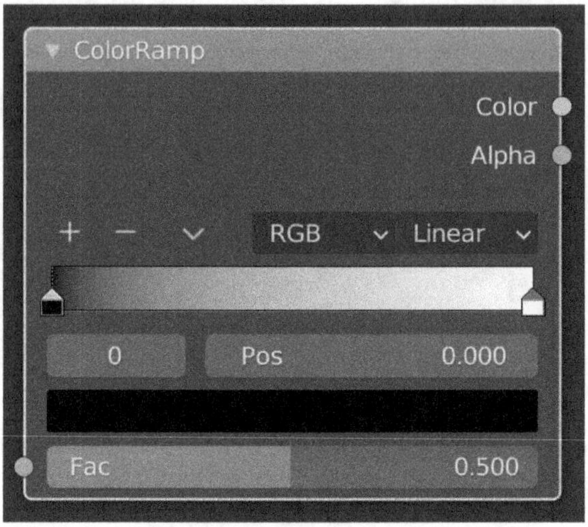

Figure 4.10: Adding a color ramp

11. I changed the white color on the right to a more grayish color and then pulled the right slider over almost next to the left slider.

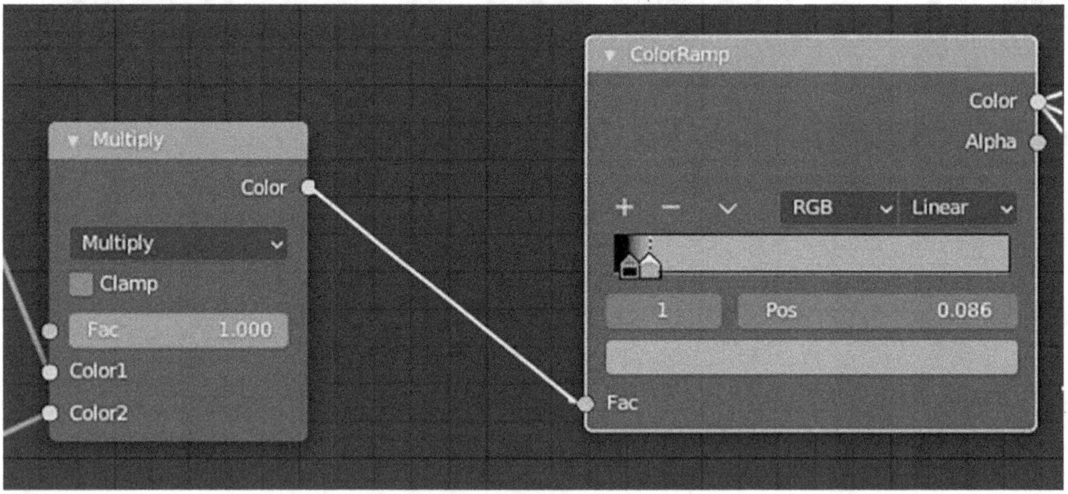

Figure 4.11: Adding a color ramp

My preview of the color ramp now looks like this in the viewport.

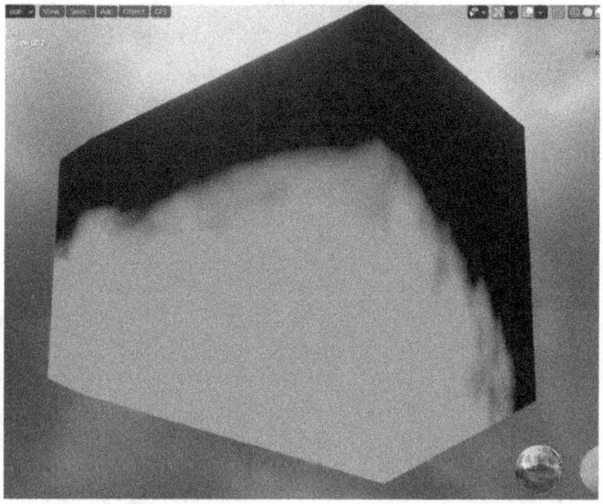

Figure 4.12: Noise and Gradient Texture output

12. So now that we've sketched out the rough outline of a cloud on our cube, all we have to do is use it to create the volumetric appearance of clouds. How we'll do this is a decidedly non-physically-based method, so applying this exact procedure to a photoreal scene is not advisable. We'll cover that in the next two projects. Let's take the **Color** output from the color ramp and input it into **Density** of our **Principled Volume** shader, the **Emission Strength** input, and the **Emission Color** input. So, anywhere our incoming texture is black is going to be see-through, and anywhere we have white is going to be "cloud."

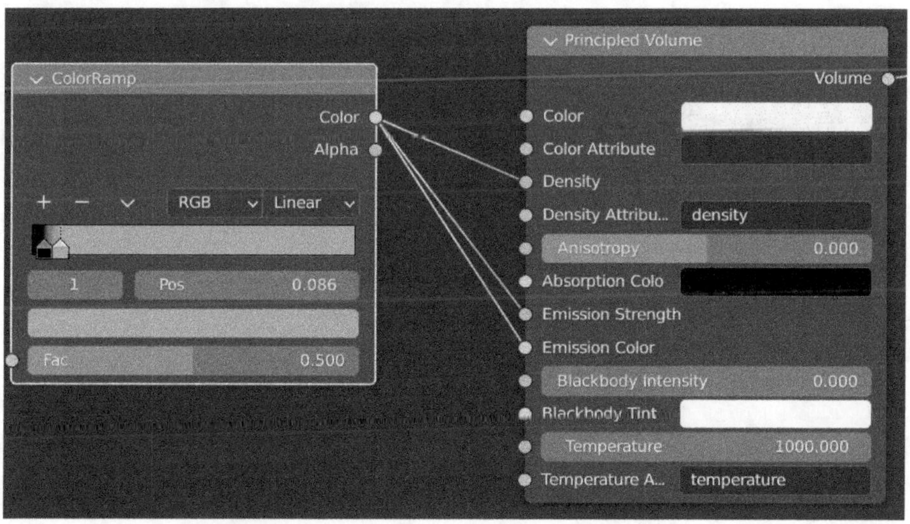

Figure 4.13: Principled Volume with inputs

13. Mine came out something like this. You can tweak the color ramp to make the cloud bigger or smaller or change the scale of **Noise Texture** to refine the raggedness of the edges. As you can see though, from the right angle it looks pretty cloud-like! Of course, if you turn the cube to look at it from another direction, the effect isn't so good, but right now we're only looking at it from one camera angle, so we won't worry about potentially seeing a cloud's "edge":

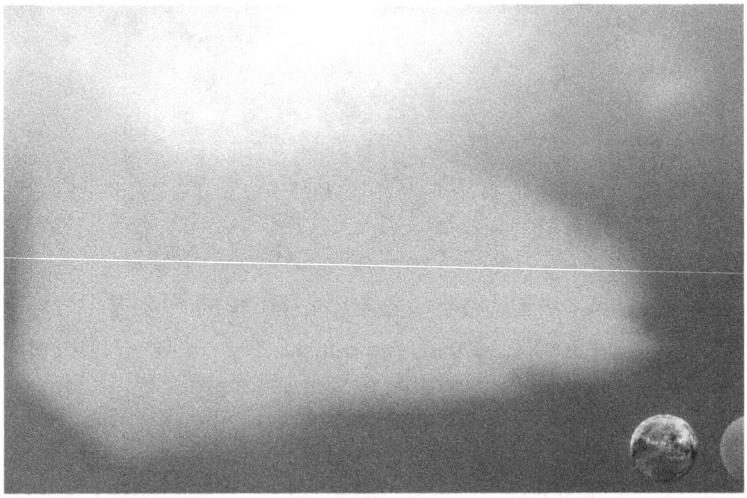

Figure 4.14: Result of Principled Shader with inputs

14. I duplicated my one cloud a few times and placed each cloud by hand, making each individual cloud bigger or smaller and rotating the cloud to get a different view of it from the camera. I ended up with something like this:

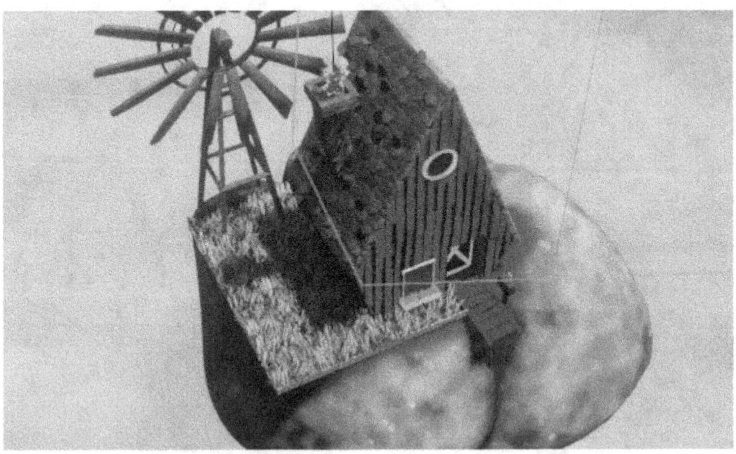

Figure 4.15: Result with clouds

15. I decided these clouds were a little too dark, so I went back into the shader, added another color ramp, and then tweaked the colors until they were more like what I wanted and plugged that into the **Emission Color** input.

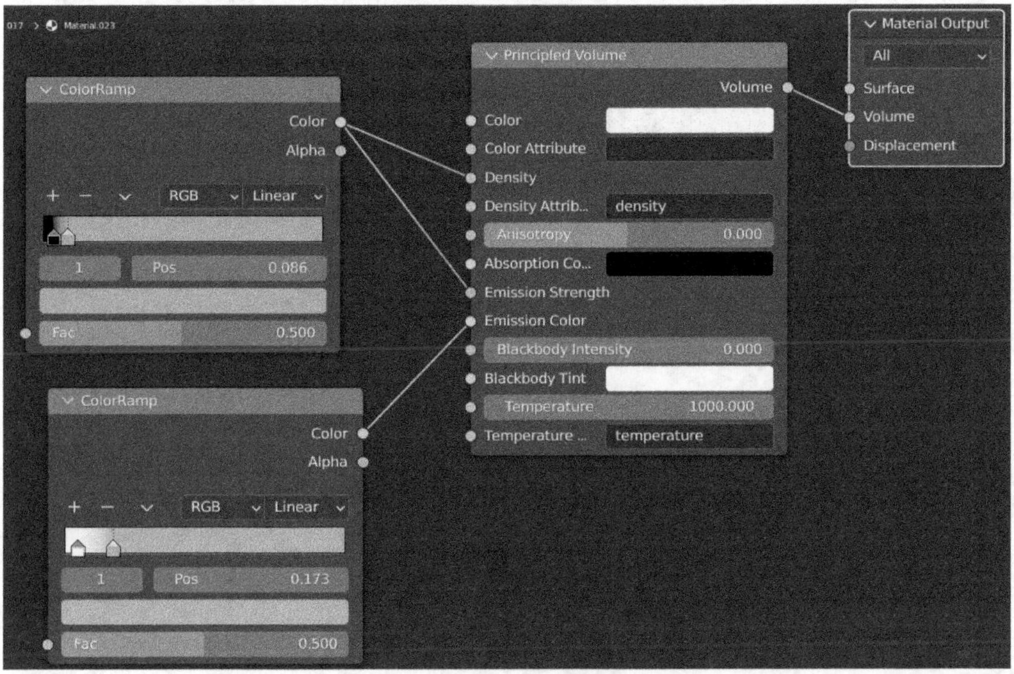

Figure 4.16: Adding more color with another color ramp

I liked the more ambient nature of the clouds when they had some blue mixed into them and I think this worked better with the overall vibe we already created in *Chapter 2*, *Creating Materials Fast with EEVEE*, and *Chapter 3*, *Lights, Camera...*.

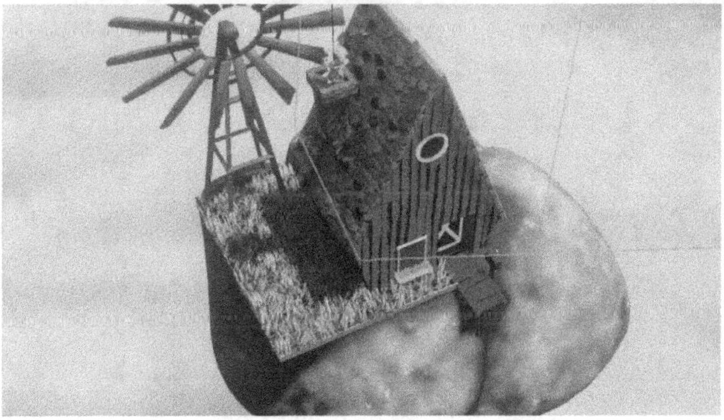

Figure 4.17: Finished clouds

16. The final stage in making our clouds look perfect involves going into the Render settings, which is why we waited until now to create the clouds. If you go to the right-hand properties panel, you'll see the Render Properties panel is the little camera at the top. Click on that, navigate down to the **Volumetrics** section, and then click the twirl-down arrow to open the **Volumetrics** options.

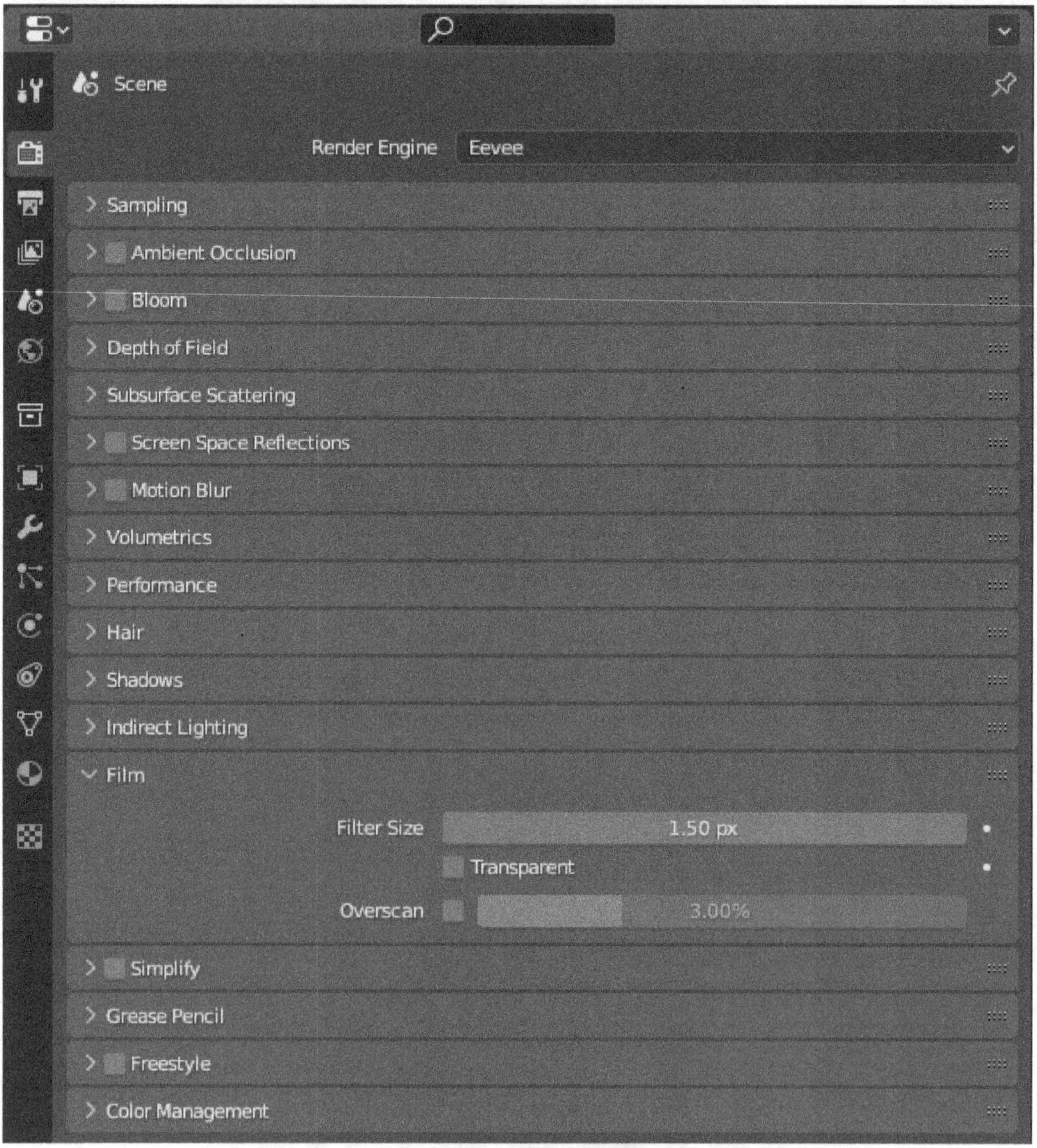

Figure 4.18: EEVEE Render panel

17. There are a number of options, most of which we'll change here. First, change the **Start** value to `15 m` and the **End** value to `95 m`. These values tell EEVEE when to start and end the volumetric zone, so EEVEE isn't rendering volumetrics that fall outside of the camera area. Following that idea, these values are based on where my camera and my clouds are, so try lowering them. The closer these numbers are together, the less volumetric rendering happens in the final render and the less computational power we'll use, so getting the optimized value for those is necessary.
18. **Tile Size** is the size of the pixel chunks used to render the volumetrics. The smaller the number, the better the resolution. I'm going to stick to **16 px** in this case, but if your computer can stand it, try using a smaller value.
19. The **Samples** value is just what it seem like it might be: the number of samples used to render the volumetrics. Try to stick to numbers compatible with a 64-bit system, such as 16, 64, 128, and 1,024. I think 128 samples is plenty to compute the clouds we have here without too many problems.
20. The **Distribution** value is the level of blending between exponential and linear sample distribution. Put simply, this means that sections closer to the camera will have more samples than sections further away from the camera. It's not something I find myself tweaking that often, so if you don't feel like you understand what this value does, just leave it at the default. I left my value on `0.8`.
21. Check the boxes next to **Volumetric Lighting** and **Volumetric Shadows**. **Samples** under **Volumetric Shadows** can be useful to tweak if your computer is having trouble rendering, but I left mine at `16`.

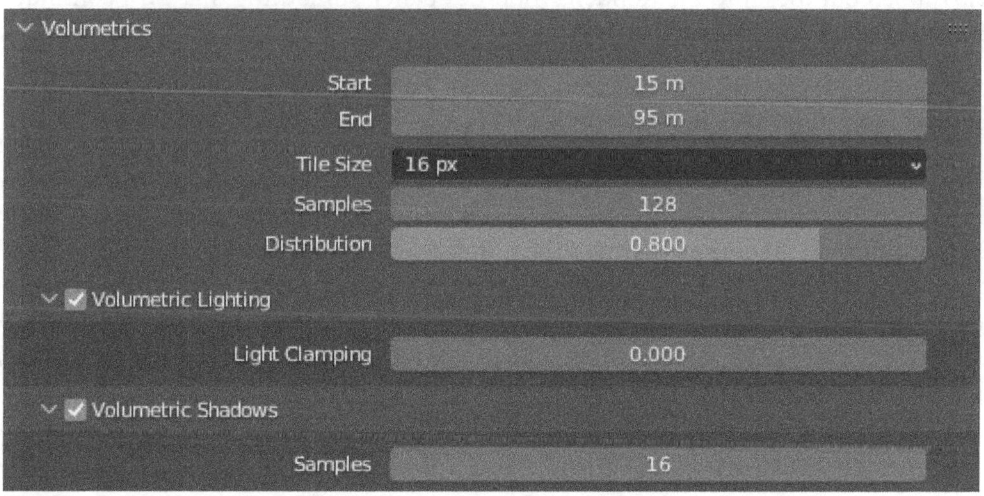

Figure 4.19: Volumetrics options in the Render panel

And there you go! We have some cool clouds that utilize the Volumetrics feature of EEVEE and we managed to get a cloud-like shape, even though EEVEE can't create volumetric geometry in any way other than cubic. We'll explore other methods for creating volumetric effects later on in the book, but I think this is a great technique for creating quick and dirty clouds that can be used in a variety of situations to break up the sky a little bit and add depth.

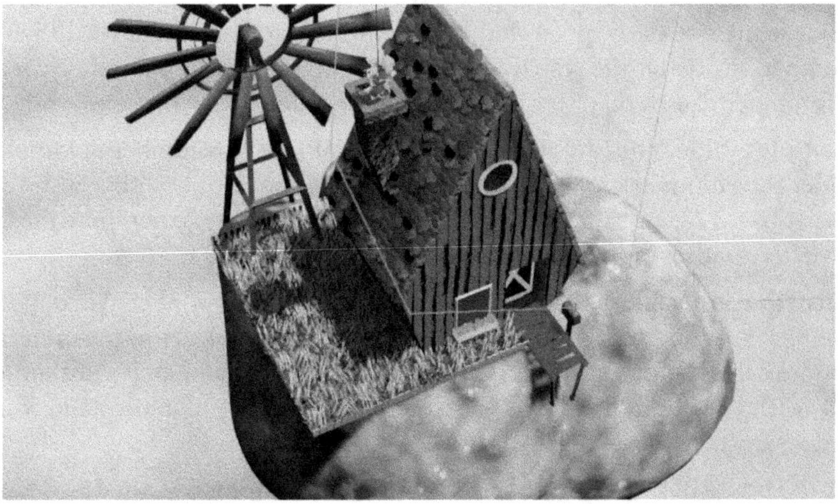

Figure 4.20: After configuring volumetrics

We also dipped our toes into the Render Properties panel, something that we'll continue to explore in the next section.

Configuring Render settings

The Render settings of any scene can take a finished product from mediocre to top-notch. Hopefully, you'll have some experience with Render settings from previous projects in Cycles, but in EEVEE, the importance of the Render settings becomes even greater. This is because, in a rasterized real-time renderer, a lot of the settings that really make a scene pop are at the default setting of **off**. So we, as artists, need to know which settings to use to make sure we get the most out of EEVEE, but also which ones to skip in order to maintain as much efficiency as we can.

Let's look at the options in order, explaining how each affects our render with examples. The Render Properties panel contains all the Render settings that we'll be looking at for now. The Render Properties panel should be on the right-hand side of the screen in the Properties editor. Select the Camera icon if you don't see the Render settings in your Editor panel.

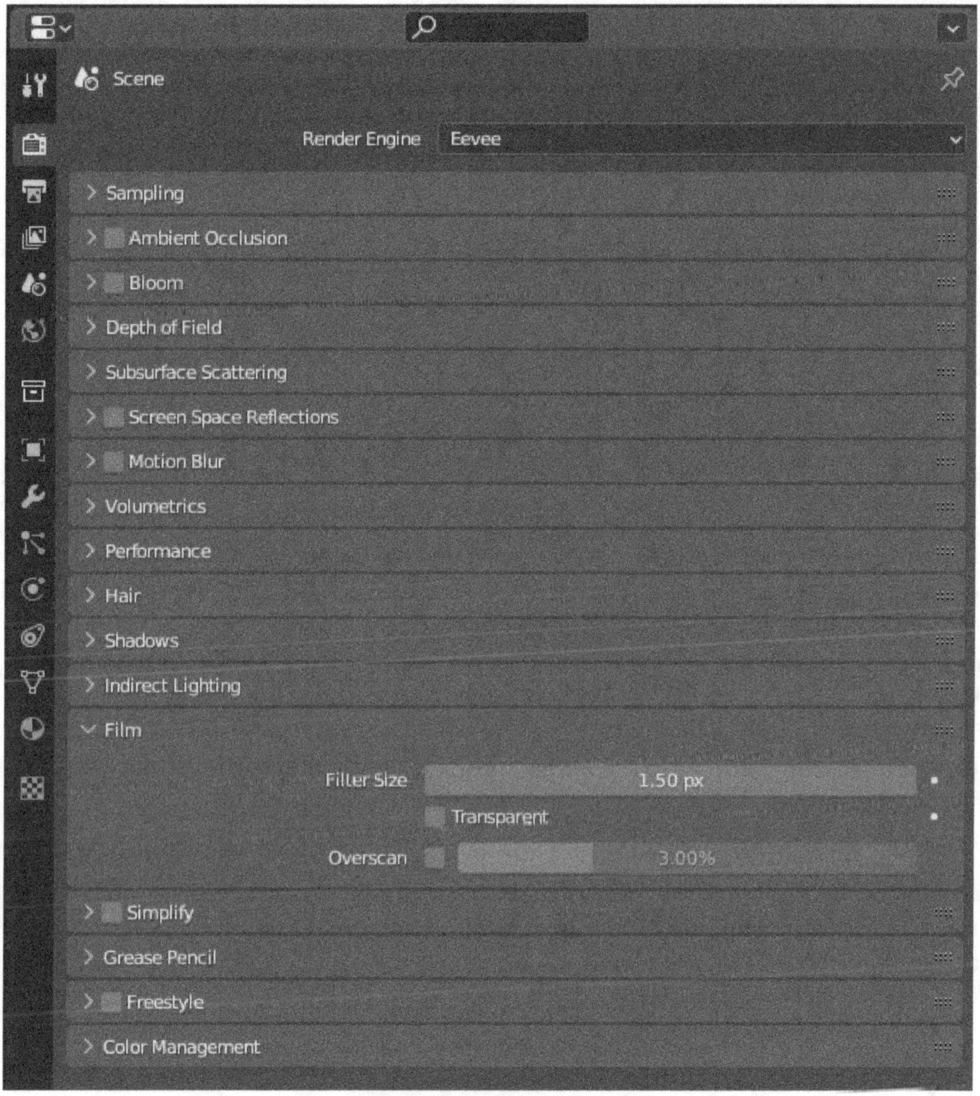

Figure 4.21: Render panel (redux)

Let's go through each setting that pertains to our current scene. In this chapter, we'll be looking at the **Sampling**, **Ambient Occlusion**, **Bloom**, and **Screen Space Reflections** sections. If we skip something, assume that it doesn't have any bearing on our current scene.

Sampling

Sampling is a measure of how many samples the rendering engine will take in one frame. A sample is one calculation of how the lighting is bouncing around the scene. So, if we have more samples, we're bouncing more light around the scene and getting a more accurate output of what the scene actually looks like. Since we're using EEVEE and not Cycles, our samples are actually calculating the approximate behavior of the light so that we can view our scene faster.

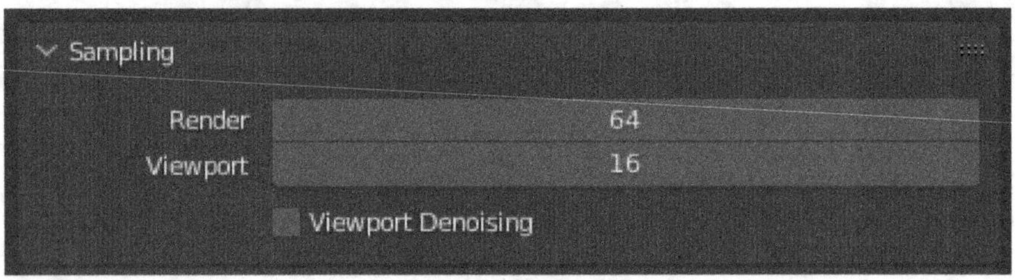

Figure 4.22: Sampling options

So, it follows, the more samples, the more refined our final output will be. But more samples also equals a longer render time. So, we need to dial in our **Render** number so we don't wait too long for the render, but we also get a good final product. The **Viewport** number in this section is the number of samples from the viewport. I find the best way to decide how many samples you might need is by testing it out in the viewport. Right now, we have 16 samples in the viewport, which is looking pretty good in my output preview. I'm going to push my **Render** sample number to `128` (following the rule of 8-bit numbers), just because I think we can afford more samples with how fast 16 samples are rendering.

This is really a trial-and-error stage, which will get easier as you get more experience. So, try out some numbers and render them and see how things turn out. Luckily, EEVEE is lightning fast and you really won't have to wait too long until you want something insane, such as a million samples.

Ambient Occlusion

Ambient Occlusion is a really useful thing in 3D. It pretty much means that where two meshes are close together, shadows will be added. This mimics what happens in real life, where two objects will throw shadows on each other that get deeper when the objects get closer. Ambient Occlusion is a setting inside of EEVEE that defaults to off, so we need to turn it on by clicking the box next to **Ambient Occlusion**.

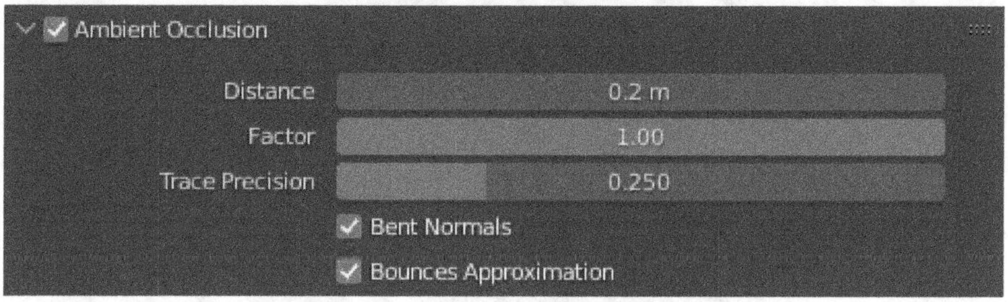

Figure 4.23: Ambient Occlusion options

I find most often that **Distance** is the only number I end up playing with. If I want a more pronounced ambient occlusion, I'll pump that number up to `1 m`.

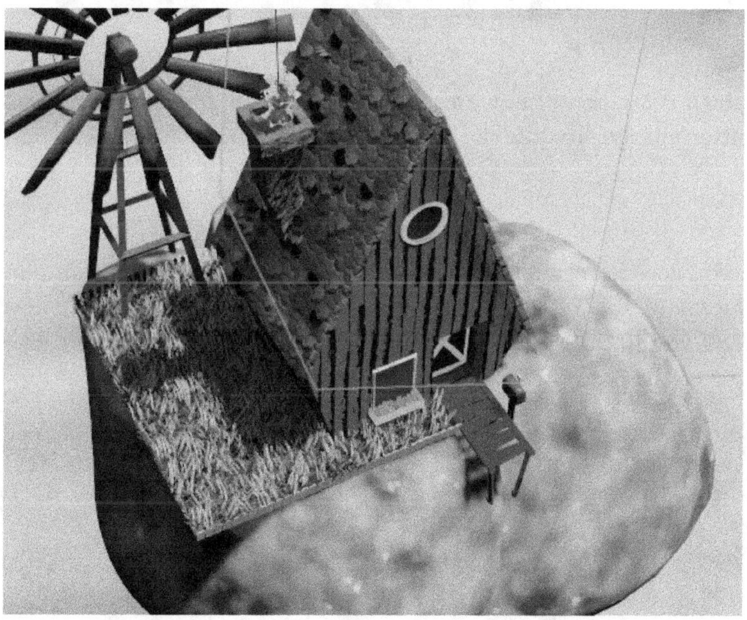

Figure 4.24: Before ambient occlusion

Now we'll look at the effect ambient occlusion has on the scene.

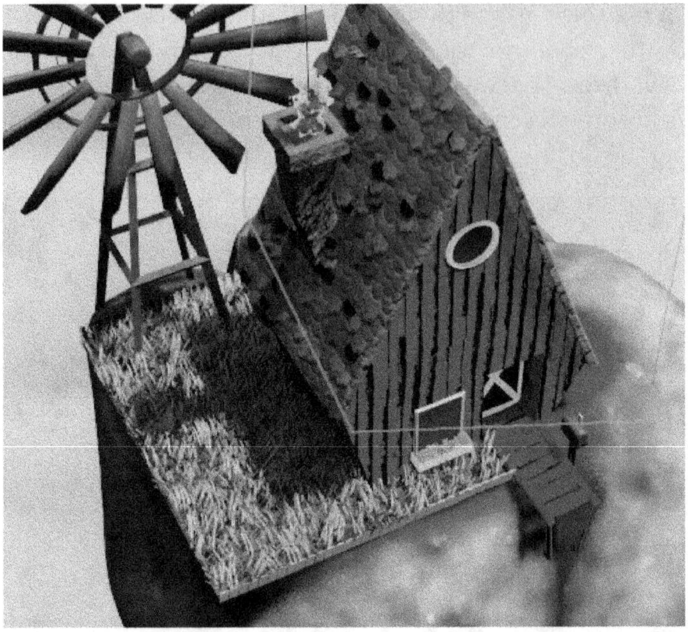

Figure 4.25: After ambient occlusion

As you can see, the areas where the two rocks overlap are now more shadowed, and we have more definition on the shadow of the house.

Bloom

Let's turn **Bloom** on as well by clicking on the checkbox for **Bloom**. Bloom has to do with the lighting in the scene. It simulates a light bleed effect from the lights we have and gives the whole scene a softer look.

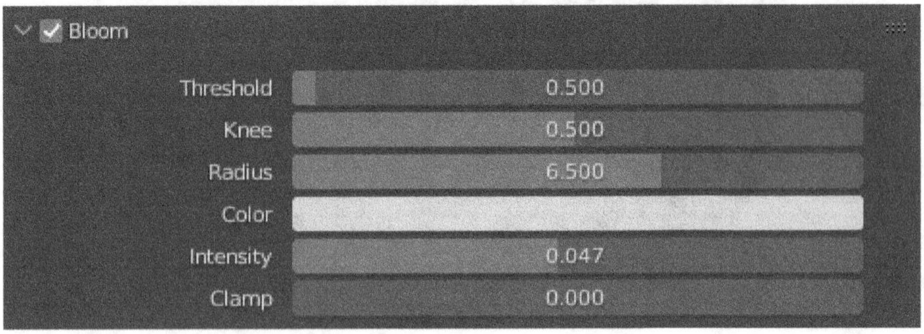

Figure 4.26: Bloom options

Changing the value of the **Threshold** setting is most useful. A higher threshold means less bloom, while a lower threshold means more bloom. It's subtle, but a very low number such as `0.2` definitely gives it a hazy look that a higher number such as `1` will not.

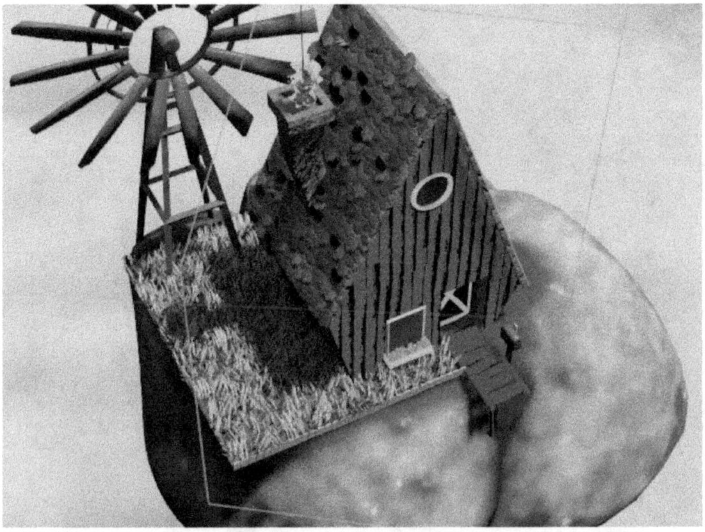

Figure 4.27: Before Bloom

And now let's see how **Bloom** has changed what we see in the viewport:

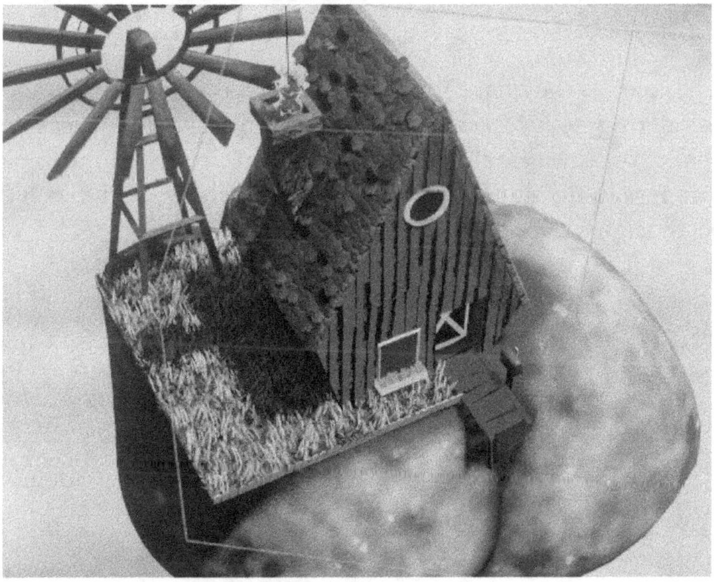

Figure 4.28: After Bloom

The other thing I like to play with is the color of the bloom. The overall look really changes if you input a cold color, such as blue, instead of a warm color, such as orange, that we had as the default.

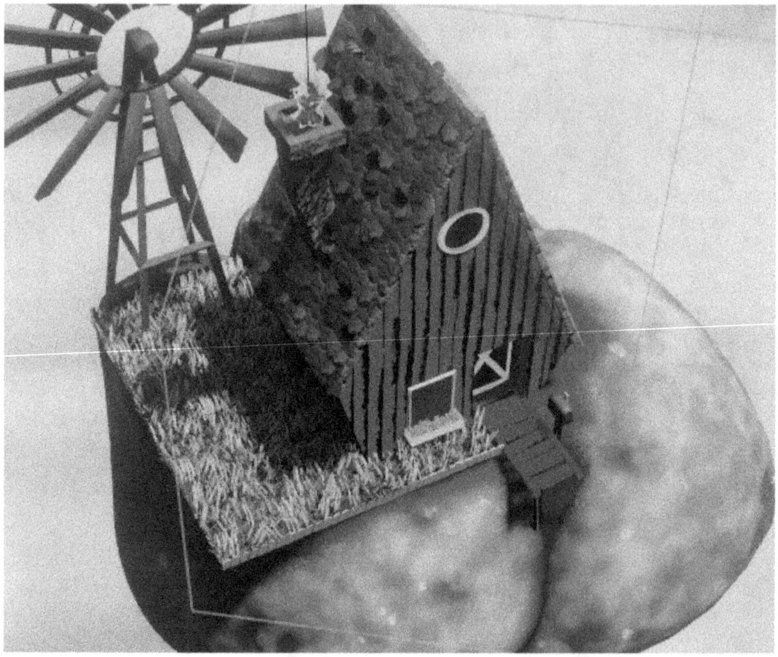

Figure 4.29: Green bloom

I kept a light orange color as the final color of my bloom and kept the threshold at `0.3`. This is a stylized rendering, so having a little more bloom will help us to achieve that style, but in a more realistic scene, we would probably not want to have so much bloom. We'll look at bloom a lot more in the third mini-project, in *Chapter 9, Lighting an Interior Scene*, as a way to get specific lights to pop.

Screen Space Reflections

Turning on **Screen Space Reflections** will just change one small thing in our scene: the windows.

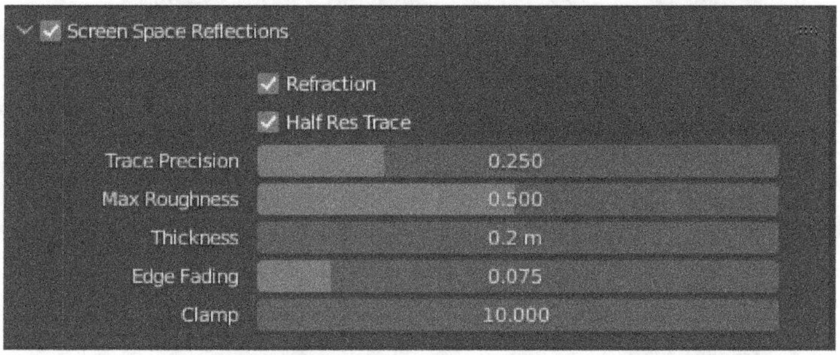

Figure 4.30: Screen Space Reflections options

Screen Space Reflections makes any surface that is above a certain threshold of reflectivity reflect light. It's a complicated notion, one that we'll talk a lot more about in *Chapter 7, Faking Camera Effects for Better Renders*, when we create a whole lake of water that we'll need to be reflective.

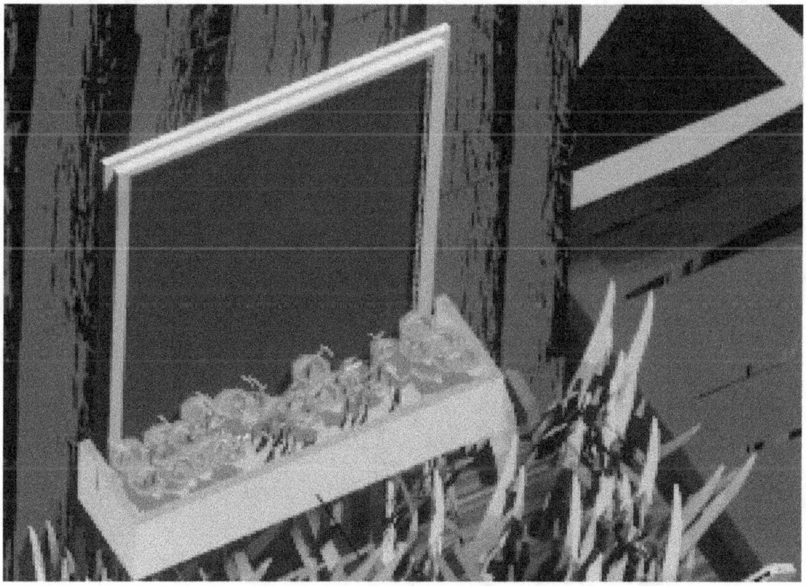

Figure 4.31: Before Screen Space Reflections

Now look at the **Screen Space Reflections** addition, with refraction on:

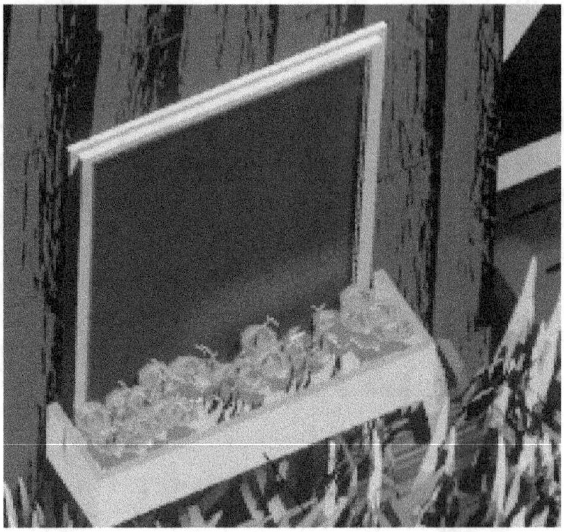

Figure 4.32: After Screen Space Reflections

Pretty subtle huh? From this angle, we can only see the way the window is now reflecting the flower box. This isn't a truly significant difference at the moment. We can increase the window's ability to reflect at this angle by unchecking the **Refraction** setting. This is not physically correct, so in more realistic scenes, we would absolutely want to keep refraction on, but in this case, where we're exercising more artistic control, I like a little more reflection on the window.

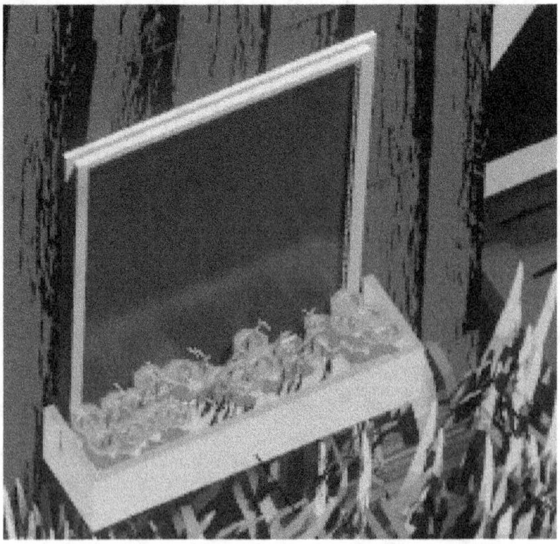

Figure 4.33: After turning off refraction

Film

The last setting we need to check is the **Film Transparent** option.

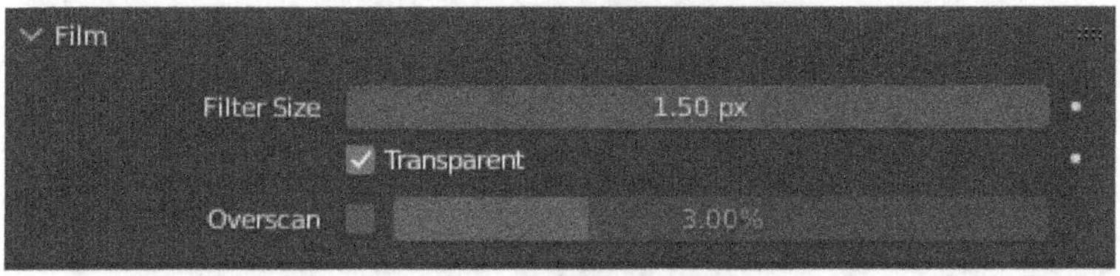

Figure 4.34: Film options

This will make the background of our scene transparent, so we can render out a good alpha channel to work with in our compositing system.

At this point, we've made all the changes we need to the settings. Let's now set ourselves up to render and composite a really cool finished piece.

Compositing Render layers

That's the extent of what we'll cover in terms of the Render panel for this project, but more will be covered in future chapters of this book, where we'll get deep into baking and other EEVEE features. At this point, we have two separate features that are going to be composited together to create something really cool. If you remember from the previous chapter, we made some line art to add some lines to the outer edges of the geometry in the models to get more of a comic book feel. Let's add those back into our preview by unhiding them from the Render view. So this looks pretty cool, as is, but if we want to take it one step further and render the clouds and the geometry of the scene separately, it will give us a lot more flexibility in the final composite. Feel free to start this section from your own work that you've done in previous chapters, or download my prepared `.blend` file from GitHub, named `MiniProject1_Compositing.blend`.

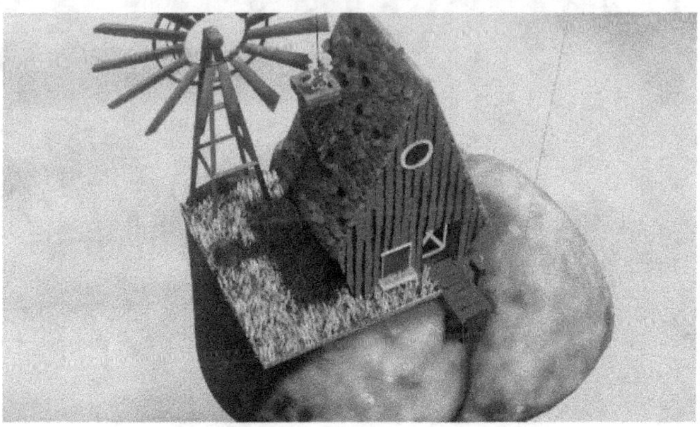

Figure 4.35: Starting the compositing

To start our composition we need to go to the outliner and create another View Layer.

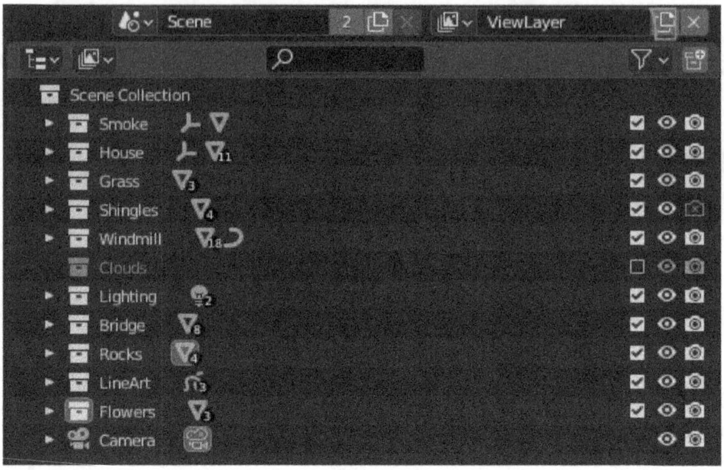

Figure 4.36: Creating a new View Layer

View Layers are ways in which we can render certain parts of our scene so that we can combine them in interesting and creative ways. We'll use View Layers to separate the clouds from the house and then recombine them later:

1. Hit **New** in the menu options and that should add a new View Layer to our scene.
2. Click on the title of the View Layer to rename it to **Clouds**.
3. Next, uncheck every collection in the scene except for **Clouds** and the **Lighting** collection.

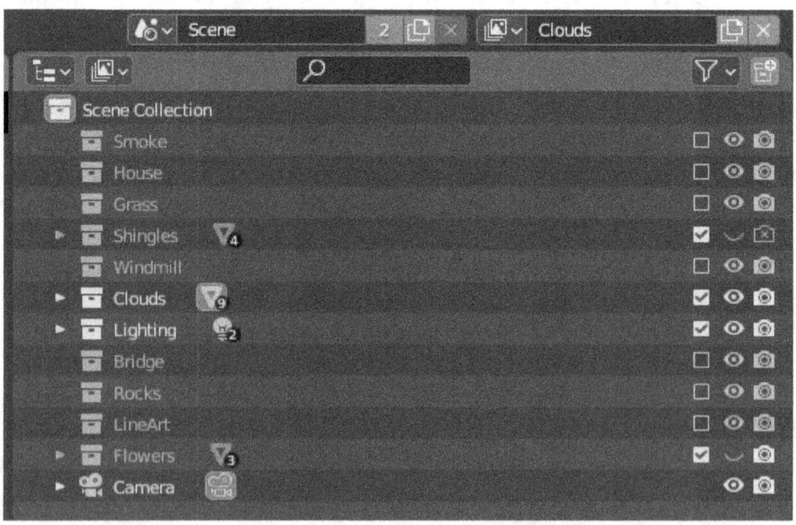

Figure 4.37: The Clouds layer

This deactivates them from the render of this scene, so we will only render out **Clouds** in this View Layer.

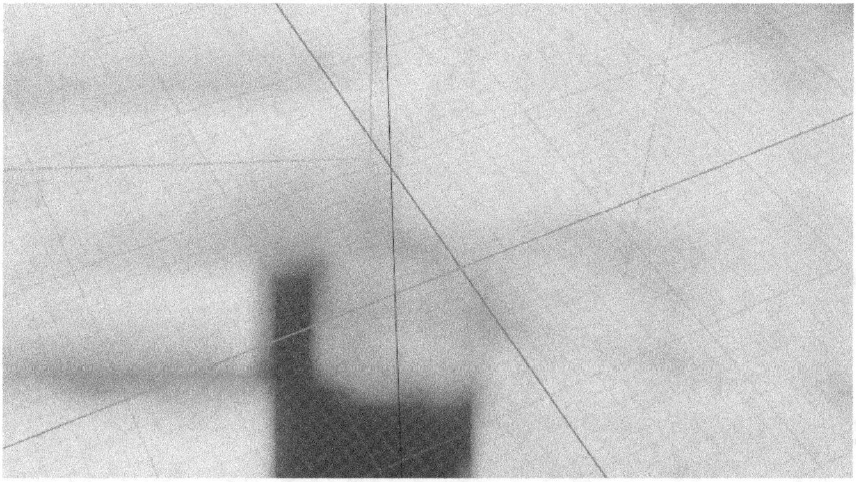

Figure 4.38: Result of the Clouds layer

4. Next, go back up to the top right and change the active View Layer back to the default View Layer with the drop-down menu button.
5. Then, go to the collection where we're holding all the clouds.
6. Click the checkmark on the right that corresponds with **Clouds** to deactivate it from the default View Layer.

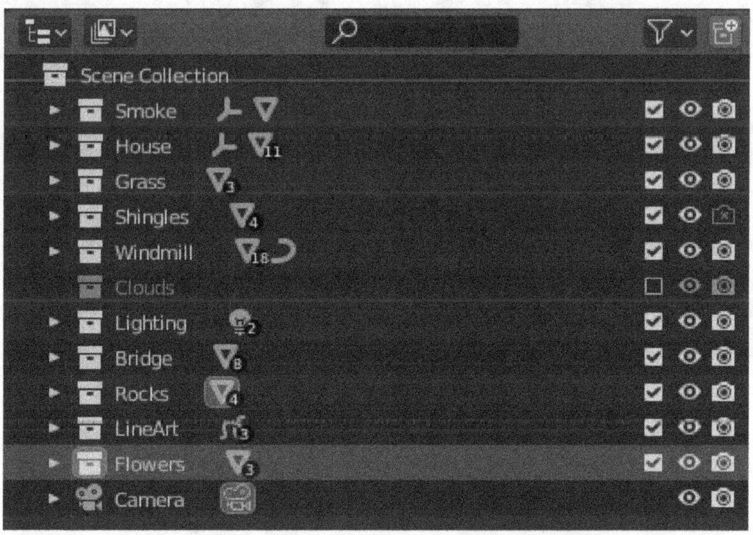

Figure 4.39: The collections visible in the default View Layer

Notice that when we deactivate the clouds from the default View Layer, they no longer appear in the render.

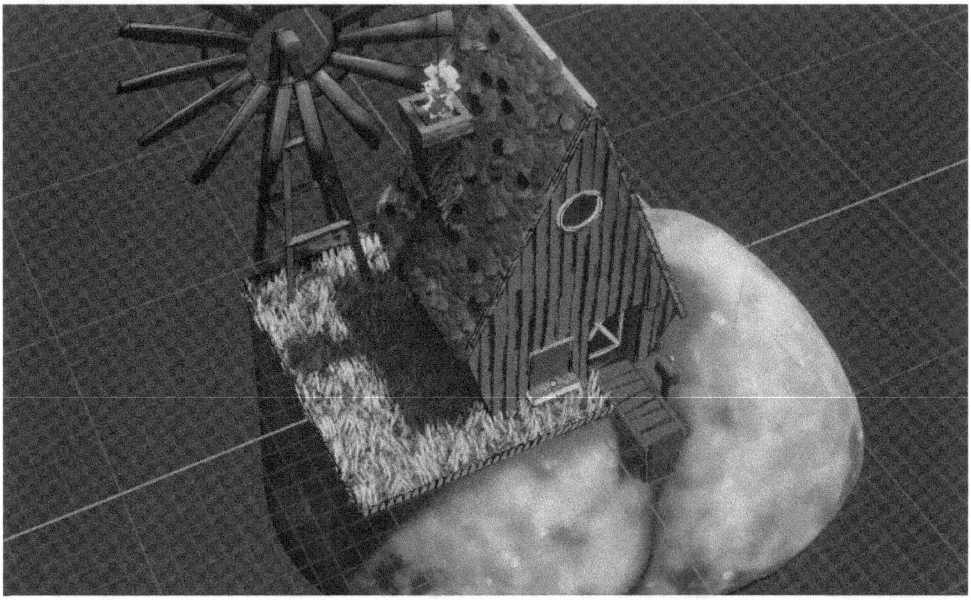

Figure 4.40: The default View Layer result

Now we've set up the right View Layers, let's select the **Compositing** workspace from the workspace tabs at the top of the screen.

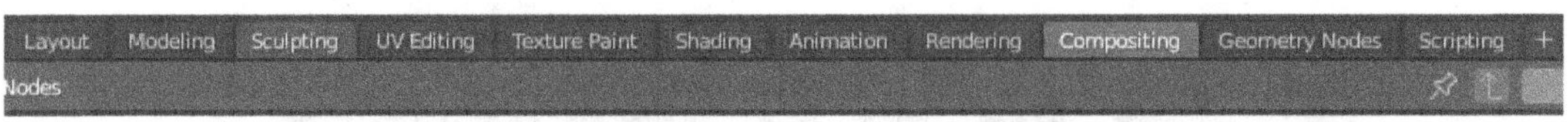

Figure 4.41: The Compositing workspace

7. Enable the compositing nodes by selecting the checkbox called **Use Nodes** in the top menu area.

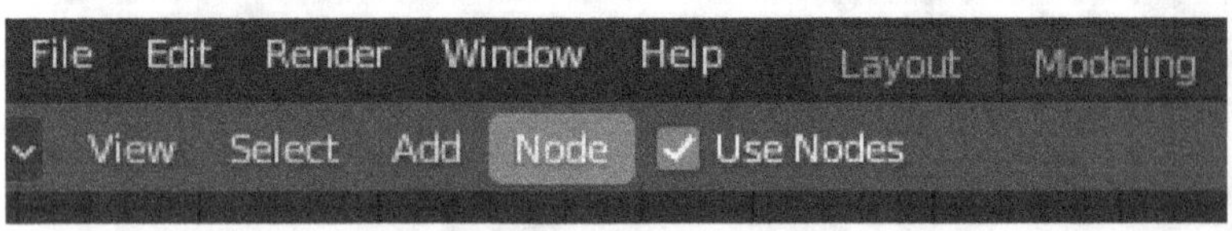

Figure 4.42: Use Nodes option

8. You should see the nodes open up in the workspace. We want to select the **Render Layers** node and copy it with *Shift* + *D*.

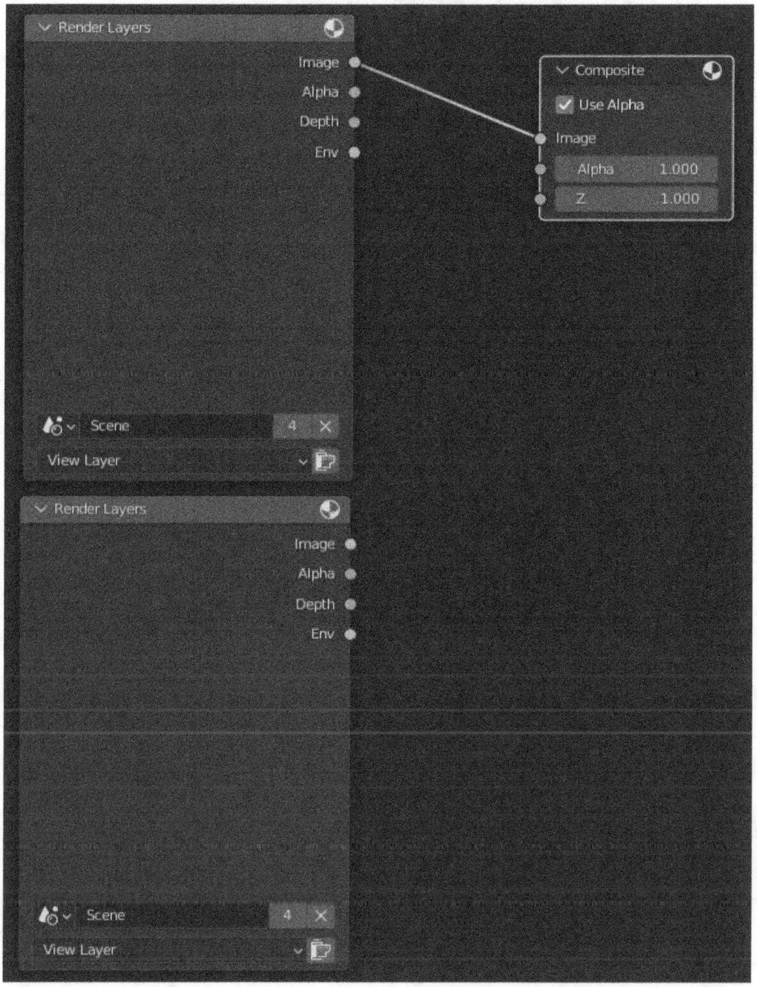

Figure 4.43: Duplicating the render layers

9. Change the View Layer for the second render layer to the cloud layer we made.

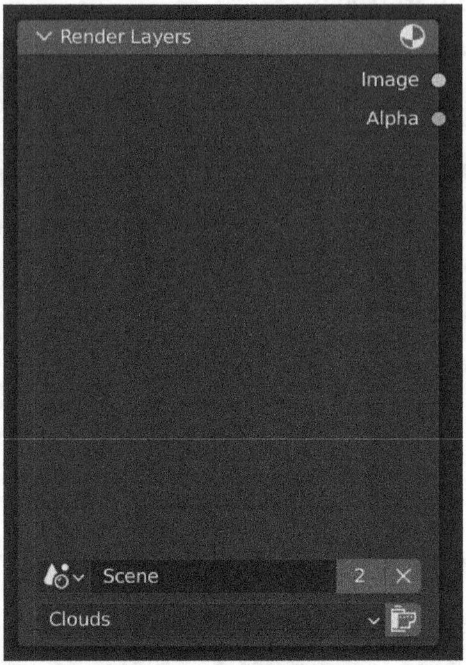

Figure 4.44: Render layers with the Clouds option selection

10. Next, we'll add three **File Output** nodes (with the **Add** menu accessed from our usual shortcut, *Shift* + *A*).

11. Attach the **Image** output to the **Image** input of **File Output** and select a path for your image to be saved out to. There should still be one **File Output** node available to attach an input to. We need to render out an environment pass so that we can put the background into our composite.

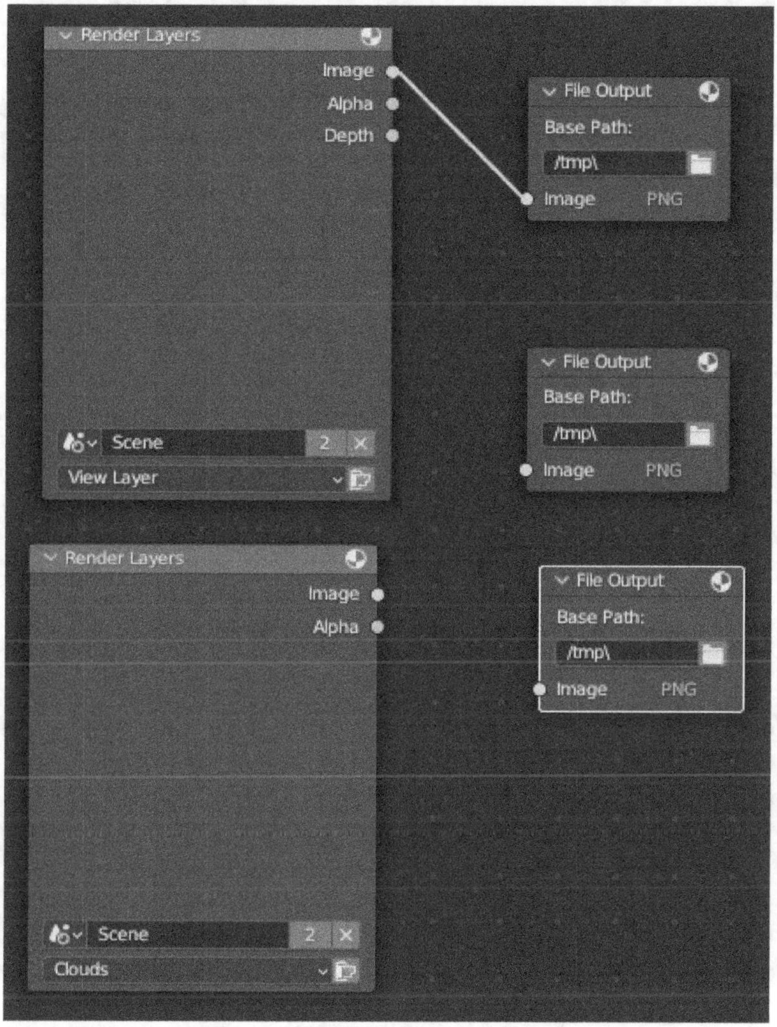

Figure 4.45: Adding more file outputs

12. Let's now go to the **View Layer** properties, which is inside the **Properties** panel (on the right side of the screen) and looks like a little picture.

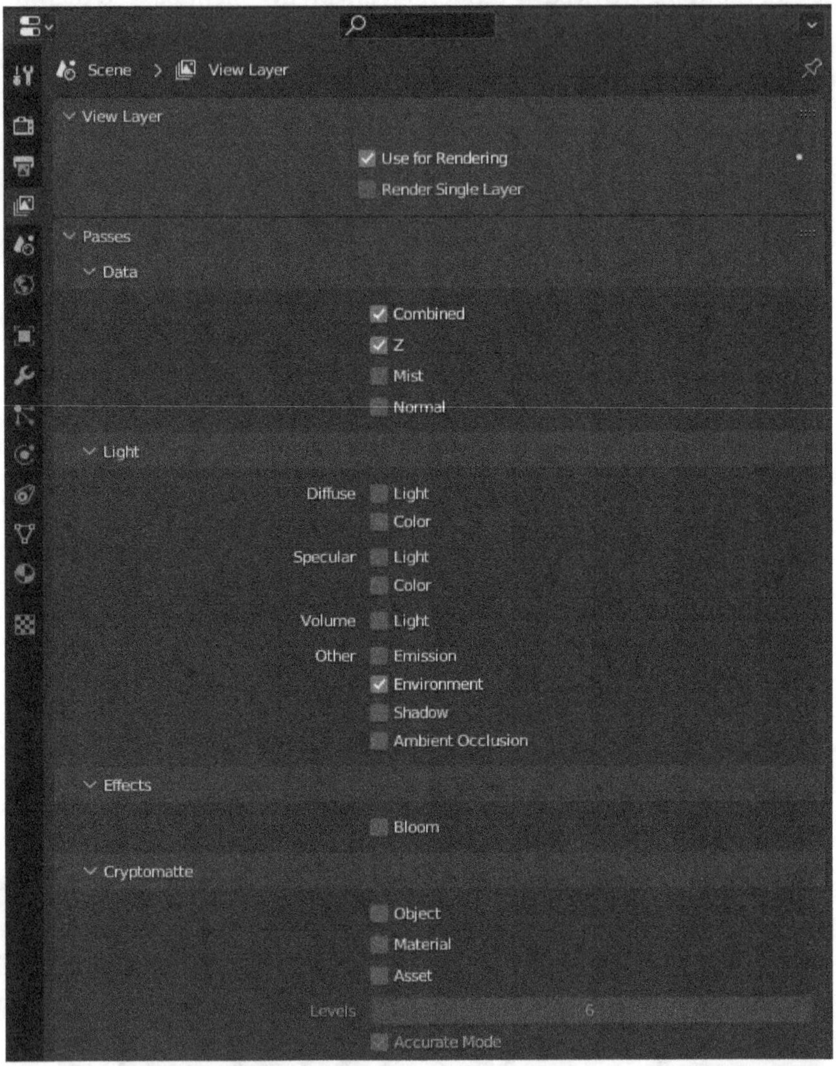

Figure 4.46: The Passes options

13. Make sure you've selected the first View Layer (not the clouds). Check that the **Combined** and **Z** passes are selected, as **Line Art Modifier** needs this information to render out properly. Then, select the **Environment** pass in the **Light** category. We'll revisit passes in more depth later in the book.

14. Take the output of the environment in the first View Layer and put it into the third **File Output** image input.

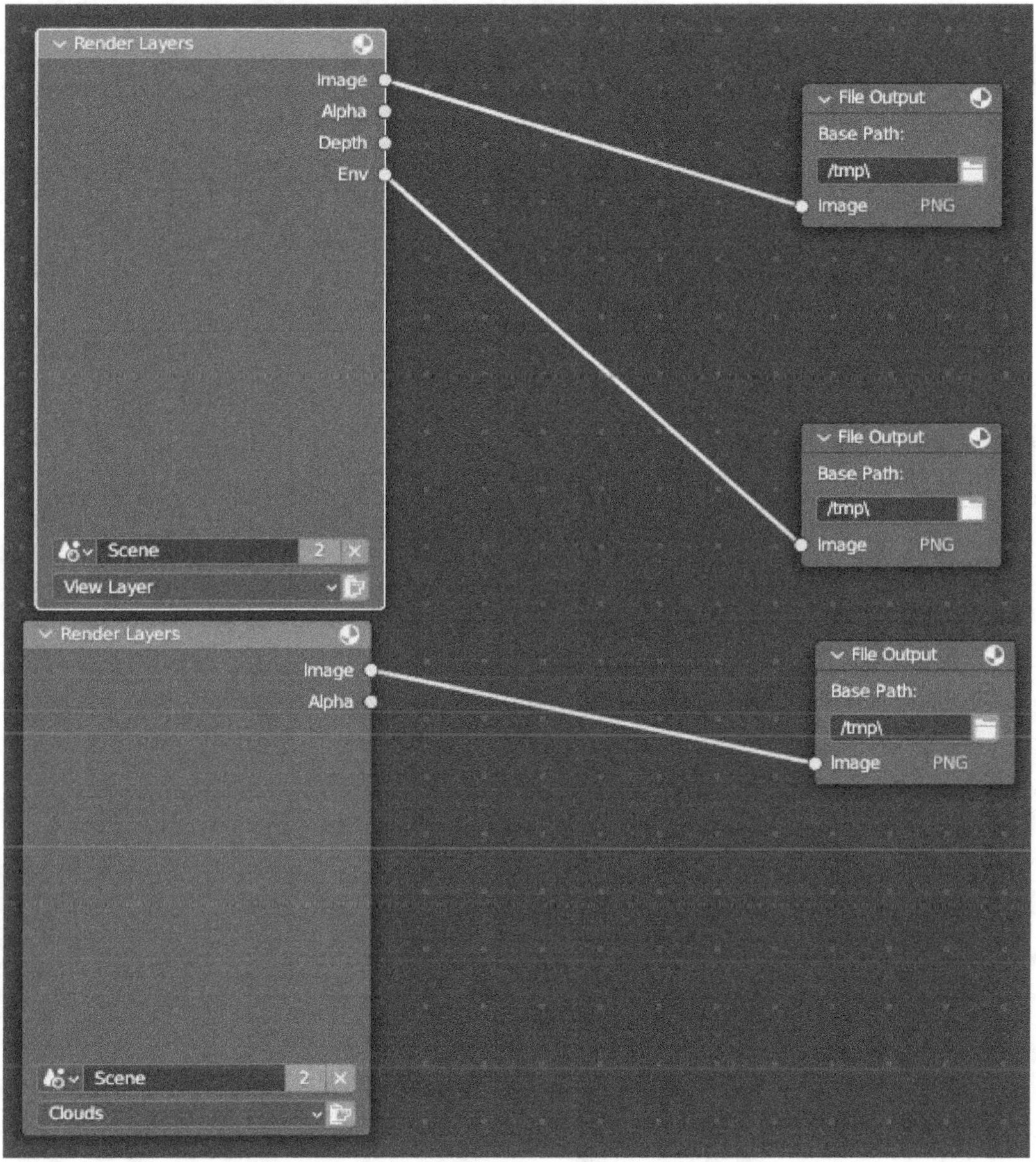

Figure 4.47: Adding the Environment pass

15. The shortcut to render is *F12*. Let's give it a whirl!

I now have three separate passes – the default View Layer, the cloud View Layer, and the environment. These images can now be combined any way we want. If you like Photoshop or Krita, you can use those to combine these three passes, or if you want to stay in Blender, we have the option to combine those three images natively in our compositor. I'll show you the Blender way, but you should do what is comfortable for you.

> **Side Note**
> If you want to use Krita (another awesome open source program), they have great documentation to get you started on compositing in their program: `https://docs.krita.org/en/user_manual/getting_started/basic_concepts.html`.

Final compositing

We're on the home stretch! In this final section, we'll look at how to add the two images we rendered out together inside Blender so that you can see how powerful the use of separate passes is. Let's get started:

1. I like to open a new fresh Blender window to composite, just in case I still need to make tweaks to the original render. This way, we can save our `Mini-Project 1` file as is and come back to it later if we want to add or remove something.
2. Let's go to the **Compositing** tab again and select **Use nodes** (again).
3. Import the three images we rendered out. I like to drag and drop them from the `File` folder into the compositing window, but you can also use **Add** and select **Image** and import them with File Manager.

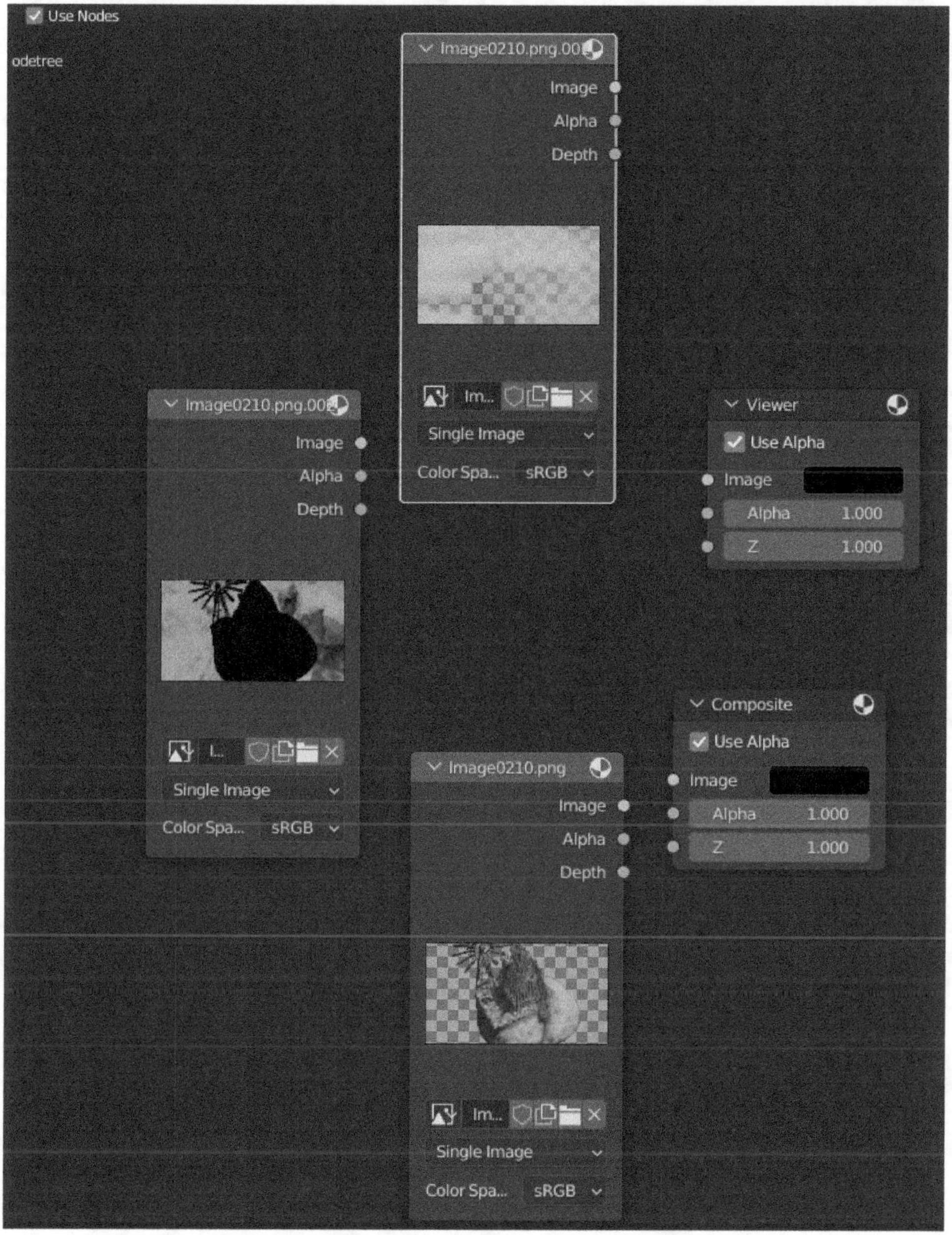

Figure 4.48: Starting the final compositing

4. Hit the *N* key to pull up the **Backdrop** option. Check the box that says **Backdrop** and click on the **Fit** option once. This inputs the viewer output into the background of our scene so we can see what we're doing as we work. Use the **Node Wrangler** add-on shortcut, *Ctrl* + *Shift* + *Click*, to preview a specific node.

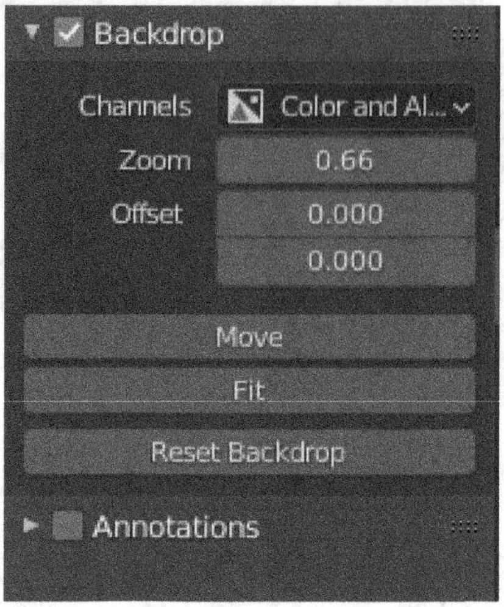

Figure 4.49: Turning on Backdrop in the compositor

5. Add two **Alpha Over** nodes to the compositor.

6. Put the environment pass into the top of the first **Alpha Over Image** input, and the cloud pass into the second **Alpha Over Image** input. Then, take the second **Alpha Over** node and do the same with the output of **Cloud** and **Environment** combined and the house pass.

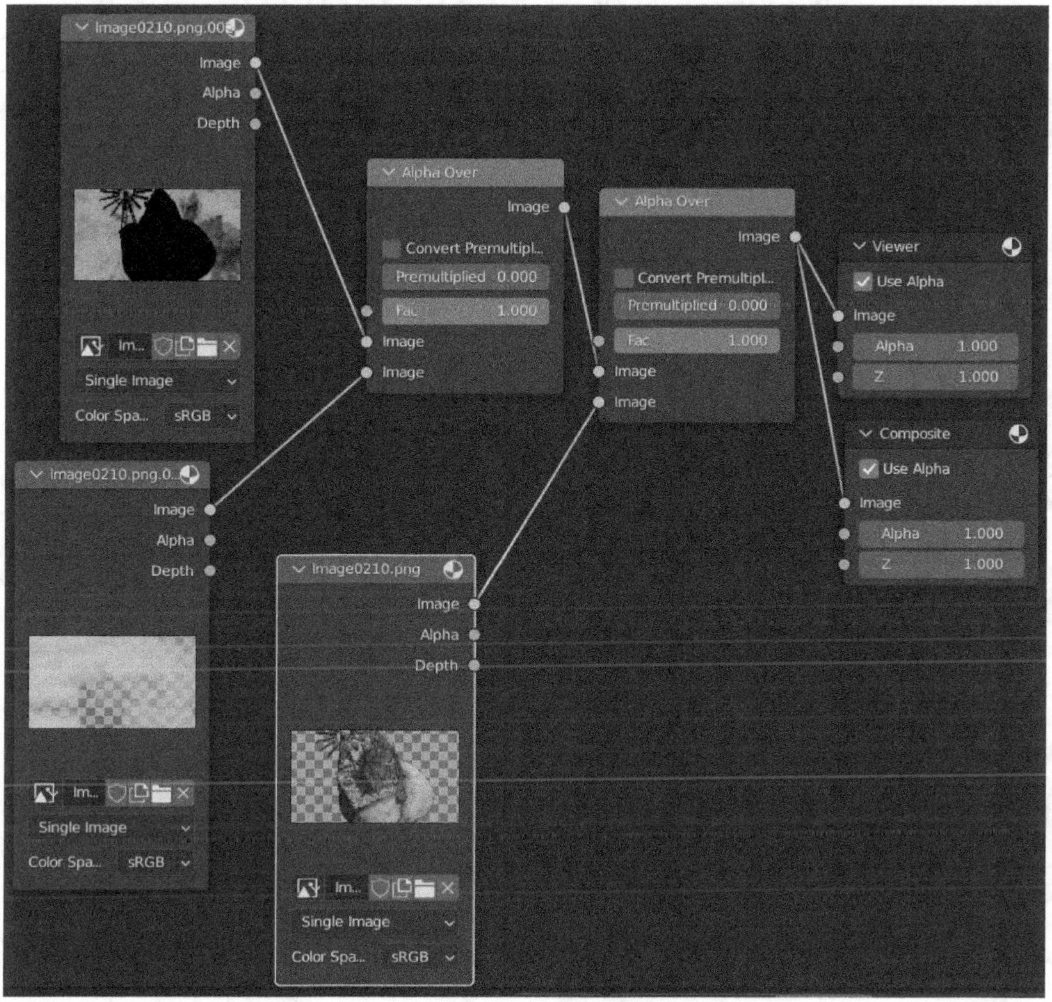

Figure 4.50: Using the Alpha Over nodes to connect

Now we have pretty much recreated the original render. Why did we go through the trouble of rendering three separate passes to create the exact same thing as we had at the beginning?

Well, the magic of compositing is the ability to tweak parts separately. Let's put a **Hue Saturation Value** node in between the **Cloud** pass and the first **Alpha Over** node.

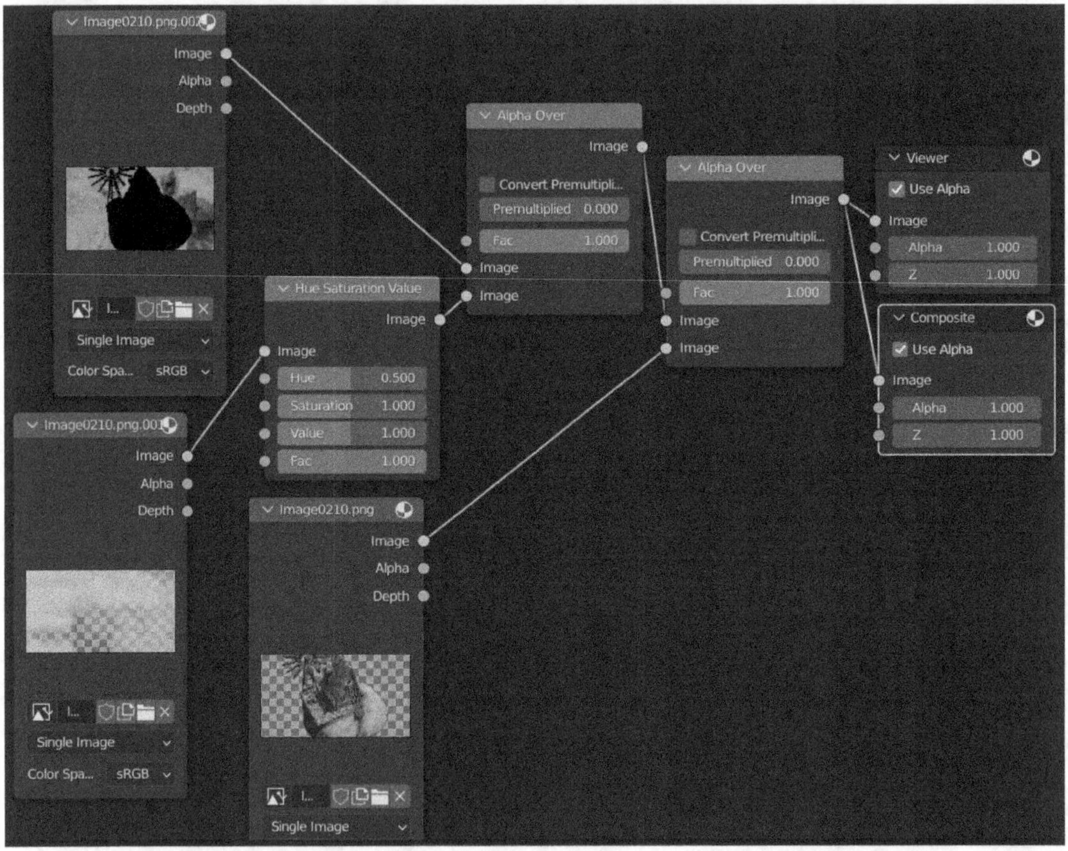

Figure 4.51: Using the Hue and Saturation nodes to change the render

If we change the values of **Hue Saturation Value**, we can affect just the clouds. Or, if we incorporate an RGB curve in between the **House** pass and the second **Alpha Out** node, we can change the color of just the house, making it a little bluer. We can also change the factors of the **Alpha Over** nodes to show more or less sky, make the clouds more obvious; basically, we can do anything we want!

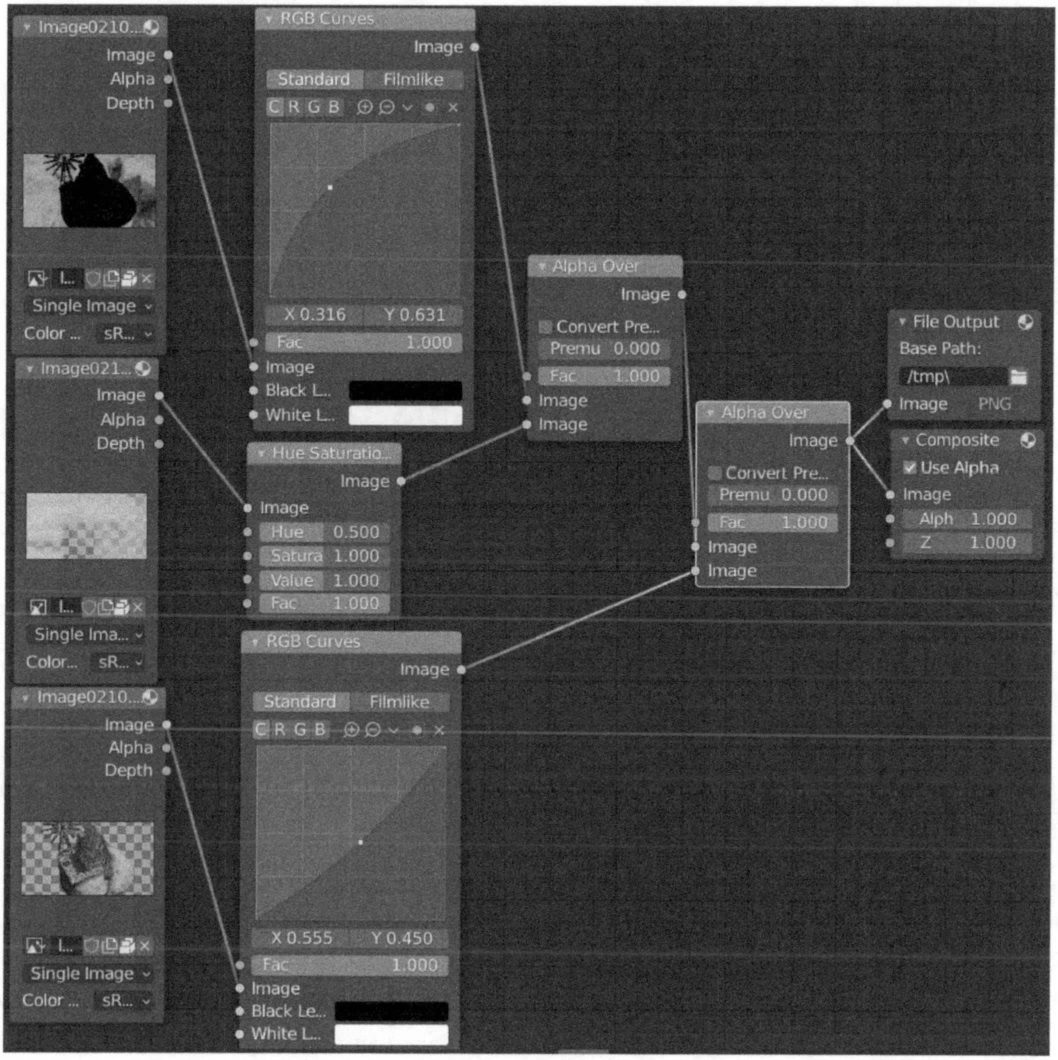

Figure 4.52: Tweaking our layers

After playing with some values and making some small tweaks, I ended up using a **Hue Saturation Value** node on the house to make it more richly colored and cartoony, and then used RGB curves on the clouds and sky to tweak them until I liked how it was all blending together. I added another **File Output** node and then pressed **Render** again. Here's how my finished product looks:

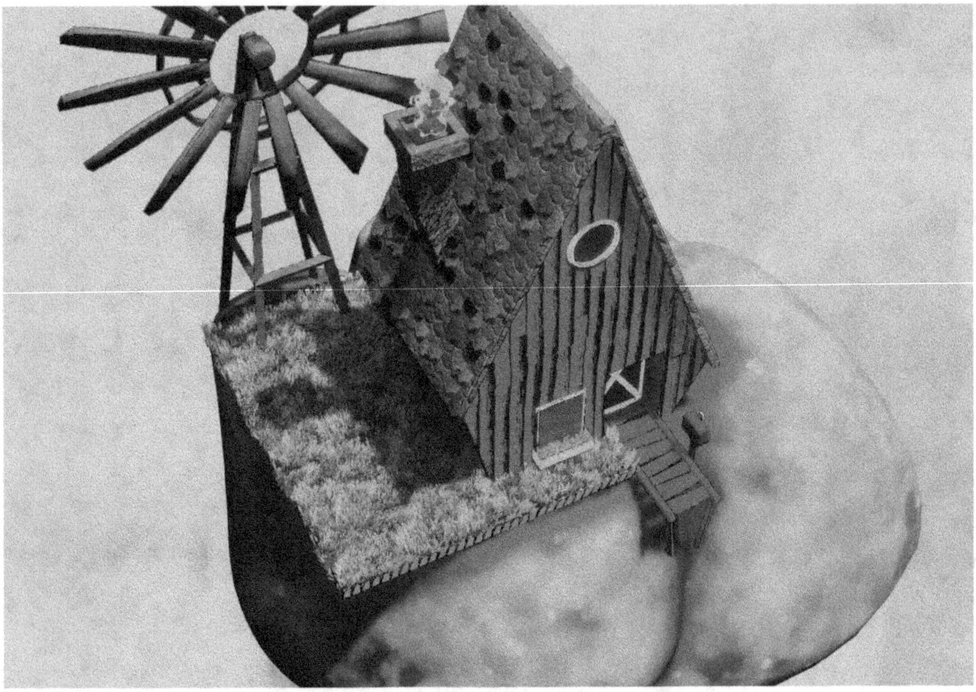

Figure 4.53: The final render

The huge advantage of rendering out passes is worth the little extra time to set them up. Imagine your boss, the art director, comes to you saying she wants this finished product to look a little more green, and the background a little less bright. All you need to do is go back to the composite, tweak two values, and save it out again. If you hadn't saved each layer separately, you'd have to go all the way back to the original file and change the lighting or materials or any number of time-consuming things to get the right look for the shot. So, don't discount the practice of being organized and planning for future changes.

Summary

I really hope you enjoyed working through this process of our first mini-project. I think we ended up with a really cool stylized scene that laid down some of the fundamental practices of working with EEVEE. We created materials, lights, effects, and more to pull this really fun, simple scene together. A lot of the components we touched on in this chapter will be important in the next mini-project, so go over some of these workflows, use them to create other projects, and make sure you feel confident in working with EEVEE before you move on to the next mini-project, which will involve creating an environment landscape, complete with trees, grass, and water.

In the next chapter, we will go over Geometry Nodes, an amazing, powerful new feature in Blender, and see how we can use them to create grass, rock, and tree distributions.

Section 2: Real-Time Rendering – Mini-Project 2 – Creating a Realistic Environment Concept

Let's continue to expand our knowledge in section two. In this section, we'll be learning about EEVEE-specific lighting and diving deep into Geometry Nodes and tactics that will save you so much time in your creative journey. After learning this material, you'll have an even deeper understanding of the considerations of EEVEE.

In this section, we will cover the following chapters:

- *Chapter 5, Setting Up an Environment with Geometry Nodes*
- *Chapter 6, Screen Space Reflections – Adding Reflection to the Water*
- *Chapter 7, Faking Camera Effects for Better Renders*
- *Chapter 8, Using Alphas for Details*

5
Setting Up an Environment with Geometry Nodes

In the last three chapters, we worked toward making a non-realistic render. We covered some material editing, lighting, camera work, and rendering to get the most out of EEVEE to make a cartoony house-in-a-cloud. Now, we're going to up the ante and make an outdoor environment using some premade grass and rocks, as well as looking at some advanced aspects of Blender, including **Geometry Nodes**, which will be covered in this chapter.

Blender hasn't always been the computer graphics powerhouse that it is now. Thanks to diligent work from many amazing developers, Blender users get to work with many new and interesting tools, as Blender is constantly updated and changed so that it is the very best software that it can be. One such tool is Geometry Nodes. Added to Blender in 2020, Geometry Nodes is a system of nodes that we can string together to create geometry. The Blender Material Editor that we used in *Chapter 2, Creating Materials Fast with EEVEE*, operates on the same principle, using nodes that we can string together to create something – in that case, materials. So, you already have some experience in this style of working! I find that many 3D programs are moving toward implementing (or already have implemented!) the same kind of system that Geometry Nodes works on. As a result, learning how to use Geometry Nodes will be very helpful if you ever decide to learn Houdini, Unreal, or any other number of programs that have node systems. Geometry Nodes is flexible, easy to understand, and will be useful in any number of projects you undertake in your career. Let's jump right in and start using it to create a procedural dispersal system for the grass that will be growing on top of our land.

In this chapter, we will cover the following:

- Setting up the scene – adding grass and rocks to the Asset Browser
- Creating a Geometry Nodes system to scatter our objects
- Adding more complexity and applying a modifier to other objects

Technical requirements

Make sure to download the file from GitHub called `MiniProject2_Start.blend`.

We'll use this as our main `.blend` file and add more things to it. As you can see, it already has a landscape, water plane, camera, and sun set up inside of it. We covered all these aspects in the last three chapters, so I don't want to repeat the information already presented there. Feel free to poke around the project and see how things work and how I've applied the previously covered principles to this file.

The other files we need to download for this chapter are the grass and rock assets. I find that recreating rocks and grass every time you need them is very tedious and doesn't really teach much. So, we're going to download `Nature_Assets.blend`, and make sure you have them saved in a place you'll be able to find them. Don't worry about opening them; we can transfer objects between files very easily with the **Asset Manager**. As with the previous chapter, most of the textures I will be using are downloaded from `Ambientcg.com`; they have an amazingly vast library of CC0 textures that you can use for free and without attribution. You may consider donating to their cause if you find them as useful as I do.

> **Grass and Nature Resources**
>
> After you've made one rock, you've made them all. I recommend trying to create pieces of nature (trees, rocks, grass, and so on) at least once or twice so that you get the hang of it, but overall, they're very time-consuming and really, really hard to do well. If you have a little bit of money to spend on assets or add-ons, buying grass and trees is a good idea. They are always going to look so much better (3D add-on developers have the time and energy to spend making sure that trees look perfect!) and save you time. To me, and many others, it's way worth the money to skip that part of developing a nature scene. So, don't waste hundreds of hours perfecting your trees when the forest is the more important part.

The supporting files for this chapter can be found here: `https://github.com/PacktPublishing/Shading-Lighting-and-Rendering-with-Blenders-EEVEE/tree/main/Chapter05`.

Setting up the scene - adding grass and rocks to the Asset Browser

In this section, we'll look at importing the assets that we just downloaded to the main `Mini-Project2` scene that we'll be working with in this chapter and setting up the scene so that we can get to the fun stuff – Geometry Nodes! The Asset Browser is a brand-new addition to Blender 3.0, and we're going to use it to add the assets we downloaded to the main scene and also make them available in any other `.blend` file on our computer.

The first thing we'll do is mark the nature assets as **Assets**, which then lets us add them to a library that we can reuse at any point:

1. Create a folder in the file explorer you use that you'll easily have access to. I created one in my `Documents` folder called `Blender Assets`:

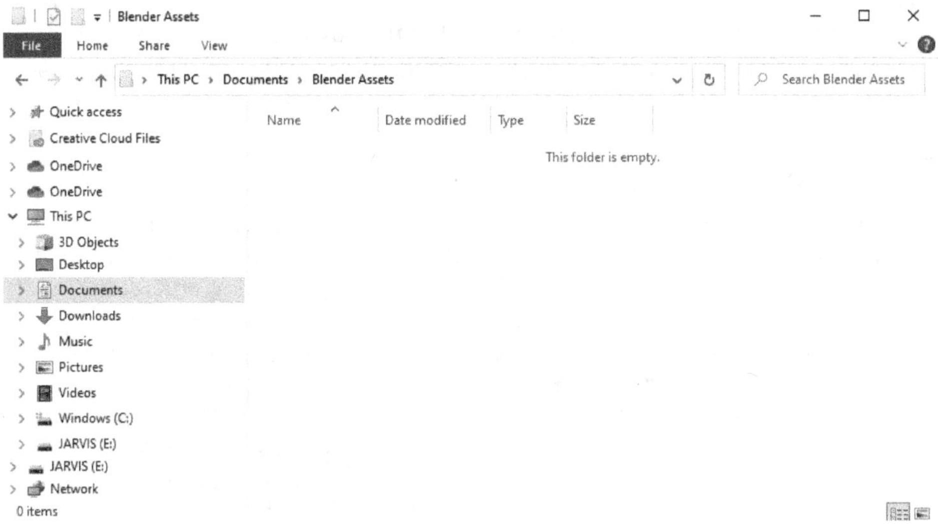

Figure 5.1: An empty folder to use as an asset library

2. Copy the `Nature_Assets.blend` file to the new folder you just made.
3. Open the `Nature_Assets.blend` file. You'll see we have two rocks and one grass object:

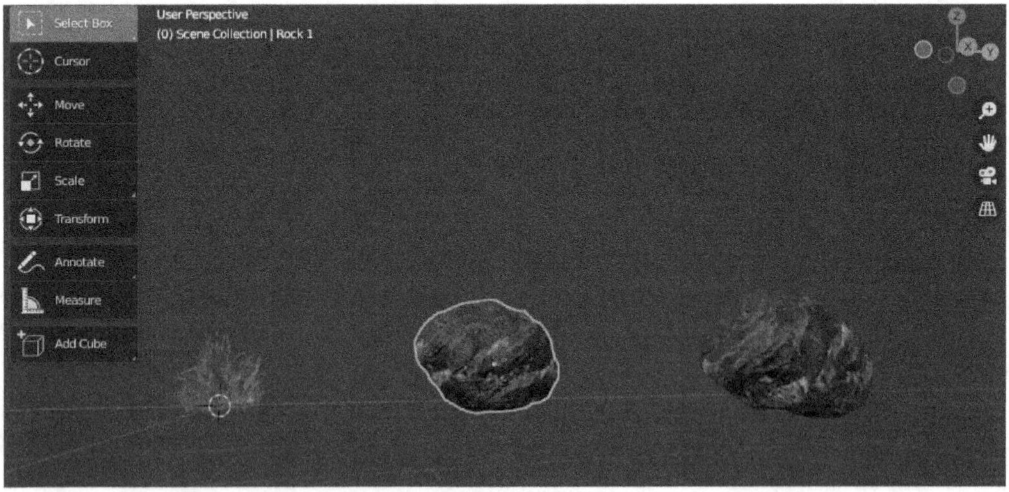

Figure 5.2: Objects in the Nature_Assets.blend file

4. Select an object and then go to the Outliner at the top-right corner; right-click on the object, and then click **Mark as Asset**. This tells Blender that we want to make the object available for the asset library:

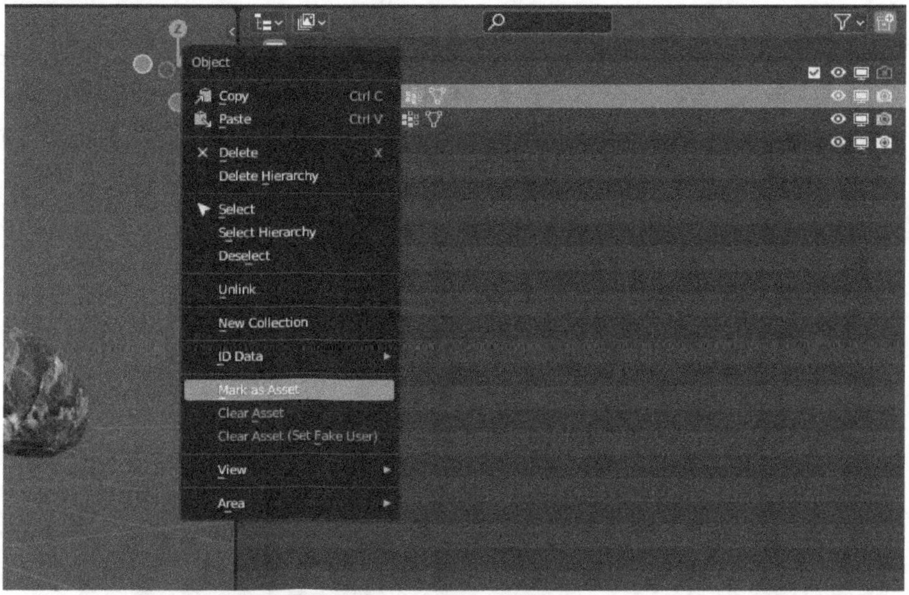

Figure 5.3: The Mark as Asset option

5. Right-click the other two objects in turn and mark each one as an asset. Each object should have a little bookshelf icon next to it now that denotes it has been *marked as an asset*:

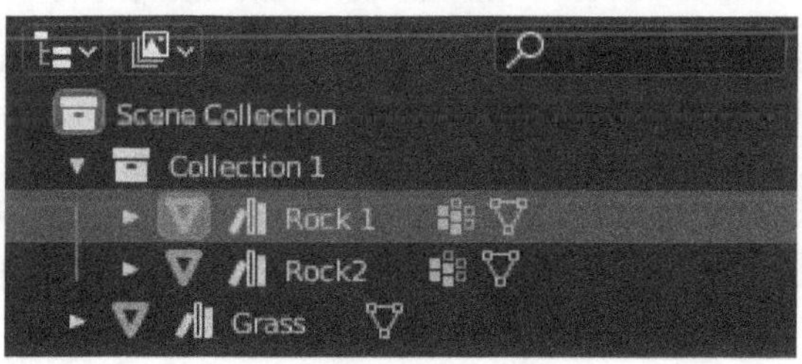

Figure 5.4: The bookshelf icon

Save the `Nature_Assets.blend` file and close it. We'll now open the `Mini-Project 2-Start.blend` file.

To import the marked assets into the `Mini-Project 2-Start.blend` file, we need to tell Blender where to look for our assets:

1. In the toolbar, select the **Edit** menu and then select **Preferences...**:

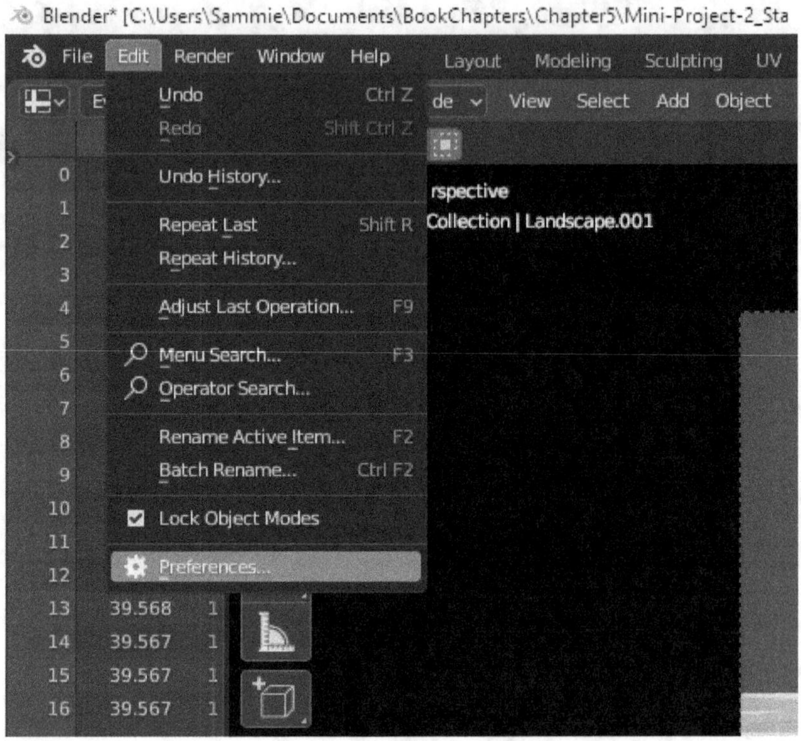

Figure 5.5: Opening the Blender Preferences menu

2. Navigate to the **File Paths** section in the **Blender Preferences** menu. At the bottom of the options in the **File Path** section, there is an option to add a path to **Asset Libraries**. Either copy and paste the path into the box or use the folder button on the side of the box to navigate to the right folder:

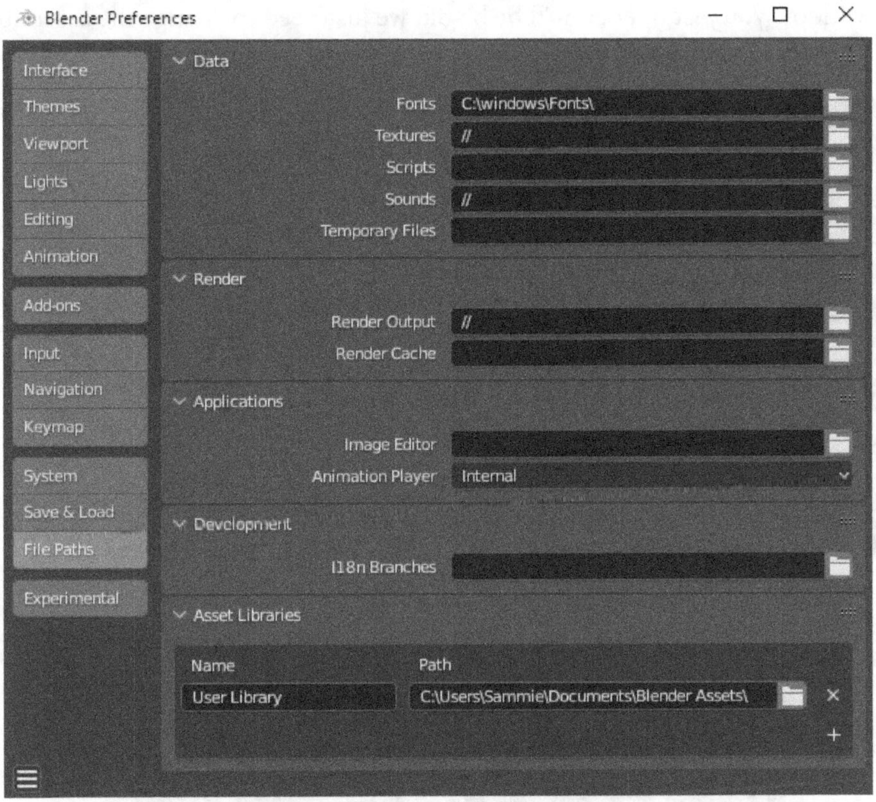

Figure 5.6: The File Paths options

3. In the left window, use the window editor type button to change the window type to **Asset Browser**:

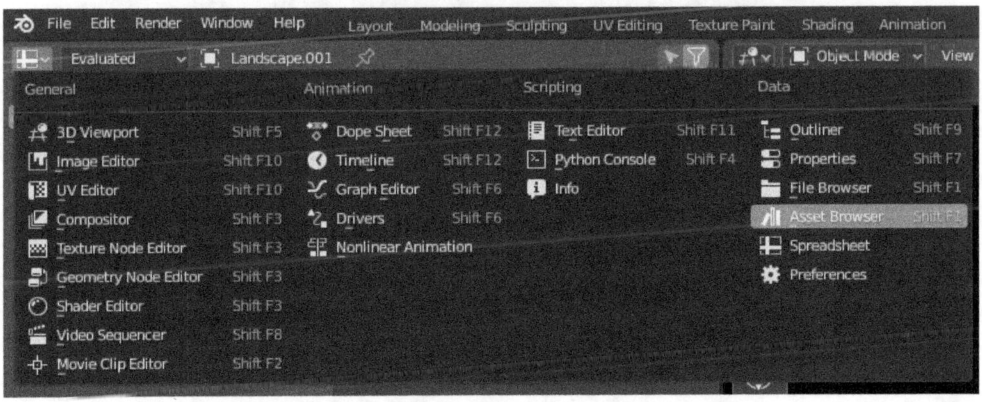

Figure 5.7: Changing the window to the Asset Browser

The window you just opened will be blank; we just need to change the asset library source from **Current File** to the asset library we just designated:

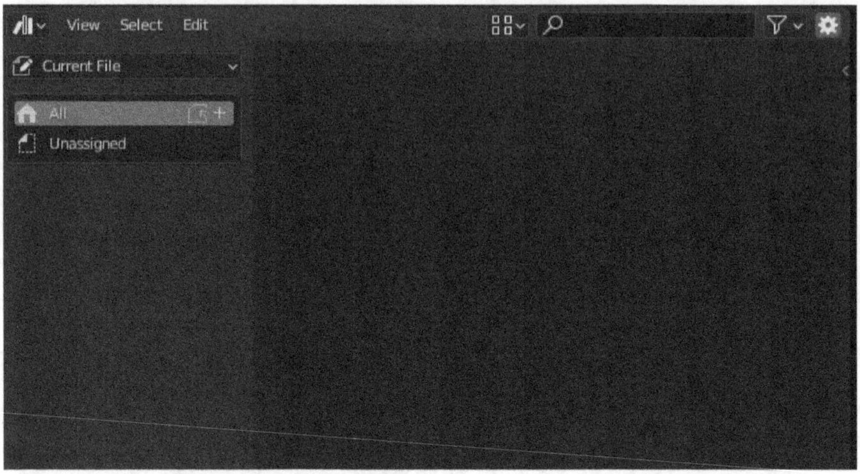

Figure 5.8: The asset library upon first opening

4. Click on the **Current File** dropdown and change it to **User Library**:

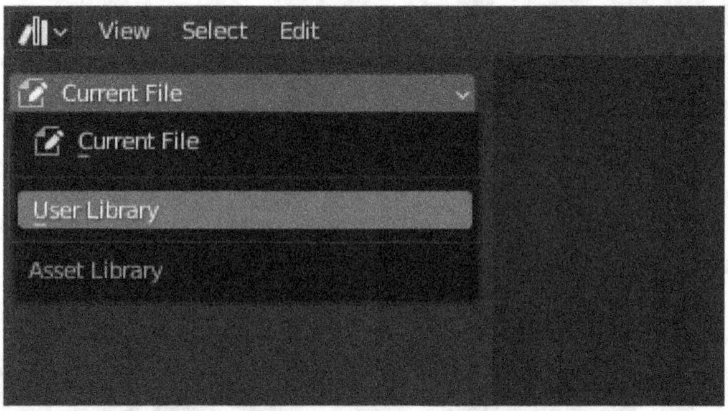

Figure 5.9: Changing to a user library

You should now see the three files that we marked as assets:

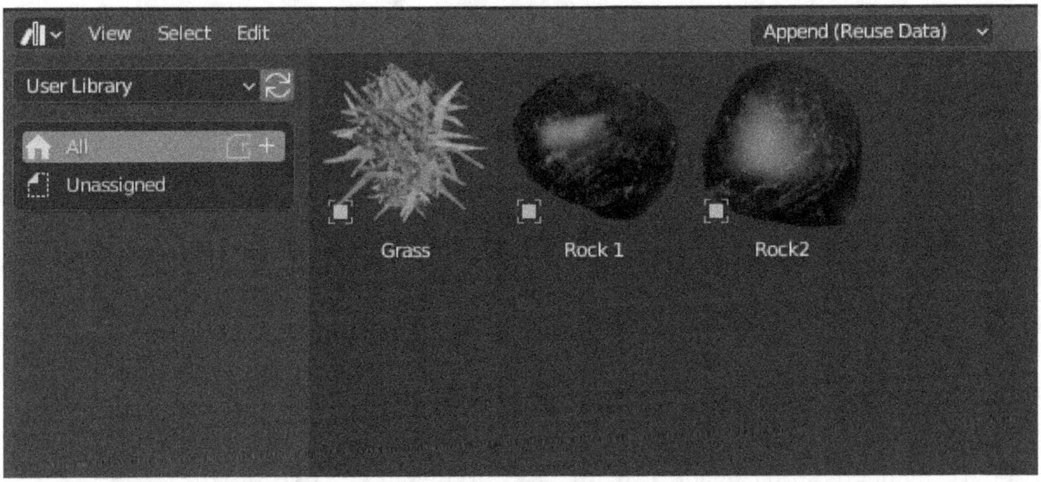

Figure 5.10: The marked assets in our library

5. To import the assets into the scene, all you have to do is drag and drop the assets into the open 3D window:

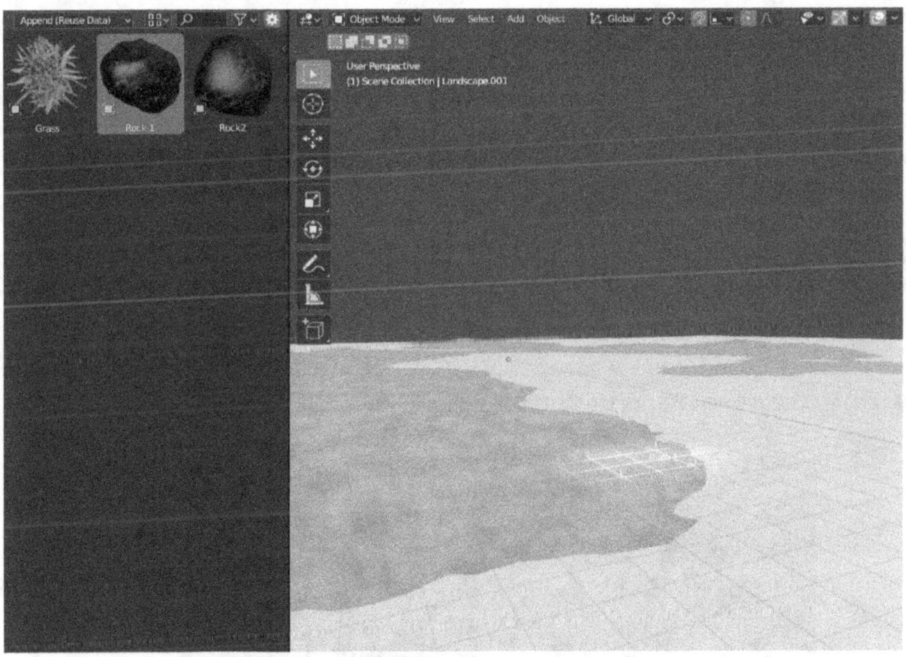

Figure 5.11: Adding the rock asset to the scene

Drag and drop all three objects into the scene:

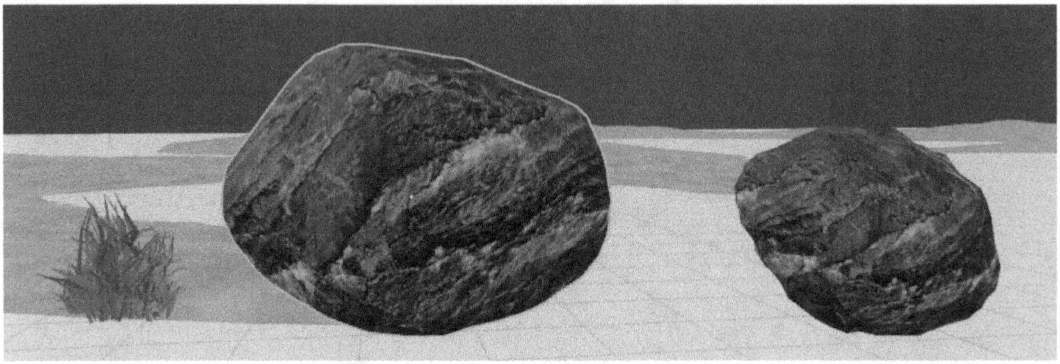

Figure 5.12: The assets in the scene

This method of adding objects into a scene may seem like more work now, but the effort pays dividends. You can add as many `.blend` files as you like into the `Blender Assets` folder that we just created, mark any type of data as an asset, and then reuse it on any file you want! This means that if you spend the time creating a robust library, you can have access to any object you've ever made with ease. This asset library addition to Blender 3.0 is a game-changer, but another game-changer in Blender 3.0 is Geometry Nodes. We'll scatter these three objects with the Geometry Nodes modifier in the next chapter. Don't worry if you've never used Geometry Nodes before; we'll be starting from a beginner level, since Geometry Nodes is new for everyone who uses Blender.

In the upcoming section, we'll go over the Geometry Nodes workspace, the workflow, and how to create flexible node trees to scatter objects on top of a landscape.

Setting up the scene – adding grass and rocks

The first step in using Geometry Nodes is getting access to the Geometry Nodes workspace. Luckily, Blender has a handy workspace tab already set up for us. It's at the top of the screen, in the same row as the **Shading** workspace tab that we already accessed:

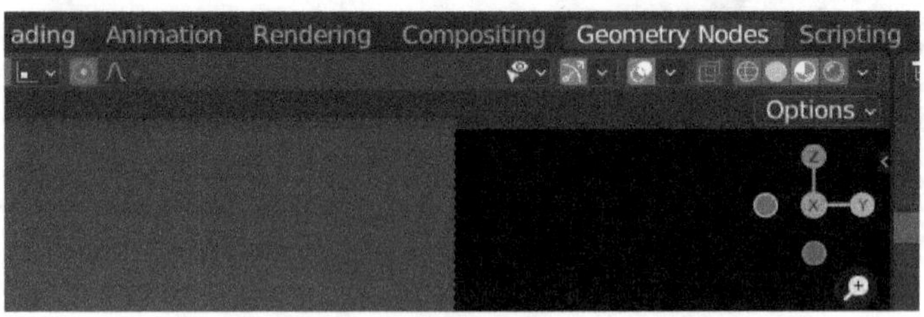

Figure 5.13: Geometry Nodes workspace

After clicking on it, you should have a workspace similar to the following visible, with a Spreadsheet window at the top left, the 3D viewport at the top right, and the Geometry Node editor at the bottom of the screen:

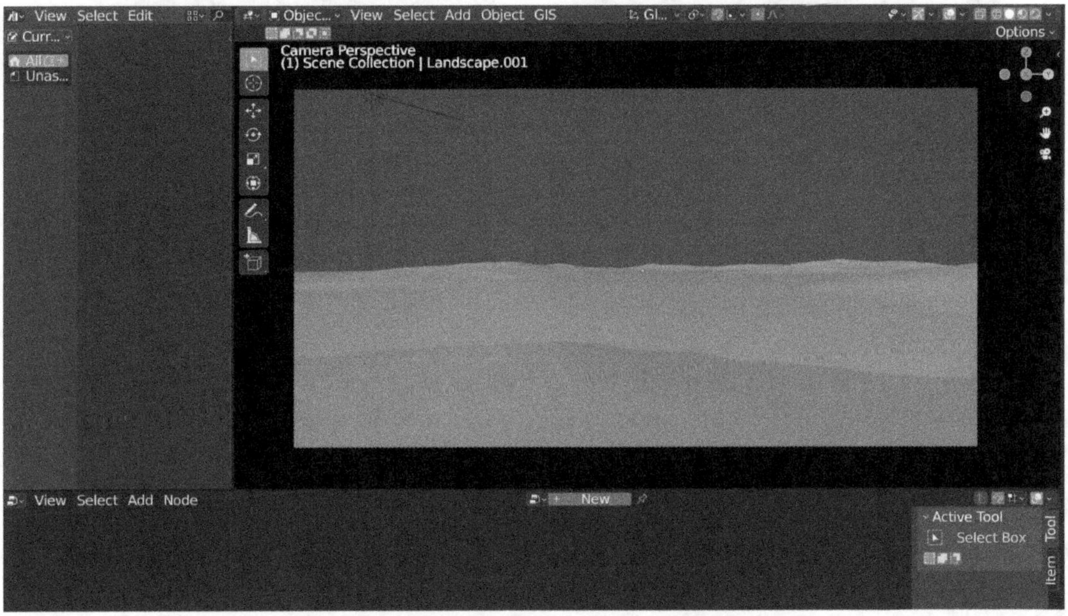

Figure 5.14 : The Geometry Nodes workspace layout

Let's start by adding a new Geometry Nodes network. This works similarly to the material network that we covered in *Chapter 2*, *Creating Materials Fast with EEVEE*:

1. The first thing to do is select the object we want to apply the **Geometry Nodes** modifier to. Since we want to distribute the objects around the landscape, we'll select the **Landscape** object in our Outliner.
2. Click the **New** button on the **Geometry Nodes** menu:

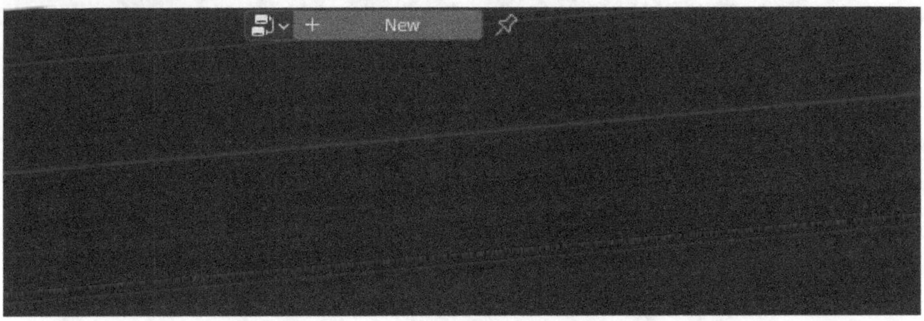

Figure 5.15: The New button on the Geometry Nodes work area

3. We should now have a **Geometry Nodes** modifier added to the object and be able to see **Group Input** and **Group Output** generated as default for **Geometry** Nodes:

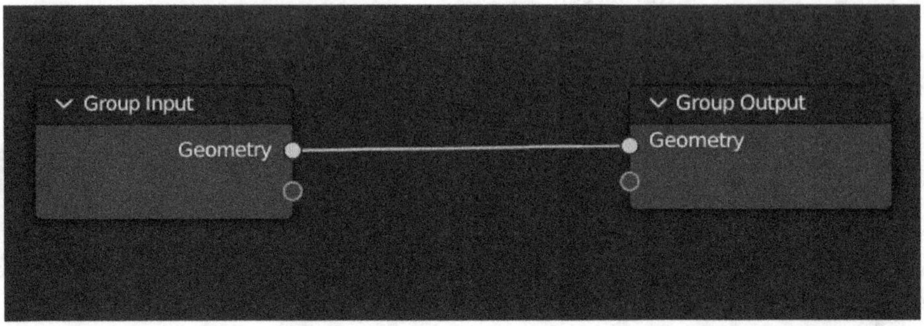

Figure 5.16: Input and output defaults for the new Geometry Nodes system

4. The next thing we want to do is add scattered points to the **Geometry Nodes** network so that we can then tell Blender that we want to add a `Grass` object to every scattered point on the landscape. Let's add a node, using *Shift* + *A*. Instead of looking through the different node categories to find that node, we can just type the title of the node into the search bar at the top of the **Add** menu. Let's add a **Distribute Points on Faces** node. By dropping the node on the line connecting **Group Input** to **Group Output**, we can effectively scatter points on top of the surface of our object:

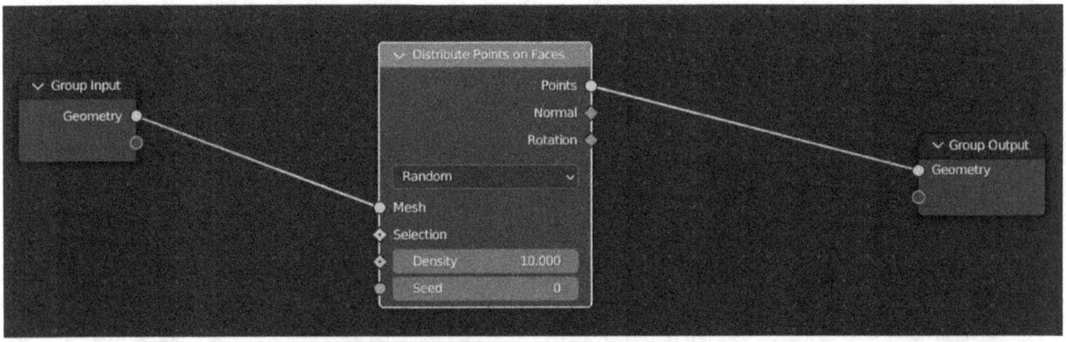

Figure 5.17: Distribute Points on Faces

Geometry Nodes are computed left to right, just like the Material Editor or Compositor that we've used so far. So, we're telling the computer with this node group to take our group input (the landscape object), distribute points on the surface, and then display that in our viewport. Looking at the viewport, you can visualize the points that we're distributing as little orange diamonds:

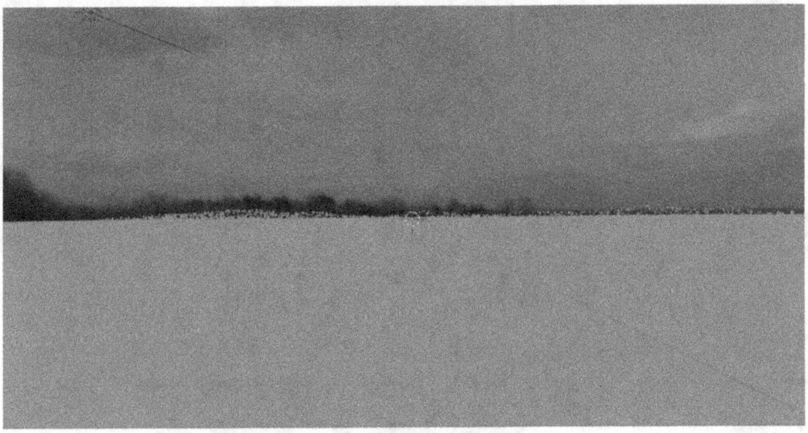

Figure 5.18: Scattered points

5. So, now we need to connect the `Grass` object to the points we've scattered. Let's do this by adding **Instance on Points** after **Distribute Points on Faces**. The **Instance on Points** node takes each point we scattered with **Distribute Points on Faces** and adds an instanced object to it. An instanced object can be any mesh we designate:

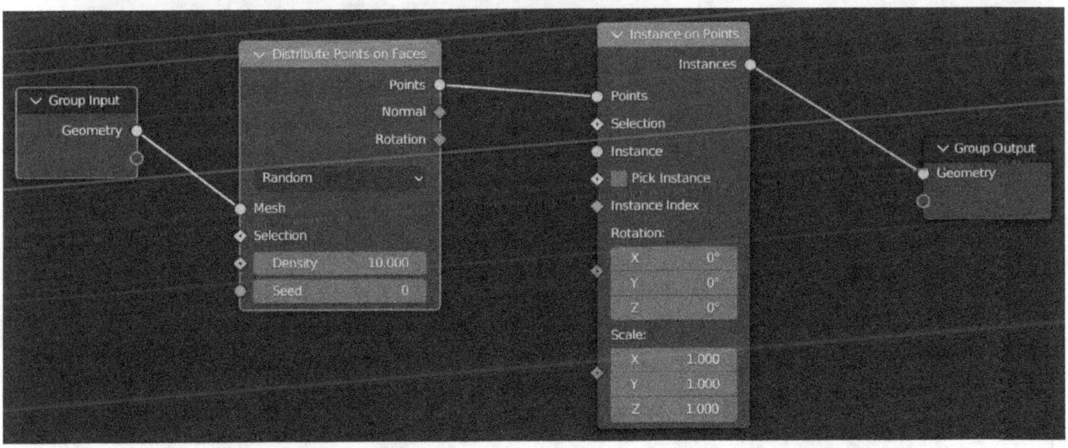

Figure 5.19: Distribute Points on Faces and Instance on Points

6. Then, we need to add an object to distribute. Add an **Object Info** node and connect it to the **Instance** input on the **Instance on Points** node:

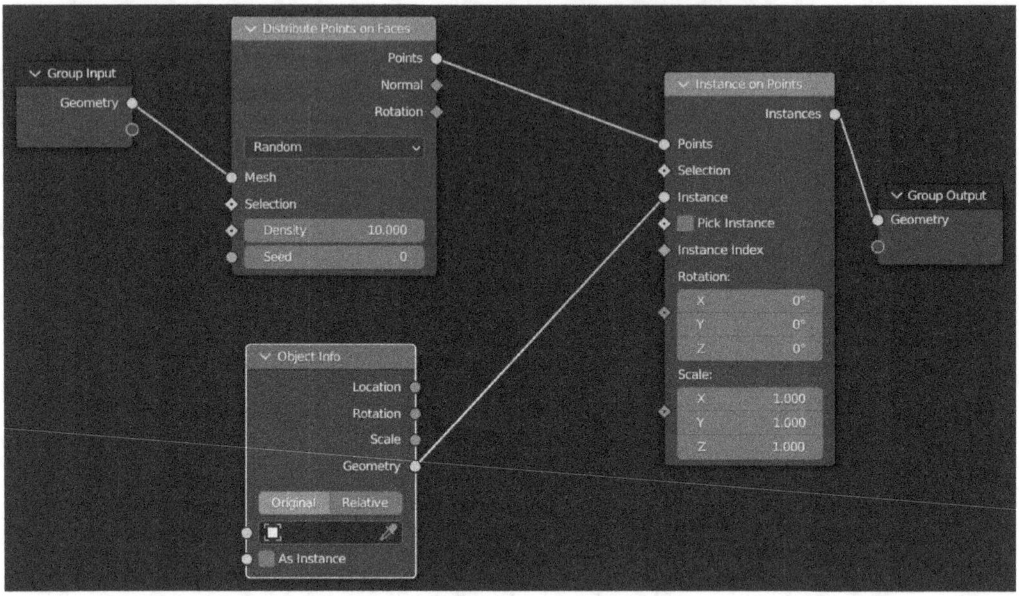

Figure 5.20: Adding the Grass object to the point instance

7. Using the eyedropper on the object box, we can select the `Grass` object as the object that we want to populate on our landscape:

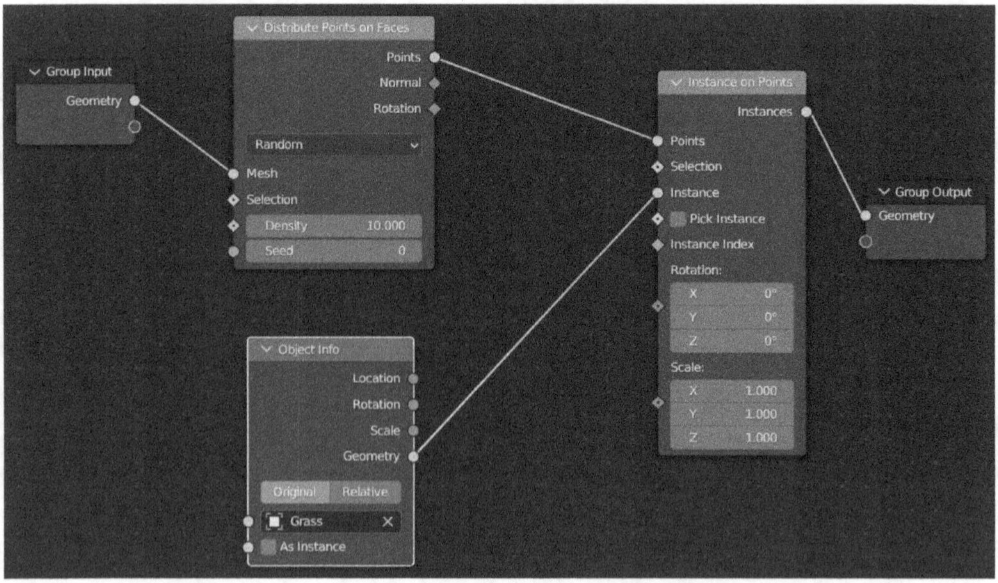

Figure 5.21: Adding the Grass object to the Object Info node

Woah! We have grass suddenly everywhere in the viewport! That isn't exactly what we want, so we'll have to figure out how to make our `Grass` object a little bit smaller. We can definitely do this by just editing the size of the original object, but I want to show you how to control the size of scattered objects inside of the **Geometry Node** editor:

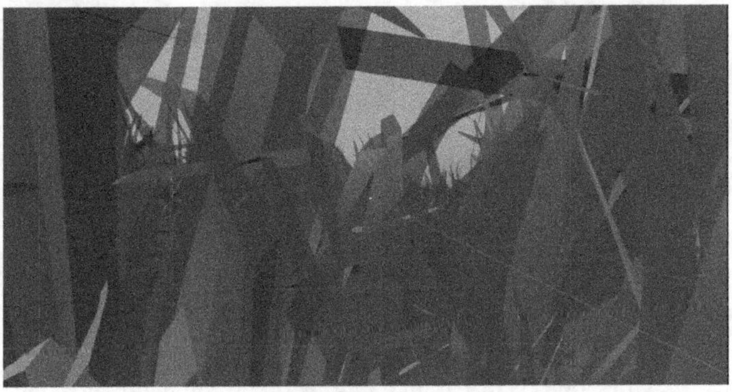

Figure 5.22: The camera view after adding the Grass object to the Instance node

8. We can change the **Scale** value on the **Instance on Points** node to **0.100**:

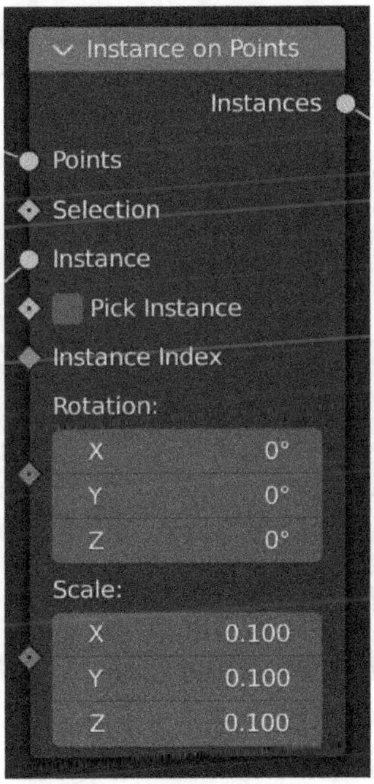

Figure 5.23: Changing the point scale

This changes the grass objects to a 10th of their original size, making them decidedly more grass-sized:

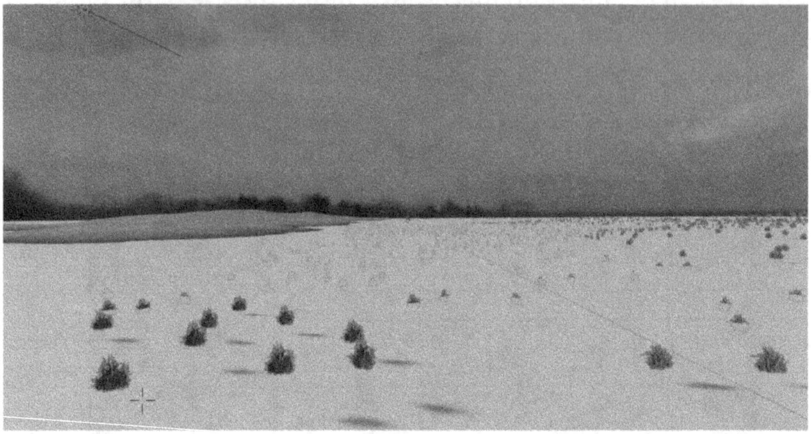

Figure 5.24: Grass objects distributed on the foreground landscape object

9. We now have some cool plants to populate our scene. But where did the `Foreground Landscape` object go? It's completely disappeared in favor of our plants, which isn't what we want. Let's make sure we can see the landscape plane. Add a **Join Geometry** node and attach it between **Instance on Points** and the **Group Output** node. Take the output from the first node, **Group Input | Geometry**, and connect it to the same input on the **Join Geometry** node:

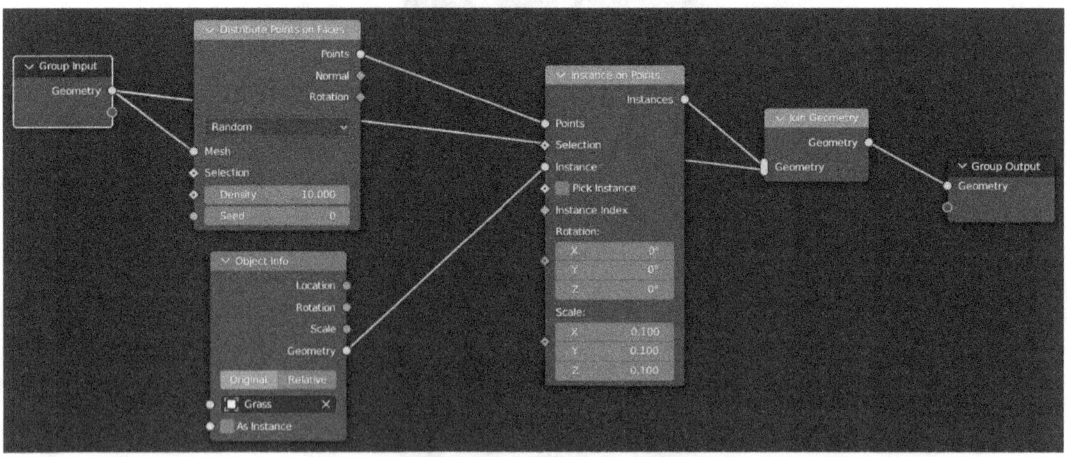

Figure 5.25: Joining it all together

We should now see both the landscape and the scattered grass objects together on the screen:

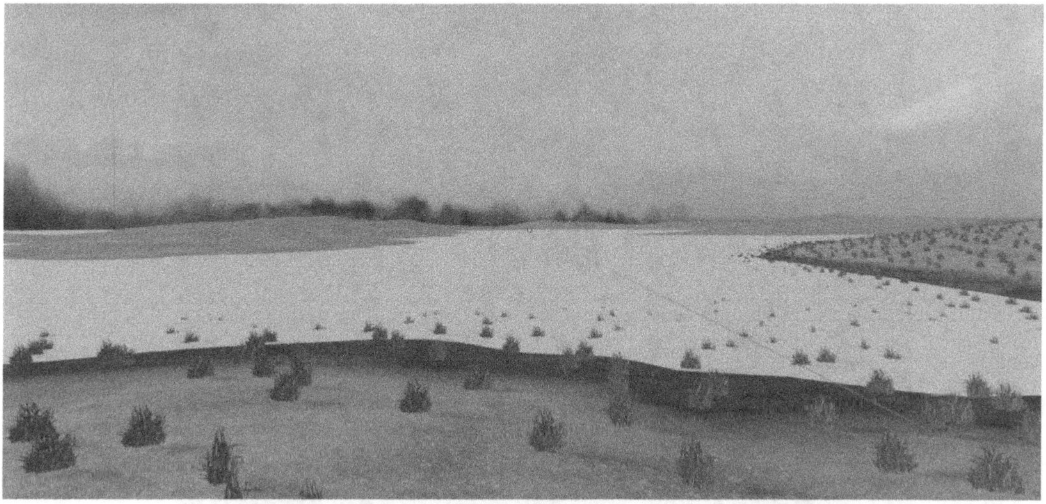

Figure 5.26: The landscape and scattered grass joined together

10. This scattering looks alright, but we probably don't want to have grass appearing underneath the water; it's a waste of computing power. We'll add a **Density** map now to control where the plants can be scattered. First, we want to connect the empty socket on **Group Input** to **Density** on the **Distribute Points on Faces** node:

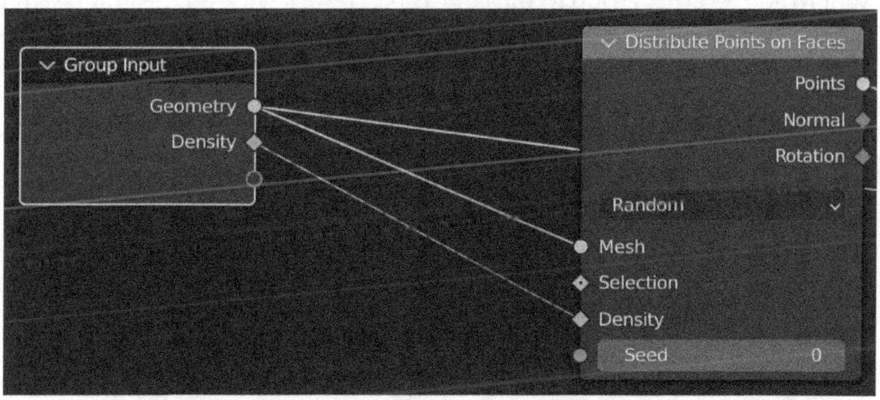

Figure 5.27: Adding Density to Group Input

11. Let's go to the **Properties** menu at the right-hand side of the screen and select the Modifier panel:

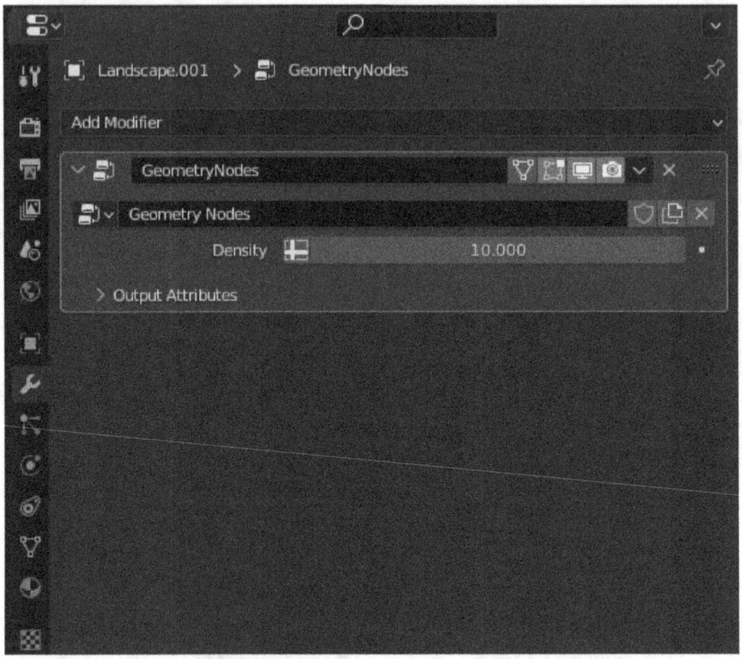

Figure 5.28: The Modifier panel

12. We want to add a vertex group to the landscape, so we'll click on the graph sign next to **Density**. This should result in the previous number being cleared from the **Density** value. We can now add a vertex group that we can paint to control the density:

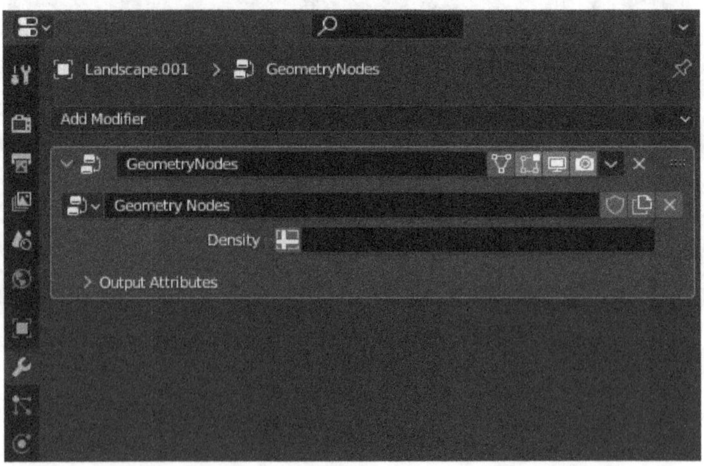

Figure 5.29: Creating a field for the vertex group

13. We need to create the vertex group now. Let's go to **Object Data Properties** (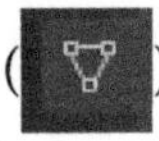) and add a vertex group using the plus sign on the **Vertex Groups** section:

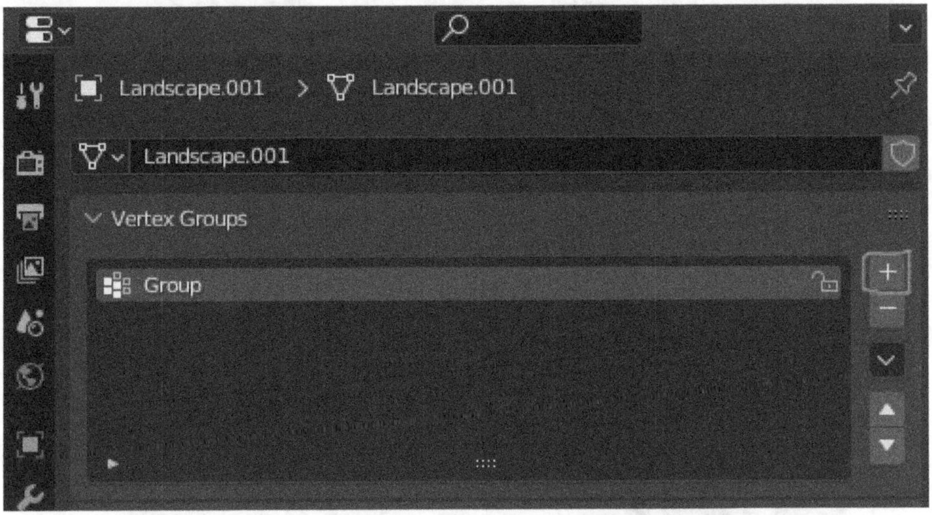

Figure 5.30: Creating the vertex group

14. It should give us a vertex group called **Group**. Going back to the Geometry Nodes modifier, we can now click on the **Density** field and select **Group** from the list of options:

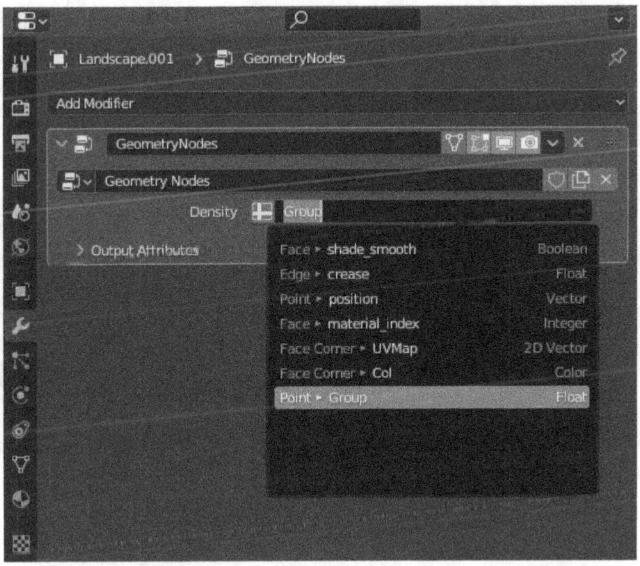

Figure 5.31: Selecting the vertex group as the Density field

15. With that **vertex group** set, we can now change to **Weight Paint** mode from the drop-down menu at the top-left corner:

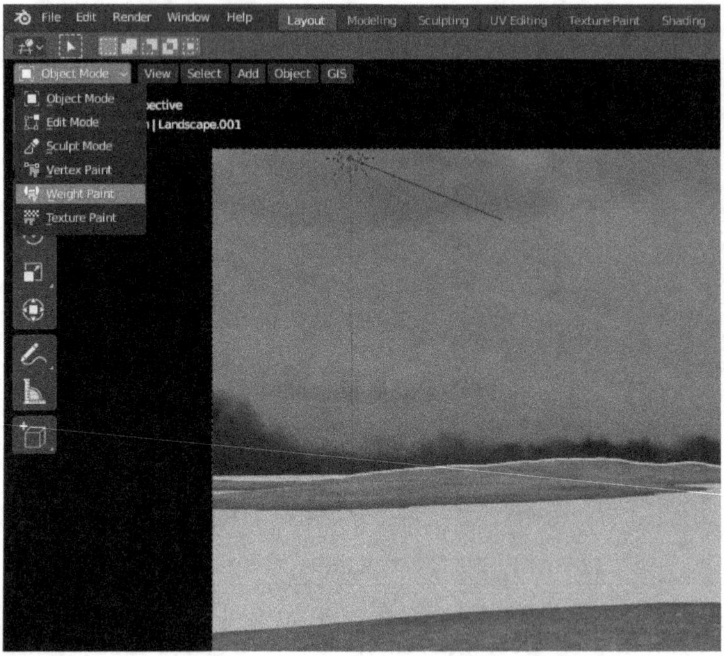

Figure 5.32: Weight Paint mode

16. The 3D viewport should now show your landscape as entirely blue. Try painting on top of the landscape with your cursor. The landscape object should change to red (with other shades of yellow and green) as you paint. If this doesn't happen, try changing the **Weight** and **Strength** values located at the top left of the screen to **1.000**:

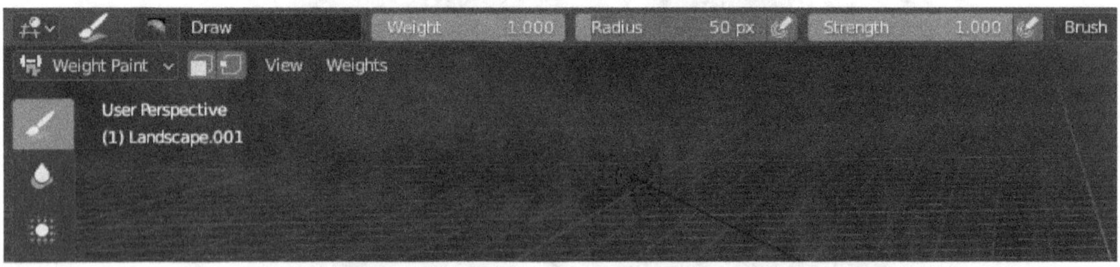

Figure 5.33: Weight and Strength toggles

17. In a weight paint map, all red areas indicate where the grass will appear, and all the blue areas indicate where the grass will not appear. I tried to paint all the places that are visible in the camera view red and left anywhere not visible from the camera as the default blue color:

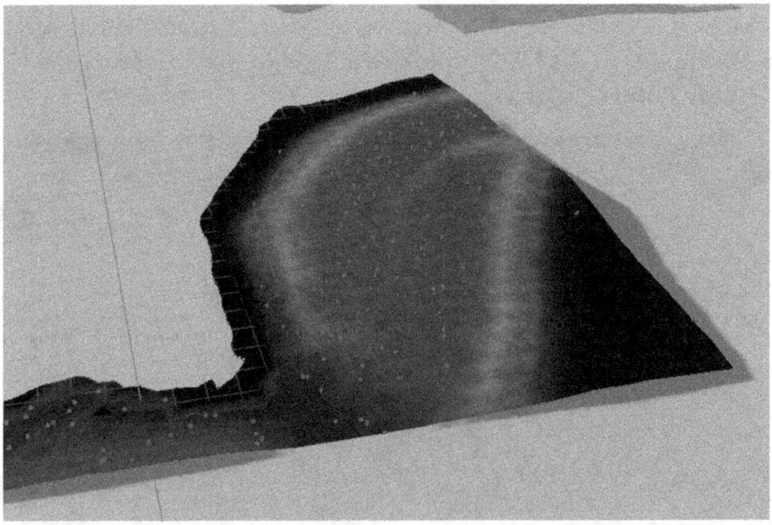

Figure 5.34: Weight painted on the landscape

18. We have plants! If you are still getting grass showing up under the `Water Volume` object, just jump back into **Weight Paint** mode and readjust the values so that you get the grass showing up where you want it:

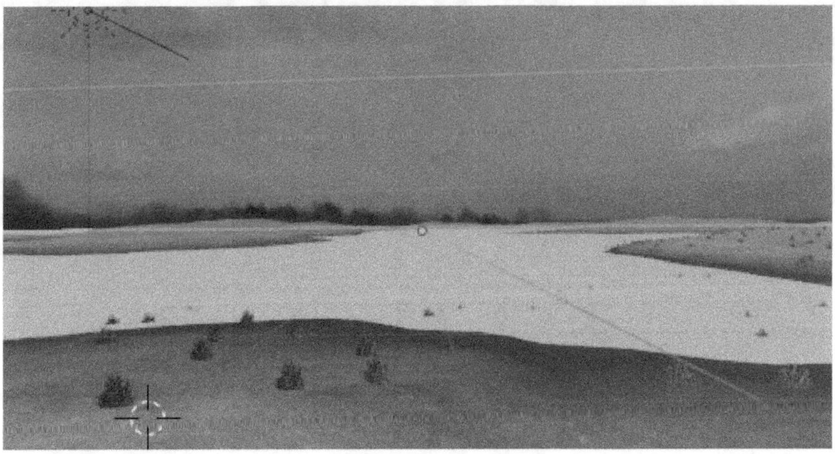

Figure 5.35: Scattered grass after applying the vertex group

19. The last step we'll do in this section is playing with the Density Multiplier. Since this piece of land is close to the camera, we probably want to add more density than, say, the landscape pieces that are farther away from the camera. This way, we can be more efficient, as every grass object has to be calculated by the computer, so if we have four separate pieces of geometry, we can let the background pieces be more sparse, while the foreground pieces are denser. We can change our density by adding a **Math** node to the Node editor, adding it between **Group Input | Density** and **Distribute Points on Faces | Density**:

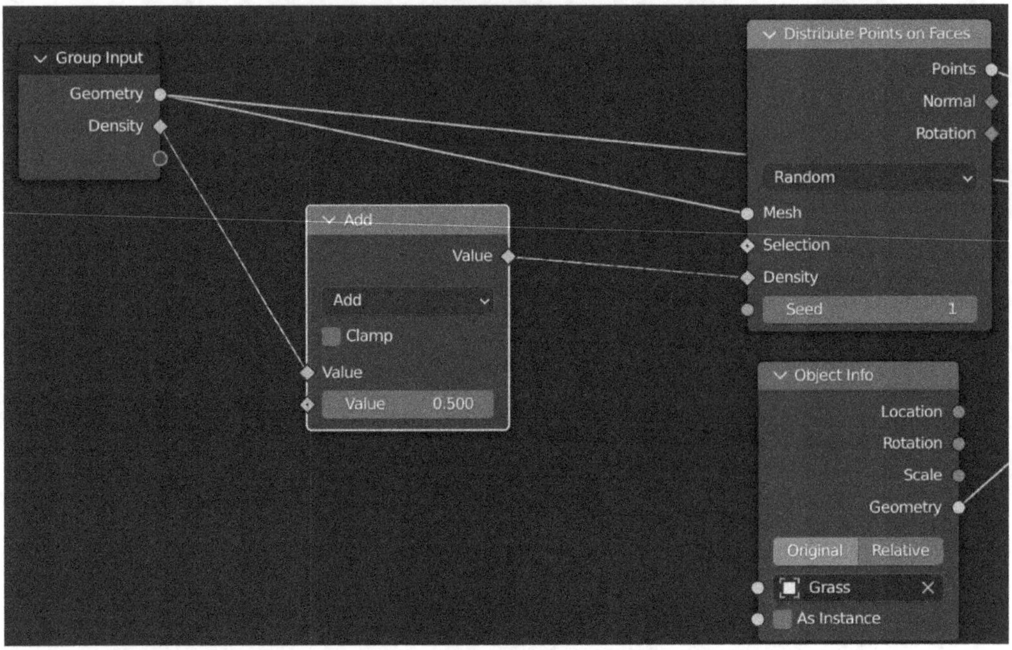

Figure 5.36: Adding a Math node

20. The default for the **Math** node is the **Add** operation. If we click the **Add** dropdown and switch the operation to **Multiply**, we can now effectively increase the density of our grass without getting plants under the lake. If you think about it, multiplying by zero is still zero, so therefore, we still have no plants under the water, but we can multiply the amount we're getting on land:

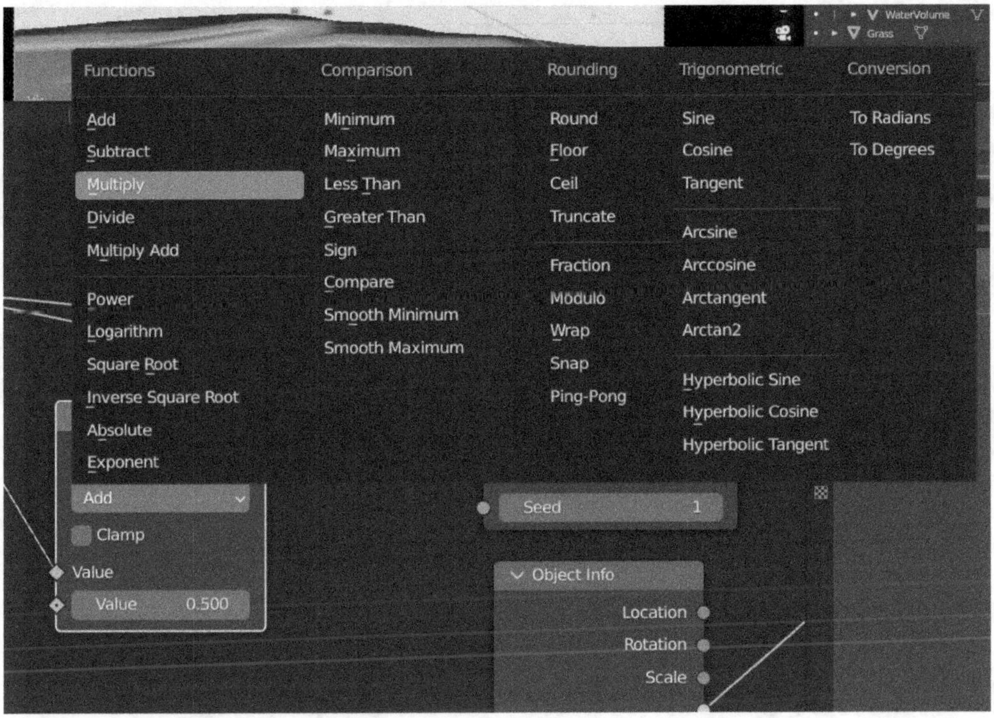

Figure 5.37: Changing the Math node to Multiply

I changed my value to `100.000` and got a result I liked. Feel free to try other values and see how they compare for you:

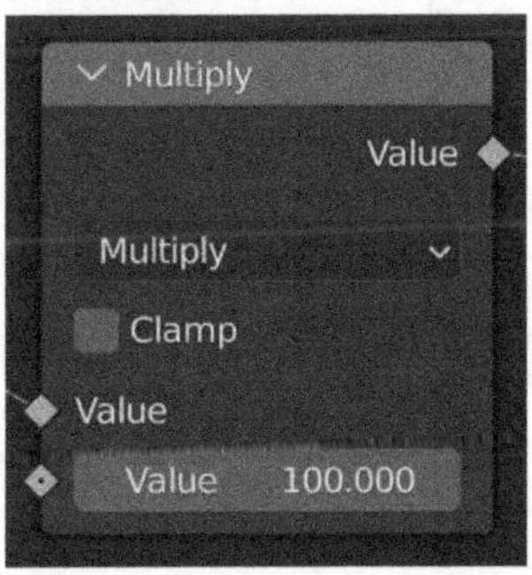

Figure 5.38: Changing the value to 100.000

After some fiddling with my vertex map, I dialed in my vegetation to create something like the following screenshot:

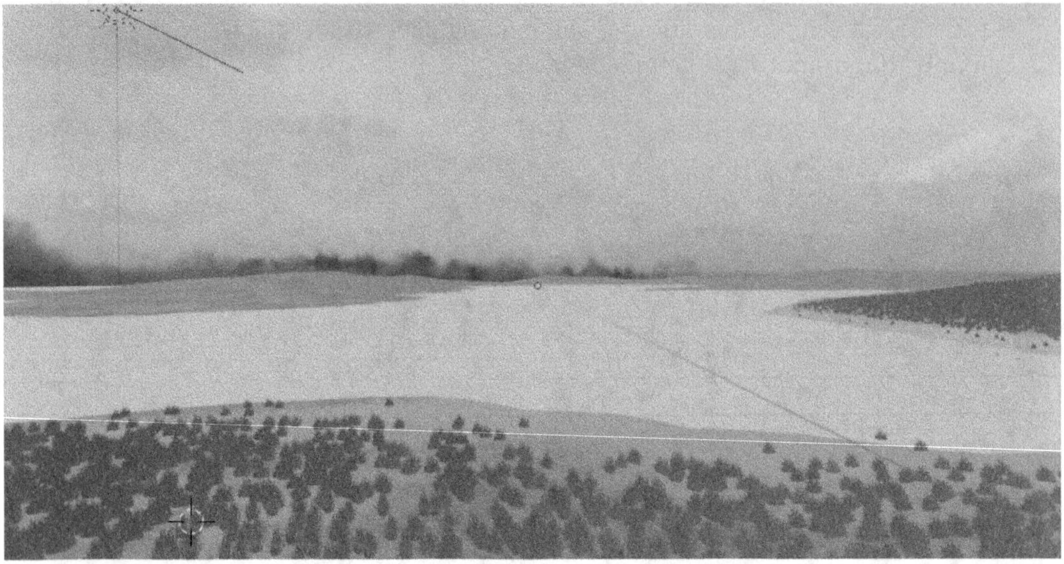

Figure 5.39: Adding density to the grass scatter

In the next section, we'll add some random variation to the grass objects, add `Rocks` to the node tree, and then create a reusable system so that anyone can use our system without knowing how to use Geometry Nodes.

Adding more complexity and applying the modifier to other objects

We have an interesting scattering of grass in the scene now. I'm not sure if you noticed, but every single grass object is pointing in the same direction, which isn't very natural. If we want to add randomization to the rotation of the grass, all we need to do is add a randomized value.

Let's get started:

1. Using *Shift* + *A*, add a **Random Value** node and connect it to the **Rotation** input on the **Instance on Points** node:

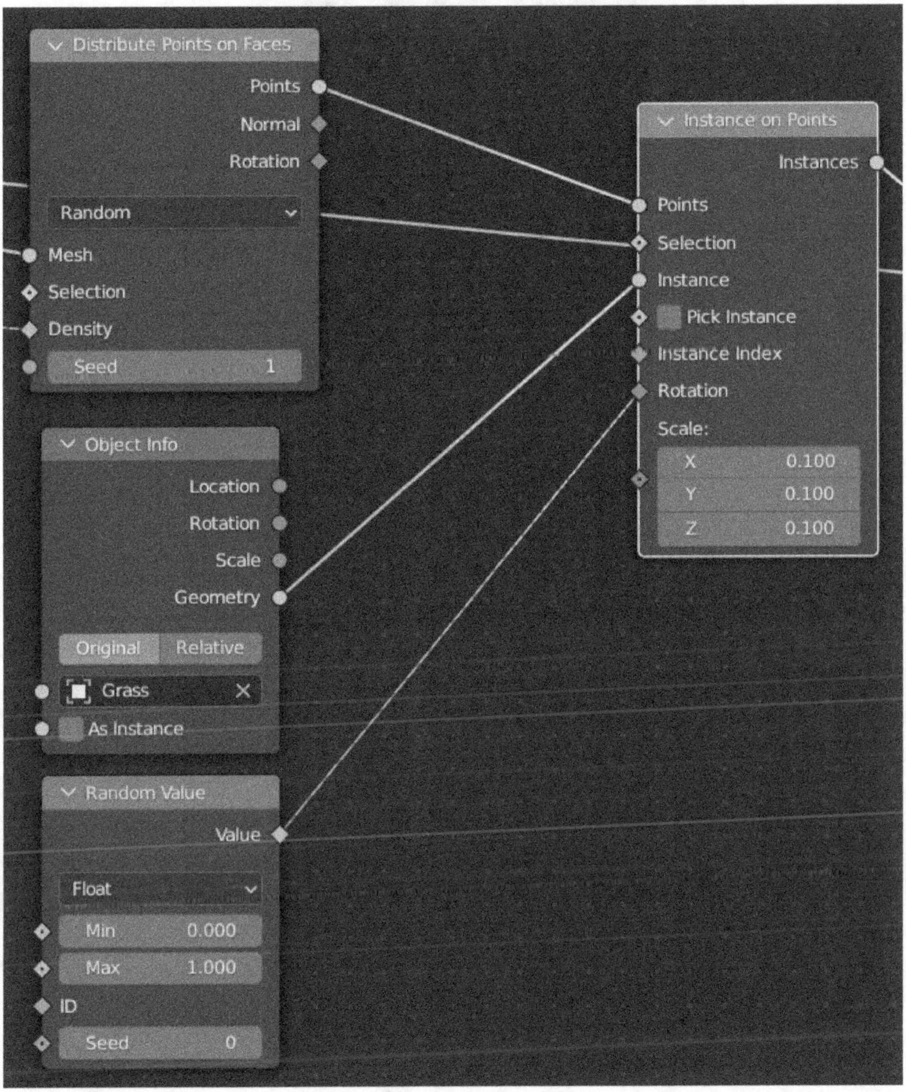

Figure 5.40: The node tree with Random Value added

2. Change the drop-down box from **Float** to **Vector**. You may need to reattach the value to the **Rotation** input after changing to **Vector**:

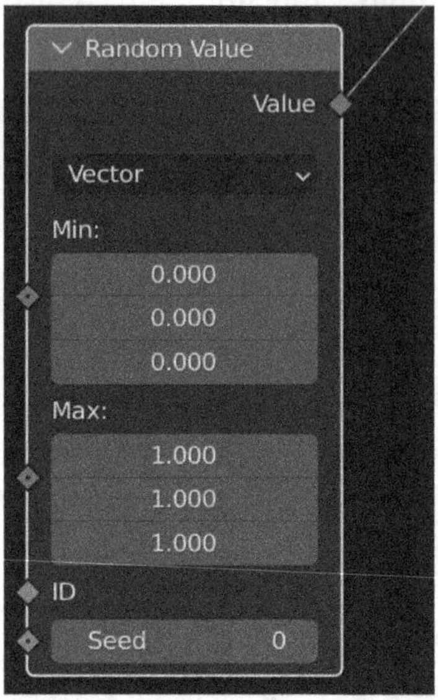

Figure 5.41: Random Value changed to Vector

3. There should be random rotation happening to the grass particles now. But the vector that we designated has three **Max** inputs and three **Min** inputs. These inputs are *x*, *y*, and *z*, in that order. So, we have *x* min, *y* min, and *z* min as numbers we can set, as well as *x* max, *y* max, and *z* max, which we can set as well, all from the **Random Value** node. These numbers are so we can tell the computer the domain in which to randomize. So, for example, if we set the *x* min to `0.000` and then *x* max to `1.000`, we'll get rotation values between `0.000` and `1.000` for the *x* axis. So, we can see that the default **Random Value** setting is to have rotation from `0.000` to `1.000` on all three axes. But we probably only want the grass rotation to be about a 10th of that on two axes (grass doesn't generally grow upside down!). So, if we change the *x* **Max** and *y* **Max** values to `0.100`, we should get a better result:

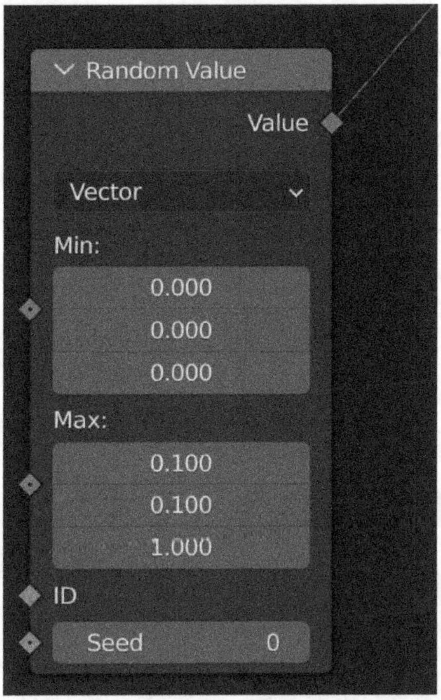

Figure 5.42: Changes to the max values on the x and y axes

So now, we have some random variation happening in the rotation of our grass objects:

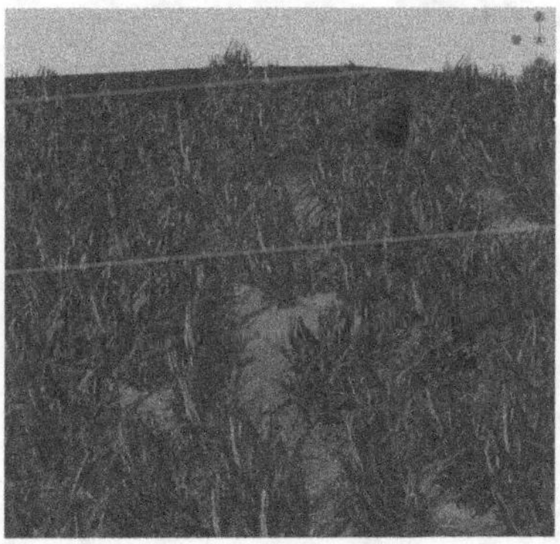

Figure 5.43: Randomly rotated scattered grass

Scale, position, and so on can all be randomized in this way, so try to experiment and see what you can get to work. Try attaching another **Random Value** node to the scale value and randomize the scale values of the grass as well.

Adding rocks to the node tree

Okay, we've worked in some random variation. Now, let's add our rocks to the node tree. This is where some of the magic happens in the Geometry Nodes process because now that we've got the grass working, we can just copy part of the node network, exchange the grass for rocks, and we'll have an awesome result! Let's get started:

1. Click and drag inside of the **Geometry Nodes** workspace to select nodes. We want to select **Multiply Node**, **Distribute Points on Faces**, **Object Info**, **Random Value**, and **Instance on Points**, so if we click at the top-left corner of the node tree workspace and drag over the nodes we want to select, we should get all of those nodes selected.
2. Use the *Ctrl* + *Shift* + *D* shortcut to copy these nodes while maintaining their connection to **Group Input**:

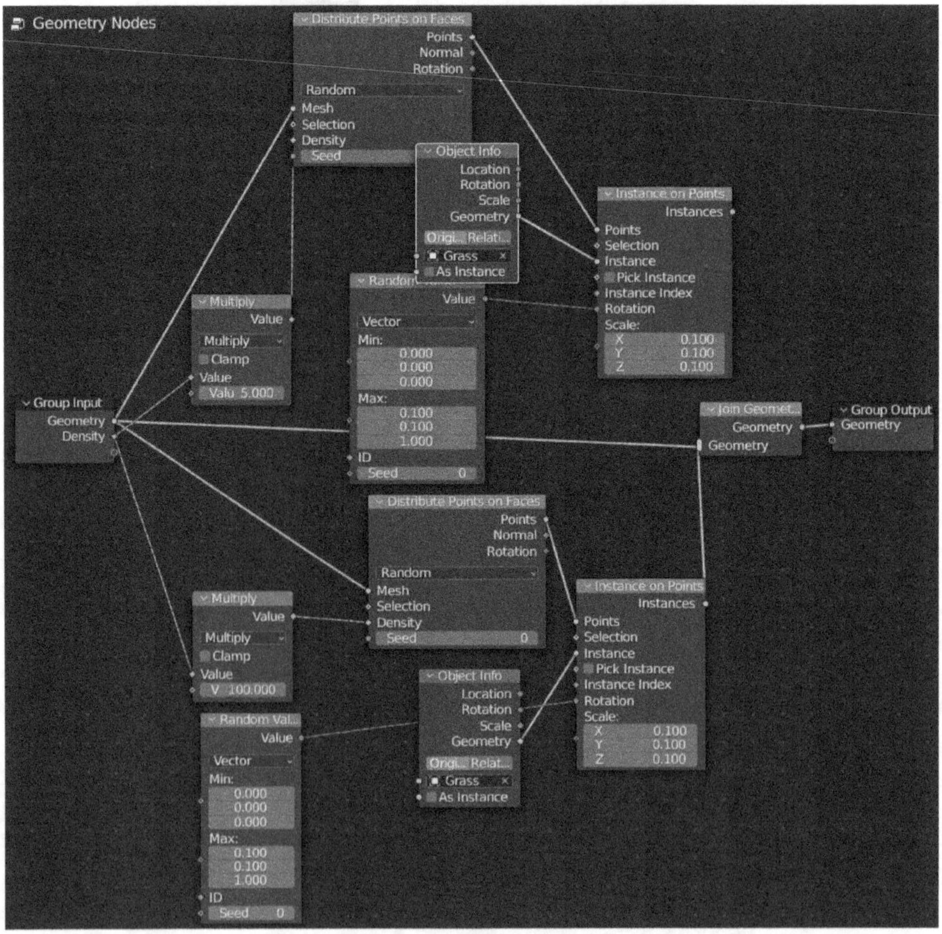

Figure 5.44: Copying the nodes

3. In the copied system, we want to delete the **Object Info** node and replace it with a **Collection Info** node. Using the **Collection Info** node, we get the opportunity to add an entire collection to the system, so we can input multiple objects and get several different variations on the object being scattered on the landscape, instead of just the single object:

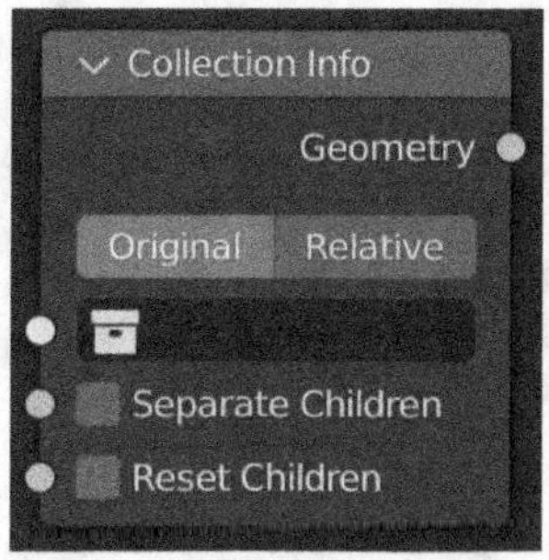

Figure 5.45: The Collection Info node

4. We need to make a collection with the rocks. Select our two rock objects in the Outliner and use the *M* shortcut key to open the **Collection** menu. Select **New Collection** and then name the collection `Rocks`. The two rock objects will be moved there:

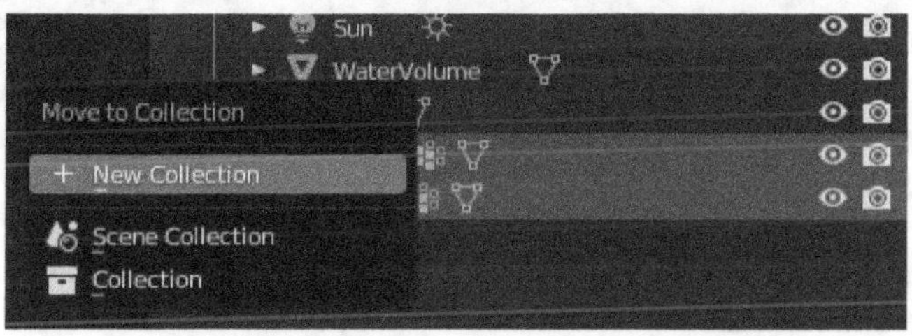

Figure 5.46: The Move to Collection menu

5. Go back to the **Collection Info** node and select the new **Rock** collection in the drop-down menu.

6. Connect the **Geometry** output on the **Collection Info** node to the **Instance** input on the **Instance on Points** node. Check the **Separate Children** and **Reset Children** boxes on the **Collection Info** node. This means that each rock will be spawned as separate objects, instead of spawning the whole collection at every point:

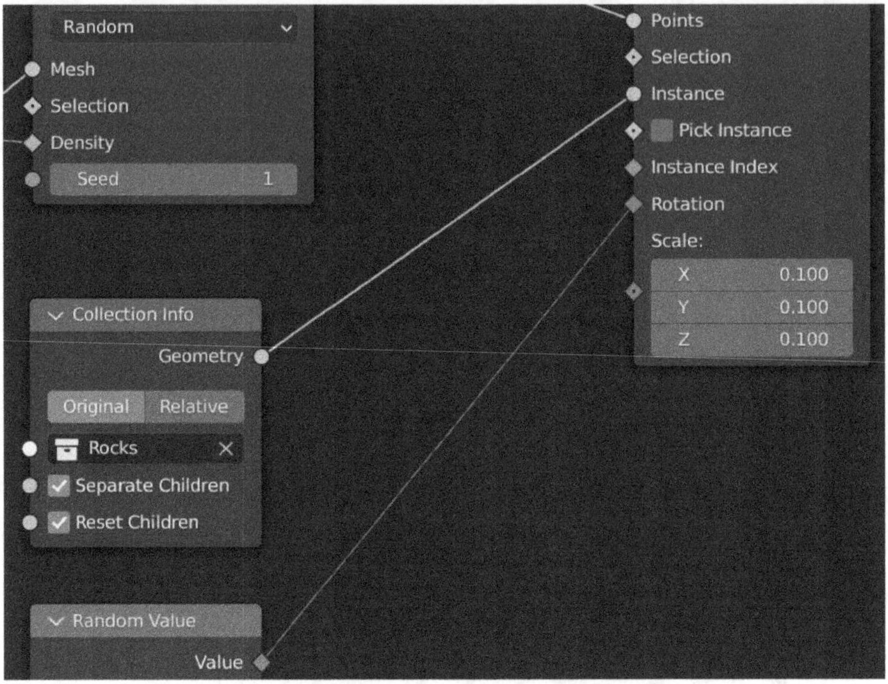

Figure 5.47: The Collection Info node

7. Connect the whole thing up to the **Join Geometry** node:

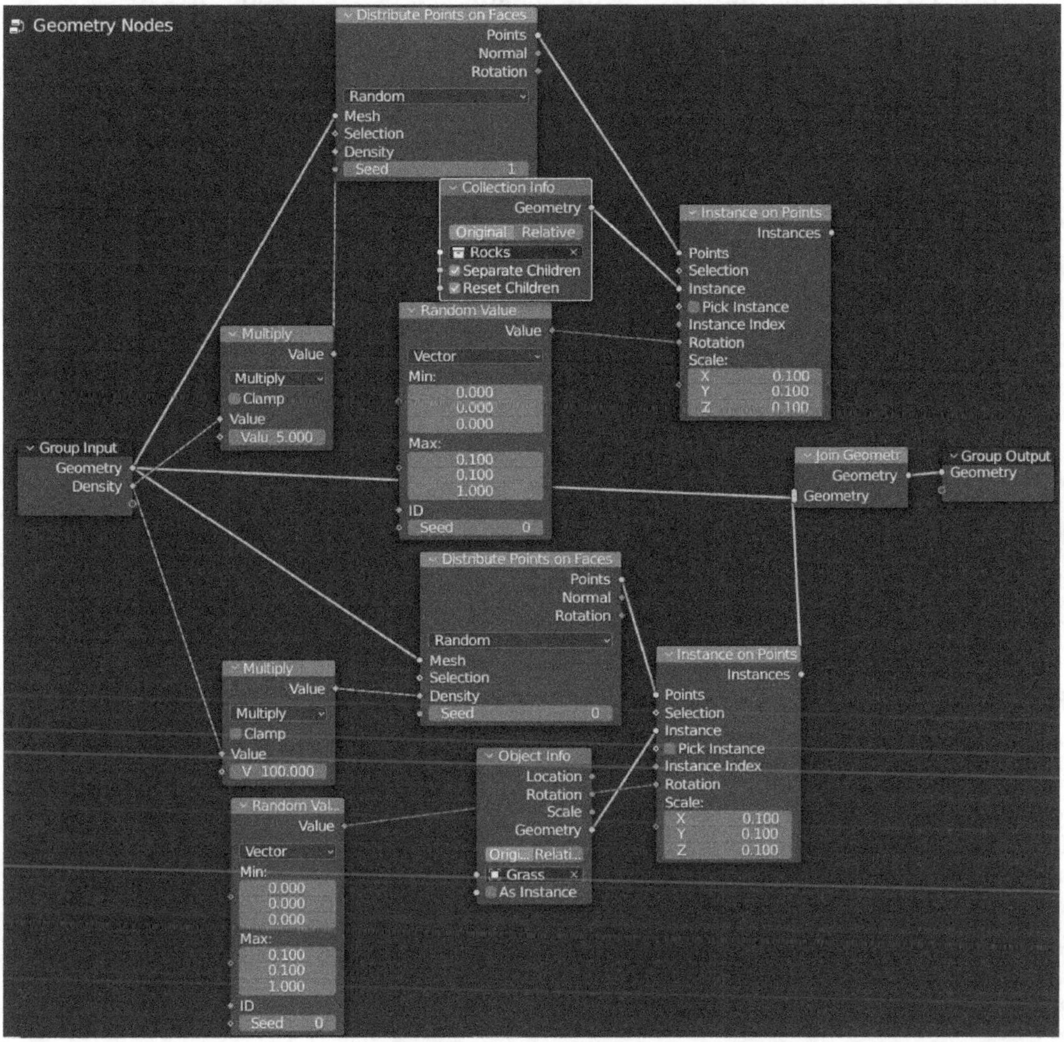

Figure 5.48: The finished node tree

8. You may notice some problems now. There are so many rocks, we can't see any grass. Let's lower the **Multiply** value of the **Rock** section of the node tree to something more like `5`:

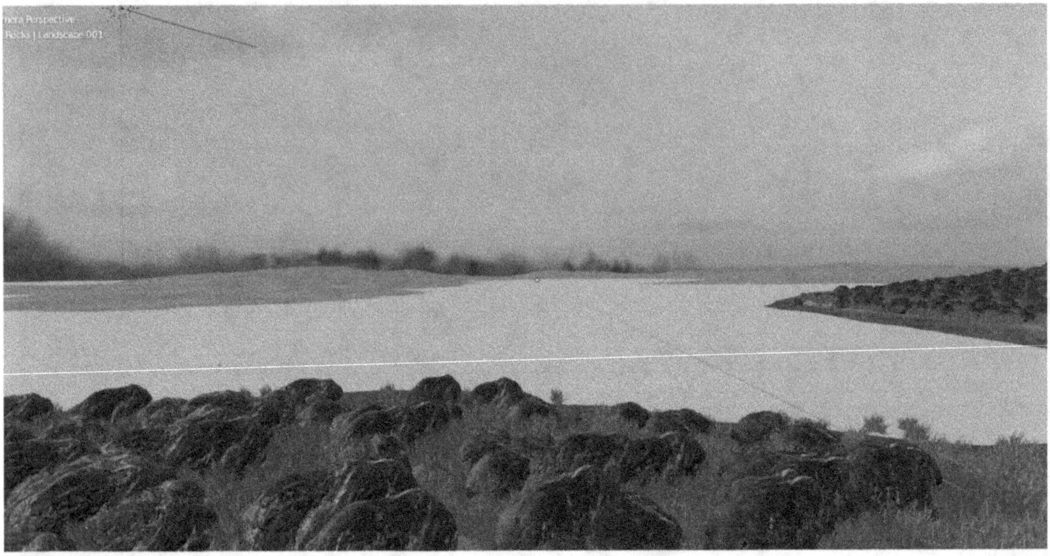

Figure 5.49: Rocks with the density at 5

That's looking pretty good; we have rocks and grass and some really interesting variations that didn't take much time to set up. But you may be asking, why move to Geometry Nodes when we have a perfectly good particle system that we can use just as easily? Well, Geometry Nodes has infinitely more control. It's a steeper learning curve, that's for sure, but it's incredibly powerful. And it can be extremely customizable, with ways to expose values so that you don't even need to look at a Geometry Nodes system if you want to change how many rocks appear in the scene, or their size. Let's add some customizability to our Geometry Nodes system to finish this chapter.

Customizing our Geometry Nodes system

Let's get started:

1. You may have noticed that there was another blank output on the **Group Input** node, but it's gray. This designates an inactive socket that can be activated, just as we added the **Density** vertex group. Let's add the value output for the **Multiply** node on our `Grass` object to **Group Input**. Do this by simply grabbing the **Multiply** | **Value** socket and dragging it over to hook up with the unused socket on **Group Input**. The unused socket should now have changed its name to **Value**:

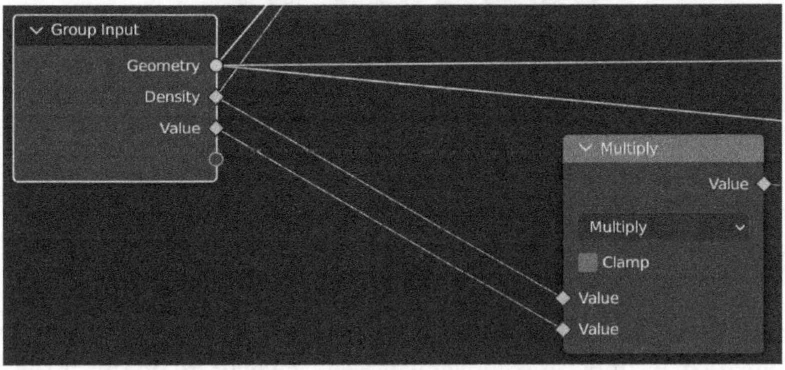

Figure 5.50: Connecting the Density multiplier to Group Input

2. Let's change the name of the socket so we can understand that this is the grass density, not the rock density. Hit *N* on the keyboard, and the Geometry Nodes menu should fly out on the right side of the panel. You should see **Inputs** and **Outputs** listed:

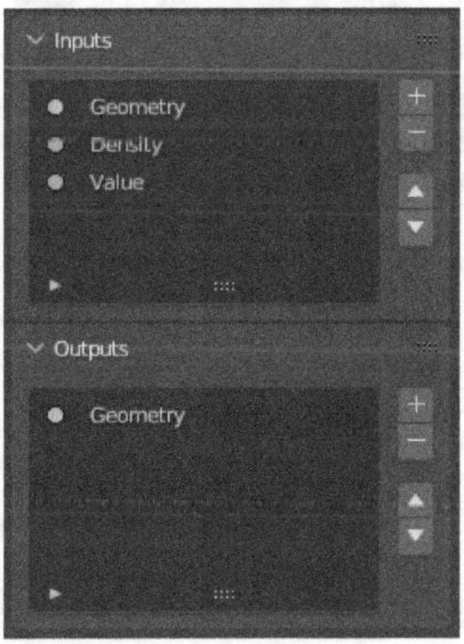

Figure 5.51: Inputs and Outputs in the Group tab of Node options

3. If you click on **Value**, it should open up a dropdown. Inside the **Name** box, you can rename it. I'm going to change mine to `Grass Density`:

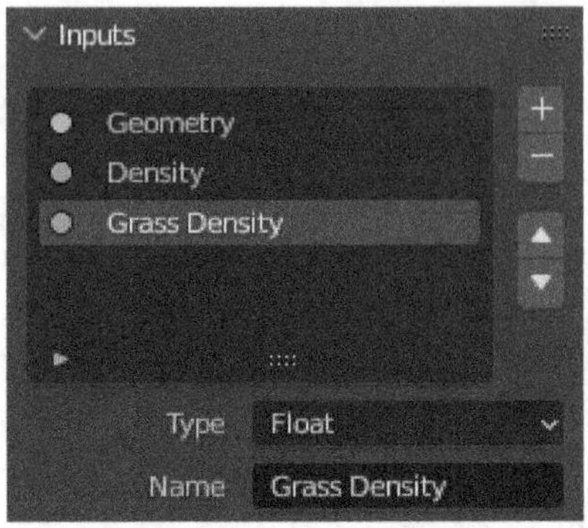

Figure 5.52: Renaming to Grass Density

As you can see, the input is renamed so that I can tell what it is. It's possible to add a great variety of customizable inputs to the **Group Input** node. It allows you to designate what is important to be tweaked and what can be left alone.

4. So, we've added **Grass Density** as an input, but we need to find where we can edit **Grass Density** in a simple and convenient way. The place to do this is the **Modifier** tab! If we click on the **Modifier** tab (), we can see the **Geometry Nodes** system that is being applied to this object, with **Grass Density** labeled and exposed, as with any other value we can change in Blender:

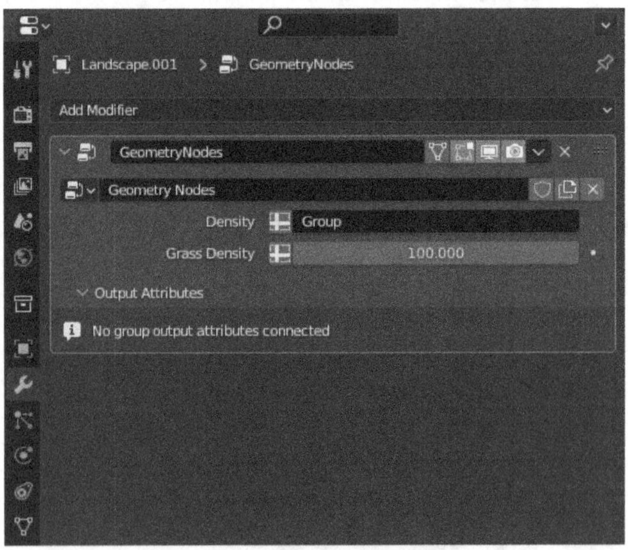

Figure 5.53: The Geometry Nodes modifier with the added Grass Density option

5. We've just created our own custom modifier that anyone can come in and use. Say we're working on a file, and we need to hand it over to a colleague. Well, there's no need to worry that they won't understand our mess of a Geometry Node network. All they need to do is click into the **Geometry Nodes** modifier we made and tweak values to their heart's content. I added a few more inputs to the **Group Input** node that I thought would be useful. Simply follow the same procedure I just outlined to add any value to the **Input** field of the **Geometry Nodes** modifier:

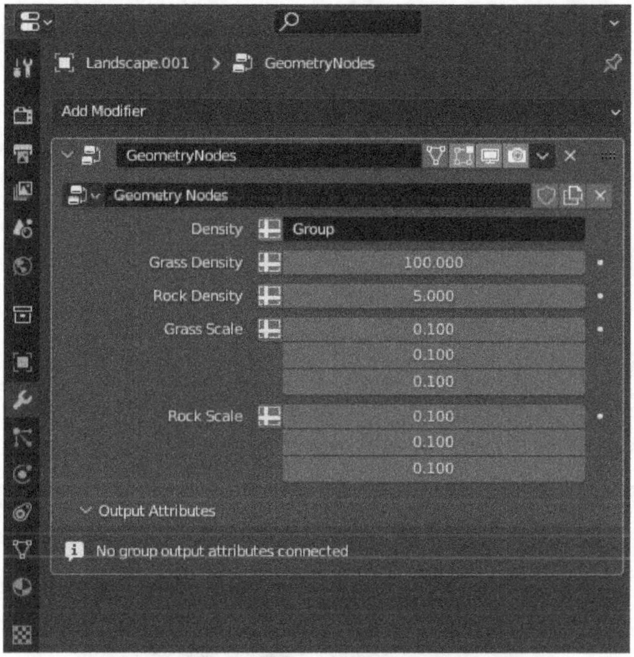

Figure 5.54: The Geometry Node modifier with more options added

6. The last thing we need to do so that we don't accidentally crash our computer when we reuse this node group is edit the **Default** values for each input. This way, when we add this Geometry Nodes group, only a few rocks and grass will be scattered. We can then turn up the values that we want. If we leave the default values at `100` every time we add a new modifier, the computer will try to add hundreds of objects instantly and cause our file to crash or severely lag. So, let's select the first **Density** value and change the default density to `0.000`, which is located with the **Name** and **Type** options in the **Inputs** menu:

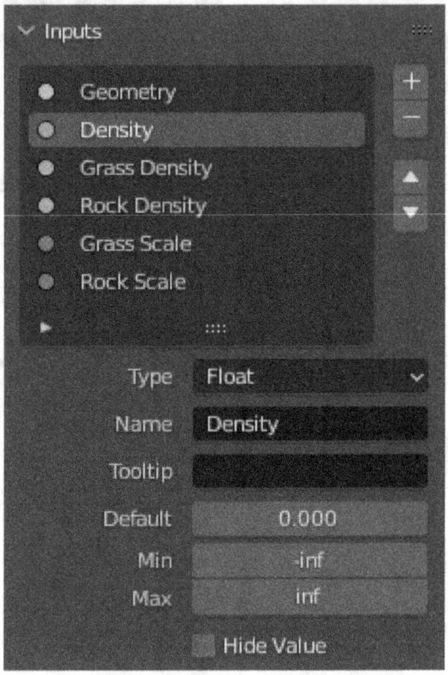

Figure 5.55: Added inputs to the Inputs menu

Do the same for **Grass Density** and **Rock Density**; change them to something small such as `1` or `2`.

The other thing we can do that makes Geometry Nodes amazing is apply it to all our other landscape pieces with ease, all with the ability to change anything we want. Let's add some rocks and grass to **LeftPlane** in our scene:

1. Select **LeftPlane** in the scene.
2. Go to **Weight Paint** mode and paint a **Density** map for the left plane.
3. Go to the **Modifier** tab, select the **Add Modifier** dropdown, and select the **Geometry Nodes** option. This adds a new **Geometry Nodes** modifier, not the one we just worked on. So, we need to link the old node tree to this new modifier.

4. Select the **Browse Node Tree to be linked** button (it looks like two little nodes connected by a line, next to the **Geometry Nodes** name):

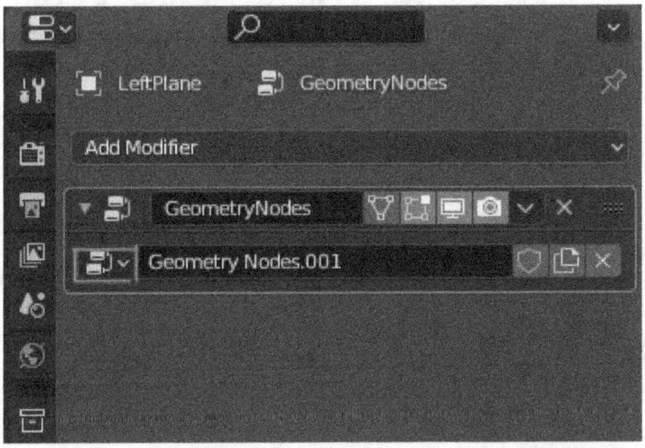

Figure 5.56: Browsing to another Geometry Nodes tree

5. Select the first entry, the original Geometry Node network we just made. Feel free to rename it if it helps you to keep organized:

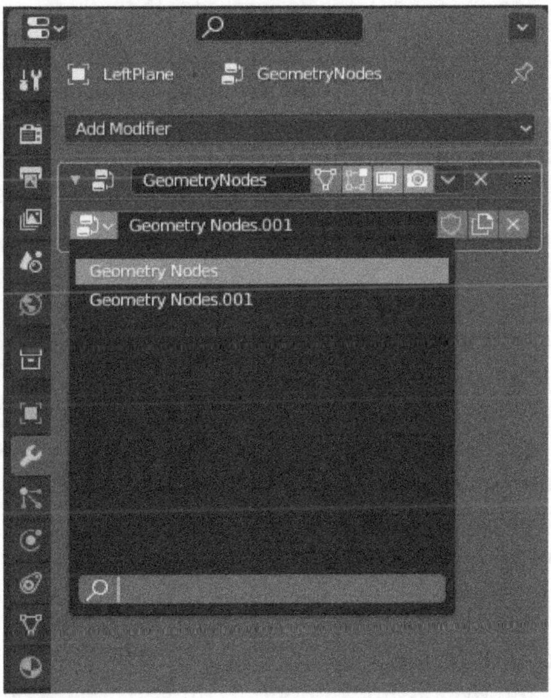

Figure 5.57: Changing the Geometry Nodes tree dropdown

6. We should now see the rocks and grass appearing on the left plane. Change the **Density** map to the one we just painted for this land object using the same method we did for the first landscape object. Try increasing **Grass Density** or **Rock Scale**, and see how it affects the objects scattered on the left plane but not the objects on the plane closest to us:

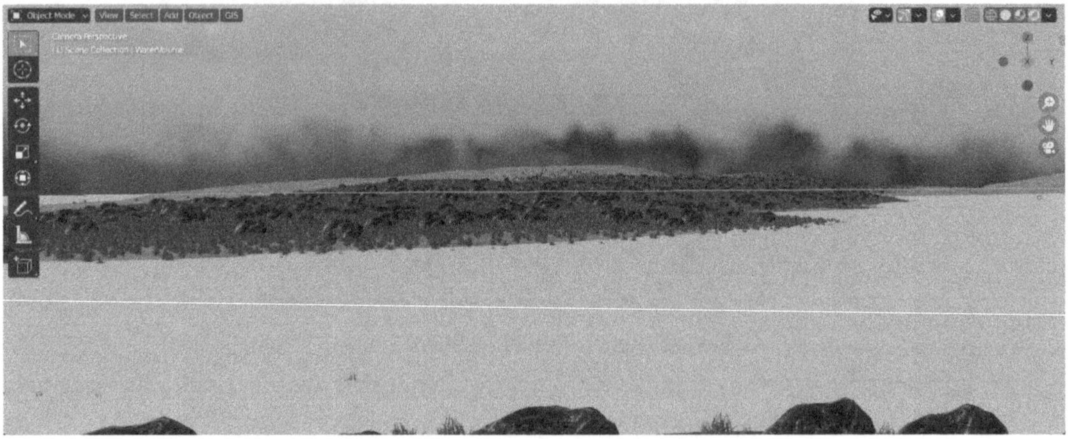

Figure 5.58: The same node tree being applied to the background object

Projecting all these objects is pretty hard on the computer, so try to only work on one plane at a time, disabling the **Geometry Nodes** modifier on planes that you're not working on as you focus on others. This is why the landscape is broken up into pieces – so that we can work on the foreground and background at separate points in time, and not have the whole scene full of plants trying to show in the viewport all at one time. EEVEE is good, but it's not that good!

Summary

I hope you are as excited as I am about this new step in Blender's development program. Geometry Nodes provides an artist with infinite variation, customization, and adaptability. It's also faster in the long run; next time you want to scatter objects on another plane, all you have to do is import the network and tweak it as needed. We've just scratched the surface on what is possible with this amazing tool, and I hope you feel motivated after looking at this simple introduction to the subject to learn more. We just created an amazing node network that scatters grass, rocks, or anything on a landscape; then, we learned how to add random rotation and control the size of the grass and rocks directly inside of the **Geometry Node** network. Then, we customized our network so that we can reuse it over and over again, without needing to create copies or fake users to change the values.

That's all we'll do with Geometry Nodes for this project. In the next chapter, we're going to make a shader for the water and then learn about how to add reflections so that we get an accurate reflection of the sky and the surrounding environment, making our scene look more realistic.

6

Screen Space Reflections – Adding Reflection to the Water

Now that we have some rocks and grass set up in the scene, I want to explore another element that often comes up when creating a realistic environment: water. Water can be very hard to get right, especially in EEVEE. Considering EEVEE only uses approximations of light and reflection, it can be really difficult to create a lake or ocean that really accurately reflects your surroundings. Also, because humans are deeply attuned to nature, it can be really easy to spot a fake environment if something is just not quite right. In this chapter, we're going to set up the water shader and then tune the settings of our render to get perfect results. A new concept that we haven't covered yet that I'll start to introduce in this chapter is the usage of **light probes**. Using light probes is an alternative way to calculate light in EEVEE and should help us in this chapter to create a really nice lake that adds to the natural beauty of the environment we're trying to create.

In this chapter, we will cover the following:

- Screen space reflections
- Reflection plane light probes
- Adding volume and transparency to the water

Technical requirements

Download the starting file of this chapter, `MiniProject 2-Chapter6-Start.blend`, or use the project we worked on in the last chapter to start. I want to give the choice to skip chapters, which is why I provide a starting file for each chapter, but if you worked through *Chapter 5*, *Setting Up an Environment with Geometry Nodes*, you should have a file that is ready to start from, without needing to download it from GitHub. We'll be using procedural methods to add some noise to the water in this chapter, so there are no extra files to download.

The sample files used in this chapter are available here:

`https://github.com/PacktPublishing/Shading-Lighting-and-Rendering-with-Blenders-EEVEE/tree/main/Chapter06`

Screen space reflections

Before we start to create the water shader, it's pertinent to go over what exactly screen space reflection means. Screen space reflection is a method of creating a reflection in a real-time rendering engine. The reflection is calculated using a depth buffer (a way of representing depth in 3D graphics) to calculate reflections based on the screen view we are using. As a result, reflections from a point of view other than the camera in a render might not be accurate. Screen space reflections are much more accurate than using reflection probes and also allow us to use a reflection plane to further inform the direction of the reflection effect. We'll use screen space reflections in this chapter to create a reflection effect on the surface of the water. Let's jump into creating the water shader. I started this chapter by disabling the Geometry Nodes Modifier we created in *Chapter 5*, *Setting Up an Environment with Geometry Nodes*, by clicking the **Monitor** button for each system.

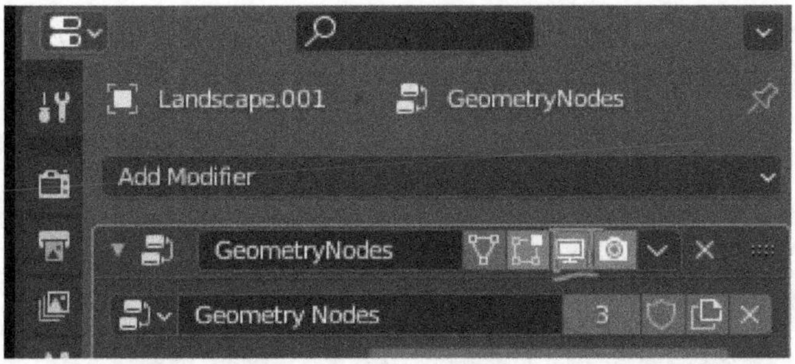

Figure 6.1: Turning off the Geometry Nodes

This hides them from the viewport so that our computer doesn't lag while we're trying to create water. My rule of thumb is to hide anything from the viewport that doesn't affect the part of the scene we're working on. That way, we can create small pieces of a complex scene and then render them all together at the end, reducing the strain on our computer.

The first thing we'll do is add a shader that creates a reflective surface for our WaterVolume object:

1. Select the **WaterVolume** object and add a new material by clicking the **New** button in the Shader panel.

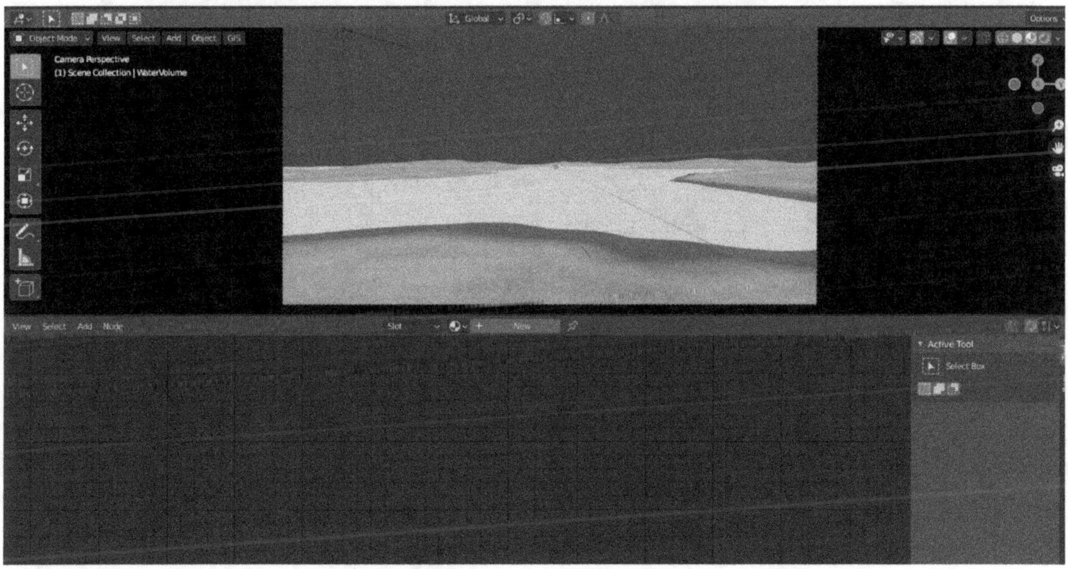

Figure 6.2: Adding a new material

2. The water shader will utilize the default **Principled BSDF** shader, but we need to decrease the **Roughness** value and then change the **Base Color** value to full black.

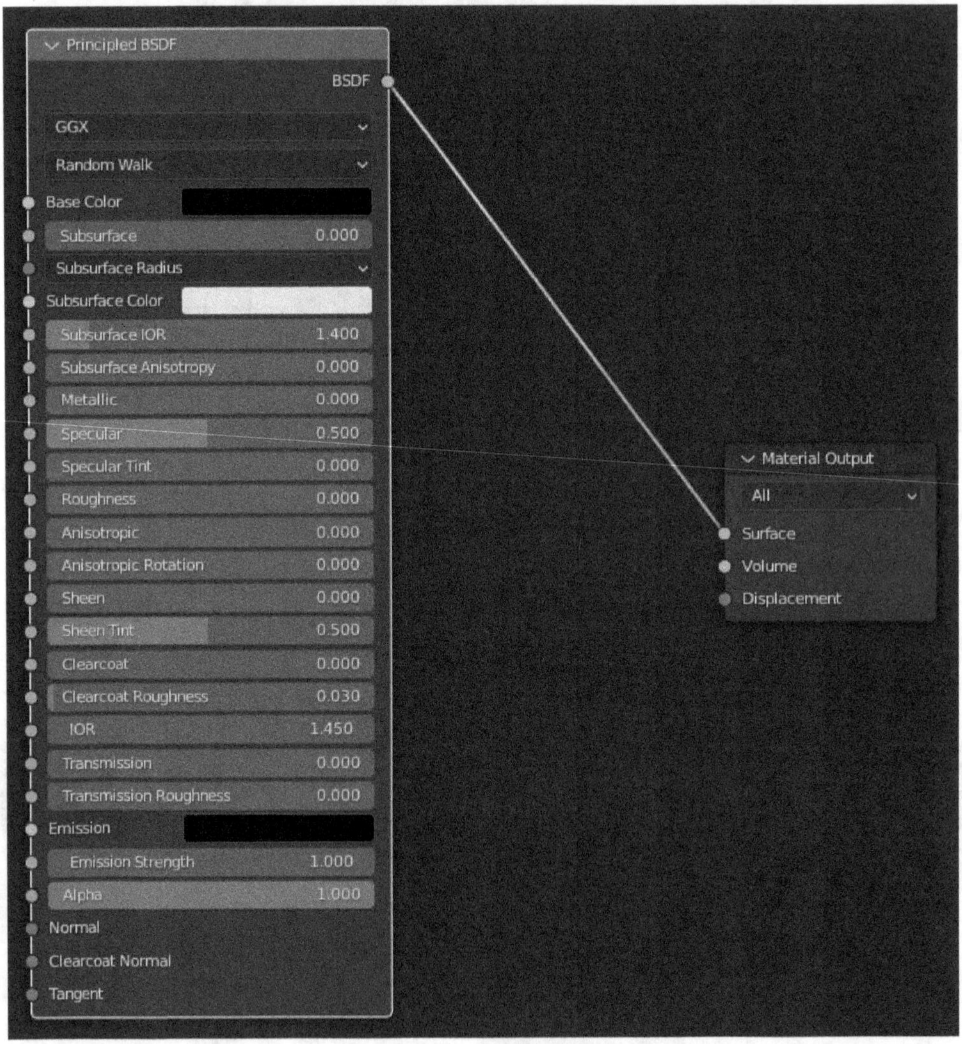

Figure 6.3: Material settings

The water shader will now look like it's reflecting the sky! This is pretty cool, considering all we did was change two aspects of the **Principled** shader.

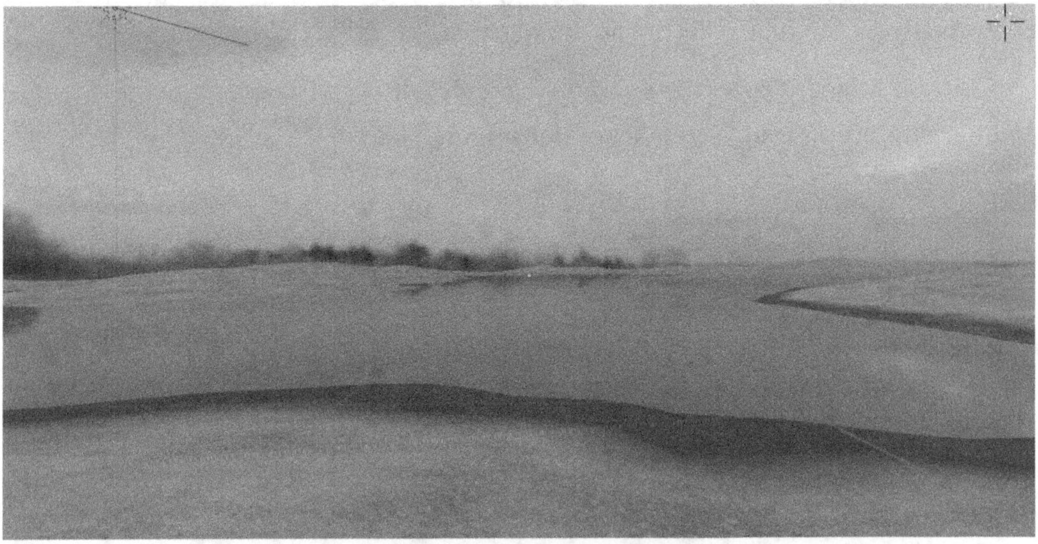

Figure 6.4: Results of the Principled shader

From this image, we could call it a day, consider our water shader done, and go home. But let's test it first, to make sure we have true reflectivity. Create a `Cube` object (or any other object of your choice) and suspend it over the water.

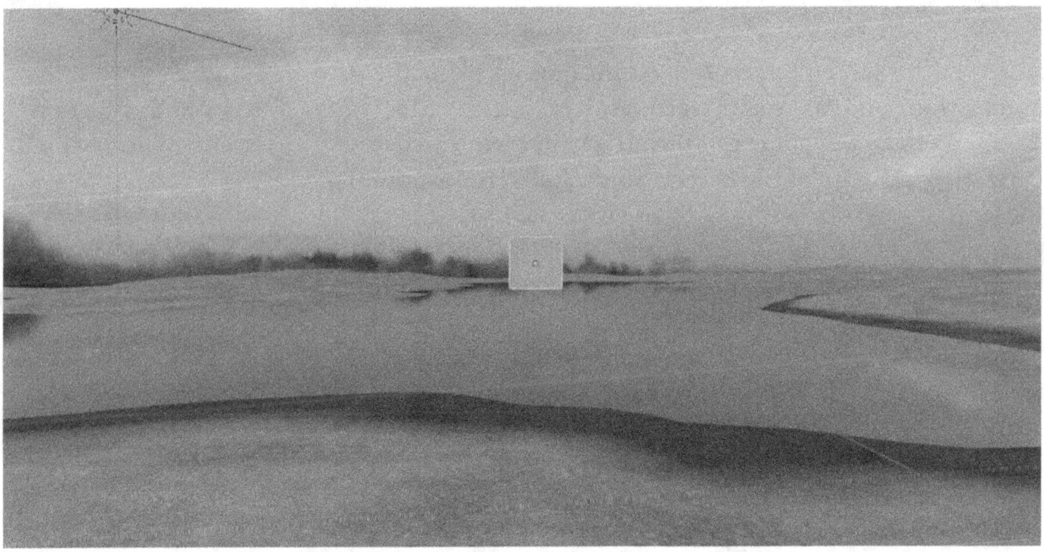

Figure 6.5: No reflections!

There are no reflections! True water would reflect an object, the cube, and we would see the reflection on the water. So, obviously, this water shader isn't working exactly as we want. The way to fix this behavior in EEVEE is to turn on **Screen Space Reflections** so that we actually get the cube reflecting in the water. Let's try that right now:

1. Go to the **Render Properties** panel on the right side of the screen.
2. Check the box next to **Screen Space Reflections**.

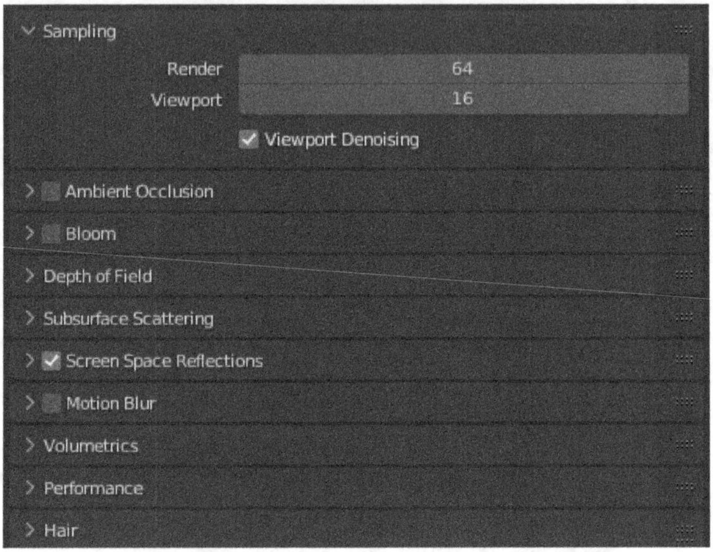

Figure 6.6: Screen Space Reflections

3. Open the **Screen Space Reflections** options using the twirl-down arrow next to the checkbox and make sure **Refraction** is checked. Most of the defaults in this section are pretty good, but experimenting with them can definitely be useful to understand the full capacity of the **Screen Space Reflections** option.

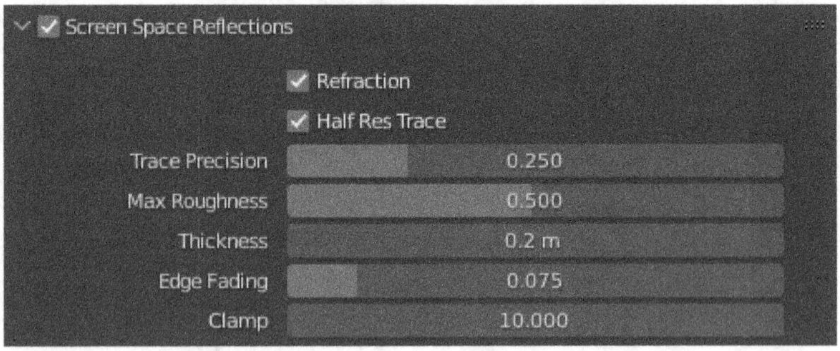

Figure 6.7: Screen space properties

Now, if we look at the viewport, the cube is being reflected in the water!

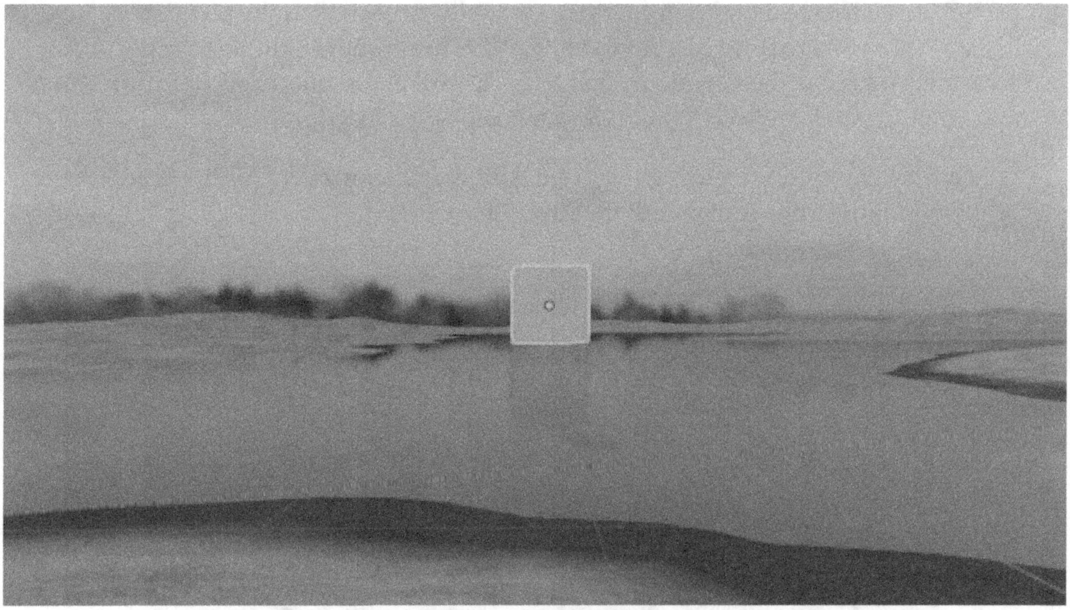

Figure 6.8: Reflection!

Screen Space Reflections can enhance any reflective material, from windows to water, so make sure you use it when needed. I think it gives great results, but as usual, we could always make them better. Let's try using a reflection light probe in the next section and refine this reflection even further!

Light probes - reflection planes

Light probes, as we touched on briefly earlier, are auxiliary objects in the scene (they won't be visible in the render) that we can use to tell EEVEE to compute lighting or reflectivity more accurately than just the default. In this section, we'll use a reflection plane probe to add more accuracy to the reflectivity of the water. Let's get started:

1. Add a reflection probe by using the usual **Add** menu shortcut of *Shift* + *A* and then selecting **Light Probe**, then the **Reflection Plane** option.

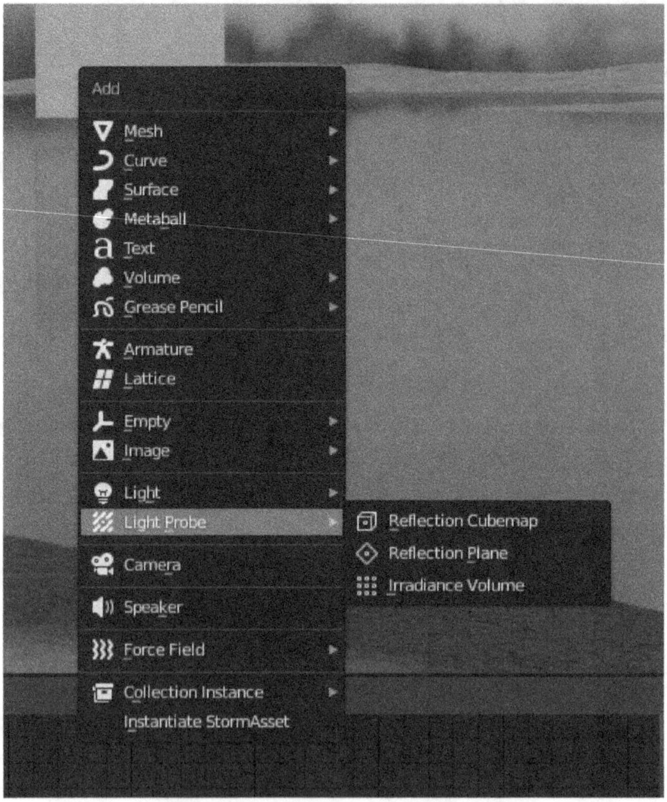

Figure 6.9: Adding the light probe

2. The reflection plane should look like a flat box with an arrow pointing in the direction we want reflections to be calculated. Make sure that the arrow is pointed up (as should be the default) and the box is slightly on top of our lake.

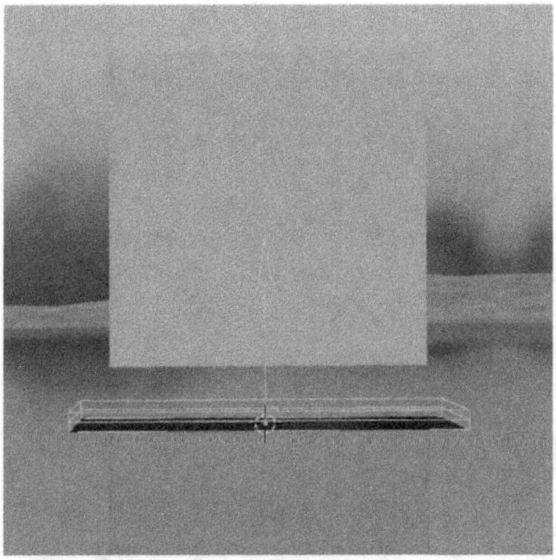

Figure 6.10: The light probe in the scene

3. Next, we'll scale up the reflection plane by using the *S* shortcut. Scale it so it covers most of the water area we can see in the camera view. If you aren't getting something similar to what I get, try moving your reflection plane up or down a little bit. Or you can experiment with moving the cube up and down as I have in *Figure 6.11*. Reflection planes only have a limited sphere of influence, so the cube might be outside of the plane's influence. The best way to understand this is to experiment and see how the reflection reacts as you change things.

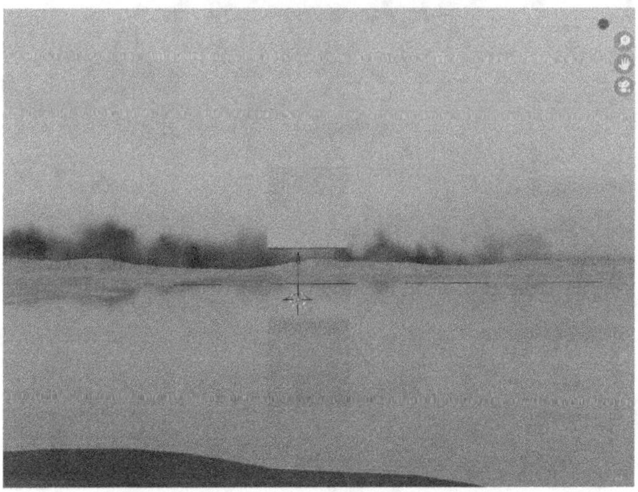

Figure 6.11: Scaling up the reflection plane

4. We can now specify the range of the reflectivity. As you can see from the previous screenshot, the reflection plane doesn't really seem to have changed much. But now, we can tweak our reflection by going to the properties sidebar and selecting the **Object Data Properties** option for **Light Probe**.

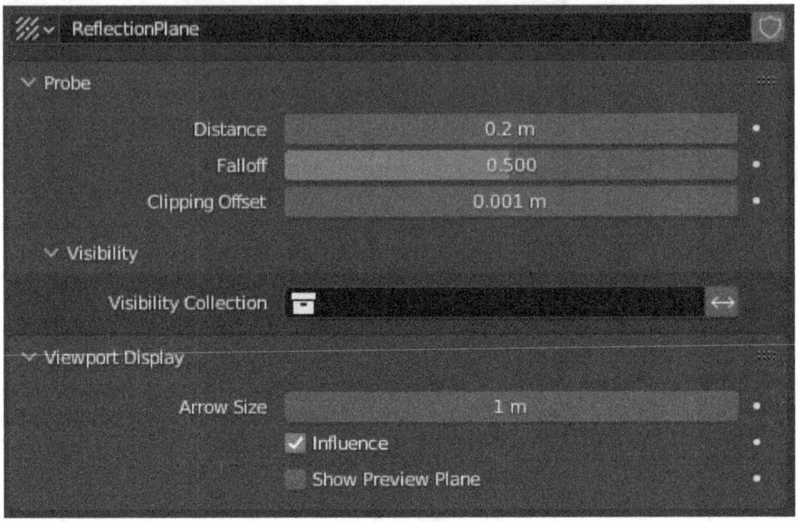

Figure 6.12: Reflection plane properties

5. By changing the **Distance** value to something such as `8 m`, you can see that the area the reflection plane is affecting changes to encompass the cube object that I'm using to test the reflectivity of the lake.

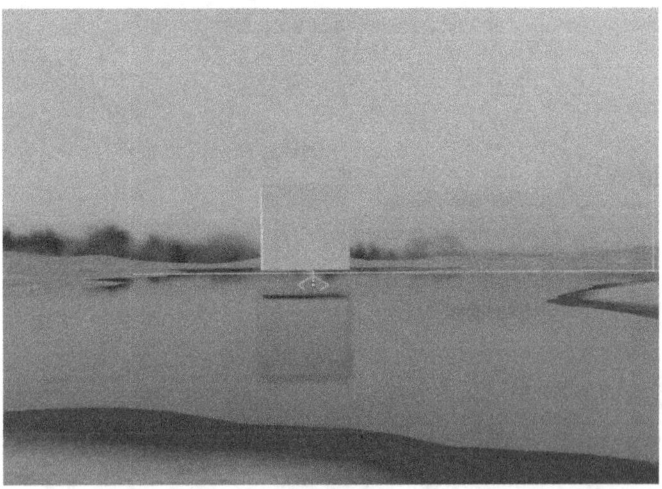

Figure 6.13: Changing the Distance property

Try comparing the result with the reflection plane enabled and the previous reflection, before you added the light probe, as shown in *Figure 6.8*. The reflection plane enables us to get much more accuracy on reflections and even allows us to tweak the reflection with the **Light Probe** properties, so we have much more control over our scene. We'll explore light probes more in future chapters. Now, we're going to move back to the water shader and create a more advanced version that takes into account the real physical properties of water to make our water really over the top.

Advanced water – volume and transparency

What we have so far for the water is pretty good, but let's not let ourselves settle for "pretty good"! Let's make it completely amazing. We'll start by changing some of the properties of our water shader, so let's select the **WaterVolume** object and get back to the Material Editor:

1. Let's change the **Base Color** value of the water to something that fits our scene a little more. I went with a dark turquoise blue, but experiment and see what fits for you. I also changed the **IOR** value to `1.33`, as this is the correct **Index of Refraction** (**IOR**) for water.

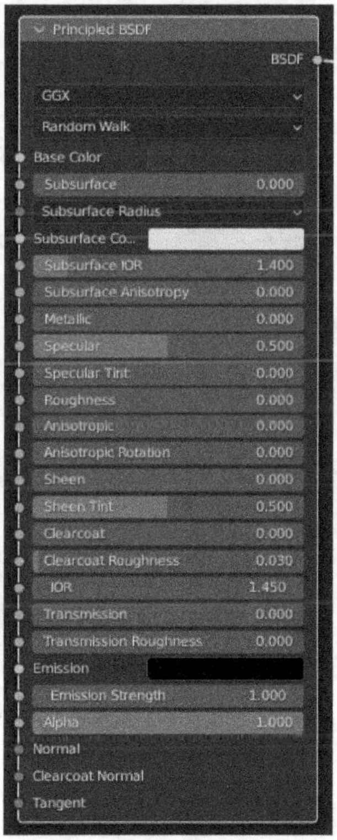

Figure 6.14: Changing the color and IOR

2. Next, we'll add some transparency to the water material. We'll do this using a concept called Fresnel. Fresnel is the equation for how reflective water is at a certain angle. If you've ever looked at a lake from the shore, you'll notice the water close to you is quite transparent because you're looking at it almost from above, whereas the water further away is quite reflective, because you're viewing it at a more oblique angle. We can mimic this property using a **Fresnel** node, so let's add a **Fresnel** node, change the value to `0.5`, and connect it to the **Alpha** input on the **Principled** shader.

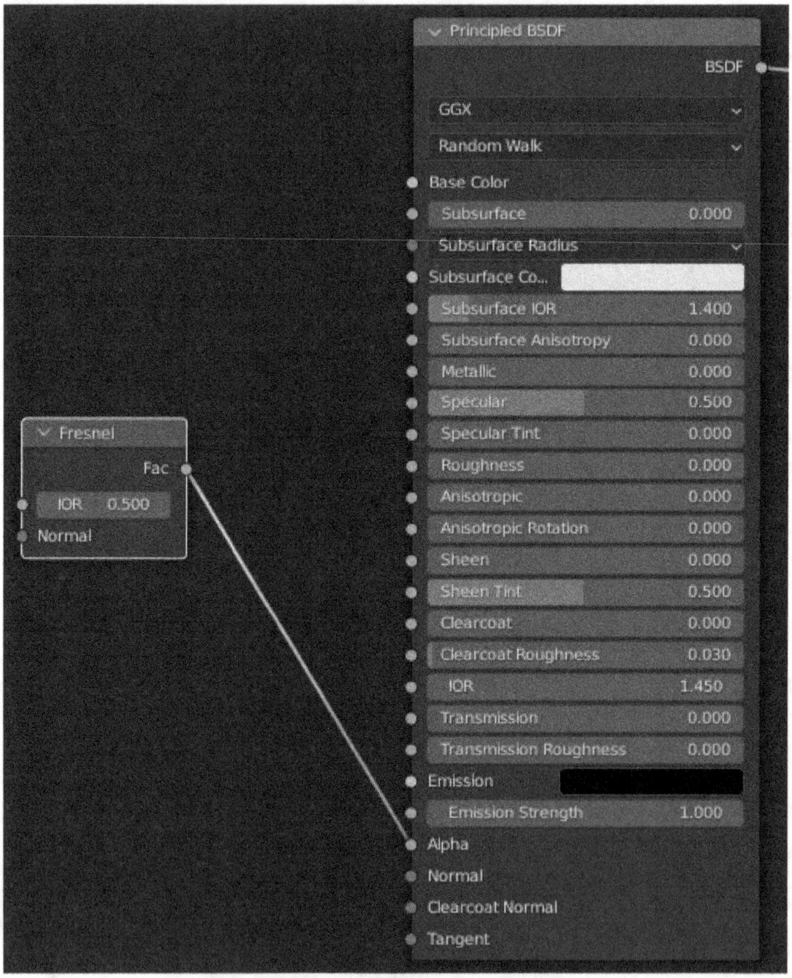

Figure 6.15: Adding transparency

3. You'll notice this seems to do nothing. We need to tell EEVEE what kind of transparency we want. If you scroll down in the **Material Properties** on the right side of the screen, you'll see the settings where we can change **Blend Mode** to **Alpha Blend**. The `0.5` value for the Fresnel is not a value I chose based on any real-world value, so experiment with different values and see how it affects the translucency.

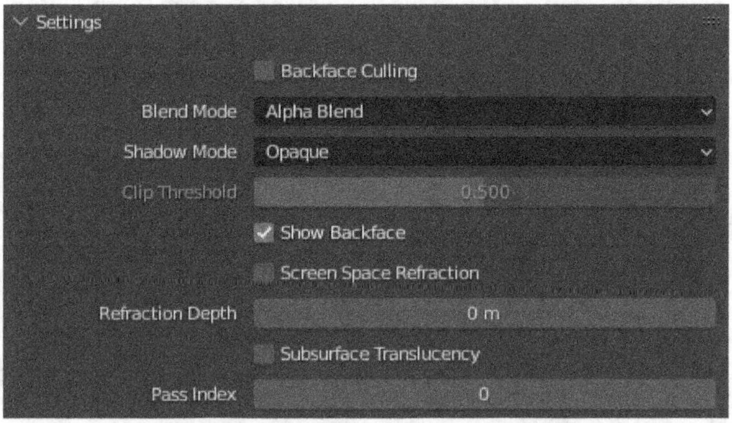

Figure 6.16: Settings for material transparency

We have some transparency in the shallows of the water now, and it changes to less transparency the further away from the camera we go.

Figure 6.17: Transparent water on the shore

4. But we can see that our water looks very flat. Let's give it a slight bump, so it looks a little more like water that's being displaced as fish or wind move it around. Add a **Noise Texture** node and change the **Scale** value to `200`. Then, add a **ColorRamp** and a **Bump** node. Connect **Noise Texture** to the **ColorRamp** and **ColorRamp** to **Bump**, and then **Bump** to the **Normal** input of the **Principled** shader. This takes the **Noise Texture** node, changes it to a black and white image (with **ColorRamp**), and then applies that as a displacement to the surface of the lake. This creates variation to the surface of our lake with minimal computational power. Change the strength of **Bump** to `0.09`.

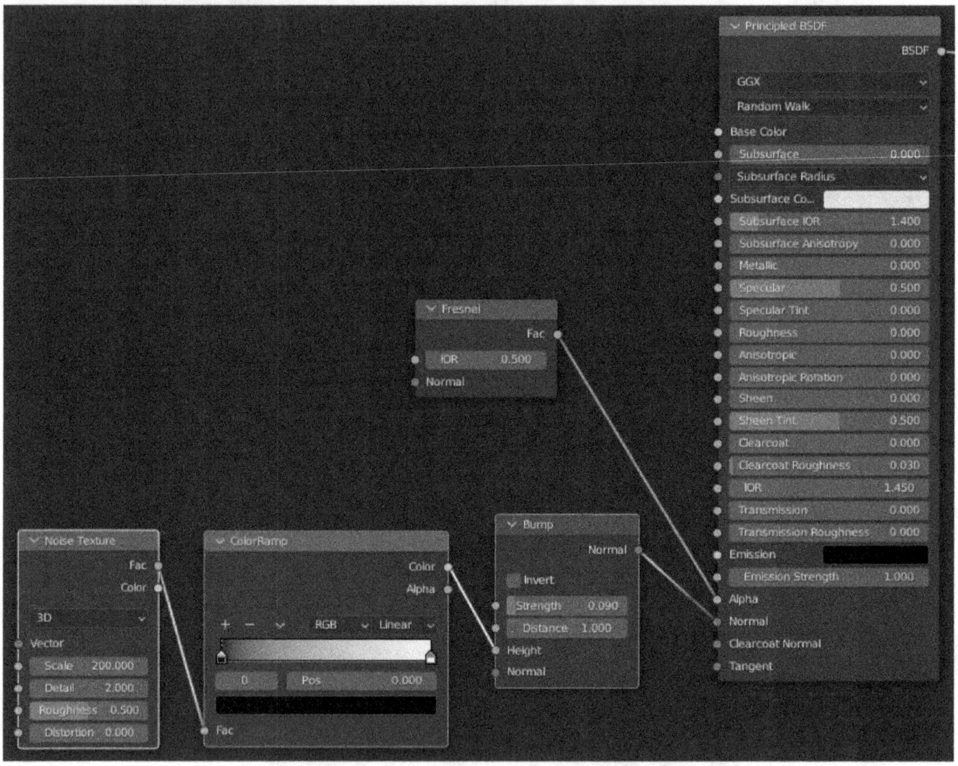

Figure 6.18: Noise bump for water

The result I have at this point is looking pretty good. The only thing I think we can improve upon is giving the water some depth.

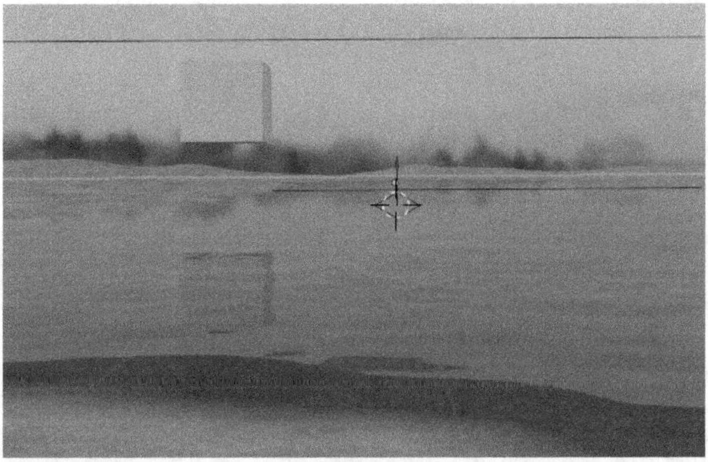

Figure 6.19: Noise bump adding waves to the water

5. The surface of the water is done at this point. Let's add some volume to the water shader. Add a **Principled Volume** shader and **Volume Absorption** to the water shader. Connect them with **Mix Shader** and connect **Mix Shader** to the **Volume** socket on **Material Output**.

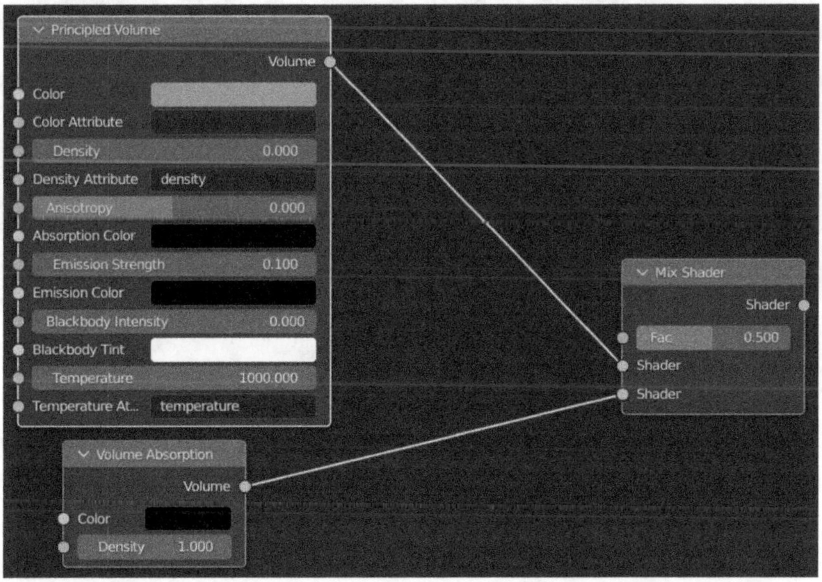

Figure 6.20: Principled Volume and Volume Absorption shaders

6. Now, let's tweak the values. Change the **Density** value on **Principled Volume** to something lower, such as `0.4`. Change the **Density** volume on **Volume Absorption** to something lower too, such as `0.3` or `0.4`. We'll also add some **Emission** to **Principled Volume**, so change **Emission Strength** to `0.1`. Finally, we'll change **Mix Shader Fac** to `0.7`.
7. We have all the numerical values dialed in, but we also don't want our water color to be just gray or white. Change **Color** and **Emission Color** on **Principled Volume** to a greenish-blue and **Color** on **Volume Absorption** to a light blue.

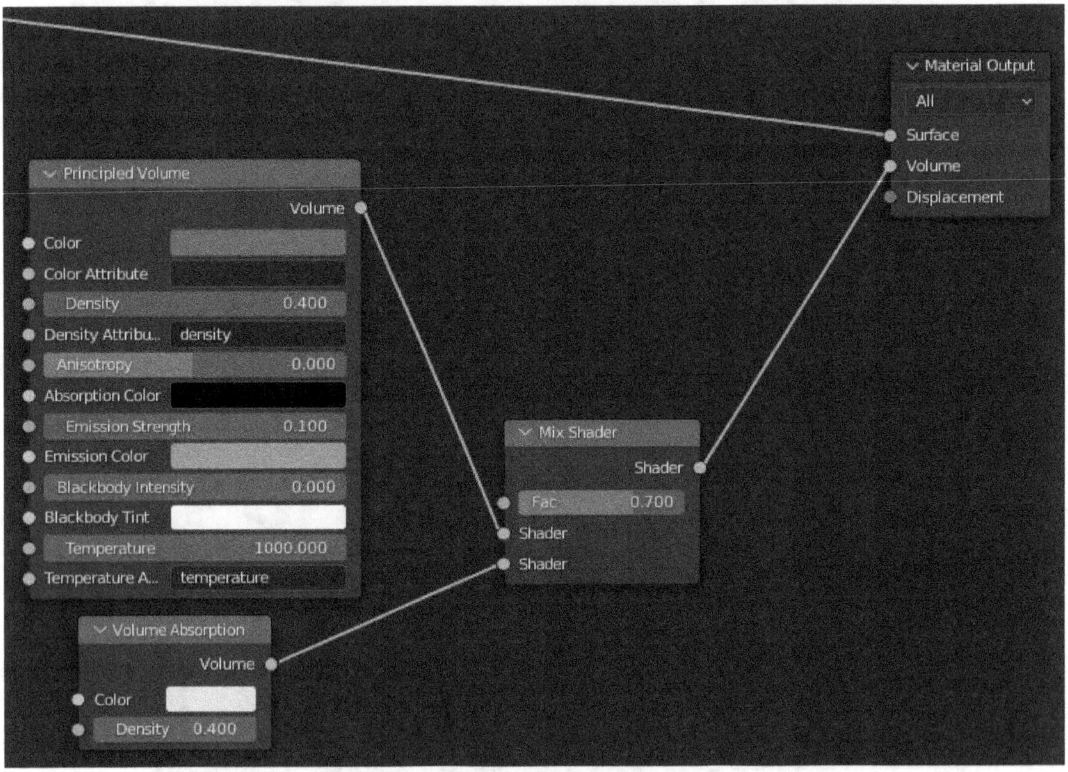

Figure 6.21: Completed water shader

You may not notice a huge change by adding volume to the water. The change is most pronounced when you want to submerge something in the water, as you'll get the correct refraction and coloration of the object as if it really were underwater.

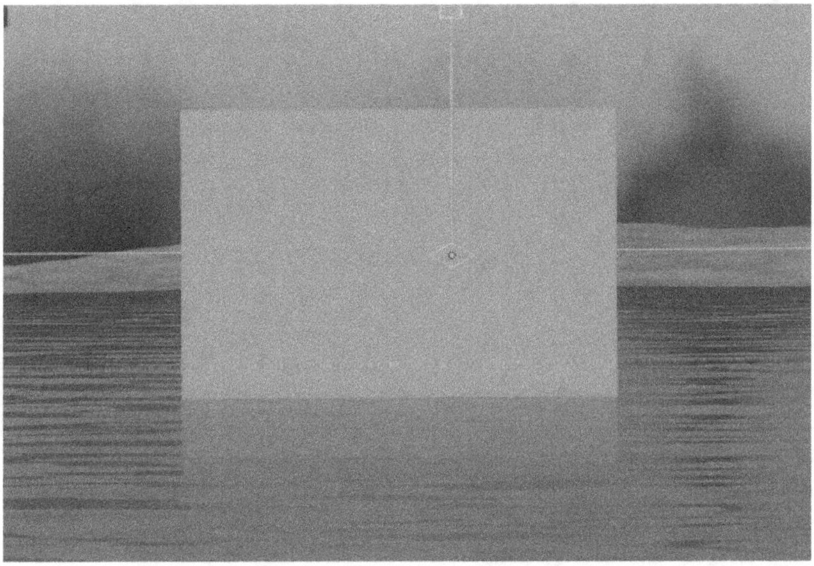

Figure 6.22: Object in the water

That finishes our water shader! In this section, we took what was just a flat water plane and turned it into a fully dimensional lake that interacts with our environment properly. This way, we can be sure the water in our scene is realistic, but also that it doesn't add too much to our render times.

Summary

At this point, I think our water shader looks amazing. Creating the more advanced version and being able to control our reflectivity through a light probe also makes this system of water shading more flexible. There's the ability to create any type of water, from ocean to swamp, depending on the scene. From this chapter, you should understand some of the principles regarding water shading in EEVEE and be able to apply them to other projects where you need water. Considering how much water there is in the world, you might find yourself using the water shader we made here a lot more than you'd think. We also dipped our toes into light probes and talked about how to optimize reflections for EEVEE.

In the next chapter, we're going to take a look at making our scene even more refined, by adding depth of field and baking some of the lighting so that EEVEE doesn't have to calculate it at runtime.

7
Faking Camera Effects for Better Renders

Now that we've created the basic building blocks for a nature scene, we can start to get a little deeper into making a *good* nature scene. What we have so far has all the elements we might want to have in a landscape: grass, rocks, water, sky. But it doesn't really look all that interesting or exciting. If we showed this to a director right now, they'd laugh and tell us to do better. So, let's take our scene up a notch. As a developing artist, it can be difficult to really hone in on this hard-to-pinpoint idea of *what will make the scene better*. With time and experience, you'll have more of an idea of what exactly you want to do to make a scene better. But for now, let's look back at the original premise of our idea. We wanted to make a realistic environment. So, let's spend this chapter and the next one looking at adding the smaller details that will make this environment look realistic. In this chapter, we'll talk about using EEVEE to fake camera effects so that our final product looks that much better. Faking camera effects is a by-product of using EEVEE. Since EEVEE only approximates our lighting using the rasterization technique, we usually need to modify our workflow for a real-time rendering engine to more explicitly specify the result we want in EEVEE. In this chapter, we'll look at **Atmospheric Lighting**, **Ambient Occlusion**, and **Depth of Field** in more detail and then cover the concept of baking indirect lighting for our scene. All of these elements can be very important to creating a more believable image. We'll start by adding some elements to the scene that will allow us to see these effects a little better and then move on to fine-tuning and talking about the reason each works.

In this chapter, we will cover the following:

- Atmospheric lighting
- Bloom
- Ambient occlusion
- Depth of field

Technical requirements

Download the `Chapter7_Start.blend` file from the `Chapter 7` repository, or if you want to build off your own file from *Chapter 6, Screen Space Reflections – Adding Reflection to the Water*, download the supplementary file (`supplements.blend`) for this chapter and append the sun object inside of it to your `Chapter 6` file. We will use the sun object to demonstrate the concept of atmospheric lighting and bloom, as well as to build our composition with depth of field. For reference, you can see how I've set up the scene to start us off in the following figure, in case you want to add the objects yourself.

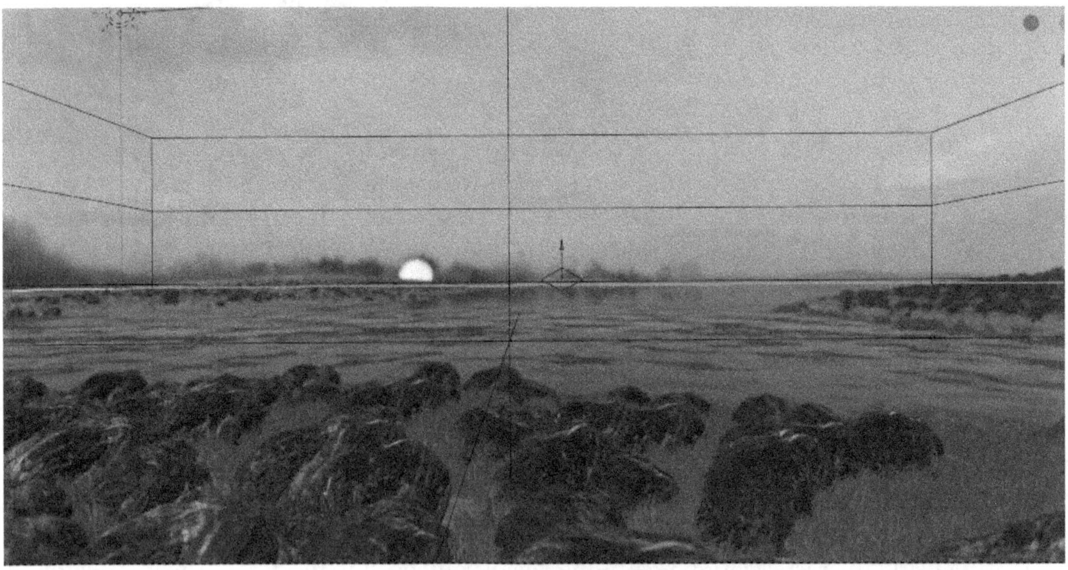

Figure 7.1: Starting the setup

Reference *Chapter 5, Setting Up an Environment with Geometry Nodes*, to go over how to add objects to our Asset Library from another `.blend` file if you feel lost, or simply start from my `Chapter 7_Start.blend` file and you will have all the pieces already put together for you.

These files can be found at `https://github.com/PacktPublishing/Shading-Lighting-and-Rendering-with-Blenders-EEVEE/tree/main/Chapter07`.

> **Side Note**
>
> If modeling and scene creation on a more granular level is something you'd like to learn more about, you'll probably be a little disappointed as I tend to gloss over it in this book. Modeling is outside the scope of this book, but I would recommend looking into YouTuber *tutor4u*, who has many simple modeling tutorials that could help bootstrap your understanding of how to model. Other paid resources I would recommend are *Udemy* or *CG Boost*. The latter has an amazingly comprehensive tutorial on sculpting that I would recommend to any budding character artist. Hopefully, the fact that I'm providing some of these models will highlight the concept that time is money, if you have to model something yourself, think of the time it will take you. We're creating concept art in EEVEE to be fast, and it can sometimes ruin the idea of "fast" if you have to model every single thing yourself. Don't be adverse to spending some money to save you some time, if you think it'll be worth it in the end.

Atmospheric lighting

Atmospheric lighting is using lighting from the atmosphere (the sky) and using it to light our scene. We did something like this with the first mini-project, as using an HDRI isn't viable in EEVEE for anything other than background. But if you think about it, we didn't really get any real atmosphere in our last project. Atmosphere means that the air in the scene is not 100% transluscent. It means we can see the light in the air, just as we can in real life. Elements of the air catch light differently, reflect elements, or provide haziness. That is what we are creating with atmospheric lighting. Unfortunately, EEVEE makes this a little more difficult to implement than Cycles, but to add real atmosphere to our piece, let's create an atmosphere to make something a little less sterile and a little more lifelike. In doing this, we'll also add some bounced lighting to the scene that will facilitate some of the faked lighting effects in the scene.

Let's start by adding a volume cube to serve as our:

1. Add a cube using the usual *Shift* + *A* method:

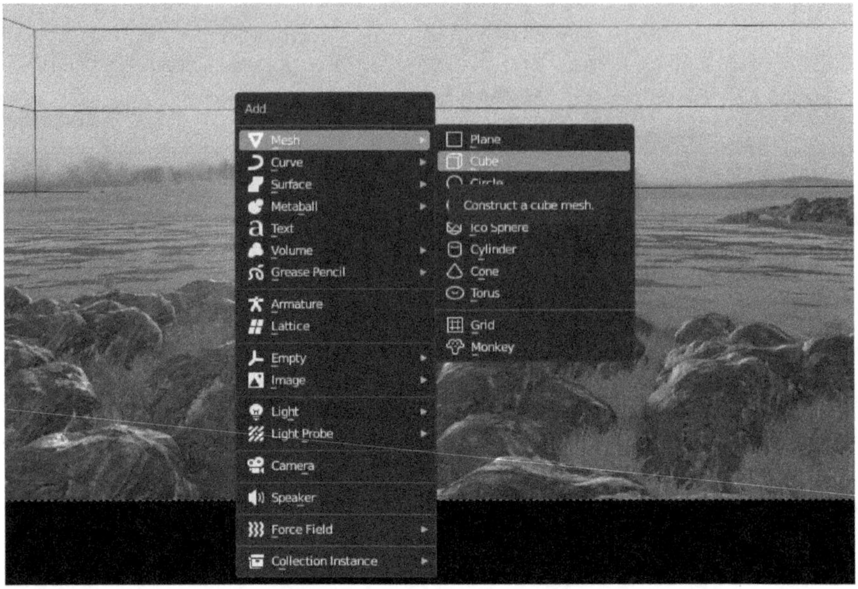

Figure 7.2: The Add Cube menu

2. Use the *S* Key to scale the cube so it covers the area of land that we can see in the camera viewport, until about the end of the reflection cube map. After we add the **Principled Volume** shader, we can tweak the size of this cube, because we want it to be big enough to cover the area the camera sees, but not so big that it will increase our rendering time.

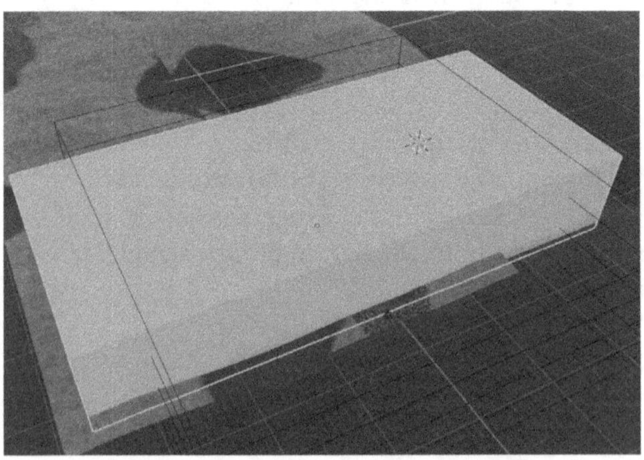

Figure 7.3: Area of the cube from above

3. Add a shader to the cube, delete the **Principled** shader, and add a **Principled Volume** shader.
4. Connect the **Principled Volume** shader to the **Volume** input of the **Material Output**.

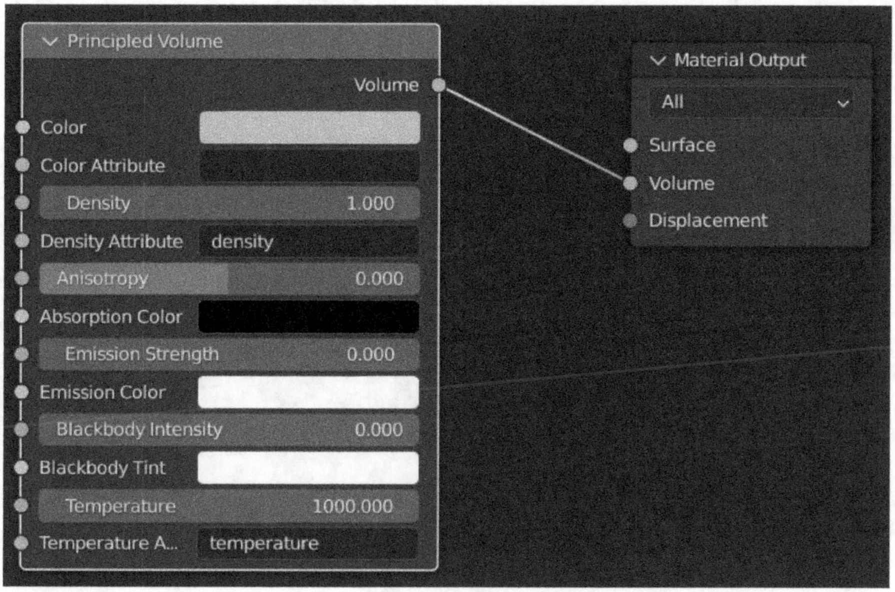

Figure 7.4: Principled Volume Shader

5. You'll notice this is the same general workflow as when we made our clouds. But, instead of using the clouds in our composition, we'll add this volumetric shader to refract light through the air, exactly like our atmosphere does. Notice that the color of our sunlight is the color of the mist in our viewport now.

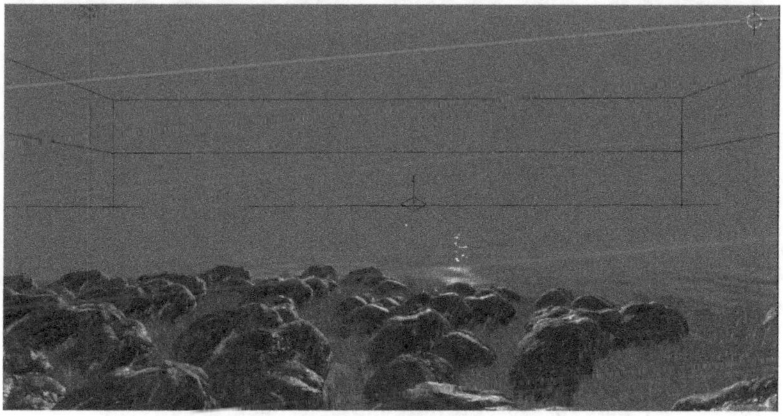

Figure 7.5: The Volume Shader with 1.0 density

6. Obviously, the mist is too thick at the moment. We can't see any of the elements further away from the camera! Let's add a **Density** mask for the **Principled Volume** shader. Add a **Noise Texture** node and a **Color Ramp**. Connect the **Noise Texture** node **Fac** output to the **ColorRamp** node input. Then connect the **ColorRamp** node output to the **Density** input on the **Principled Volume** shader. We won't change any other values but **Color** and **Density** at this point, but it can be useful to experiment and see how each value can affect the scene.

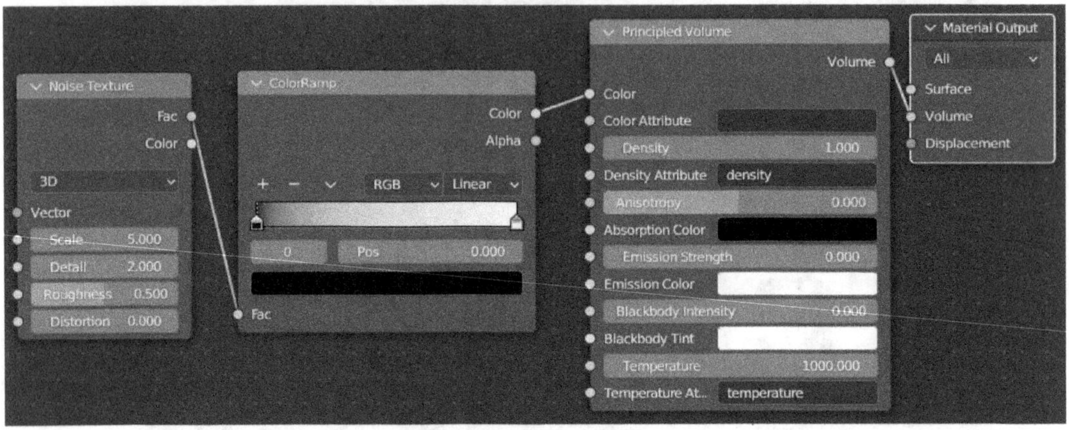

Figure 7.6: Adding the noise and ColorRamp

7. Use the **ColorRamp** sliders to change the contrast of **Noise Texture**. I usually change the white end of the ramp to gray (I used hex `424242` here), which lessens the overall density of the **Principled Volume** shader, but try a different combination of the slider positions and colors.

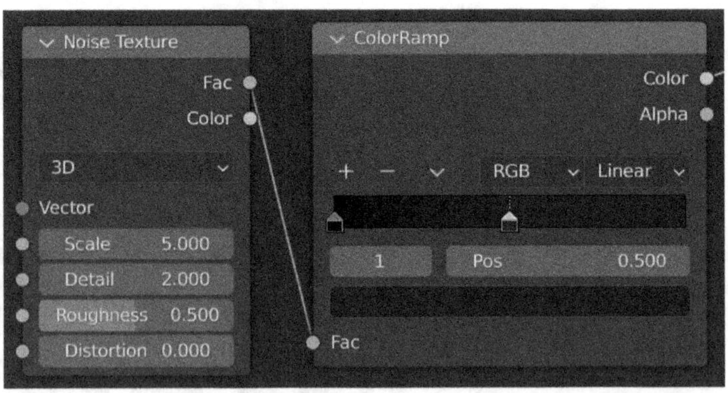

Figure 7.7: Noise Texture and ColorRamp edits

8. As you can see in *Figure 7.7*, I also increased the **Scale** for the **Noise Texture** node so that we get more variation in the mist.
9. You should see now that we have something that adds to the overall feel of the scene. It's subtle but you can see that the air is tangible and also allows us to be a little less focused on the objects that are far away from the camera, now you can't see them as clearly.

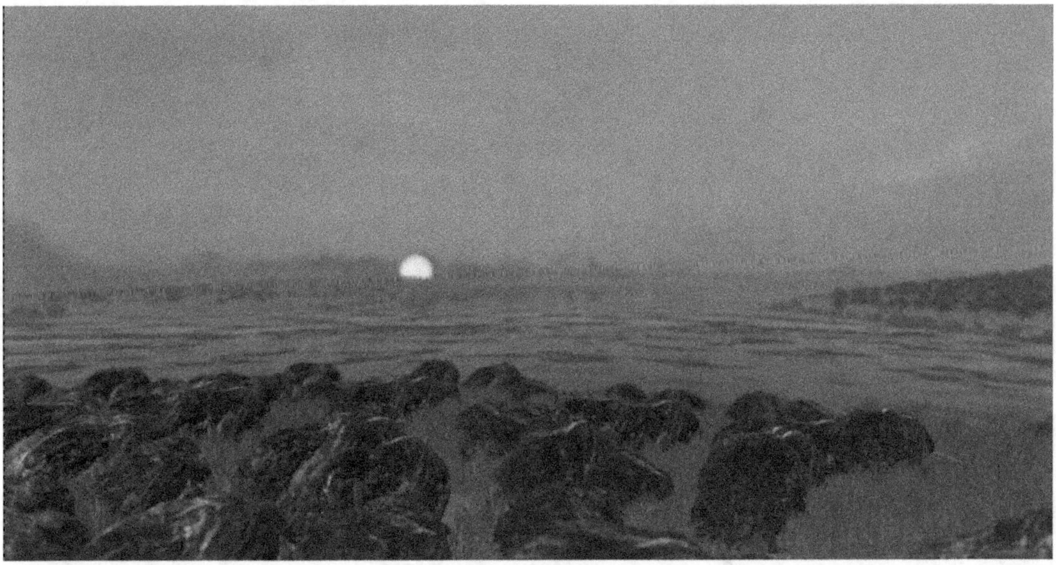

Figure 7.8: The mist in the scene

Let's take this up a notch. Since the sun is so low in the sky, it should reflect off the water, due to the angle of the light. We'll edit the sunlight we have in the scene so that when we turn on the **Bloom** option, the sun will look more natural:

1. Select **Sun Light** (the light, not the object we added to the scene at the start of this chapter!) and then rotate it until it's almost entirely horizontal and points towards the camera.

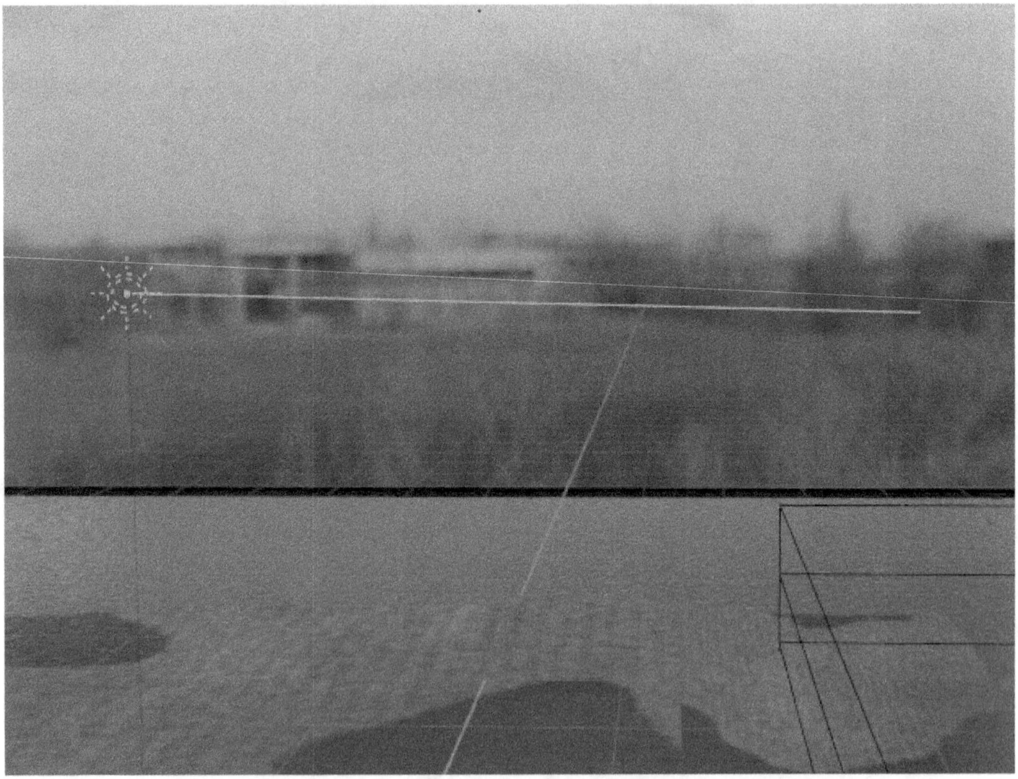

Figure 7.9: Changing the angle of the sun

2. You should be able to rotate (using the *R* shortcut) and line it up as necessary, but in case you have trouble, here are the values I used for my sun:

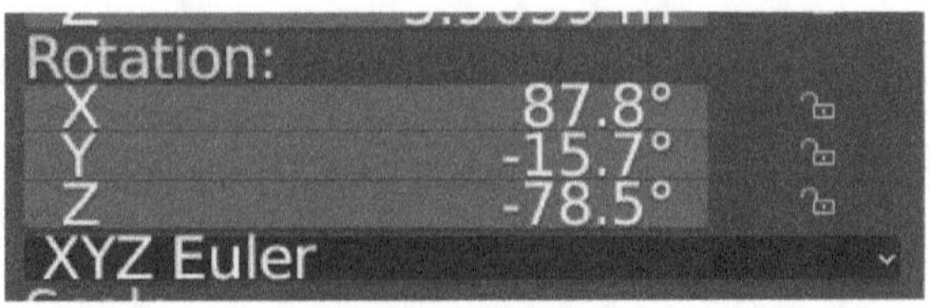

Figure 7.10: The sun values in the Item panel

3. While **Sun Light** is still selected, let's go to the Light Data Panel (the tab that looks like a little light bulb). Change the light to a color that is closer to the sun we added. You can use the color picker to select the color from the scene or choose your own from the color wheel by clicking on the wheel to select the color you want. Alternatively, you could type in the hex code I show in *Figure 7.11* to get the exact same color I did.

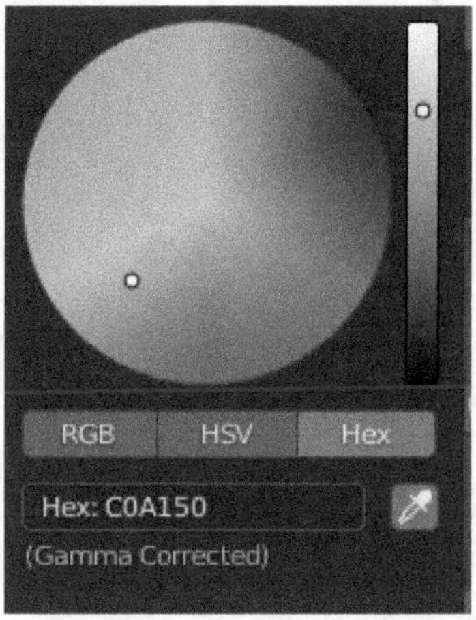

Figure 7.11: The light color picker and wheel

4. Let's also turn **Strength** up for the light. I changed mine to `5`, to really get the highlights from the water.

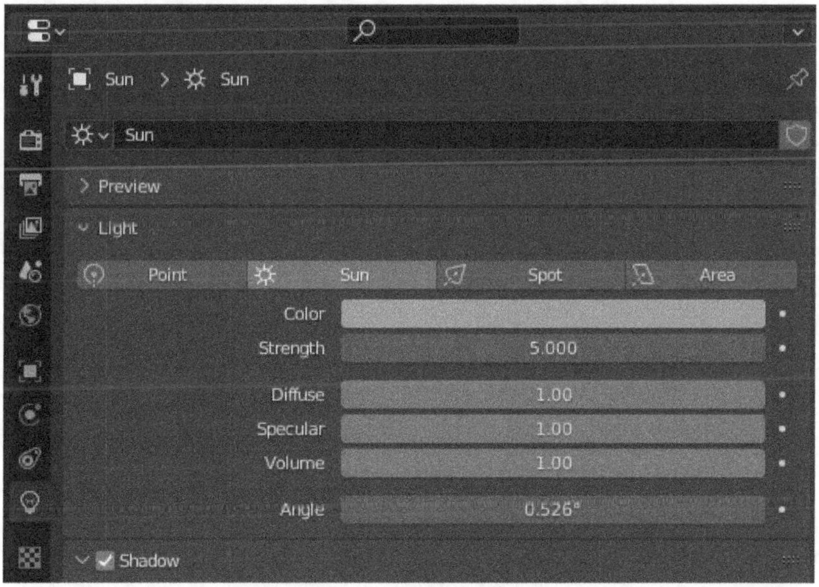

Figure 7.12: The Light Data Panel

After changing our light and tweaking the **Volume** Shader, the viewport should look a little more dramatic, with the light of the sun glancing off the water.

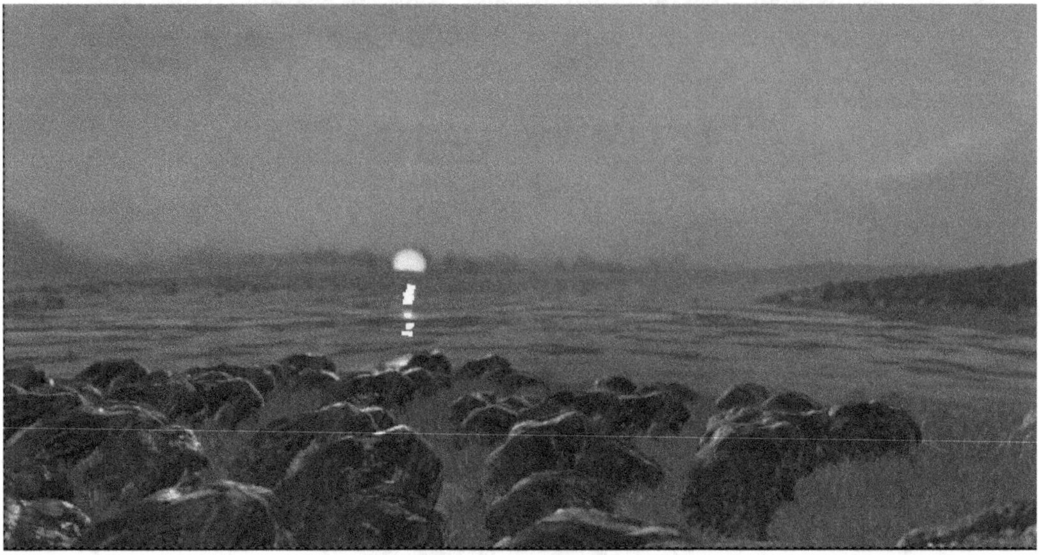

Figure 7.13: The scene so far

In this section, we've effectively used a volume cube to create a fake atmosphere for our fake sun to reflect light through, diffusing the areas far away in the scene and mimicking the real-world effects of the atmosphere. In computer graphics, you have to fake it 'til you make it, and I think we're off to a great start.

In the next section, let's transition to adding **Bloom** to the scene to give our sun a realistic glow that will really make it pop.

Bloom

There's definitely still something missing. If you remember in our last mini-project, we used **Bloom** just to change the general light coloring. Now we have actual rays of light visible in our scene, we can start to use **Bloom** more effectively. Let's check the **Bloom** option in the **Render** panel and see how it changes the light we've cultivated in the scene.

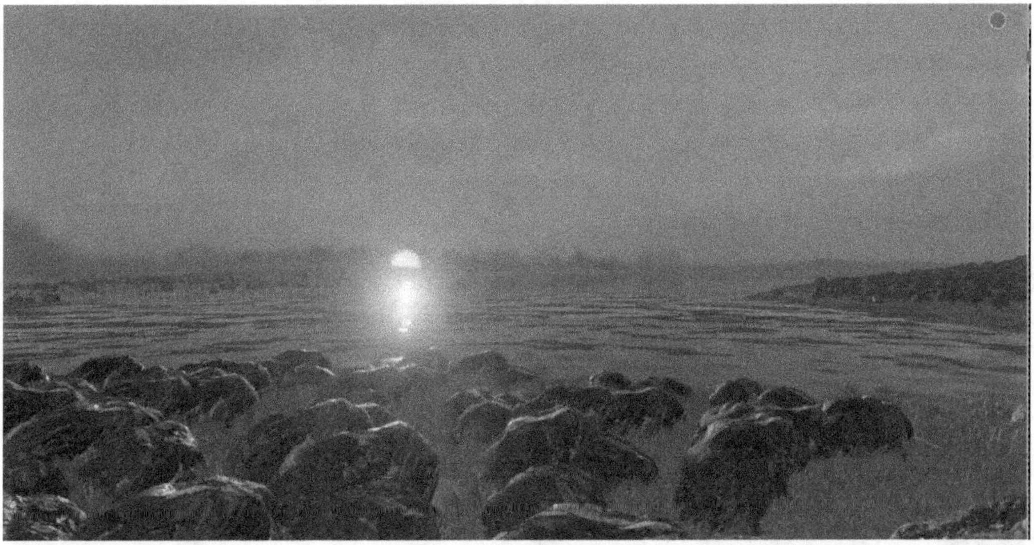

Figure 7.14: Adding Bloom

Bloom effectively mimics how a real camera lens works and fakes light refraction off the lens of our fake camera. It is a **post-processing effect** though (which means it is applied after the light is rasterized/calculated). Two major components of the **Bloom** settings are the following:

- **Threshold**: Setting this at a specific number tells EEVEE that any pixels above the threshold brightness should have a **Bloom** effect, and any below will not have the **Bloom** effect applied to them. So higher numbers mean less bloom, lower means more bloom.
- **Intensity**: This is exactly what it sounds like, how intense should the effect applied be. Higher numbers mean more bloom and lower numbers mean less here.

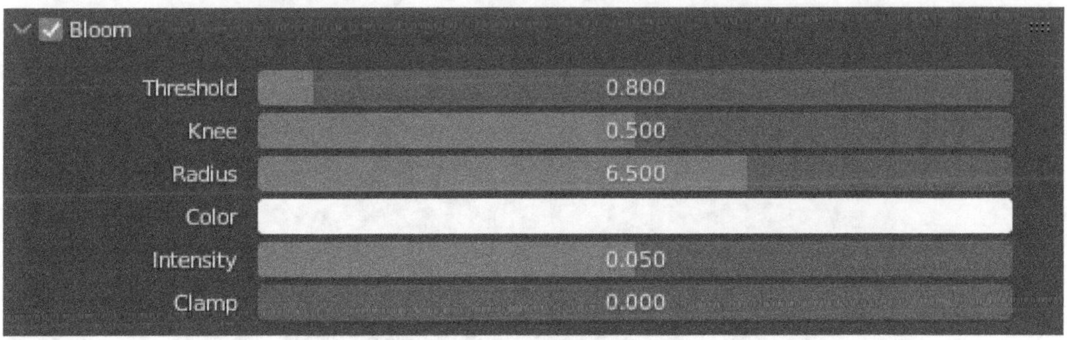

Figure 7.15: The Bloom properties

Try changing some of the values in the **Bloom** section to see how it affects the Bloom. In this short section, we covered some of the more technical aspects of **Bloom** and what values are the most important to pay attention to. In the next section, we'll add ambient occlusion to the scene.

Ambient occlusion

In this section, we'll investigate ambient occlusion further, even though we already talked about it briefly in *Chapter 4*, *Non-Physical Rendering*. We'll activate ambient occlusion (often initialized as **AO**) and then talk about some important values to change. Let's get started:

1. Go to the **Render Properties** and check the box next to **Ambient Occlusion**.

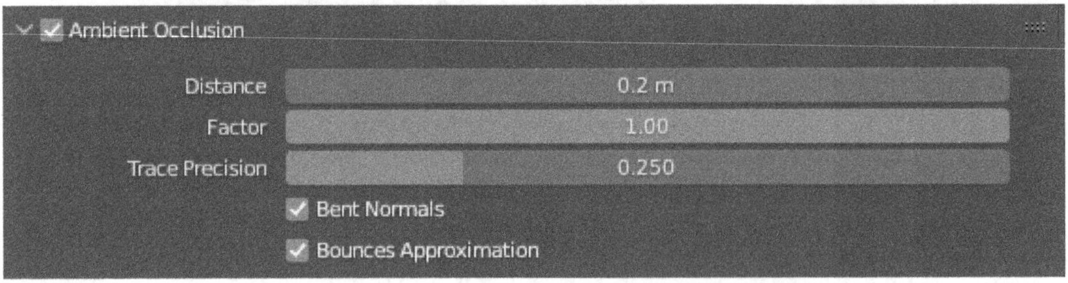

Figure 7.16: Ambient Occlusion preferences

2. You should see immediately that the rocks close to the camera become darker where they occlude with other rocks. Ambient occlusion is basically shadowing that we take for granted in real work but can be very computationally heavy in a rendering engine. In EEVEE, we approximate it so that we can see it in real time.

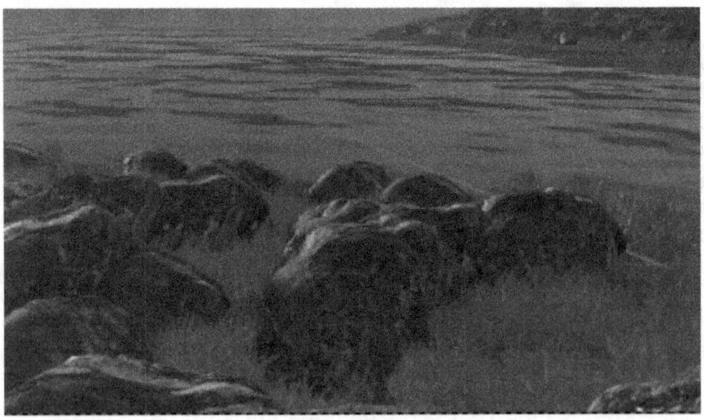

Figure 7.17: Ambient occlusion taking effect on the rocks

Refer to *Figure 7.16* to see the properties available to tweak for **Ambient Occlusion** in the **Render Properties** panel. The most important values in the **Ambient Occlusion** section are the following:

- **Distance**: This value is how far the effect should take effect. Higher values mean larger areas of ambient occlusion. I would caution you not to go overboard with this effect, as it can get very surreal very quickly. If in doubt, look for reference pictures of the type of scene you are creating and try to dial into what proves out in reality.
- **Factor**: How strongly the ambient occlusion should be shown onscreen. A higher number here would make darker ambient occlusion.
- **Bent Normals**: This can sometimes be used to increase the realism of the occlusion, as it calculates what direction should be less occluded. It can increase render times, but only marginally.

In this section, we briefly covered ambient occlusion and its necessity in creating a more realistic scene. Next, we'll talk about one of my favorites, depth of field!

Depth of field

Depth of field is something you might already understand implicitly, even if you don't recognize the term. It's available to use in Cycles, so you might have already used it in Blender before. **Depth of field** is a photography term that describes how close the sharpest object in the frame will appear. So some part of the frame will be in focus (sharp) and the rest of the frame will be out of focus (blurry). We can use this effect to highlight the parts of the frame that we want viewers to be looking at. It's also an effect that happens with taking a picture in real life, so if we use it in 3D well, it can add to the overall realism of the shot. The more we can mimic what happens with a real camera with our 3D camera, the more real the shot should look. Let's add some depth of field to the shot, keeping the rocks in the foreground in focus and the rest of the frame out of focus:

1. Head to **Render Properties** (I know, again) and scroll down to the **Depth of Field** section. If you twirl down the section, you'll see that **Depth of Field** doesn't have a box to check to tell EEVEE if you want it active in the scene. We need to do that in the **Camera** options.

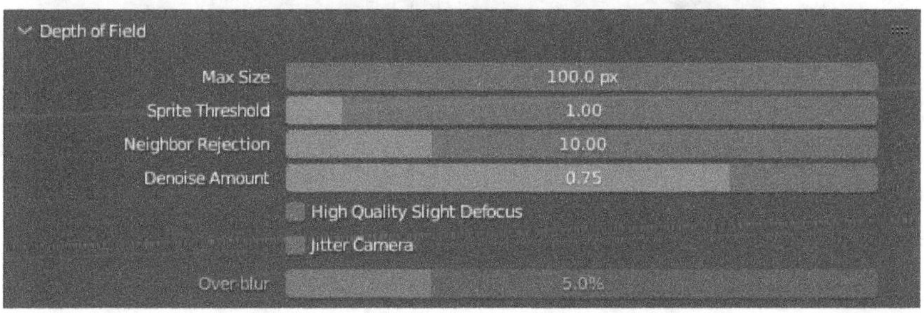

Figure 7.18: The Depth of Field options

2. Select the Camera object and then navigate to **Camera Properties** (the icon looks like an old-time camera).
3. Ah! There's the box we can check to activate **Depth of Field**. Check it and see what happens.

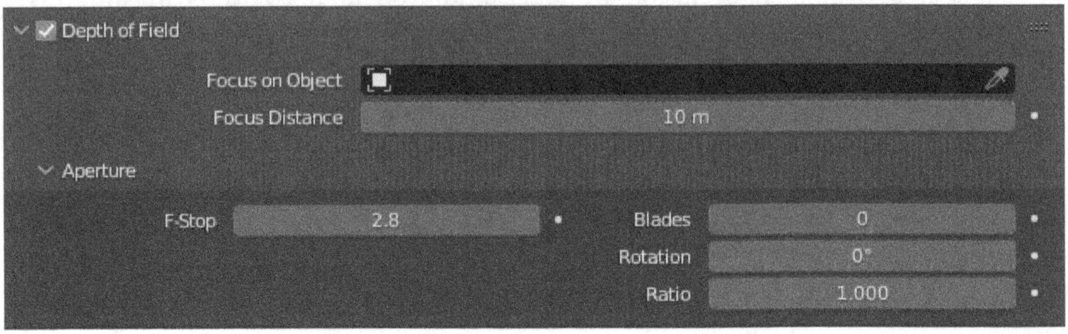

Figure 7.19: The Depth of Field camera options

4. If nothing happened...then yes, you did it right. We now need to specify the distance of the focus. You can do this through **Focus Distance** with a number, but it's a lot easier to visualize focus distance when we use the **Focus on Object** option.
5. Create a new **Empty** object in your scene using *Shift* + *A* | **Empty** | **Plain Axes**. An empty object is one that will not show up in the final render but can be used to hold coordinates, scale, or rotational values. Let's put our **Empty** object right up close to the camera using the *G* shortcut to move the object.

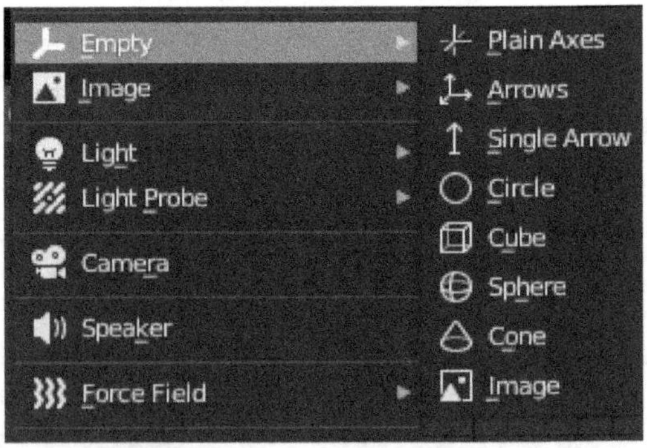

Figure 7.20: The Empty object menu

6. Now click back into the Camera object. Select the eyedropper next to **Focus on Object** and select the **Empty** object we just created.

Figure 7.21: The eyedropper tool next to Focus on Object

Once we've added the **Empty** object, it should appear in the **Focus on Object** field.

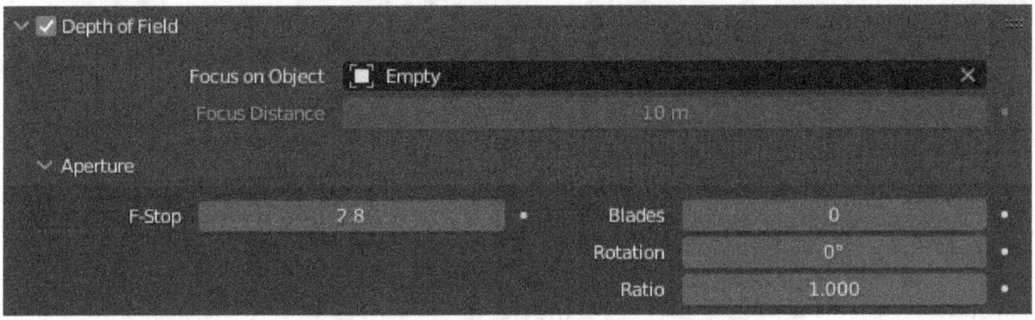

Figure 7.22: Adding Empty as our focus object

7. The **Empty** object now controls the distance of our focus object.
8. The next thing we need to change is the **F-Stop** value, which you should see in the **Depth of Field** options. A smaller value will increase the severity of the blur in the background. In real cameras, the lowest F-stop you'd reasonably use is `1.4`, so try not to go any lower than that, for the sake of keeping our camera as real as possible.

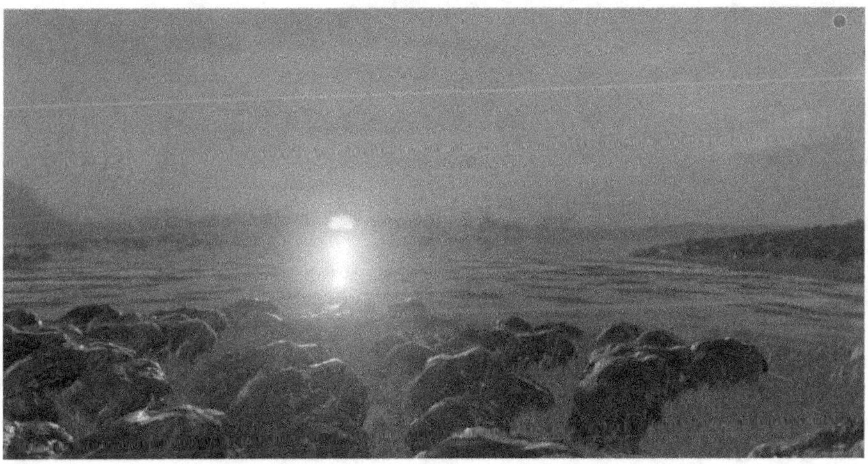

Figure 7.23: After applying depth of field

Now that we've set up our camera with the right **Depth of Field** settings, let's go back to **Render Properties** to look at the settings there.

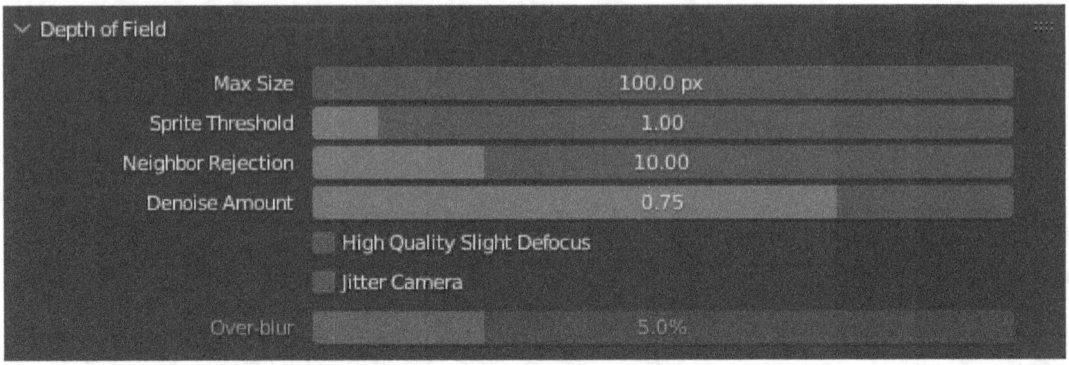

Figure 7.24: Depth of Field Render settings

Depth of Field is an interesting aspect of **Render Properties**, as it mostly controls the second pass of the **Depth of Field** filter. The first pass is the blur aspect, where the background or foreground (depending on the depth of field) is blurred. The second pass is what is controlled with this **Depth of Field** panel here in the **Render Properties** panel. This pass simply improves the highlights of the scene. **Sprite Threshold** and **Neighbor Rejection** are two aspects that can control how much of the highlight is affected. If you set **Max Size** to `0`, you can disable the second pass, and only see the effect of the first pass of the **Depth of Field** filter.

There are several important aspects of the **Depth of Field** settings. It is helpful to know about them, even if you never plan on changing them, so that you understand the inner workings of the **Depth of Field** mechanism and can plan your renders accordingly:

- **Max Size**: Maximum size of the pixel to process in the second pass.
- **Sprite Threshold**: Similar to the **Threshold** setting for **Bloom**, where it controls the cutoff for the pixel brightness to be processed.
- **Neighbor Rejection**: Controls how much of the scene is processed in that second pass.
- **High Quality Slight Defocus**: This is a really interesting effect to add. It makes areas that are slightly defocused higher quality (as the name might suggest).
- **Jitter Camera**: Be very careful using this. It jitters the camera to different positions in order for the sample pattern of the **Depth of Field** pass to be more irregular. This changes how many samples are being rendered in each frame. I would recommend not turning this on unless you're very certain you need it.

My settings for this scene:

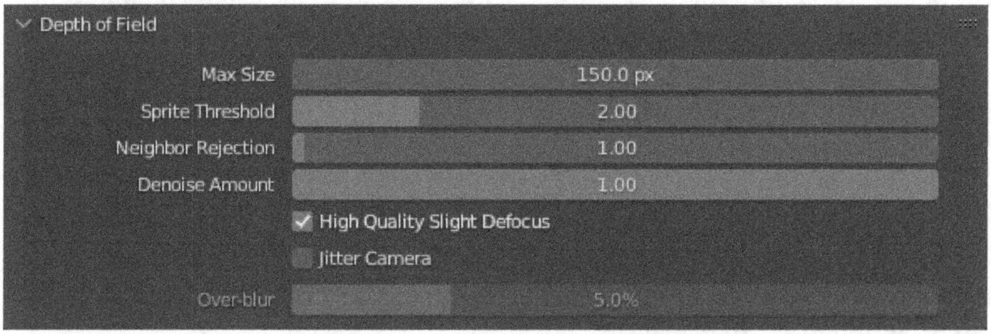

Figure 7.25: Depth of Field settings for the scene

Don't feel like you need to copy mine, and you probably won't notice much difference in your render after changing these specific values. You can use the trick of changing **Max Size** to `0` to toggle the effect of these options on and off. In this section, we went over a really cool effect, depth of field. It's a nice thing to use to direct the viewers to a specific part of the scene or mimic the way that things become out of focus as they fade into the background. Hopefully, you'll enjoy using this effect in EEVEE just as much as in Cycles.

Summary

Here's what we have so far!

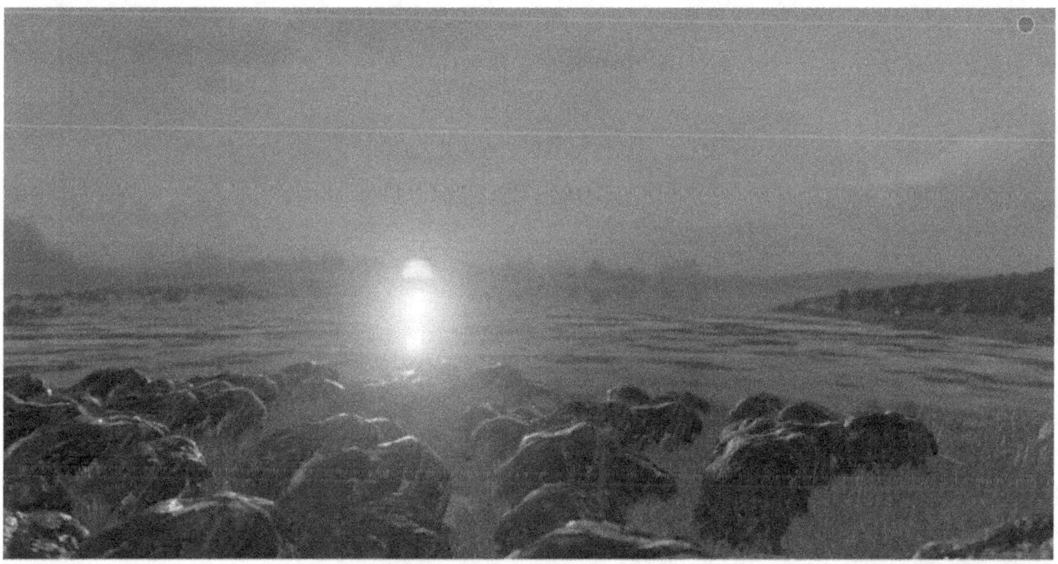

Figure 7.26: The scene so far!

I think it looks a million times better than what we had at the beginning. In the four sections of this chapter, we got to use a whole suite of effects to make our computer generated camera more like a real camera. We made it so that the background of our scene fades away, the light in the scene reflects appropriately off the lake, and the ambient occlusion and the depth of field matches what we would see in real life. The more we can mimic real life, the more we start to make images that look so real they can fool the average person. I hope you are as amazed as I am that this free software can make something so good with such little work. But, we still have more to do to make this scene really pop!

In the next chapter, we'll add small details such as birds, fake mist, and other little things that can really add to a scene's realism.

8
Using Alphas for Details

I think you'll agree that our realistic environment scene is really coming together at this point, but there might be something missing. It's really common to work on a scene for a long time and then realize that it just doesn't look right, but you actually aren't sure why! We've obviously made sure our lake is reflecting properly, and the sun and the sky are casting light correctly – we've done everything! But often, what's missing is not the big, overarching elements of a scene but the details. When we look at a natural environment, we often don't even register some of the details we're seeing; we see the scene as a whole. But as a 3D artist and designer, we need to see those details; they are what make a scene believable. So, in this chapter, we're going to create some really nice details that add to the overall composition and realism of the scene. We'll cover three different types of details: birds, mist, and backgrounds. In concept art, it can be a lot easier to add these things to your scene as images on a plane, or as **Alphas**. In creating digital images, the Alpha channel denotes the transparency aspect of the image. In an image, we have the **red channel**, the **green channel**, and the **blue channel** that create the color aspect of the image. Then, the **Alpha** channel dictates how opaque an image is. This is usually shown visually using *black* or *white*. Black means the image is completely transparent, and white means an image is completely opaque, with varying colors between those two colors denoting various levels of transparency. In this chapter, we will use various images with prepared Alpha channels, known as Alphas, to create details quickly and with ease.

In this chapter, we will cover the following topics:

- Adding detail to the scene (with birds!)
- Creating fake volumetric mist
- Adding a background and finishing up

Technical requirements

Download `Chapter 8-Start.blend` to start this chapter from my starting point, or just download the folder labeled `Images` to start the chapter from your previous file. Make sure this new image is saved in the same place that you saved the other textures from this chapter to avoid losing them. We also activated an add-on in the first chapter called **Import Images as Planes**. Make sure this is still activated, as it will be the way we import these images so that they immediately have the Alpha channel set, instead of having to set it ourselves.

You'll find the files for this chapter at this link:

`https://github.com/PacktPublishing/Shading-Lighting-and-Rendering-with-Blenders-EEVEE/tree/main/Chapter08`

Adding detail to the scene (with birds!)

In this section, we're going to add some birds to our scene. Now, one way you could go about this is to model some birds, texture them, and put them in the background, maybe by using a particle system. But that is a lot of time to create a bird that will probably make up 0.001% of the scene. Plus, each bird will add to the overall computational time of the render, so you're wasting even more time. So, let's add the Alpha of a bird flock, which will add only one extra polygon to the scene and a little extra time rendering an Alpha channel. This process will only take about 2 minutes. Let's get started:

1. Go to **File** at the left corner of the Blender window. Select **Import | Images as Planes**:

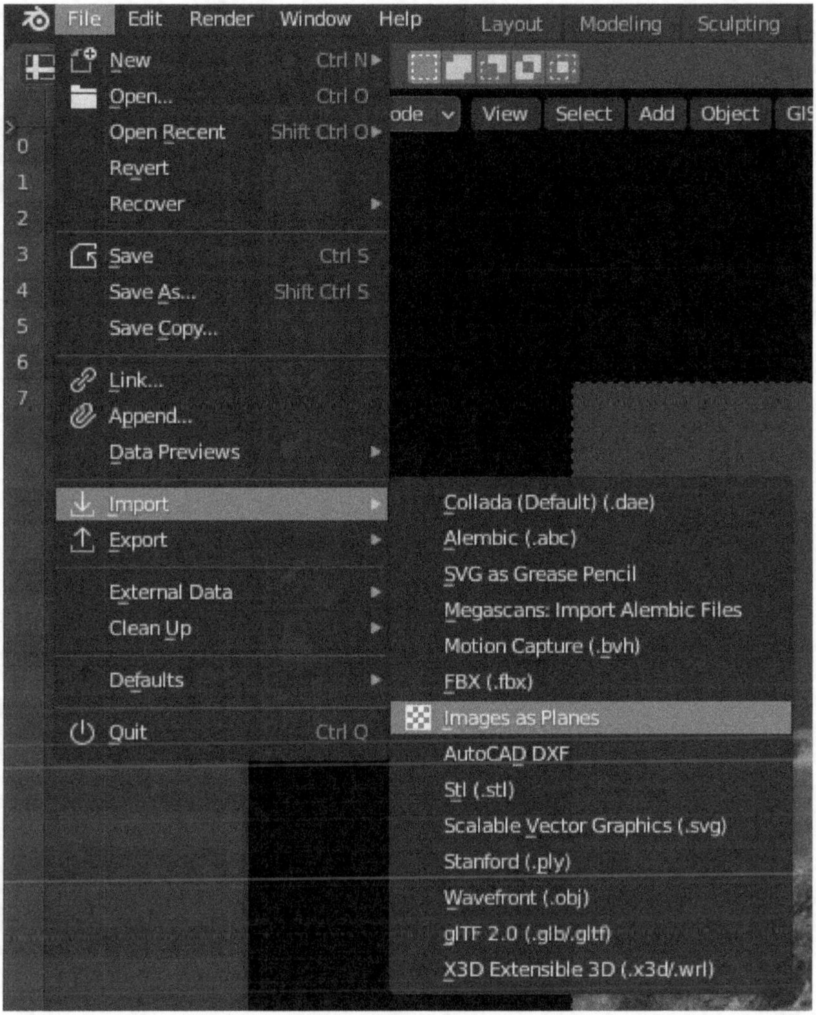

Figure 8.1: Import Images as Planes menu

Navigate to the folder in which you saved the images you downloaded for this chapter.

2. Select the **BirdAlpha** image:

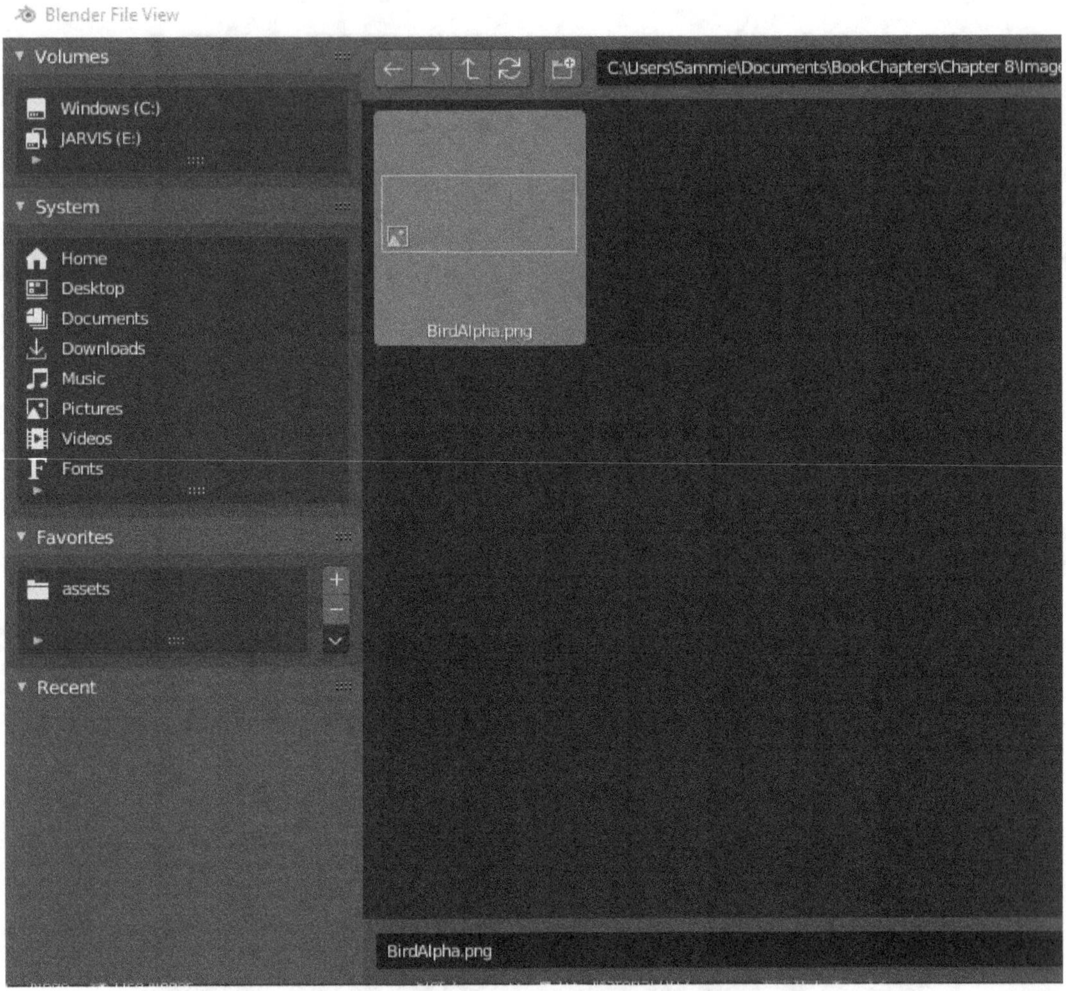

Figure 8.2: Selecting the BirdAlpha image file

3. In the right column, you'll see **Operator Presets**. Select the **Premultiplied** option in **Texture Settings** and make sure that the **Use Alpha** option is ticked, which it should be by default:

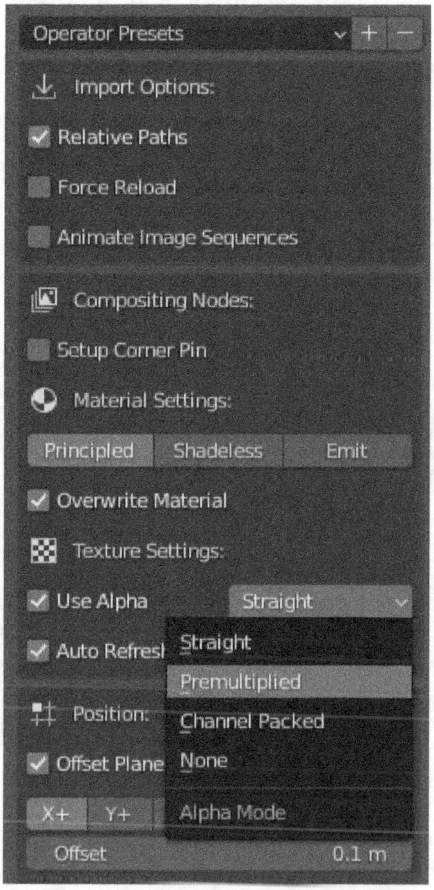

Figure 8.3: Import Images as Planes Operator Presets

Our bird Alpha should be imported into our scene. If you moved your 3D cursor, it will be imported to the point where the cursor is located, which can be annoying if the 3D cursor has moved to a place you have trouble finding. If you are having problems with the location of the 3D cursor, you can reset its location by using the *Shift* + *C* shortcut to reset the location of the 3D cursor and then re-import the `BirdAlpha` file. It should show up exactly in the center of the grid:

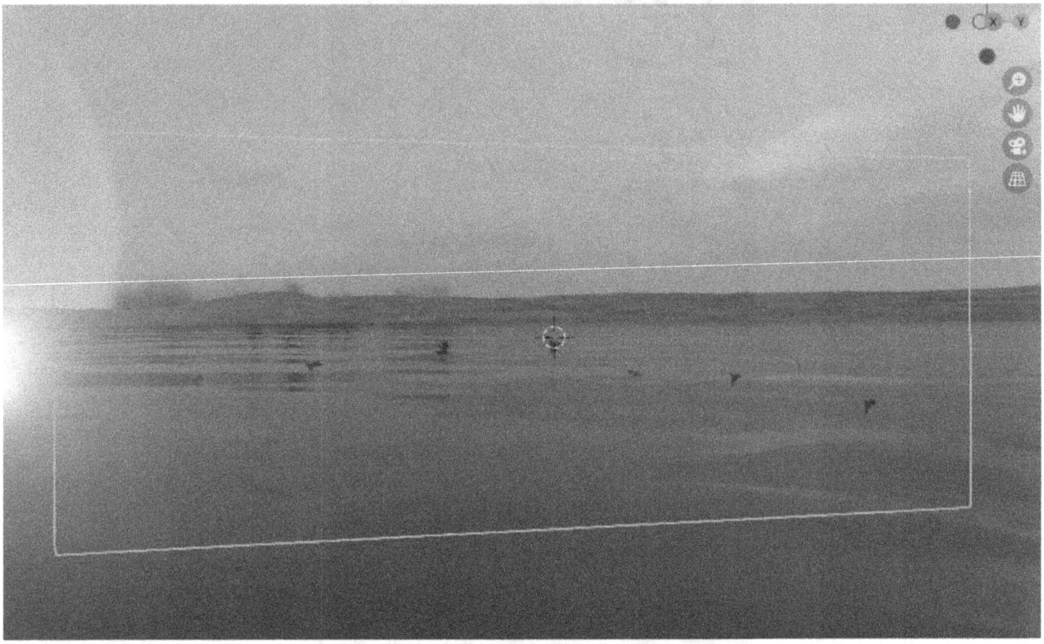

Figure 8.4: Importing the bird Alpha plane

4. As I imported it, our bird Alpha is facing the right direction, but if your bird Alpha is imported in a different orientation, use the *R* shortcut to snap the plane to the upright direction.

5. Use the *S* shortcut to size up the bird Alpha and then *G* to move it to the right location (a little bit in front of the sun but still in view of the camera). Here's where I put mine, but experiment with different placements to see whether you have a place you prefer:

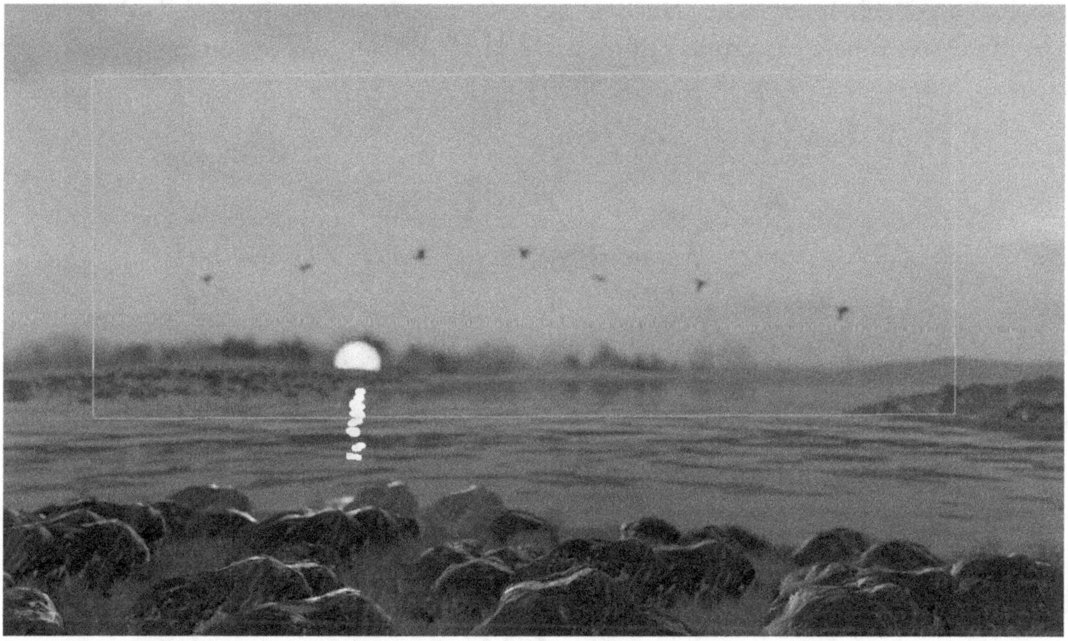

Figure 8.5: Positioning the bird Alpha plane

6. Now that we have the bird Alpha in the correct position, we can also create separate birds if we want.

   You can probably see that the Alpha is casting a shadow and has ruined the nice reflection we have from the sun in our scene. We can fix that easily. Ensuring you have the **BirdAlpha** object plane selected, go to the **Properties** panel and select **Material Properties**, scrolling down to the material's **Settings** options:

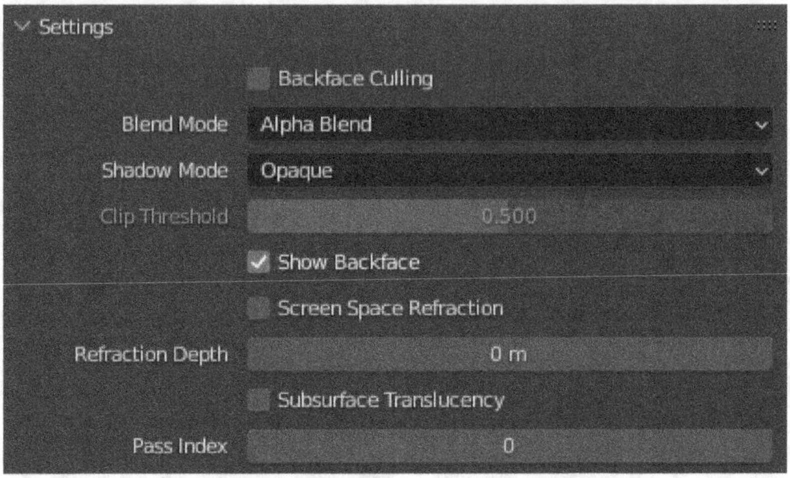

Figure 8.6: The material's Settings panel

7. Set the drop-down box next to **Shadow Mode** to **None**. Now, we don't get a shadow from the plane at all:

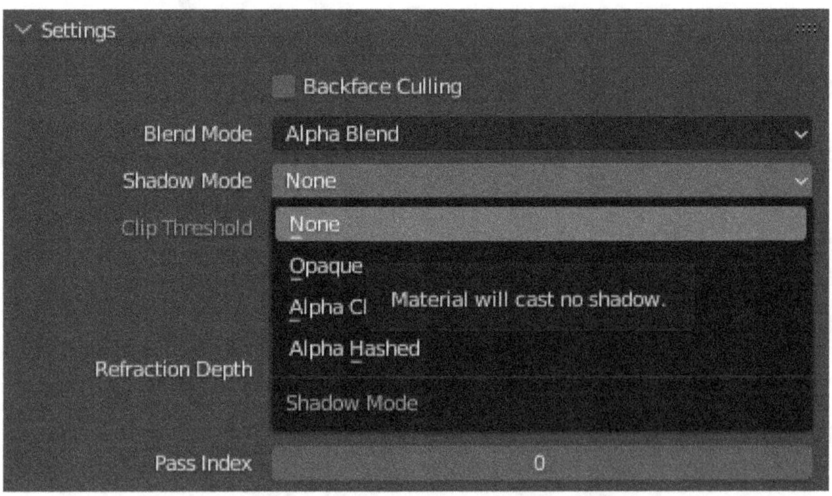

Figure 8.7: Changing Shadow Mode to None

And here's the final effect:

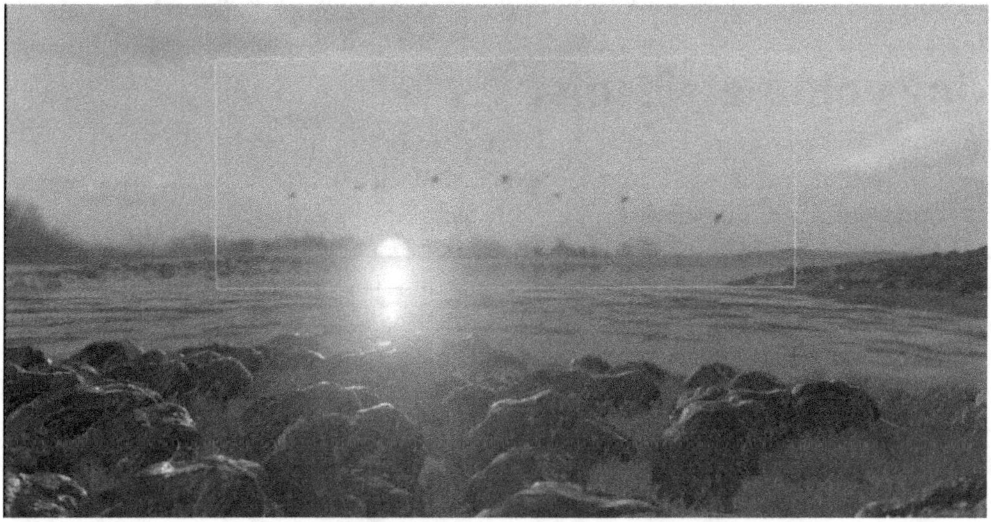

Figure 8.8: The birds added to the composition

You can probably see how easy it is to add some details to the scene, such as birds in the background. Obviously, if the main focus of the scene is a bird, you'd want to actually model and texture a bird with all the added detail and care you'd take for any other important part of the scene. But what if our birds are tiny and in the background? Use the Alpha! You can also do this for an airplane flying in the background, some trees far off in the distance, or any other small object that won't need too much detail. You can also add a simple plane, apply the bird material, and then unwrap the birds on the plane. This way, you can get more control over the scale and the appearance of the birds.

> **Making Your Own Alphas**
>
> At the risk of getting too sidetracked, I want to briefly talk about making your own Alphas. Of course, there are many packs available to buy online that people have created, but it is often really easy to create a few Alphas for yourself if all you need is a few singular Alphas for a specific purpose. If you are creating at scale, I recommend buying packs to streamline your workflow, but most people don't need such large collections of Alphas. So, to make your own Alpha, import a picture you've taken or found (I recommend *Unsplashed.com* for some great CC0 images) to Krita or Photoshop, select the area around the object you want with the lasso or magic wand tool, and then delete it. You should be left with your object surrounded by a checkerboard pattern. That pattern denotes full transparency. Make sure you export the image you just created as a PNG. JPEGs don't support an Alpha channel, so PNGs are the way to go.

Let's move on to creating Alphas procedurally in Blender with the **Shader Editor**. We'll be adding some mist to the top of our lake using a shortcut to fake **volumetrics**.

Faking volumetric mist

This time, we won't be using a pre-prepared texture to create our Alpha. We'll add a plane, use some procedural textures to create some mist, and then add them to the top of our water to simulate mist rolling off our water. This technique is extremely simplistic, so I'd say that it's often better to use a volumetric shader that actually catches the light and diffuses it as it would in the real world. However, I think it's important to understand how to do the same thing in a few different ways and why each one would apply to different situations. Using this technique to create fake volumetrics is really useful for situations where you have only small parts of a scene that need mist or smoke, but it isn't very useful in situations where you want to animate the camera, as it will become clear once the camera starts moving that the mist isn't very realistic. Take that into account if you choose to use this method of mist creation.

Let's create some mist planes to add to our scene:

1. Add a plane using the usual *Shift* + *A* method and rotate the plane so that it faces the camera. Use the *S* key to scale it along the *y* axis so that it is horizontal across the water:

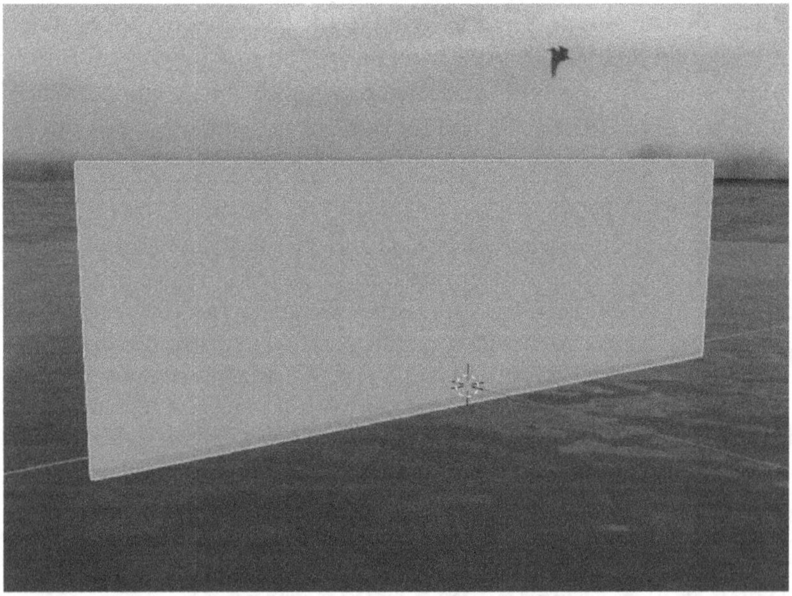

Figure 8.9: Adding a blank plane

2. Move the plane closer to the camera so that we can see how it looks in the viewport as we build the shader. Use the *G* shortcut to move and then use *X* to lock movement to the *x* axis. This makes it easier to move the plane closer to the camera without accidentally moving it up, down, left, or right:

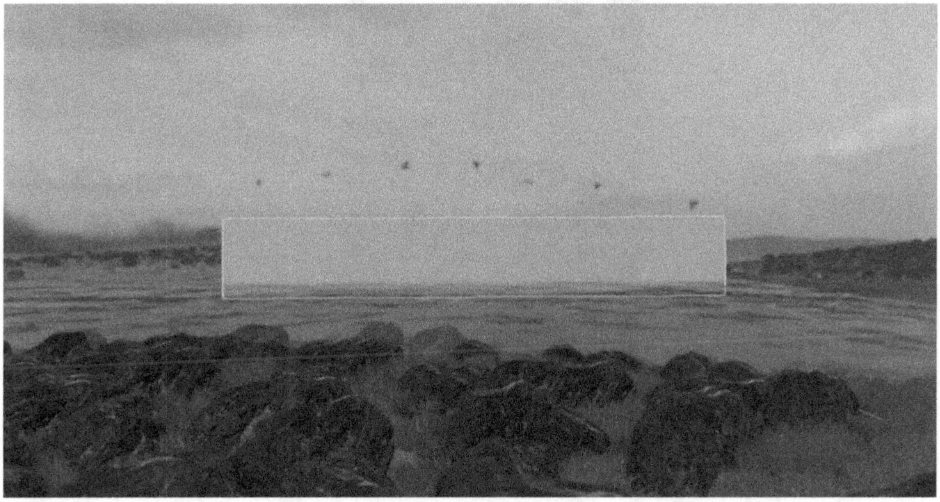

Figure 8.10: Positioning the blank plane

3. Add a shader to the plane; the **Principled** shader is added by default.
4. Add a **Noise Texture** node and a **Voronoi Texture** node to the shader and connect **Position** to the **Vector** input:

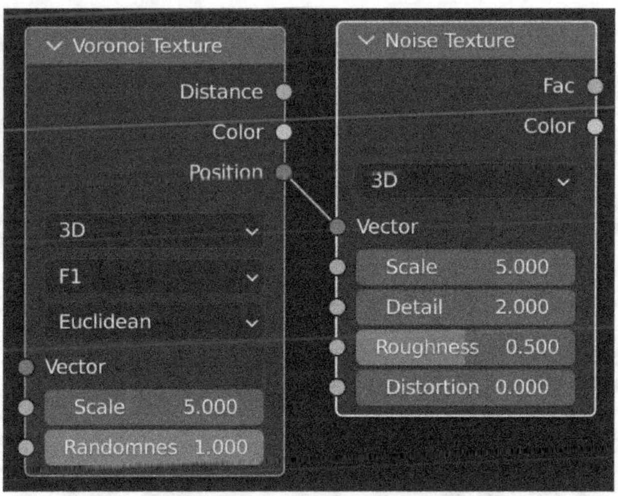

Figure 8.11: Connecting Voronoi Texture and Noise Texture

5. Let's change the **Voronoi Texture** type to **Smooth F1** and increase the **Scale** value to **25.000**:

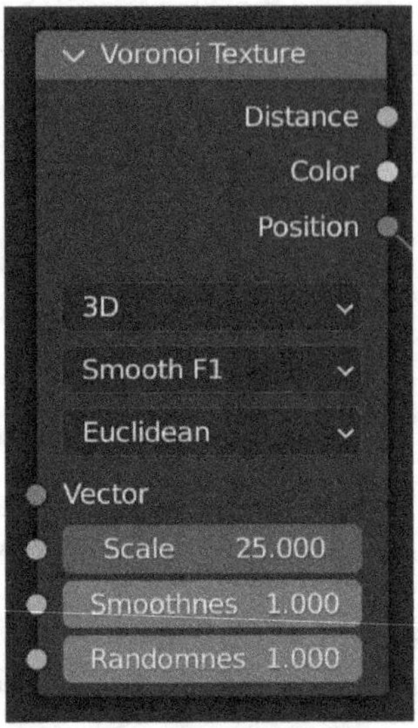

Figure 8.12: The Voronoi Texture settings

6. Add a **ColorRamp** node and pull the black marker (on the left side) down to about a quarter of the way. Black values indicate transparency, so the closer the black marker is to the white marker on the ramp, the more black will be visible on the ramp's color gradient. The more black that is visible on the gradient, the more transparency we'll get:

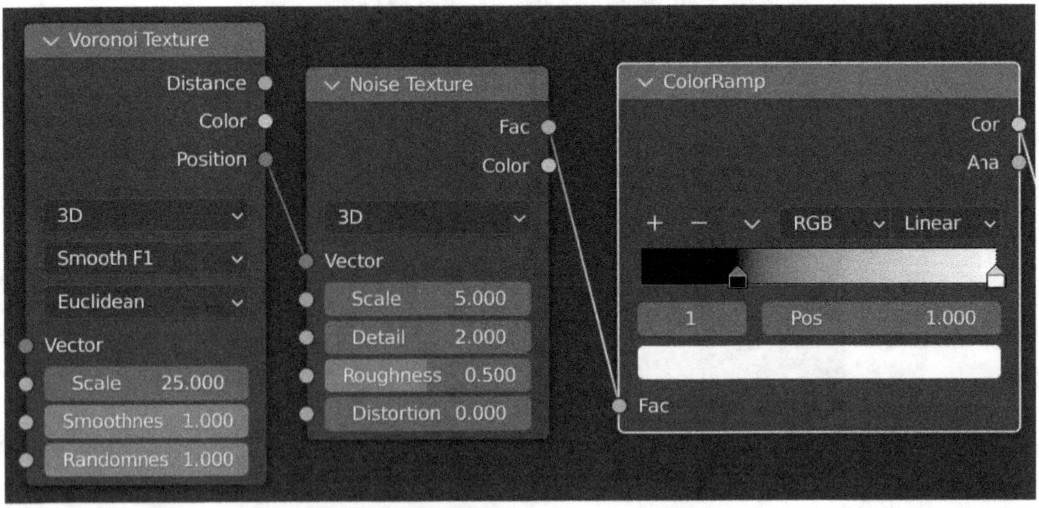

Figure 8.13: Adding ColorRamp to the shader

7. Let's take the **Color** output from **ColorRamp** and input it to **Alpha**:

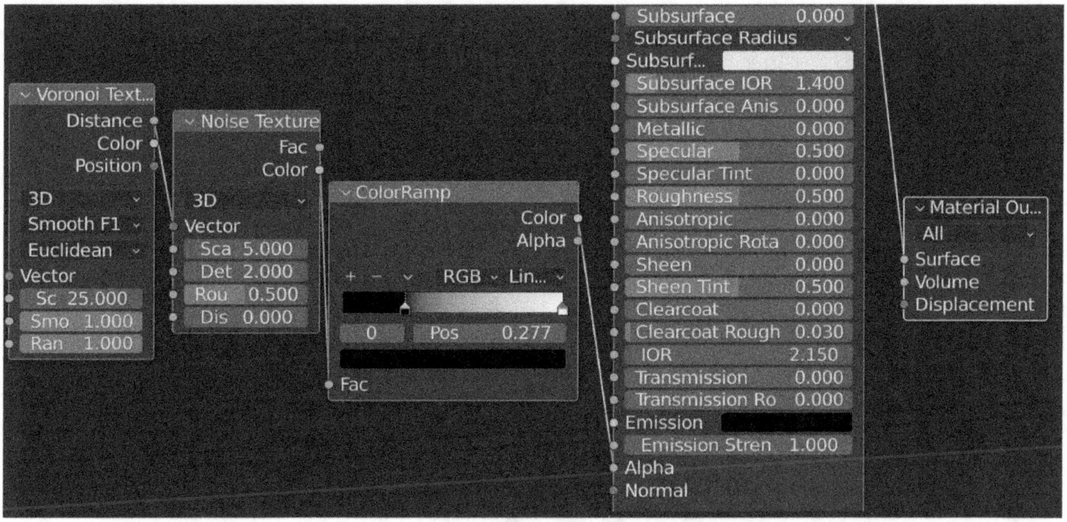

Figure 8.14: Connecting ColorRamp to Alpha

8. You'll notice that nothing happens, but we've learned that about EEVEE. You need to specify **Blend Mode** in the material's **Settings** options to actually get transparency. So, let's change **Blend Mode** to **Alpha Blend** in **Settings** (which tells EEVEE that we want areas to be rendered transparent and opaque but with mid-values of semi-transparency blended in between). We also need to set **Shadow Mode** to **None**:

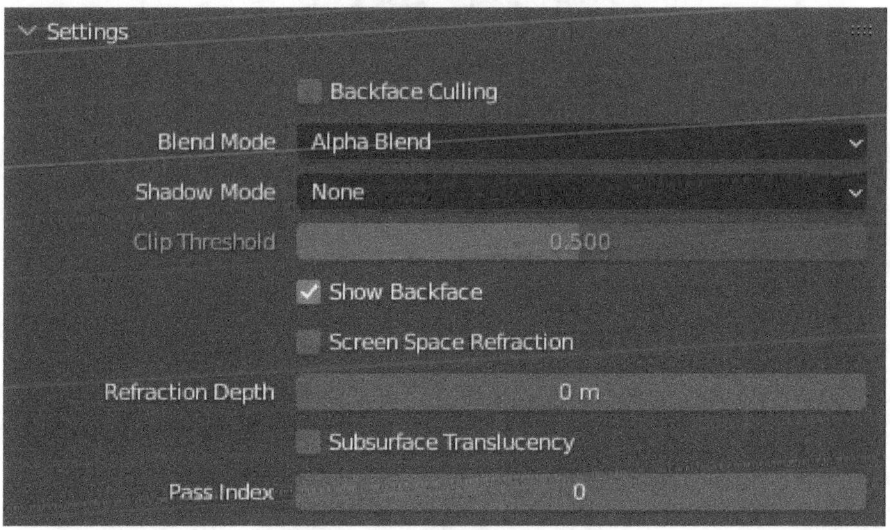

Figure 8.15: Material settings (again)

9. Now we have an okay misty effect, but it cuts off at the edge of our mist plane:

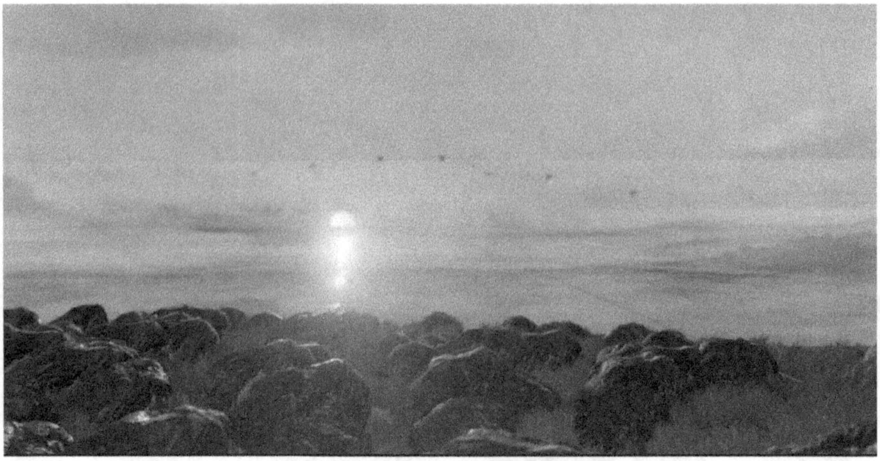

Figure 8.16: The spot where the mist ends is very obvious

10. Let's add a **Gradient Texture** node so that we can fade the texture into transparency:

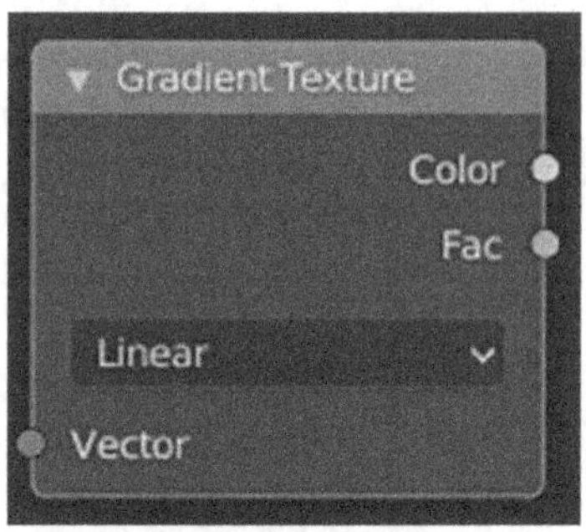

Figure 8.17: Gradient Texture

11. Add a **Mix** node and set **Mix** to **Multiply**. **Multiply** is a blend mode that adds black to the original texture, which, considering we want to add transparency to the top of the plane and transparency is represented in our texture as black, works perfectly to increase the transparency at the top end of our plane. Set **Fac** on the **Multiply** node to **1.000** so that we get the full mixture:

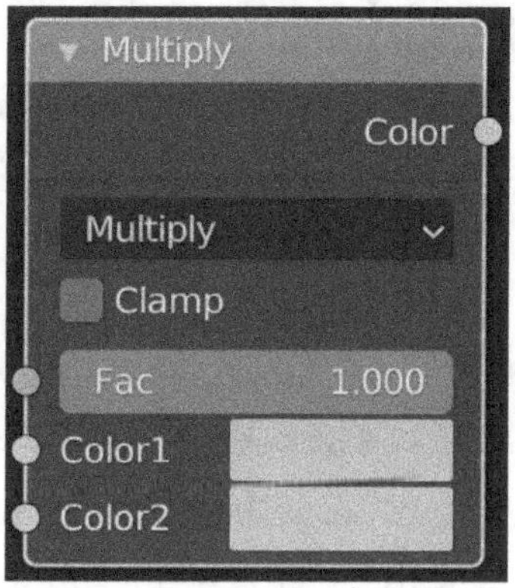

Figure 8.18: The Multiply node

12. Attach the **Gradient Texture** node's **Color** output to **Color2** on the **Multiply** node and the **ColorRamp Color** output to **Color1** on the **Multiply** node, and take the output from **Multiply** and put it into the **Alpha** input on the **Principled** shader:

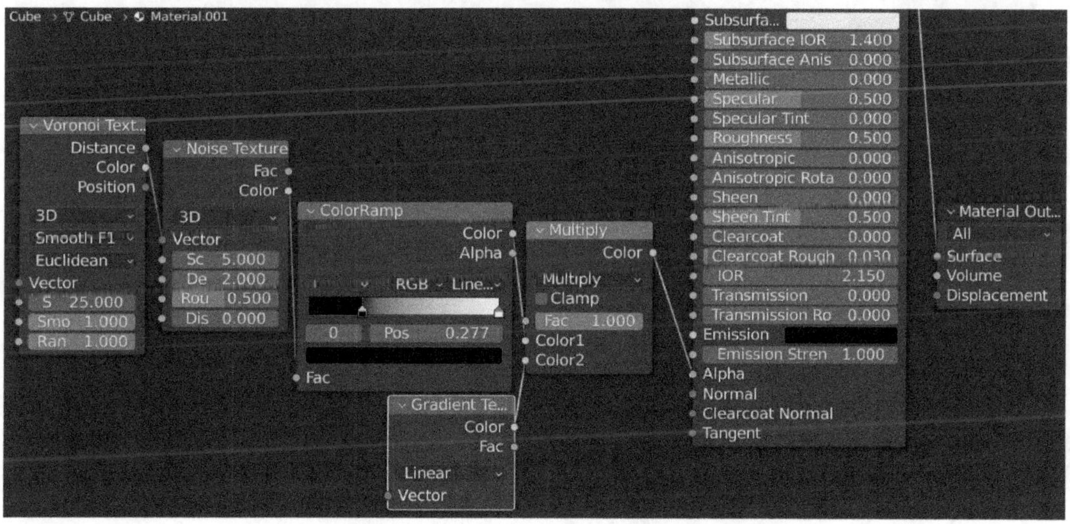

Figure 8.19: The full setup of the Alpha channel

13. I like mist with a little brightness to it, so I changed the emission color to white to give it a little more pop:

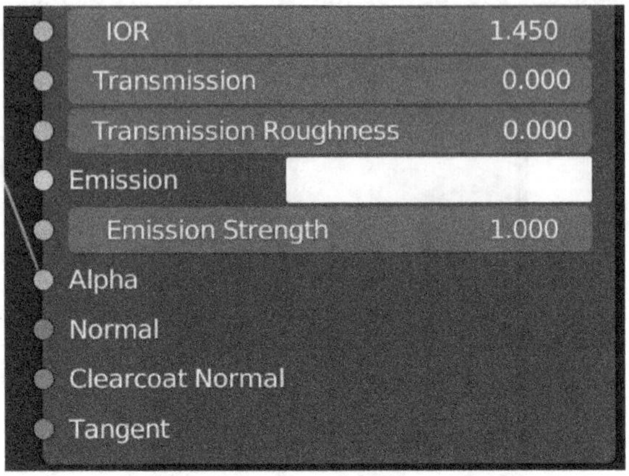

Figure 8.20: Changing the emission color

14. The only thing left to do now is to take the plane and scale it so that it stretches across the water. It's also easy to see the place where the mist plane starts if it's too far away from the land, so let's move it closer to the camera:

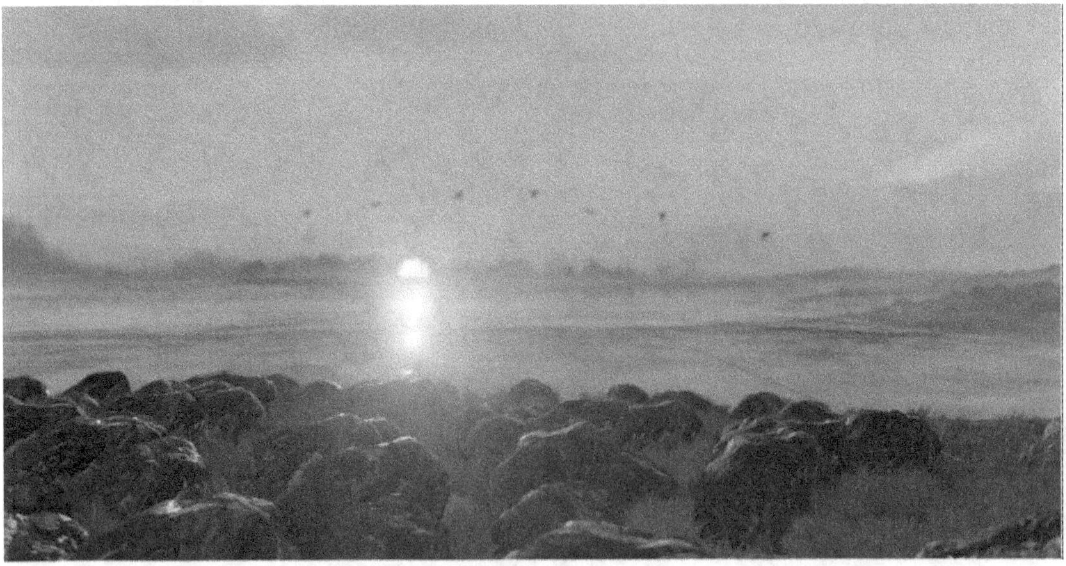

Figure 8.21: Mist planes in the scene

15. I decided the effect was a little too intense, so I changed the white marker on the **ColorRamp** node to a gray color. If we apply what we know about transparency now, we can see that a gray color gives us more transparency than white but less than black. That's why **Alpha Blend** is the best material mode for this application – we can get those shades of gray for half-transparency:

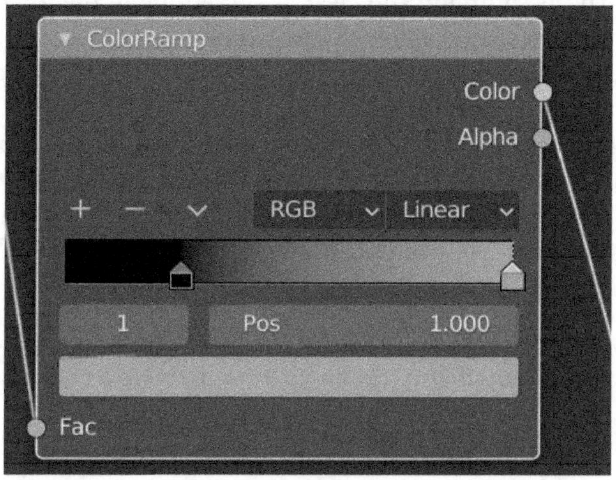

Figure 8.22: Lowering the value of the mist opacity

16. I duplicated the first mist object, moved it away from the camera, and scaled it on the *y* axis to make it stretch across the lake so that we get two layers of mist:

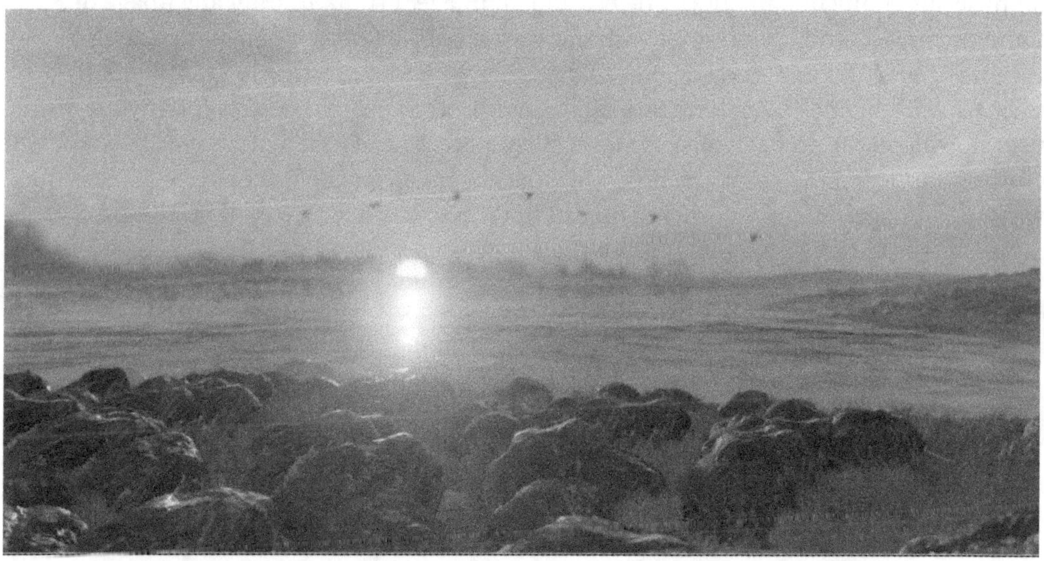

Figure 8.23: The mist in the scene after lowering the opacity

This technique is a great way of adding to the overall composition of the shot. If you look closely, you can see that the mist desaturates and makes the background harder to see, so our eye is drawn more to the foreground of the shot. Using these mist planes, we can break up the scene so that as things become further away, they seem to fade off into the background, exactly as they do in real life. Nothing in the far distance of a photograph is going to be as saturated and clear as something in the foreground, which we can artificially do with these mist planes. Now that we've looked at two different ways of adding atmosphere to a nature scene, both with volumetrics and with mist planes, we have two tools in our arsenal to create different types of effects. Imagine that instead of a lake, we were creating a dune. If we change the mist plane to a sandy color, we can imitate wind moving sand particles around the scene, something that would be very difficult with a volumetric cube. Mist planes are easier to create and faster to render but don't provide realistic light diffusion from an atmosphere. It's up to you to decide which to use or whether to use both, but both have their uses in different types of situations.

We're almost at the finish line for this image! In the next section, we'll add a background that matches the sun we've created and talk about how to make a background image as realistic as possible.

Using an image to create a background

Let's add the finishing touch to our image. I think that the HDRI we used was nice enough to work with as a background up until now, but it doesn't quite fit the type of image that I'm seeing in my imagination. So, let's add an image. I think finding any image of a sunset or sunrise would work well with our scene, but I have an image in mind. I got it from `https://kaiserbold.com/free-sky-backgrounds/`. This company creates 3D work but has been kind enough to give away some of its assets for anyone to use. Download the 25 pack of sky images if you like, or feel free to make your own. Consider supporting the company if you like the sky image pack. Make sure you store the downloaded images in a place where you can find them easily, since we'll be adding one of them to our scene right now. Let's get started:

1. We'll be adding the image the same way we added the birds Alpha. Go to **File | Import | Image as Plane**, and then select your image. I'm using sky number 14 from the `KaiserBold` pack, but any of them could look good! We don't need to worry about changing the Alpha to **Premultiplied** this time, though, as we don't need an Alpha channel in this image. Refer to *Figure 8.1* if you have forgotten how we did this initially.

2. Scale up the sky using the *S* shortcut. We want this plane to cover the entire sky, so it should be very big:

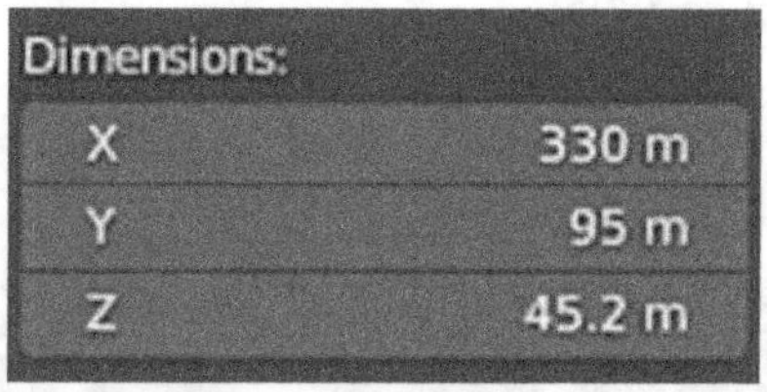

Figure 8.24: My background plane dimensions

3. Make sure the plane is facing the camera, and then rotate it on the *y* axis by about 45 degrees so that the clouds at the top of the image seem a little closer to the camera. I like to make my background images slanted toward the camera, as I think it adds a little dimensionality to the clouds:

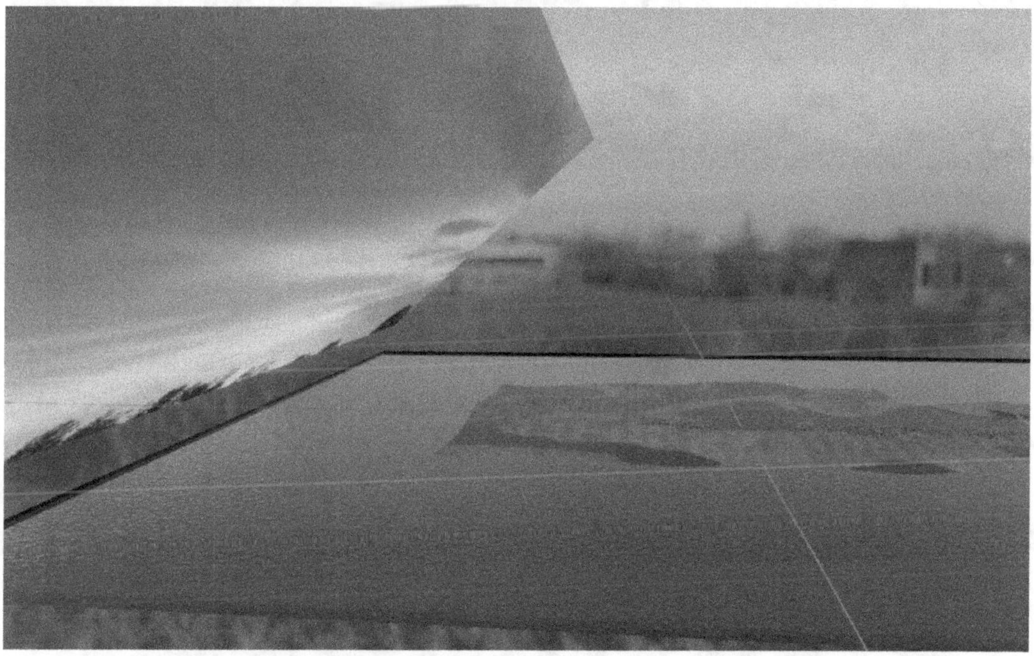

Figure 8.25: The side view of the background plane rotation

4. At this point, we should see the plane as the background behind the sun object, but it's a lot darker than I want it to be, and the background plane seems to be blocking out the light we have in the scene:

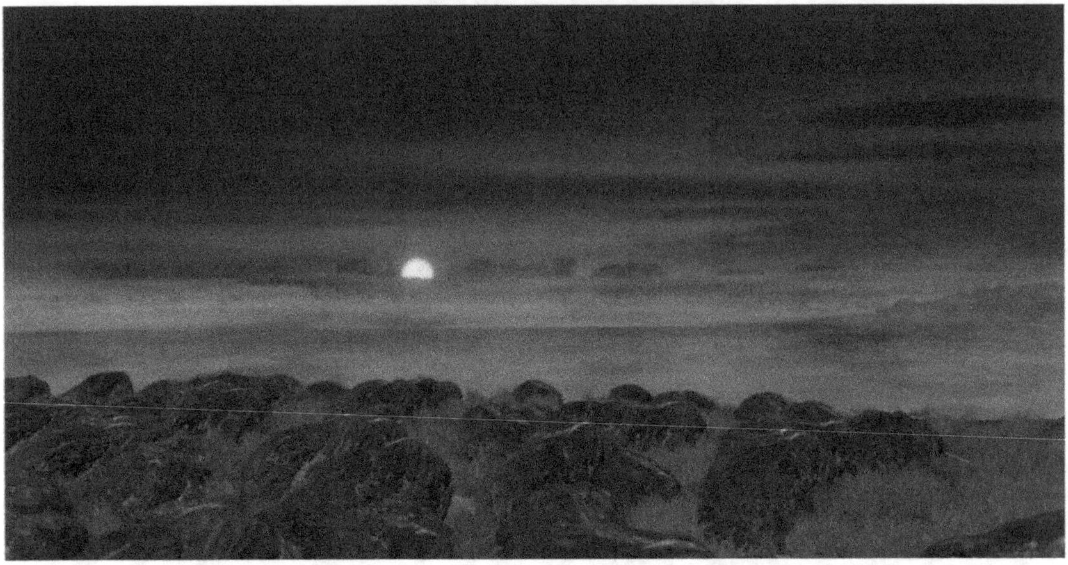

Figure 8.26: The camera view after adding the background plane

5. As we've learned in this section, if we don't want images to interact with the lighting, all we have to do is change **Shadow Mode** to **None** in the material's **Settings**, so let's do that:

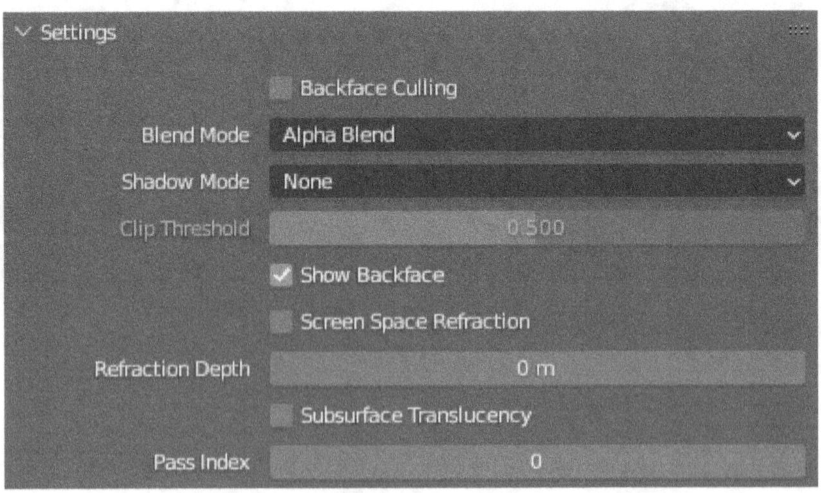

Figure 8.27: Material settings for the background plane

Our scene is instantly a lot brighter! It's still a little darker than I want it to be, though:

Figure 8.28: The camera view of the background without shadowing

6. We'll add some light emission to the background so that we can get more clarity in the background image. Simply take the image's **Color** output and attach it to the **Emission** color input on the **Principled** shader:

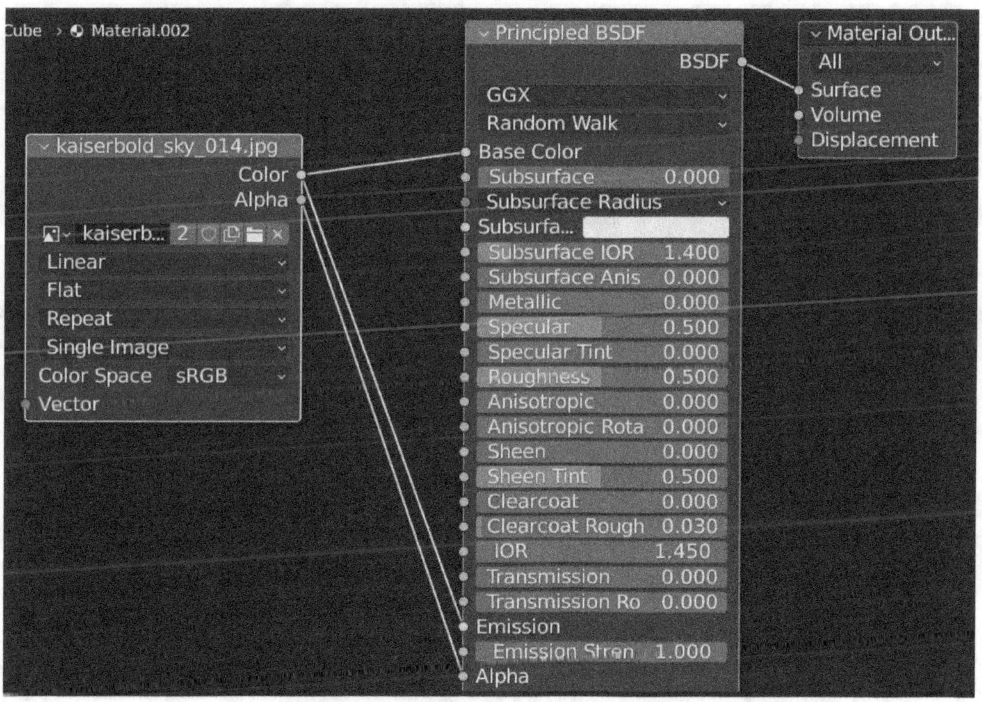

Figure 8.29: Adding some emissive-ness to the background plane

7. Our image immediately becomes a little clearer:

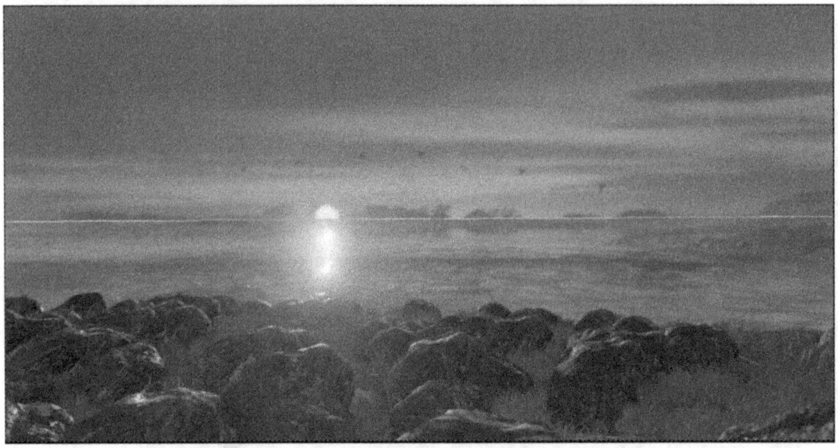

Figure 8.30: The background with some light

8. I'm still a little unsatisfied with the color of the sky; I want to make the sunlight effect really obvious. Let's go to the shader editor again and add an **RGB Curves** node between the **Color** output on the image and both the **Base Color** input and the **Emission** input on the **Principled BSDF** shader:

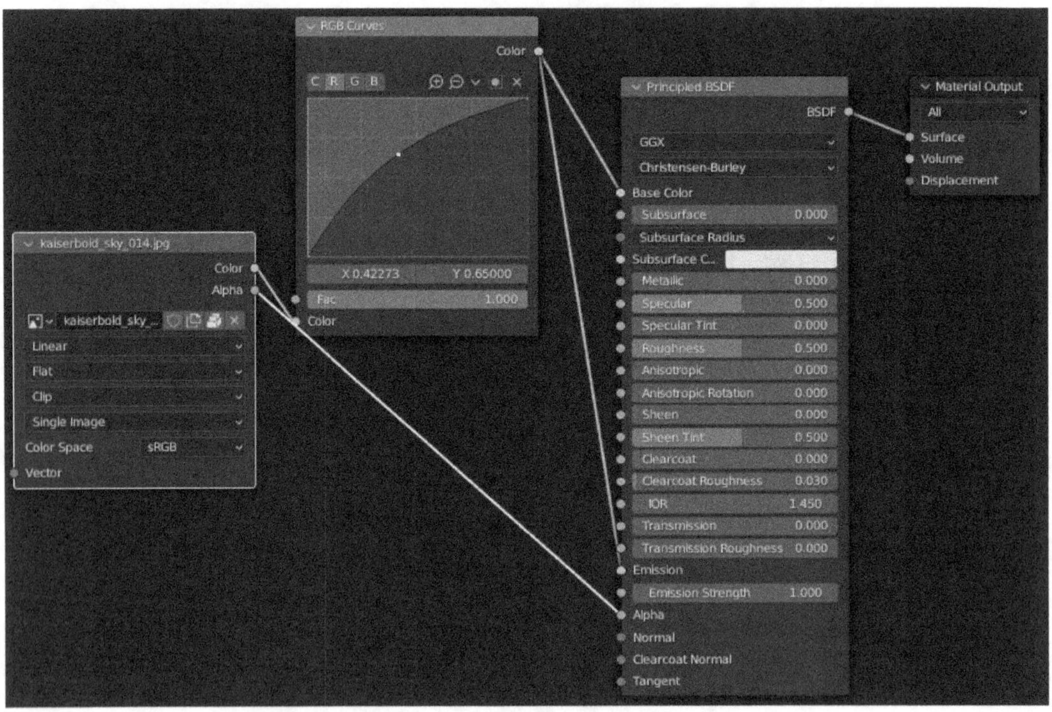

Figure 8.31: Adding the RGB Curves node to the shader

9. If we select the **R** channel in the **RGB Curves** layer list at the top left and then drag the curve up to increase the redness in the image, we'll get the image result we want:

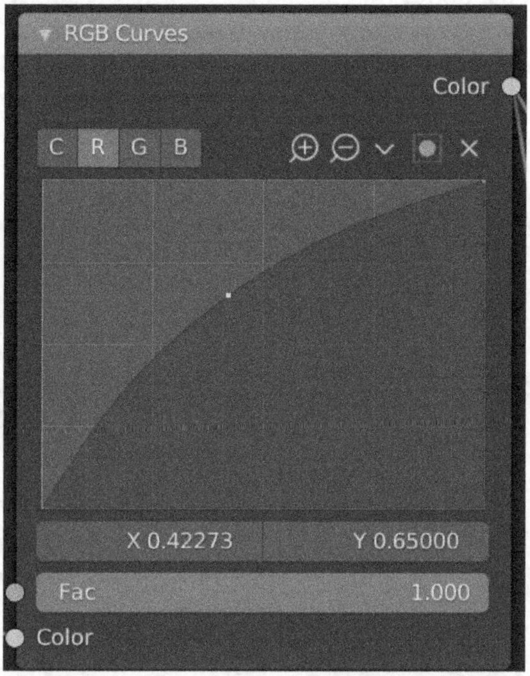

Figure 8.32: Adding redness to the image with RGB Curves

10. The very last thing we need to do is dial in our volume properties so that the light from the sun reflects off the lake properly. If you look at reference pictures of a sunset on a lake, you'll notice that the water closer to the sun reflects more of the color of the sun, whereas the water closer to the camera reflects less of the sun and is a little more blue or green (depending on the original color of the water). To replicate something similar in our scene, all we have to do is go to the **Render** panel and change the **Start** value of **Volumetrics** to `0.1` and the **End** value to `8`:

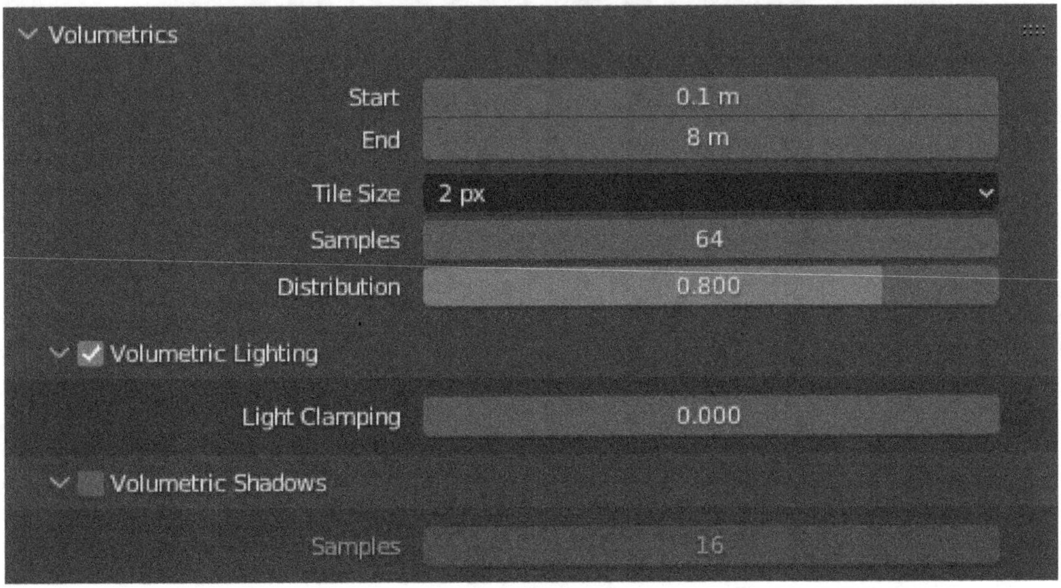

Figure 8.33: Changing the volumetric rendering

This constrains the majority of the volumetric samples to the area right in front of the camera, which means the **Volume** shader in the water is now correctly being utilized close to the camera but not far away from the camera. This creates a gradient of reflectivity to non-reflectivity that happens when a photo is taken from an oblique angle to the water. You should also notice that there is less overall mist in the scene, which you can easily introduce back into the scene by adding more of the planes that we created using Alphas in order to fake mist, as discussed earlier in this chapter. But, we now have a good reflection of the sun's light off the water. I think I'm ready to call this done! Of course, you can do a lot more work on this scene, adding more variety in vegetation or tweaking the mist in the background (we should technically get more mist planes the further away we get from the camera), but I think I'll leave that to you to experiment with.

Let's take a look at our final result!

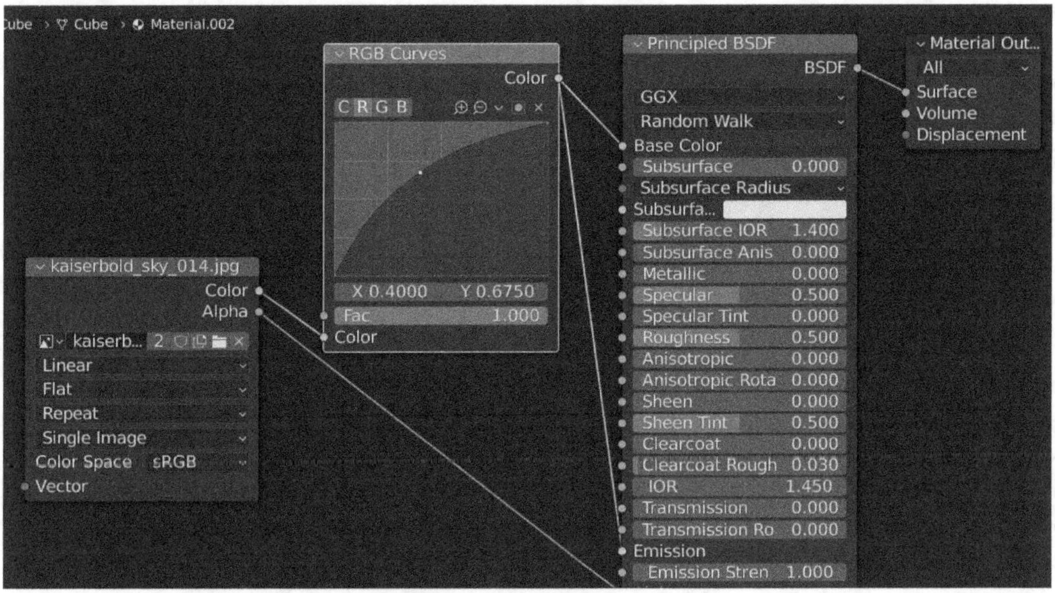

Figure 8.34: The final result

Since we talked about how to separate your layers and render them individually to composite them later in *Chapter 4, Non-Physical Rendering*, I won't go over all that again. I also lowered the opacity of the mist in my compositor to get a more subtle effect. Try experimenting with different layers of the image and how you can get them to fit together to get a more believable result! Feel free to use that workflow, or just hit **Render** and see how it turns out. My computer is fairly beefy, and this scene took almost 80% of my available GPU memory, so if you have trouble rendering this image, try experimenting with fewer rocks and grass in the **Geometry** Node modifier, or making your volumetric cube smaller.

Summary

And that's a wrap on our second mini-project! In this four-chapter arc, we looked at how to add rocks and plants to a landscape through **Geometry** Nodes, added a physically correct lake that we can reuse on any other water we use in projects, added different types of atmosphere and camera effects using volumetrics and depth of field, and then finally, learned about Alpha channels and how we can use them to create different types of details that add life to our renders. That's a lot of things that we have learned, so feel free to go back over each section and make sure you have it all down! Hopefully, you had as much fun as I did while going through all these cool techniques and solving problems as we went along. Blender can be complicated, but it can also be immensely satisfying to get the idea you had in your brain out in a render.

I'm so excited for the next chapter, where we're going to take some of the things that we've learned in the previous two mini-projects, plus even more, to start on a third mini-project. In this third and final mini-project, we'll create a sci-fi-style hangar, complete with aircraft. We'll cover how to create fire in EEVEE, some rendering effects that we haven't covered yet, and even more. We'll look at using some simple objects to create quick sci-fi renderings with **Geometry** Nodes.

Section 3: Advanced Features – Mini-Project 3 – Creating a Sci-Fi Concept

Now that we have a really deep understanding of EEVEE in Blender, let's keep diving deeper into even more advanced topics. We'll learn about more complicated lighting techniques, create special effects, and understand the next steps. After this section, you'll understand how to create amazing works both creatively and technically in EEVEE.

In this section, we will cover the following chapters:

- *Chapter 9, Lighting an Interior Scene*
- *Chapter 10, Working with Irradiance Volumes and CubeMaps for Accurate Rendering*
- *Chapter 11, Kitbashing – Adding Details Fast*
- *Chapter 12, Special Effects with EEVEE – Fire and Smoke*
- *Chapter 13, Exploring the Wide World of Blender*

9
Lighting an Interior Scene

In the first two sections of this book (*Chapter 2, Creating Materials Fast with EEVEE,* to *Chapter 8, Using Alphas for Details*), we worked on two scenes that were outside – both our **NPR** scene and the environment scene were lit mostly through HDRIs and Sun Light. In that sense, outdoor scenes are simple to light. Blender does most of the heavy lifting. The type of scene that we haven't worked on yet is an interior scene. In many ways, interior scenes can be much more difficult to work with in EEVEE. There are a number of pitfalls that an inexperienced artist can get tripped up by and can lead to a less than satisfactory final product. In this chapter and the next one, we're going to go over some of the lighting and rendering settings that are required for creating a standout interior scene, as well as some tricks and tips for overcoming common errors that occur when EEVEE is approximating light bounces inside a room or building. We'll learn how to use both **point** and **area lights** in an interior, as well as looking at some theory behind artistic lighting. We'll do this by tackling a science fiction scene, something that is an absolute staple in concept art. I have done the majority of the modeling and added materials to our scene already, using the same techniques that we went over in *Chapter 2, Creating Materials Fast with EEVEE,* so nothing fancy and nothing that you aren't already capable of doing yourself. As you begin this chapter, our scene is at the point of needing lights, and that's where we'll start to work on this scene. I have created this scene with learning in mind and therefore have created some errors for us to solve initially so that you understand what to do when you encounter them.

In this chapter, we will look at the following topics:

- Troubleshooting a common lighting error
- Designing the lighting of our interior
- Previewing render passes to inform our lighting decisions

Technical requirements

As with all the other chapters so far, I have created a scene in GitHub for this chapter called `Chapter_9-Start`. Download the entire `Chapter 9` folder to start working on the scene and make sure you save the whole folder to a safe place.

The files to work through this chapter are located here:

`https://github.com/PacktPublishing/Shading-Lighting-and-Rendering-with-Blenders-EEVEE/tree/main/Chapter09`

Troubleshooting a common lighting error

Before we start designing the lighting in our scene, I wanted to go through a common error that I know many people have come across using EEVEE while trying to light an interior scene. Because I want to show you this, I have set up the `Chapter 9` scene to allow us to troubleshoot this lighting error. Our starting file should look something like this in rendered mode:

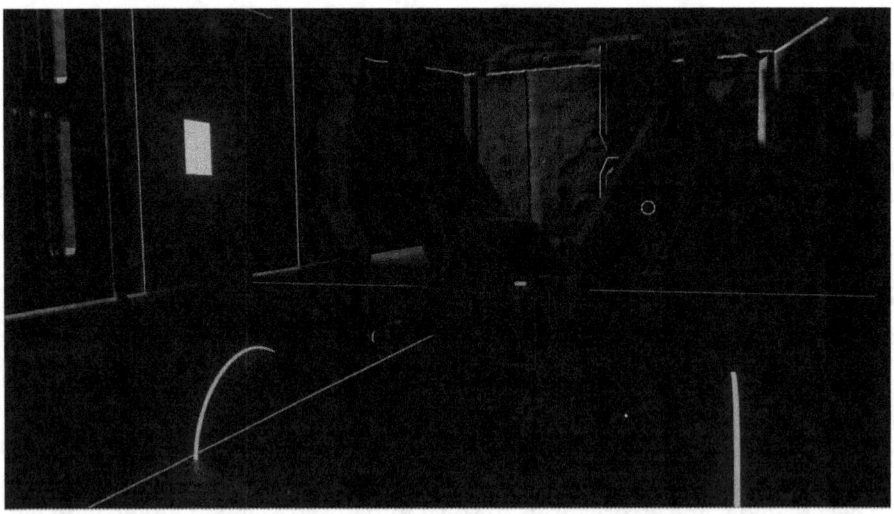

Figure 9.1: Starting scene

You might notice that I've added a **sun light** to our scene, even though we don't need one, since we'll be relying on interior lighting only and don't have any windows for the sun to come through. But as you can see in this render, we still have light coming through the solid walls of our scene! This is a very common problem in EEVEE with interior scenes, so I've added a sun light to the start of our scene so you can understand the problem and how to fix it in your own future interior scenes. This problem is called **Light Leaking**. It basically means that light is leaking through solid geometry in our scene, even when we don't want it to. It often happens when we have objects in our scene that only are one single polygon meeting with other single polygons. The way EEVEE rasterizes light means that it doesn't calculate the edges of the polygon as areas that should occlude light and as a result lets light in, and that is something we don't want. Lucky for us, there are three simple ways you can get rid of this light bleeding. Let's jump right into it:

1. Select the outer shell of our hangar. The object is called **Main Hangar** in the Outliner.

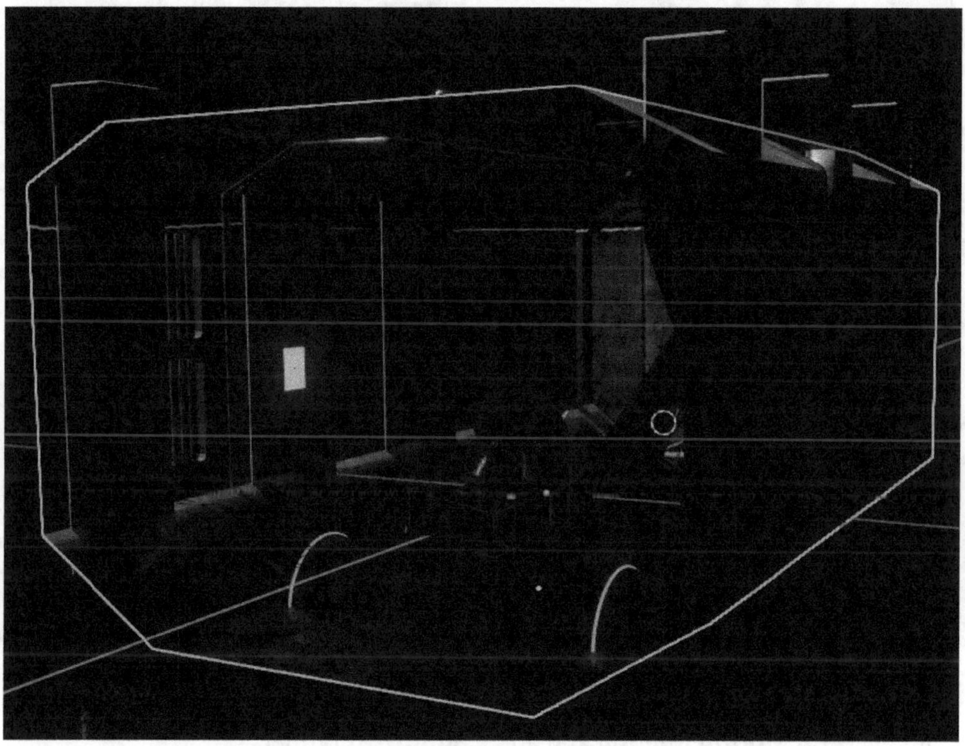

Figure 9.2: Main Hangar selected

2. Go to the modifier stack.

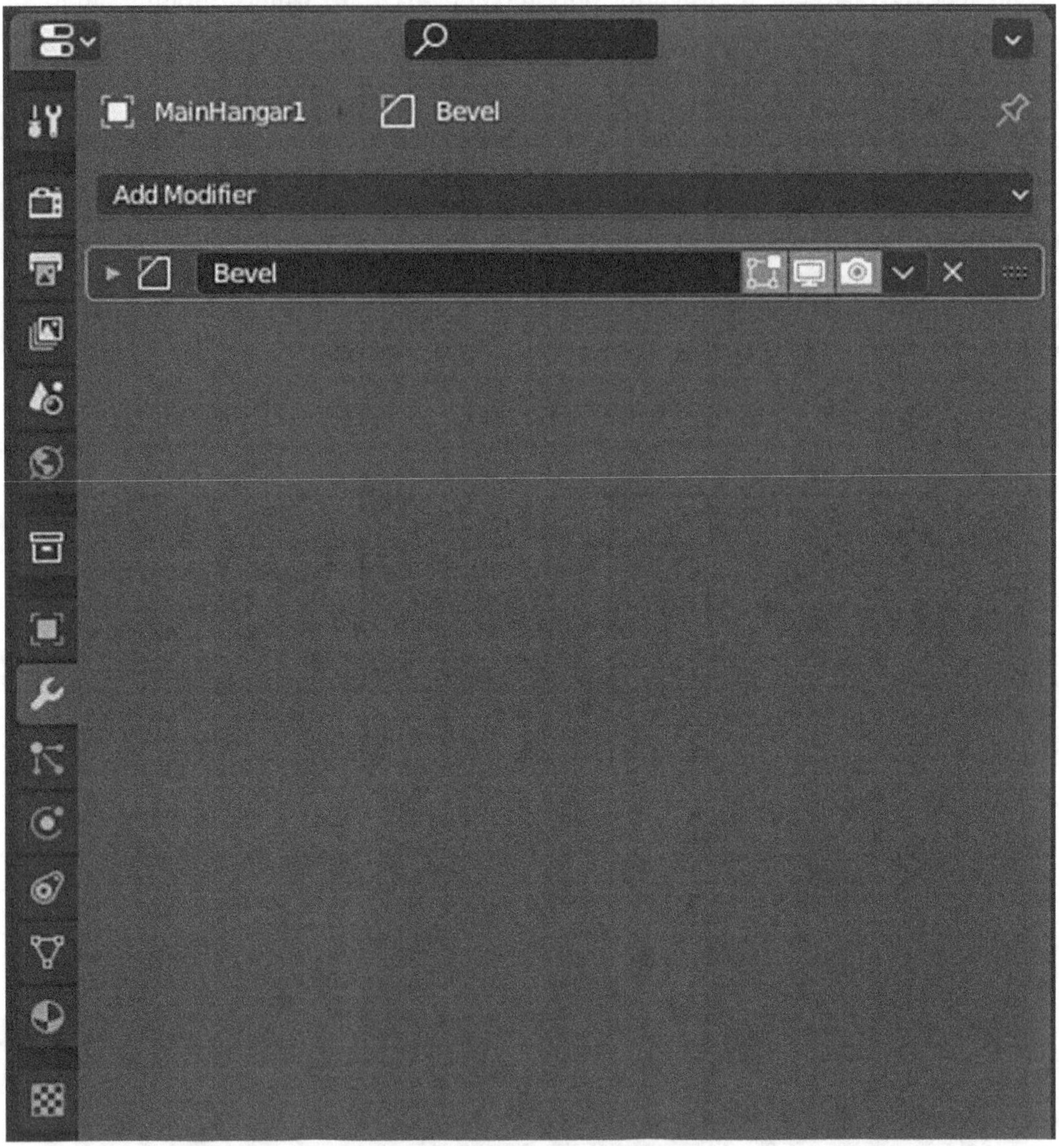

Figure 9.3: The modifier stack

3. Click the **Add Modifier** button and add a **Solidify** modifier.

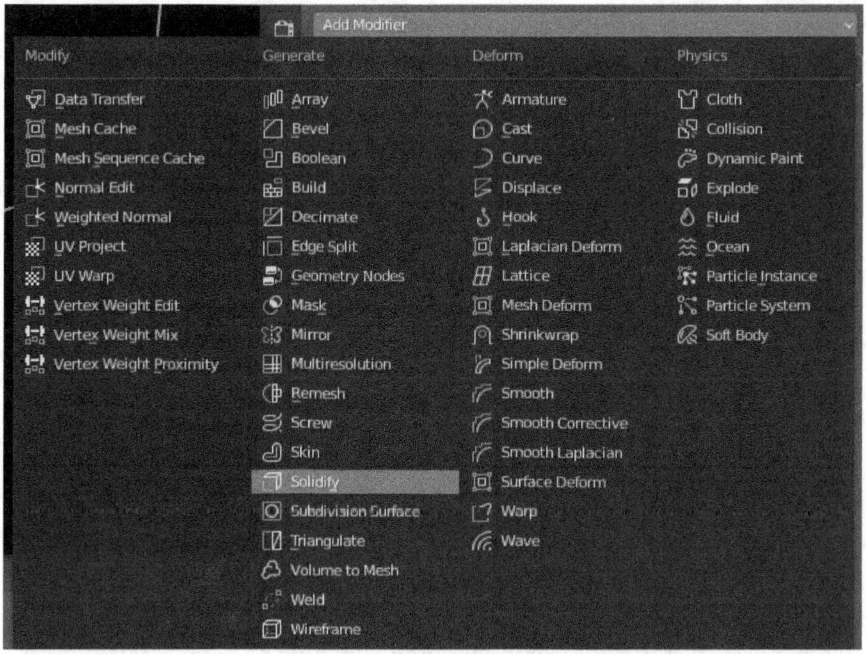

Figure 9.4: Adding a Solidify modifier

4. Change **Thickness** to -2m.

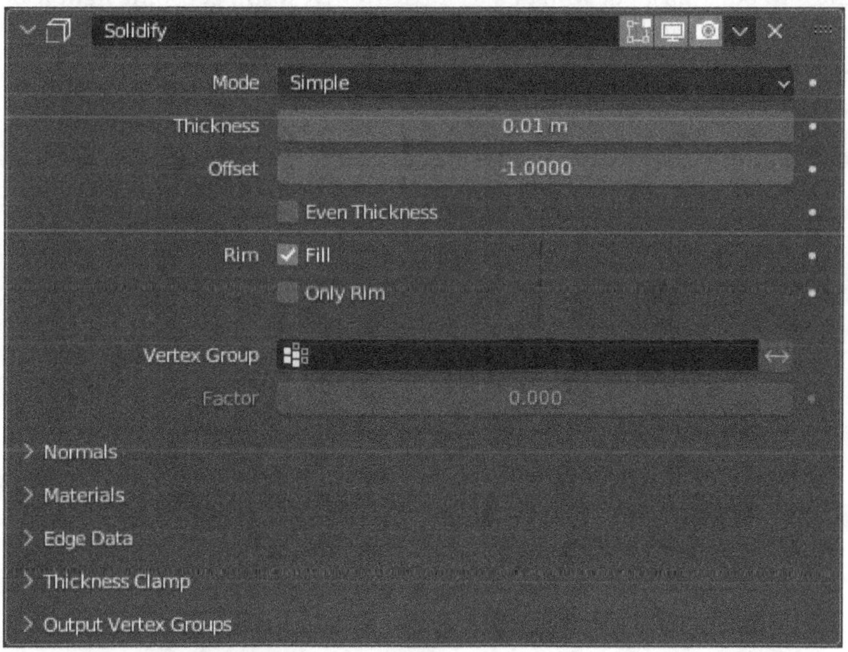

Figure 9.5: Changing Thickness

5. As you can see now, our scene no longer has light leaking in through the geometry.

Figure 9.6: No more light leak!

We've solved the problem... but looking at the scene, we've added really thick walls to the outside of the hangar, which might not be what we want. Let's try the other fix for this problem and see if we can stop light leaking without changing our geometry quite as much:

1. Let's dial back our **Solidify** modifier to `-0.33`. This should give us a little extra thickness to our walls, but won't be as intrusive. We'll still get some light leakage, but we'll see if we can improve on that with some light settings.

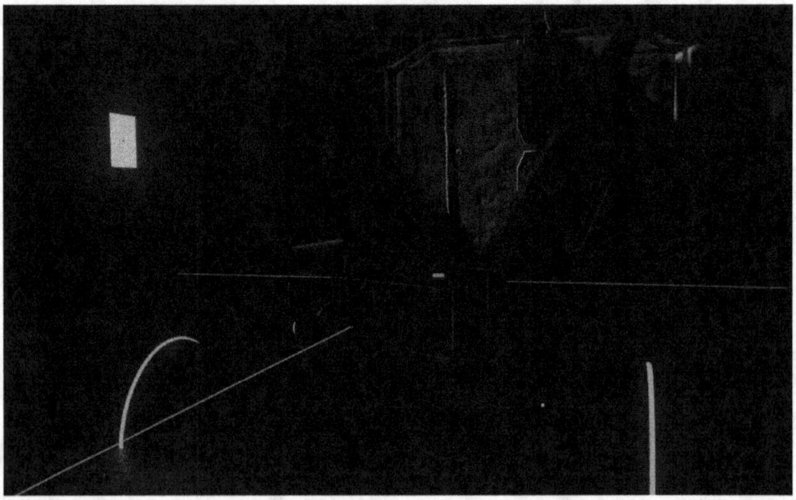

Figure 9.7: Trying another method

2. Go to the **Render** properties on the right-hand toolbar and scroll down to the **Shadows** section.

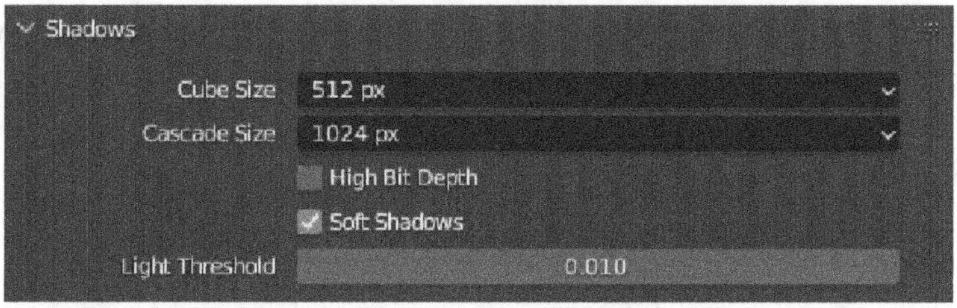

Figure 9.8: Changing the Shadows properties

3. Check **High Bit Depth**. **High Bit Depth** will increase the amount of memory we need to use for the scene, so use it with caution. But it will also decrease any shadow artifacts that might be appearing in our scene, which is exactly what we want.
   You may not notice a difference after checking **High Bit Depth**, but it also might increase the accuracy of your shadows. This will vary from scene to scene.
4. Now change **Cascade Size** to **4096 px**. This will only affect sun lights, so be aware of that. Once you have changed **Cascade Size**, you should immediately notice that the light leaking disappears. Of course, this immediately starts to use more memory for our scene, so again, only use this if you know your computer can handle it.

Either solidifying your geometry or changing the **Shadows** settings will stop light leakage fairly well. The last way to fix this problem is the most simple: delete the sun light! Since we don't have any windows in our hangar, we can create more precise and interesting lighting with a more custom solution and not have to worry about light leaking. Therefore we can just delete it. I went back and changed **Cascade Size** back to **1024 px** and unchecked **High Bit Depth** to save on some memory. A handy tip for the **Render** panel as you are experimenting with different values is the **Reset to Default Value** shortcut. You can right-click on a value in the **Render** panel and select **Reset to Default Value** and the value will be restored to its initial setting.

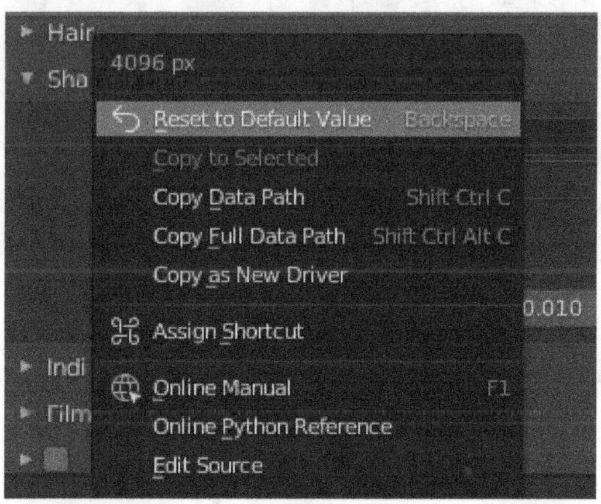

Figure 9.9: Reset the values back to the default

In this section, we went over a common problem with lighting in EEVEE that you are now well equipped to fix when it crops up in your personal projects. In the next section, we'll add lights and Emission shaders to create some awesome sci-fi lighting for this hangar.

Designing the lighting for our interior

Lighting can be something of an art, but it's also a science. We want to light something so that it looks good, but also so that it makes sense visually. In this section, we're going to add **lights** and **Emission shaders** to the scene and create an amazingly lit render, but we're also going to go through the logic of lighting a scene and how and why you should light an interior in a certain way.

To start lighting the scene, we'll start with the objects in the scene that should be emitting light. On each of the columns on the walls of the hangar, there are lightbulbs. Let's add an **Emission** shader to each lightbulb. We add an **Emission** shader so that the light looks like it's genuinely coming from the lightbulb. After adding the **Emission** shader, we'll add point lights to make light actually project from the lightbulb. Let's get started:

1. Select one of the lightbulbs on the columns.

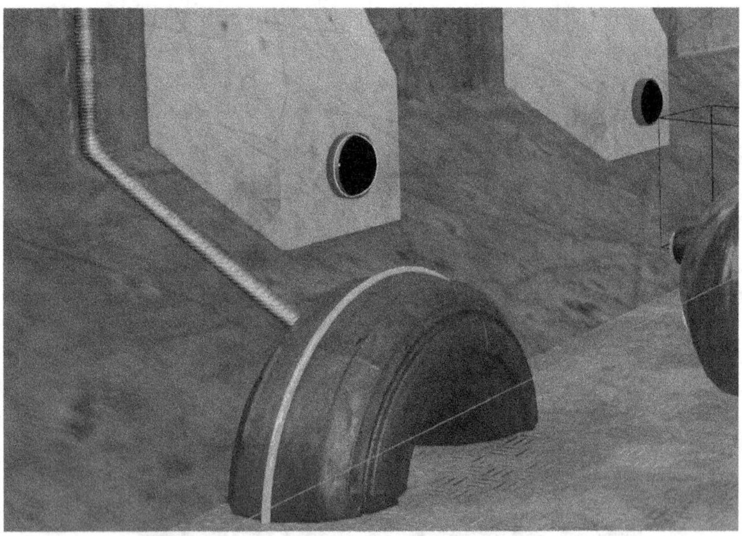

Figure 9.10: Selecting the lightbulb object

2. Go to the **Material Editor** and add a new material to the light by clicking the **New** button.

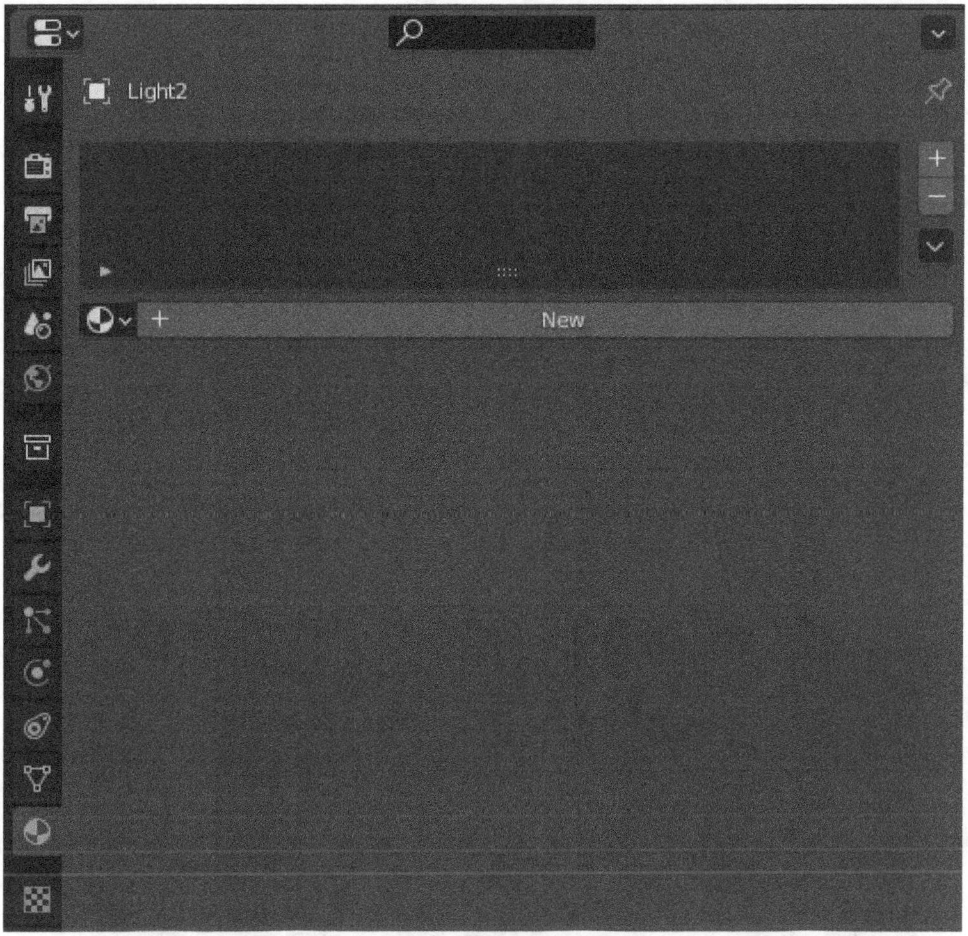

Figure 9.11: The Material Editor

3. Delete the **Principled** shader node that is added by default and add an **Emission** shader instead.

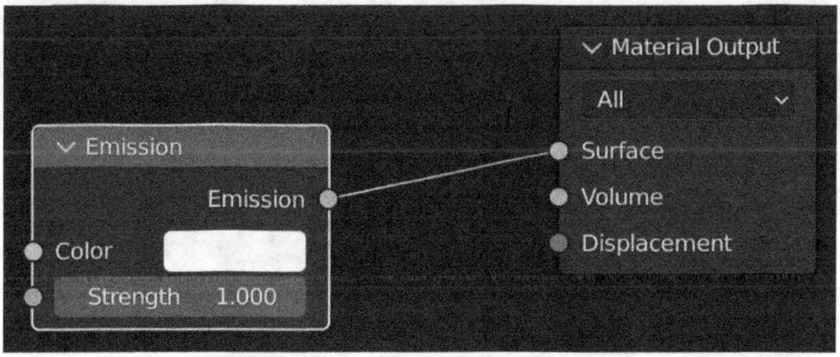

Figure 9.12: Adding an Emission shader

4. I changed my **Emission** shader's **Color** to blue, as I think blue lights will complement the colors I already have in the scene.

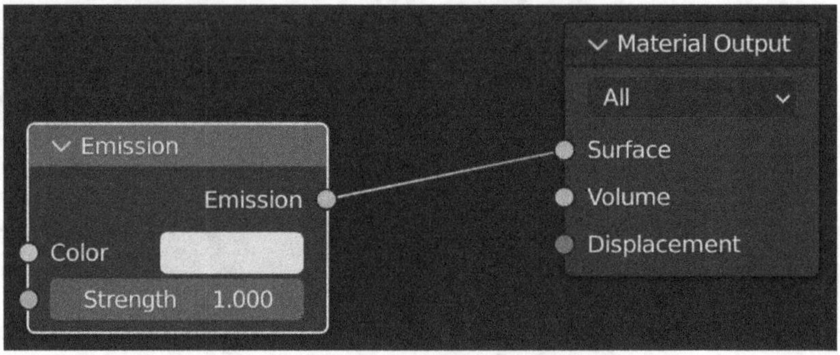

Figure 9.13: Changing the Emission color to blue

5. In rendered mode, you should be able to see light coming from the lightbulb object, but you might notice that it really doesn't project light from the surface of the bulb as a real light might.

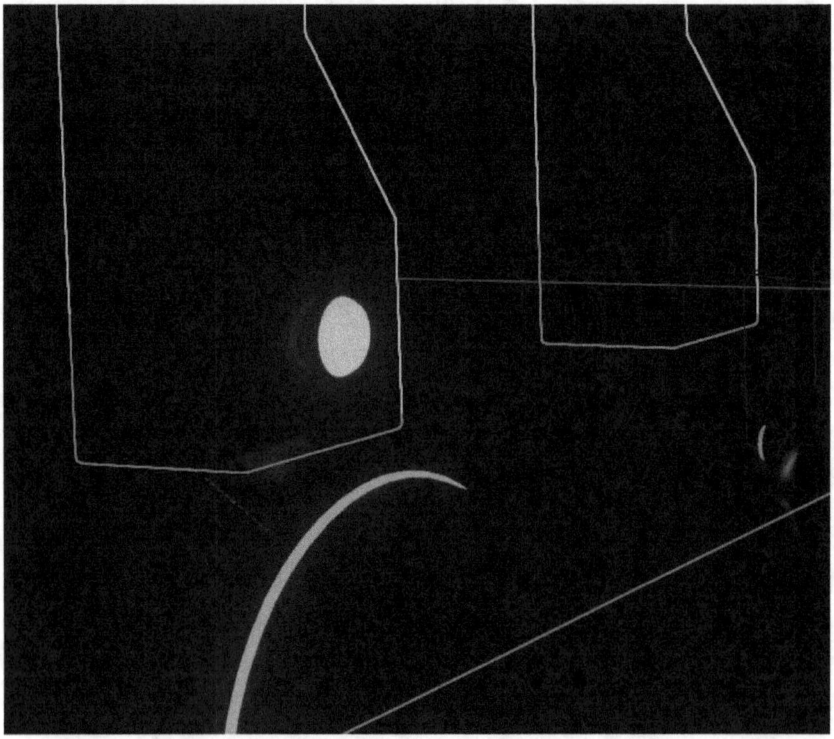

Figure 9.14: Previewing the rendered version of the Emission shader

We can try increasing the **Emission** shader's **Strength** to around `15`. But the color of our light starts to get washed out and it doesn't actually increase the ambient lighting in the scene by much. This is why we need to use a combination of Emission shaders and light objects. Light objects can be added in the **Add** menu (use *Shift* + *A* to open the **Add** menu), as we've done before with the sun light. Light objects do not appear as physical geometry in the scene. Instead, they just emit light depending on the type. The first type of light we'll add is a point light. This point light emits light in all directions from a singular point that is defined by the location of the light.

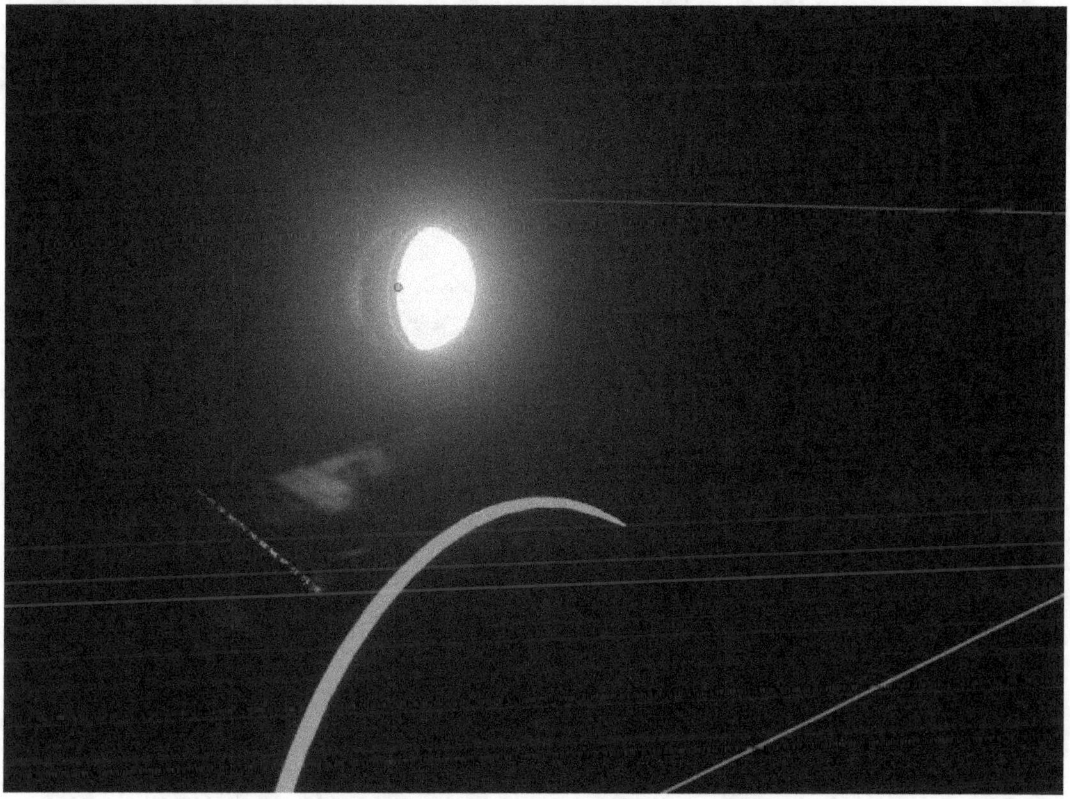

Figure 9.15: Increasing the Emission shader to 15

6. Let's keep our **Emission** shader's **Strength** at around `3` for now. We can also easily apply this **Emission** shader to the other five lightbulbs in our scene by selecting all of the lightbulb objects by holding *Shift* and left-clicking on each one, then, while still holding *Shift*, select the lightbulb that already has the **Emission** shader applied to it. While those six objects (the original light plus the five copies) are still selected, use the shortcut *Ctrl* + *L* to open the **Link** menu. Select **Link Materials** and all of the lightbulbs should now have that material applied to them.

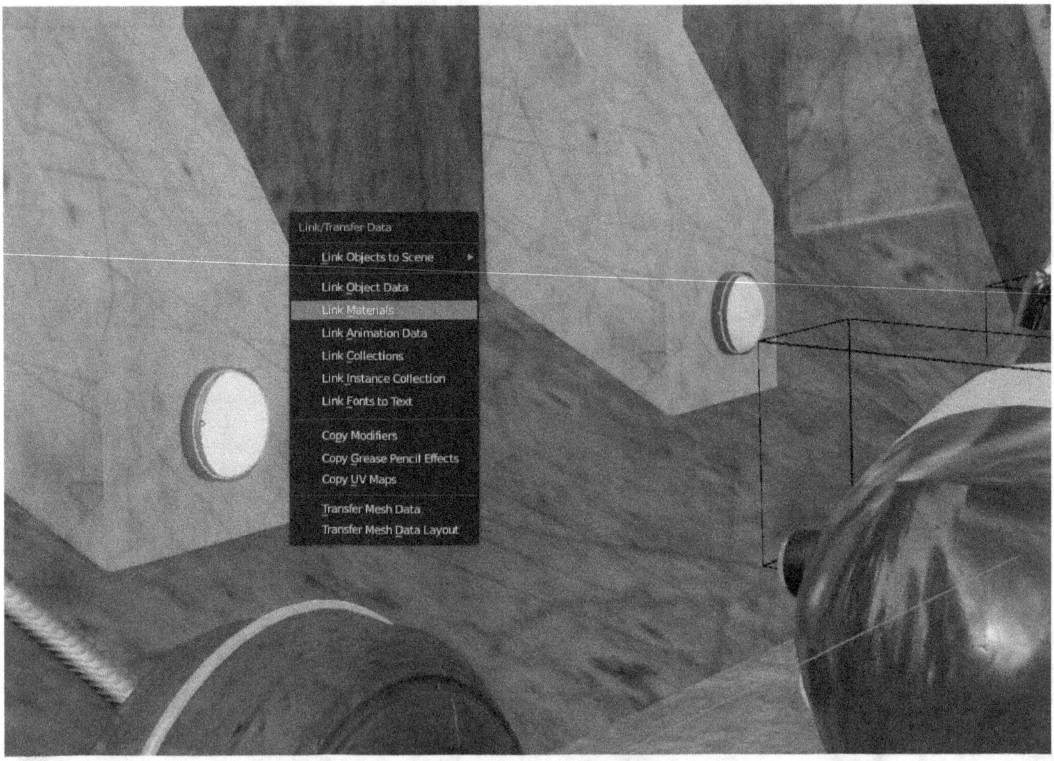

Figure 9.16: Link Materials

The next thing we're going to do is add point lights to each of our lightbulbs in the scene. This should provide some bounced lighting and start to illuminate the scene.

7. Select the lightbulb again and hit *Shift* + *S*. This should bring up the **Cursor** menu. Select the option **Cursor to Selected**.

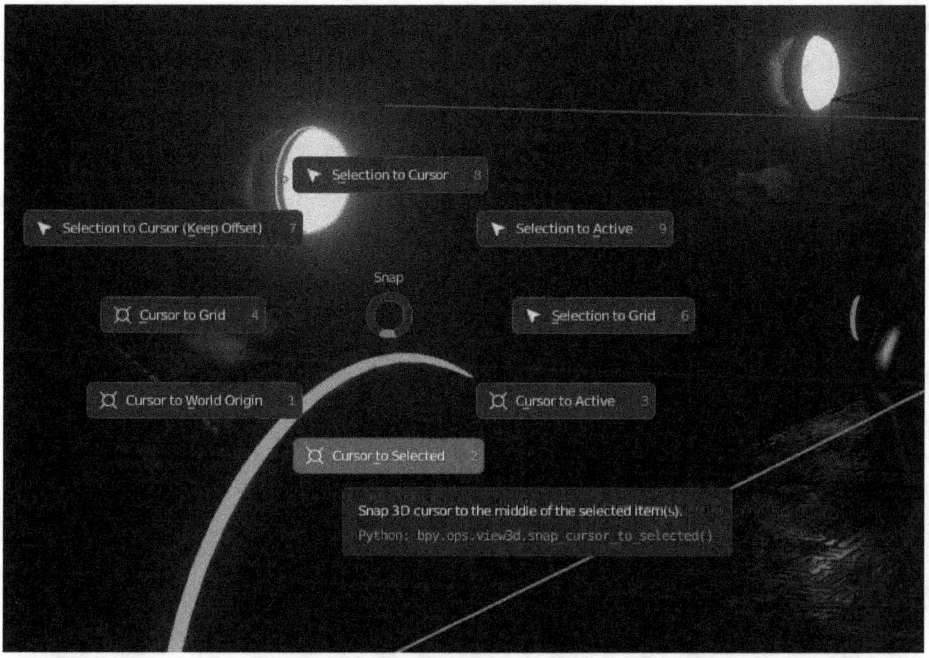

Figure 9.17: Cursor menu options

8. This moves the cursor to the lightbulb and therefore, when we add a point light using *Shift* + *A*, that point light should be added to the location of our lightbulb. Then all we have to do is use the move shortcut *G* and move it along the *X axis* so it's right in front of the lightbulb.

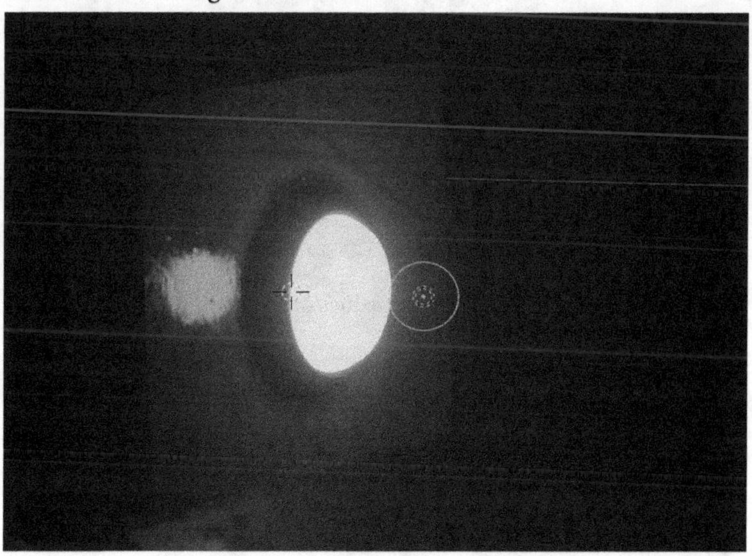

Figure 9.18: Adding the point light

9. While we still have the point light selected, let's go to the **Light** properties, in the right-hand side menu, and change **Power** to **60 W** and **Color** to something closer to the color of the **Emission** shader.

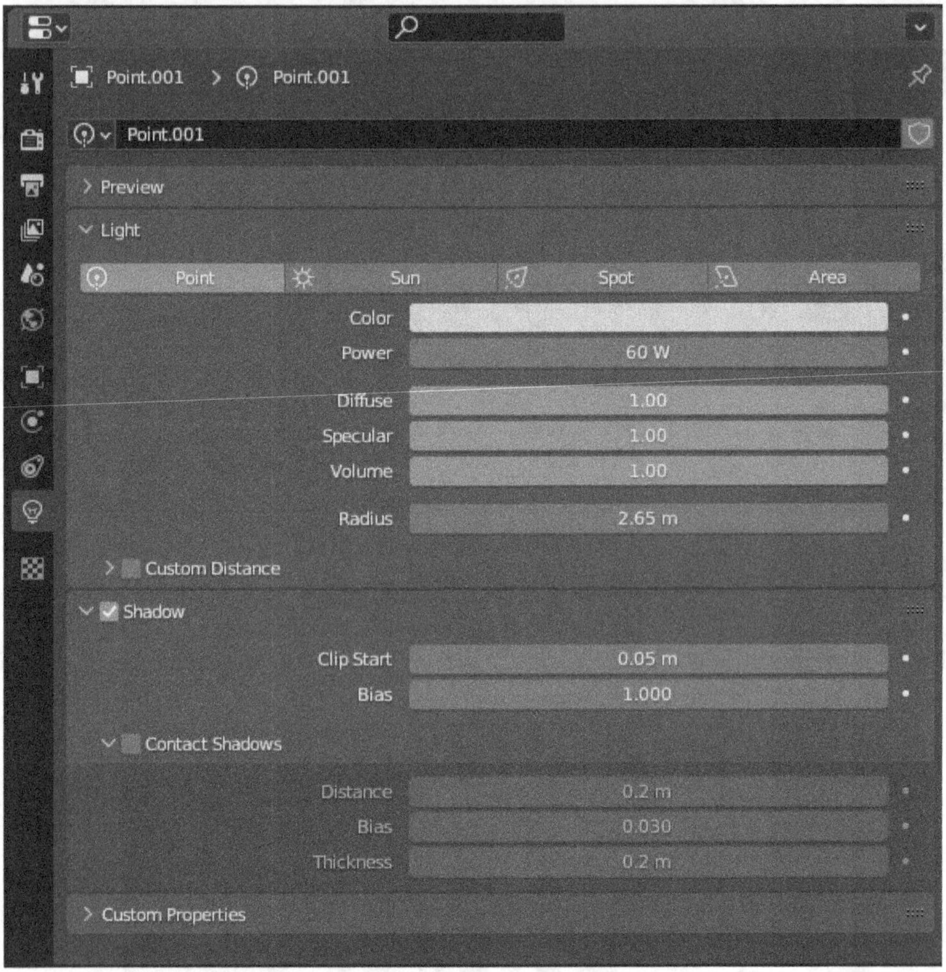

Figure 9.19: Changing the values of the point light

10. Now that we have one point light set up, all we have to do is copy it and place a point light in front of each lightbulb object with an **Emission** shader. With the point light selected, use *Shift* + *D* to duplicate it and then use the *G* key to move each light to roughly a similar position in front of each lightbulb. Do that for every lightbulb in the scene.

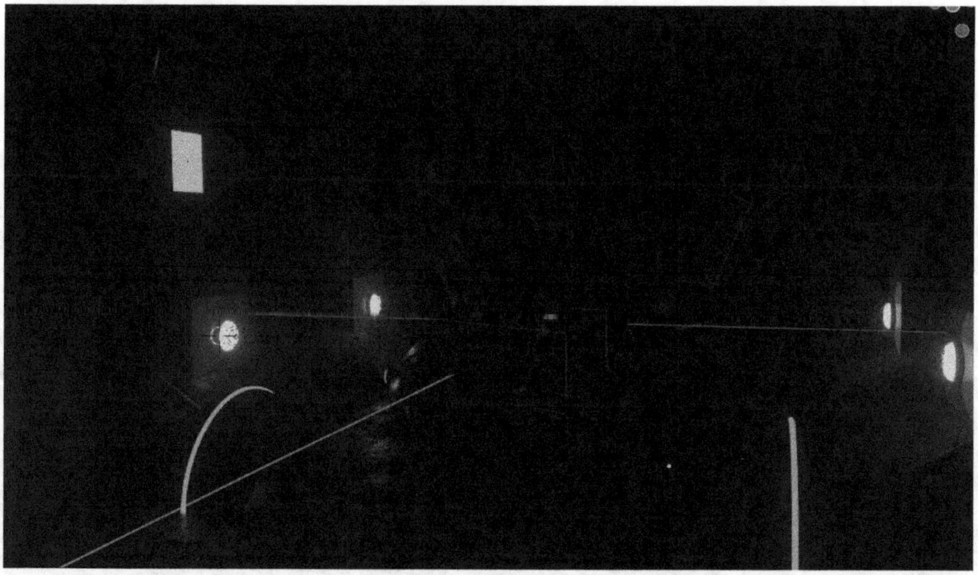

Figure 9.20: Rendered version of the point lights and Emission shader

We now have light that comes from each lightbulb. Next, we need to add lighting that comes from the roof and illuminates the rest of our room. This is a more imaginative usage of lighting. Considering we can't actually see the roof and see the lights, we have to imagine where those lights would be. Interior lighting almost always needs motivation. We saw that with the lightbulbs. In this case, we're thinking most interior spaces have lights on the ceiling, so it makes sense in the scene. If you are ever stuck when lighting a scene, always ask yourself, what makes the most sense? Of course, it's easy to break those rules and still get great artistic results, but in order to break the rules, we first need to know and consider the rules.

Let's move on to adding overhead lighting to the space. This time we'll be using area lights that will cast light from above and make sure our spaceship is easy to see. Area lights are lights that emanate light only in the direction that they are pointed. This means the rotational value of an area light is important, as it informs the direction the light is shining. Let's create some area lights and then edit them so they light the area efficiently:

1. Add an area light using *Shift* + *A* and then move it so it's directly above the cockpit of our spaceship. We can see by the way the line is pointing that our area light is emanating light down towards the spaceship.

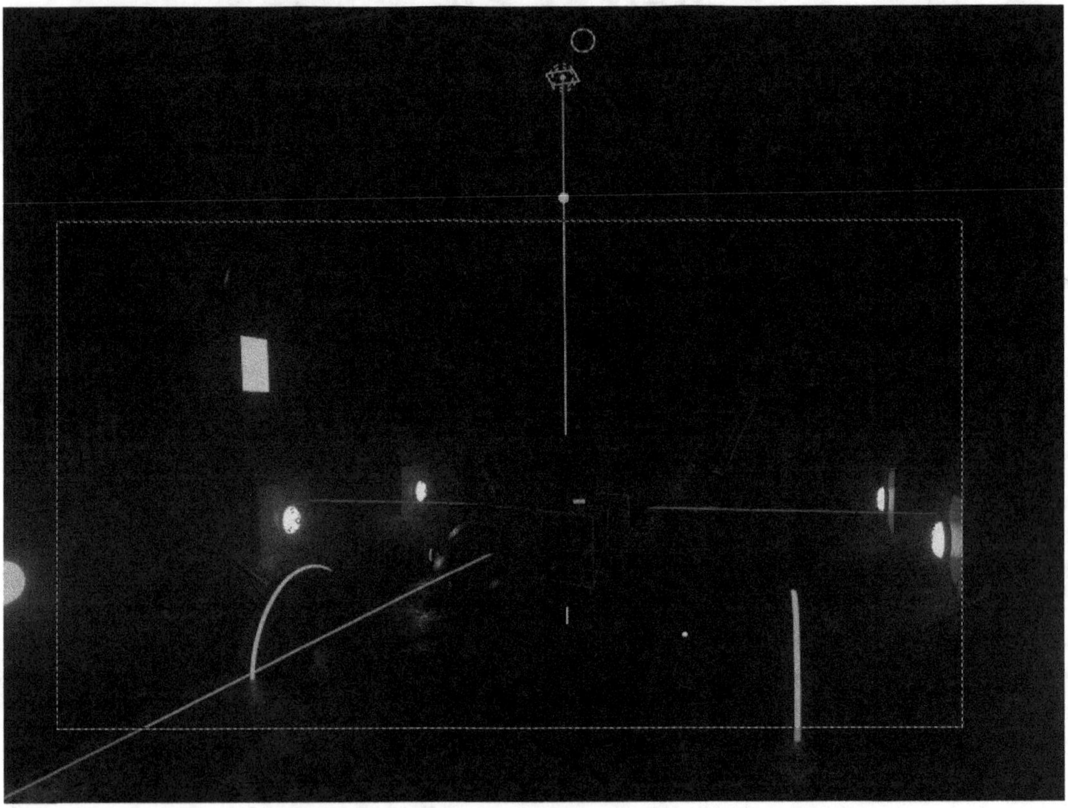

Figure 9.21: Adding an area light

2. It's not casting much light yet, so let's set the power of the light higher. While you still have the area light selected, go to the **Light** properties panel and change **Power** to **500 W**.

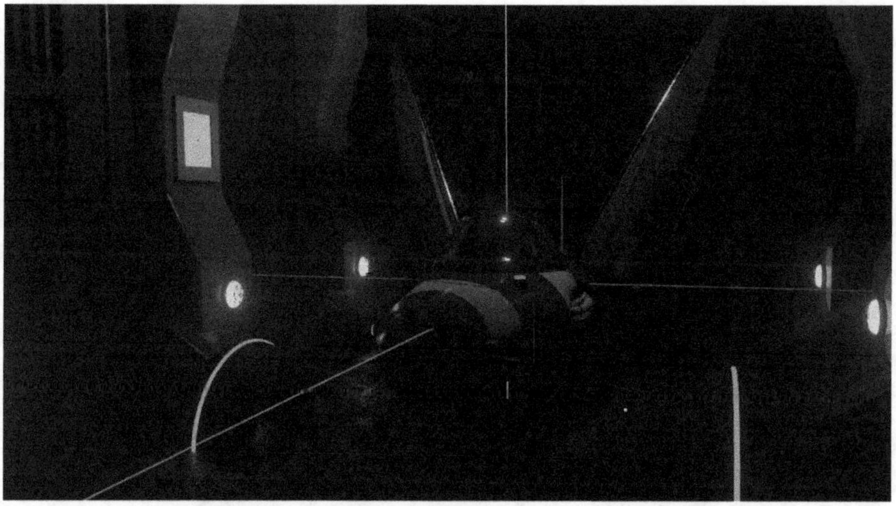

Figure 9.22: Changing the power of the area light

3. We're now starting to get some of the effects we want. In a hangar, there would often be more than one light on the ceiling. Let's duplicate the area light we already have and move it towards the camera so we can see more of the ship.

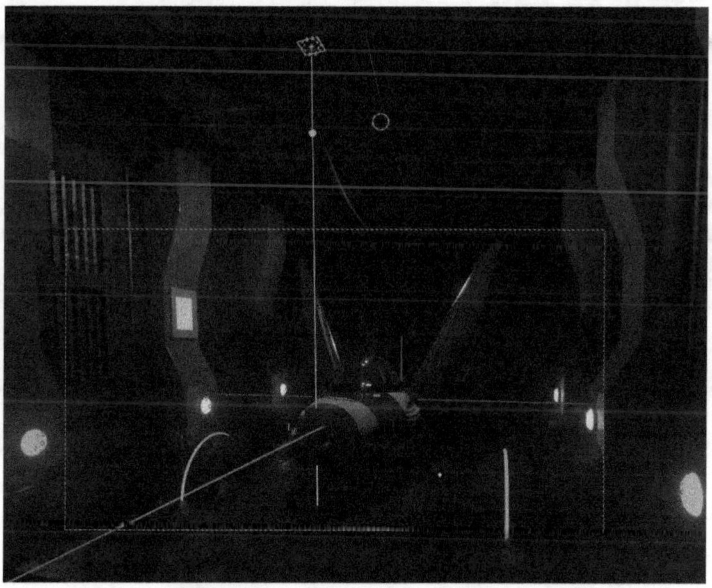

Figure 9.23: Adding more area lights

4. Area lights have two really important settings. One is the **Power** setting, which determines how much light will emanate from the light. The other is **Size**. Try increasing the **Size** setting of the area light we just duplicated.

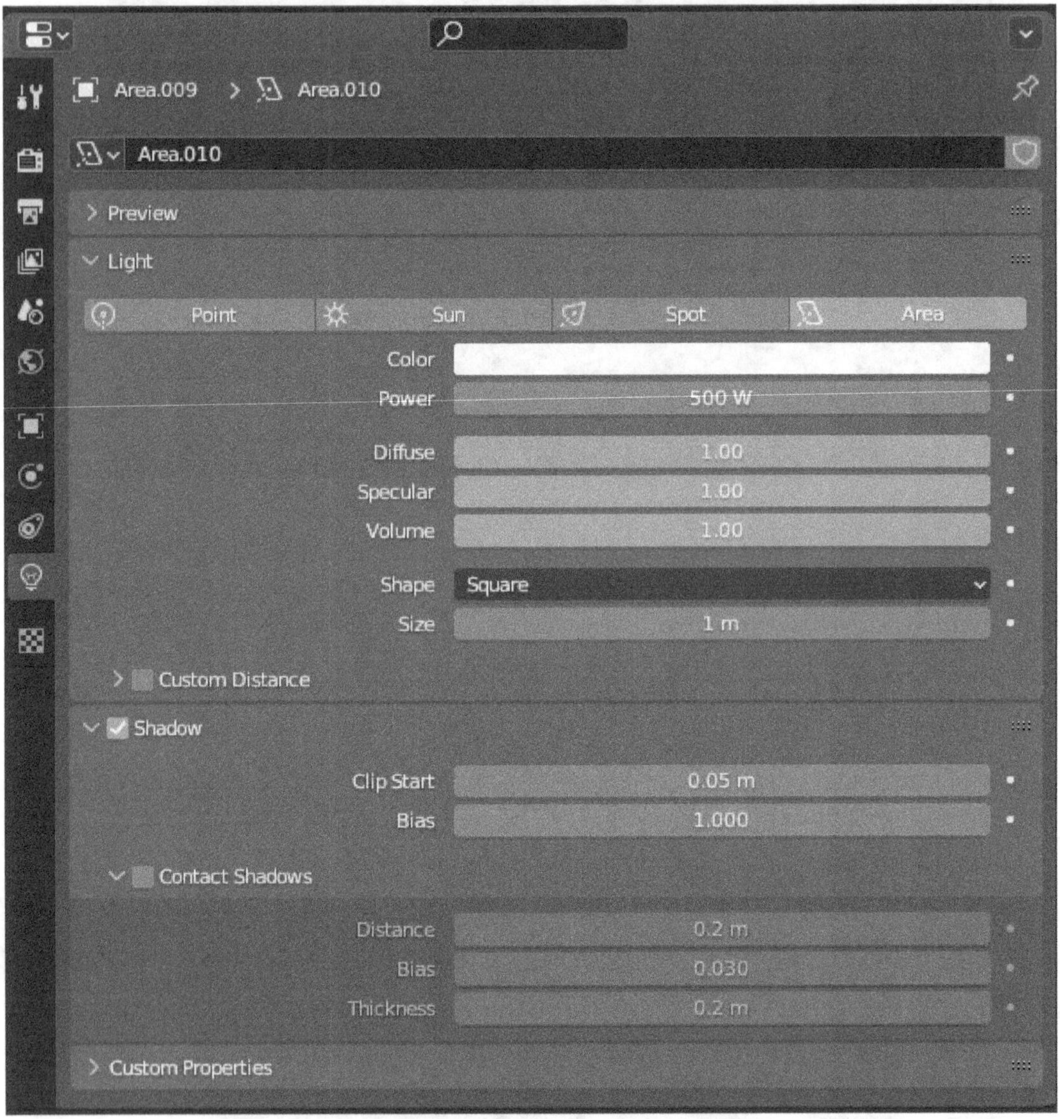

Figure 9.24: Area light values

5. You may notice that the light seems to get weaker, but also less harsh. The main idea to take away from this is that the **Power** setting of the area light is divided by the size of the light. The bigger the light, the less light is concentrated in a certain area. So having a small light with high power will result in a very harsh, highly concentrated light with lots of shadows. A light with the same power but 10 times the size will emit softer light and be less concentrated. I've created an example here to compare visually.

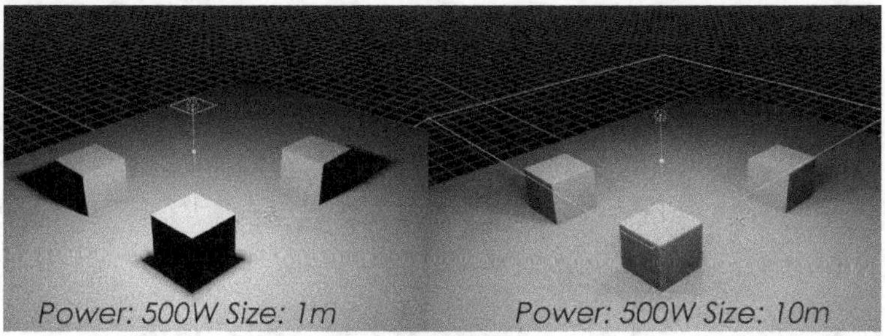

Figure 9.25: Comparing Size values for area lights with the same Power value

6. Let's add four more area lights by using the *Shift* + *D* shortcut to duplicate them and arrange them in a line above our spaceship.

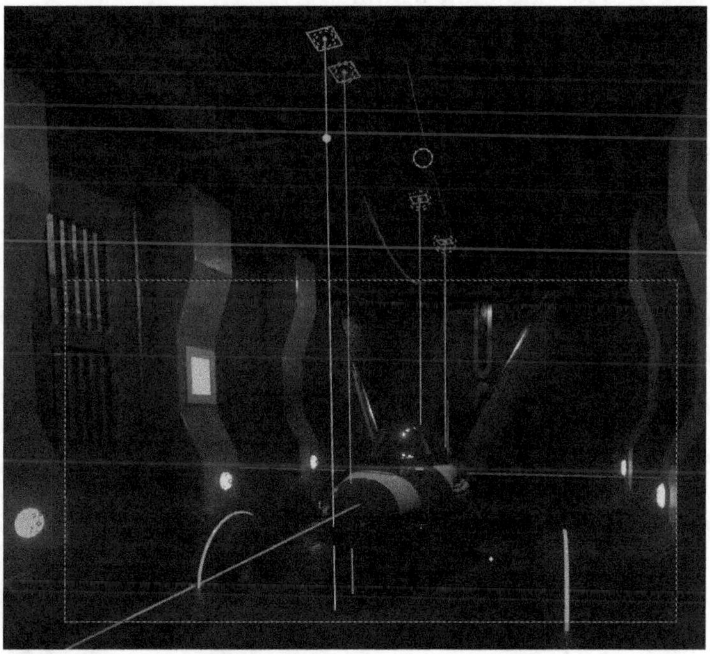

Figure 9.26: Adding more lights

Let's look at our result so far...

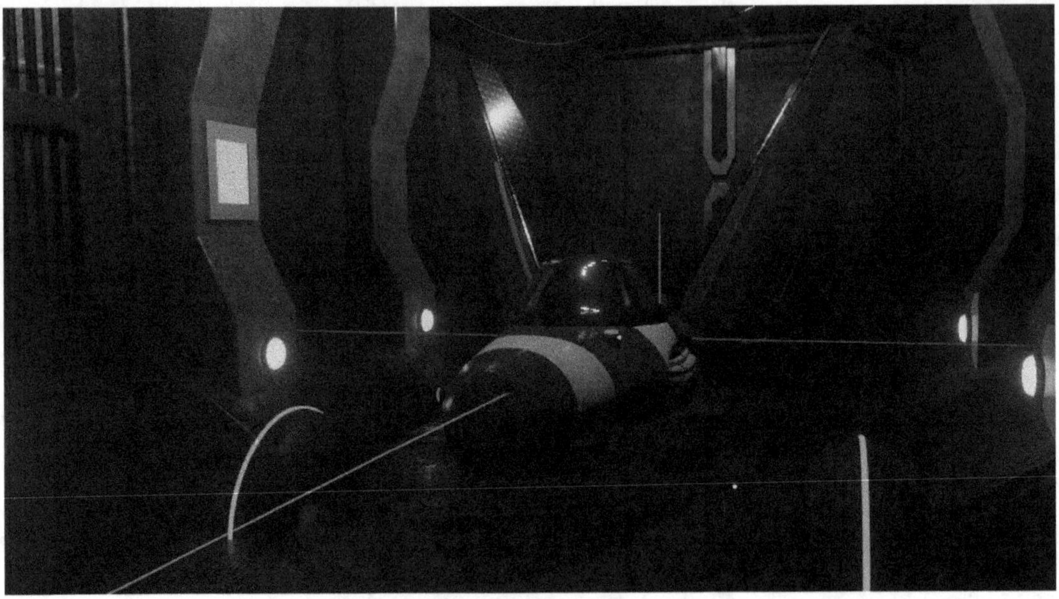

Figure 9.27: Result of our lighting so far

I think we have made a good start to the lighting!

In this section, we learned about using **Emission** shaders, the difference between point lights and area lights, and how to go about planning the lighting of an interior scene. In the next section, we'll briefly touch on previewing **Render passes** in EEVEE and how to use that to inform your lighting.

Previewing render passes to inform our lighting decisions

It can be very valuable to be able to preview sections of a render before we render it. It saves us a ton of time and energy and will also result in a better product. There's a really cool feature built into EEVEE that allows us to see individual render passes in real time that can help inform our decisions when lighting a scene. Let's activate a different **Render Pass**:

1. Make sure you're in **Rendered Shading** mode.

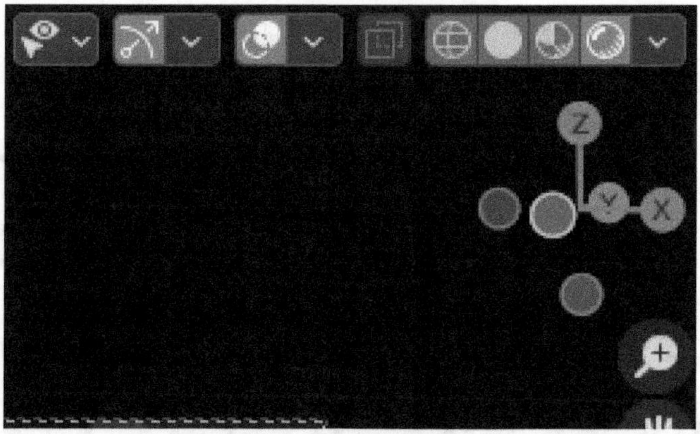

Figure 9.28: Rendered Shading mode option selected

2. In the top-right corner, you'll see a drop-down arrow, right next to the **Viewport Shading** options. Click on the down arrow:

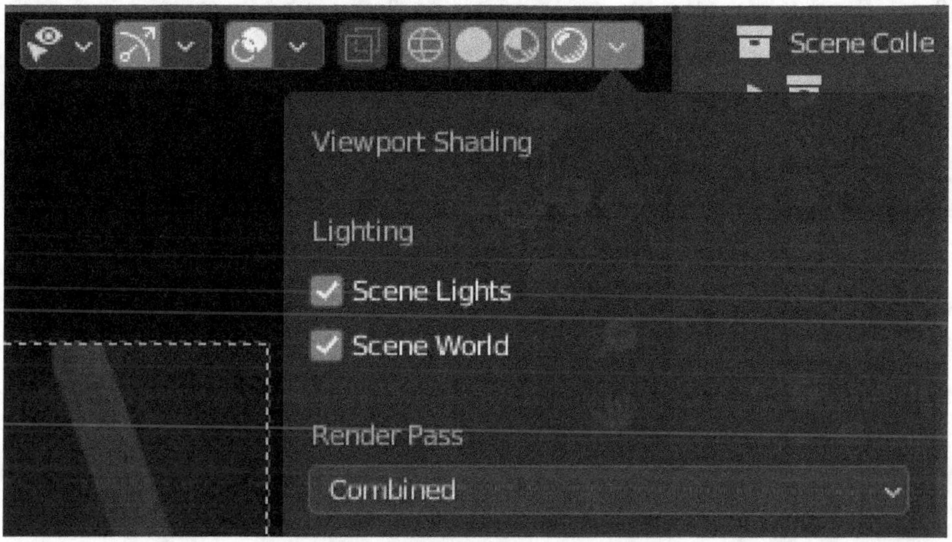

Figure 9.29: Dropdown for Viewport Shading

3. Click on the **Render Pass** dropdown and select the **Shadow** pass.

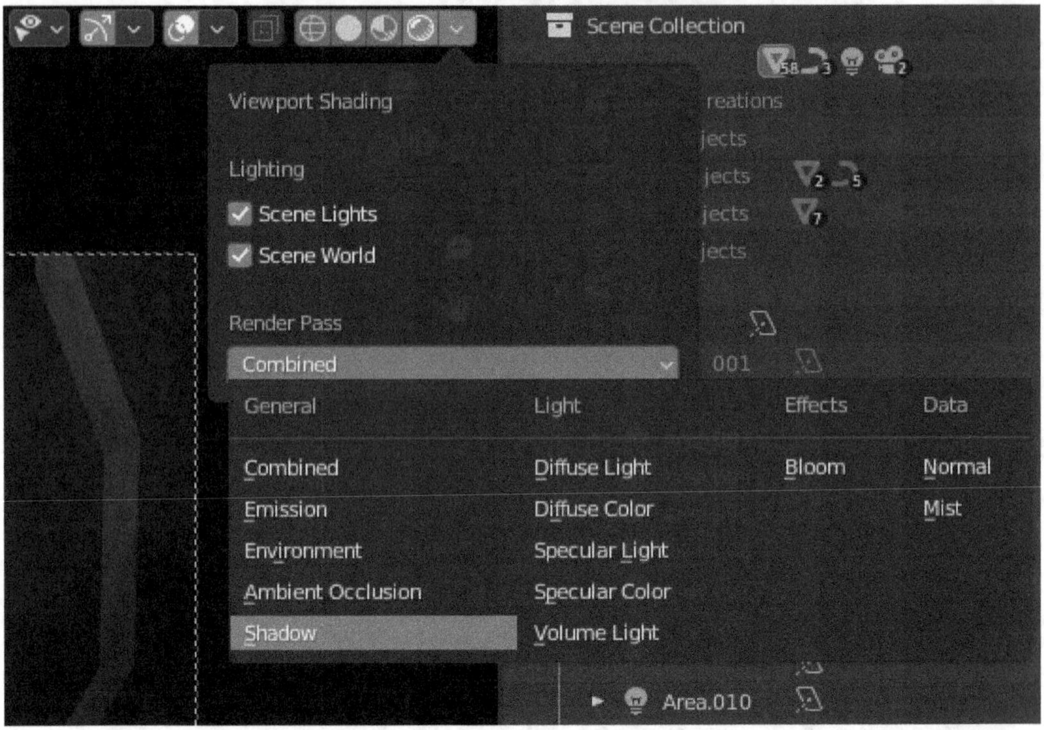

Figure 9.30: Changing to the Shadow render pass

4. We can immediately see *only* lighting information, without all the colors and materials we added.

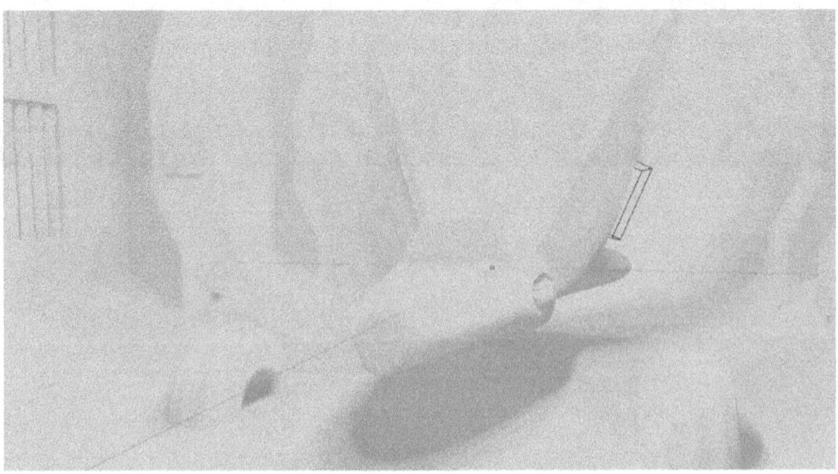

Figure 9.31: Result of the shadow pass

On the surface, this might not seem extremely valuable, but if you think about it, being able to look at only lighting information without being distracted by color or texture can be hugely helpful. You could design your entire lighting system in this mode, to get the exact right mixture of soft, sharp, and ambient lighting. It can also be valuable to explore the other render pass modes, such as **Mist**, **Emission**, and **Normal**. Take some time to experiment with the lights we just added and see how they affect the overall composition and framing of the spaceship. To change back to the normal view, select the **Combined** option. These passes are all available to render out as separate passes by going to the **View Layer** settings in the **Properties** panel and checking any render pass you might need to have as a separate render.

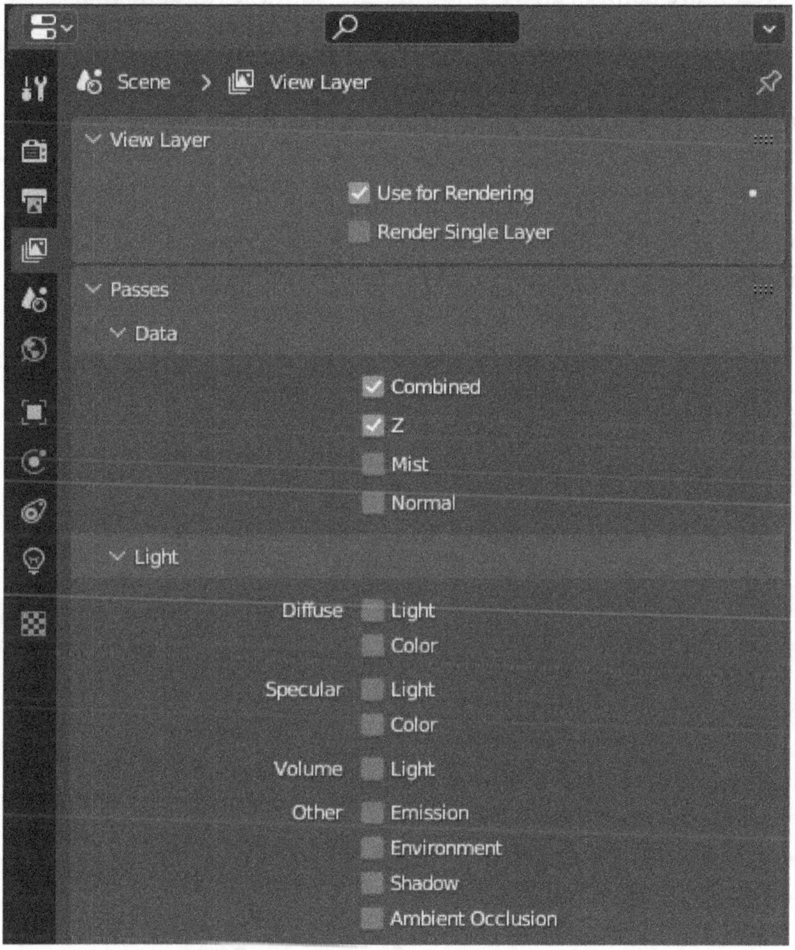

Figure 9.32: Render passes available

The render pass preview option can greatly inform your overall compositing process and lead to less time spent in rendering.

Summary

Lighting an interior scene can be a lot more difficult than an exterior scene, which is why we took the opportunity in this chapter to design the lighting and make sure our spaceship is looking the best it possibly can. Lighting is a major factor in creating an amazing scene. Often, good lighting is not even noticed, but bad lighting can completely destroy an otherwise fantastic scene. Practice creating lighting that shows off your scenes the best, and you'll slowly come to understand why lighting is one of the most important but underrated skills in the CG world. The lighting I have chosen in this scene is not the only way you could light the scene. Try experimenting with other lights in different places and create an even more complicated scene building on these fundamentals.

In this chapter, we did some troubleshooting to fix light leaking; discovered how to light an interior shot; added Emission shaders, point lights, and area lights to design the lighting for our spaceship's hangar; and then briefly touched on how to preview render passes to light a scene or to see how a pass will turn out before rendering it. At this point, you should understand how to create interesting lighting and how to use the motivation of a specific scene to add lights logically and artistically.

In the next chapter, we're going to use a different variety of light probe, called Irradiance Volume objects, to add more precision to the lighting, as well as baking some of the lighting we have to give us better real-time rendering capabilities.

10

Working with Irradiance Volumes and Cubemaps for More Accurate Rendering

Now that we've started a scene and we have the lighting set up, you may have noticed some lighting-related irregularities in the scene. Or you may not have. Honestly, EEVEE straight out of the box does a great job with approximating the lighting we're using and should already give us a great result. But sometimes it makes sense to push the boundaries of realism and we need something to look just that much more real. We have already seen this in action when we used the reflection probe in *Chapter 6, Screen Space Reflections – Adding Reflection to the Water*. We used a **Light probe** to tell EEVEE that we wanted to spend more time and energy processing the reflection on our lake because it was important to the scene. In the scene we will work on this chapter, we don't have a lake that we want to be rendered with greater accuracy, but we do have an interior scene. An interior scene, in a traditional render engine, will have the light that is bouncing off the objects, interior walls, and other obstacles, which can create more noise in a ray-tracing render engine like Cycles. In a **real-time rendering engine** like EEVEE, we have to add back some of the subtle bounced lighting that would happen in an interior scene with an **Irradiance Volume** probe.

An **Irradiance Volume** is a tool that we can use to integrate indirect lighting into a scene and therefore create a more realistic render, sacrificing some of the speed that EEVEE affords us. In this chapter, we will use an Irradiance Volume probe to calculate some of the bounced (indirect) lighting for the spaceship hangar and then go through some of the overall functionality and tweaking that can be done to get a better result. The other light probe that we will talk about in this chapter, but to a lesser degree, is the **Reflection Cubemap**. The Reflection Cubemap will result in a similar output as **Screen Space Reflections**, but it will only be localized to the area that the Reflection Cubemap is placed. This can be used if you want reflectivity in an area, but not in the entire scene. The processing gain (how easily the computer can calculate our scene) on using a Reflection Cubemap over using Screen Space Reflections is negligible, so there's not a lot of reasons to use the Cubemap over screen space functionality for most situations. But I'm sure at least once in your career you'll find a reason to use the Reflection Cubemap, so therefore we should go over it for that point in the future when you need it.

In this chapter, we will look at the following topics:

- Implementing an Irradiance Volume
- Implementing a Reflection Cubemap

Technical requirements

Download `Chapter 10-Start.blend` to start working on this chapter, or carry on from your own file we worked on in *Chapter 9, Lighting an Interior Scene*. This chapter will only use features native to Blender, so doesn't require any outside files or add ons.

Download the `Chapter 10-Start.blend` file from here: `https://github.com/PacktPublishing/Shading-Lighting-and-Rendering-with-Blender-s-EEVEE-/tree/main/Chapter10`.

Implementing an Irradiance Volume

In this section, we're going to implement an Irradiance Volume probe, which allows us to more accurately calculate the bounced lighting within our hangar. When EEVEE rasterizes lighting, it approximates the overall lighting. When we use an Irradiance Volume probe, we're telling EEVEE to calculate the light that bounces from different surfaces and create more accurate occlusion. This gets us a better result. As you can imagine, an Irradiance Volume probe is better utilized in an indoor situation where light is more likely to be bounced between objects and kept inside of a room. Let's get started and add an Irradiance Volume probe to the scene and then tune our results:

1. To add an Irradiance Volume probe to the Scene, use *Shift* + *A* to navigate to the **Light Probe** section and select **Irradiance Volume**.

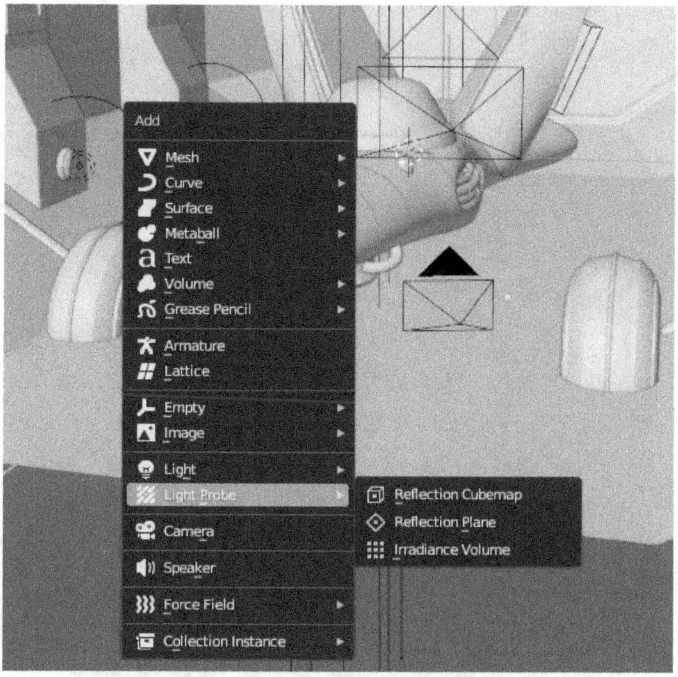

Figure 10.1: Adding an Irradiance Volume probe

2. Make the **Irradiance Volume** probe big enough to encompass our entire hangar.

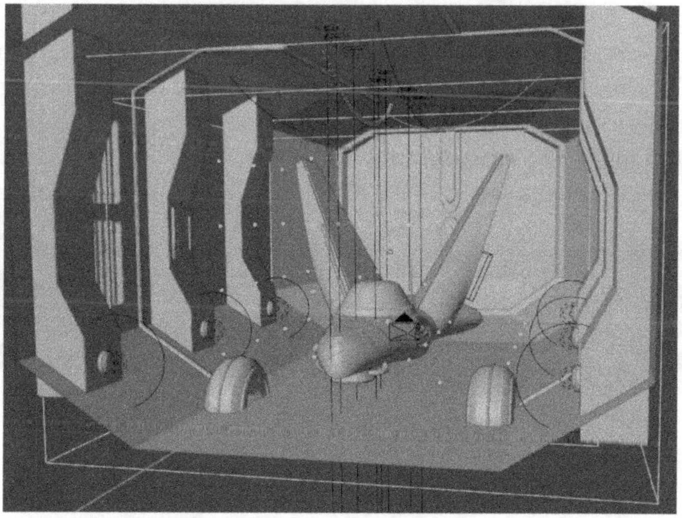

Figure 10.2: Sizing up the Irradiance Volume

3. With the **Irradiance Volume** probe still selected, navigate to the **Probe** setting in the right-hand side **Properties** menu:

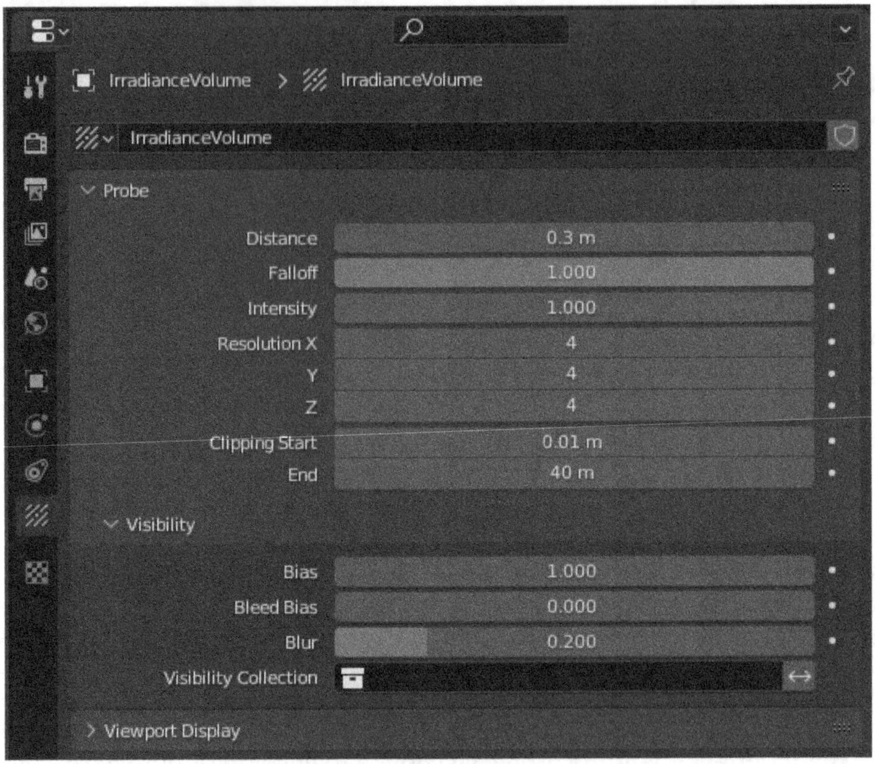

Figure 10.3: Irradiance Volume Probe options

- The most important property is **Resolution**. The **Resolution** number is the number of probes that are added to the volume. More probes mean more accurate lighting, but a slower bake time. **Resolution** is shown visually as the number of points. Try changing **Resolution** to `5` and see how it adds more points to the volume. Each represents one probe point from the **Irradiance Volume** probe.

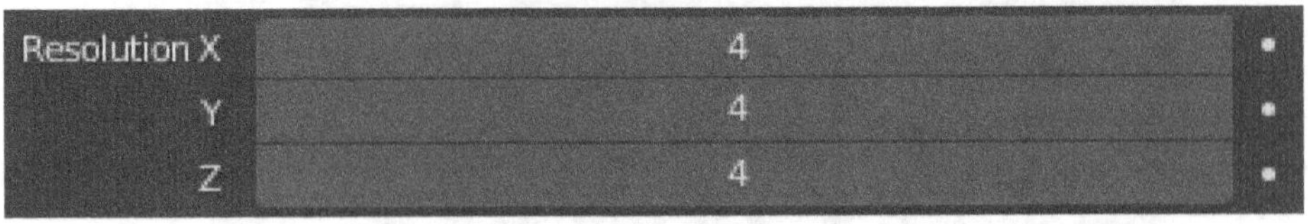

Figure 10.4: Resolution parameters

- **Distance** is the influence distance of the probe. The outer box (the larger box in *Figure 10.5*) is the end of the decay distance of the effect. The inner box (the smaller box in *Figure 10.5*) is the start of the decay zone. Anything inside of the inner box (where the probe points are) is 100% affected by the probe. The area outside the inner box, but inside the outer box lessens in effect in accordance with the **Falloff** value, reaching zero at the lower limits of the outer box.

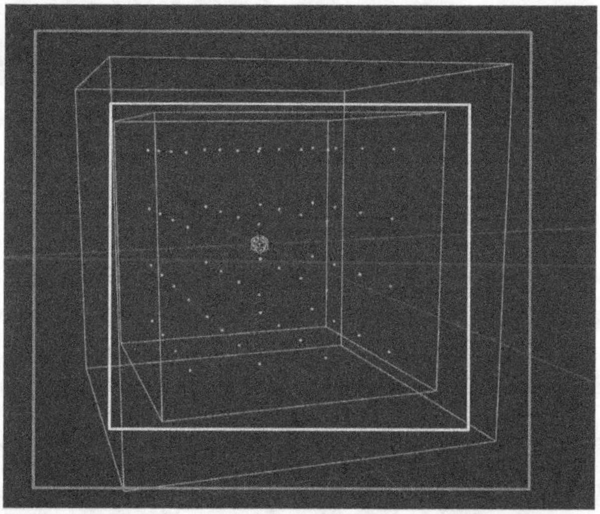

Figure 10.5: Difference between the inner and outer box

- Changing the **Falloff** value changes how fast the effect decays from 100% to 0. This is visualized by the distance between the inner box and the outer box.

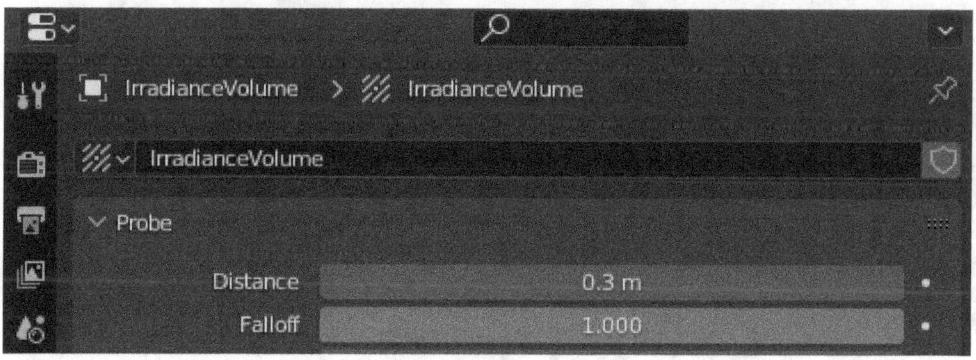

Figure 10.6: Distance and Falloff values

- The **Clipping** values can be used to change the distance at which the effect of the volume is clipped. You can use these to limit the lights that are being calculated in the Irradiance Volume probe, say if you had a light you wanted to exclude from the volume.

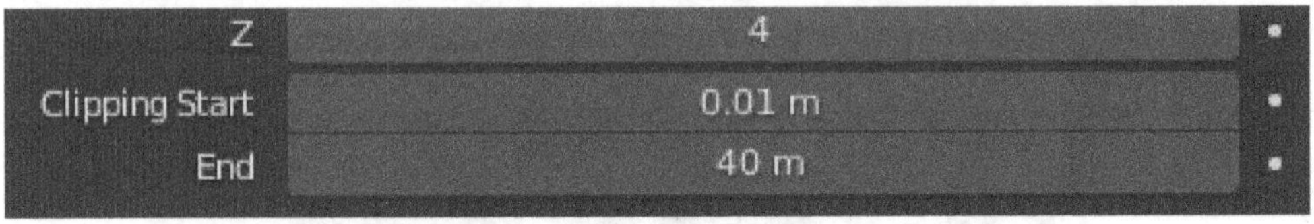

Figure 10.7: Clipping parameters

Feel free to try different things and learn what each value affects for yourself. The values in *Figure 10.3* are the ones I've used. Once we've tweaked all the settings for the Irradiance Volume, we need to go to the **Render** properties.

4. The first thing we're going to do in the **Render** properties is to make sure the **Ambient Occlusion** option in the scene is turned on, and that **Bent Normals** is activated. This makes sure that the lighting is sampled from the direction that has the fewest obstacles, ensuring that the lighting will appear more realistic.

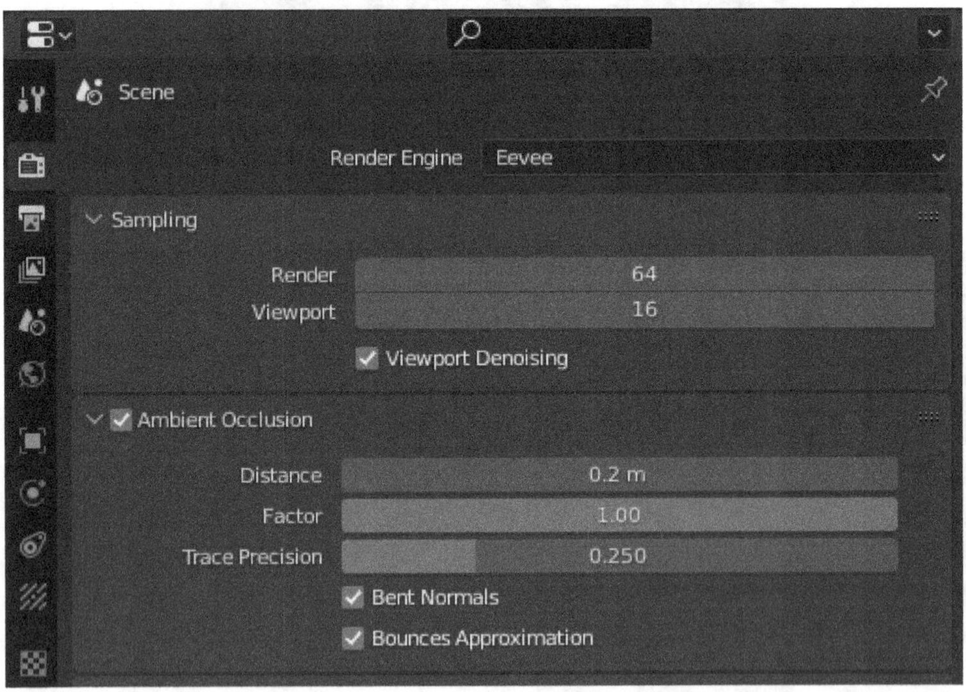

Figure 10.8: Activating Ambient Occlusion

5. Then scroll down to the **Indirect Lighting** section. Make sure you have saved recently, as there is a chance of Blender crashing, and then click the **Bake Indirect Lighting** button. This should take a couple of minutes, depending on how good your computer is. While baking it might seem like Blender is not responding, but give it some time to work through the bake.

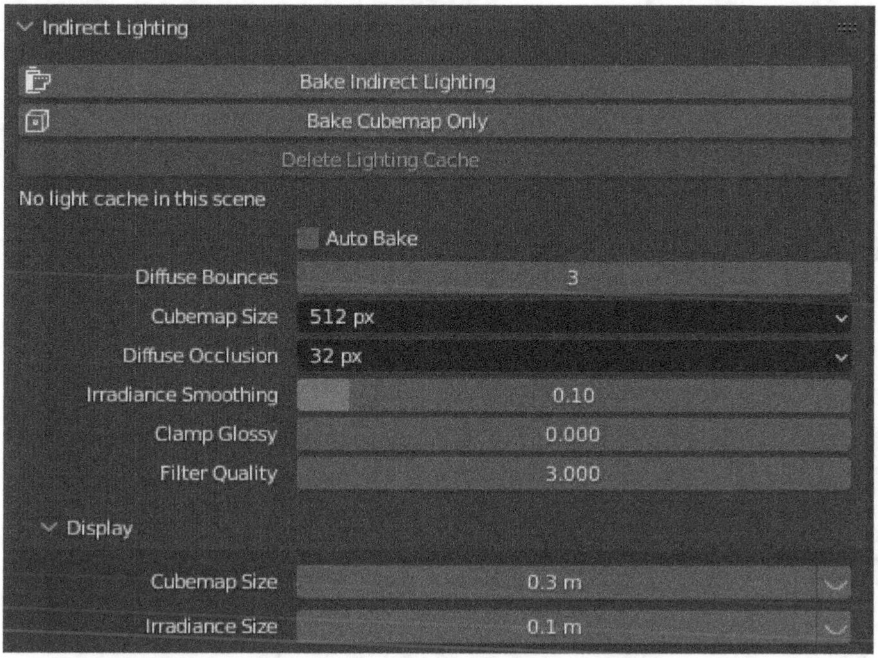

Figure 10.9: Render properties Indirect Lighting section

If you find your results less than satisfying, troubleshooting **Indirect Lighting** is fairly straightforward:

1. Firstly, probe points should be put in areas with geometry present. Try not to put the probe resolution points in empty areas, as you are then using processing power for spaces that don't need processing.
2. Use multiple Irradiance Volume probes. Small probes will always be calculated first, so if you have problem areas, or areas that have many models and lights, try putting a smaller, high-resolution cube in the problem area for better-baked lighting.
3. Another option to try is changing **Cubemap Size** in the **Indirect Lighting** section. Changing it to `1024` or `2048` should increase the resolution of the baked lighting. Also, remember this will increase the baking time.
4. It can also help to increase **Diffuse Bounces** to `5` or `6` to get more accurate light bouncing.

Baking the indirect lighting means that we're calculating the light only once – when we choose to bake. Every time we move in the viewport, EEVEE usually has to recalculate the lighting. Baking means that we decide when to calculate indirect lighting and we only have to wait for it to compute once. Then the lighting is cached and EEVEE doesn't need to spend resources on recalculating it. If we do happen to make changes to the lighting or layout of the scene, we will need to re-bake the lighting, so it is advisable to only bake the lighting when you're close to completing the scene. Look at the scene before adding the Irradiance Volume:

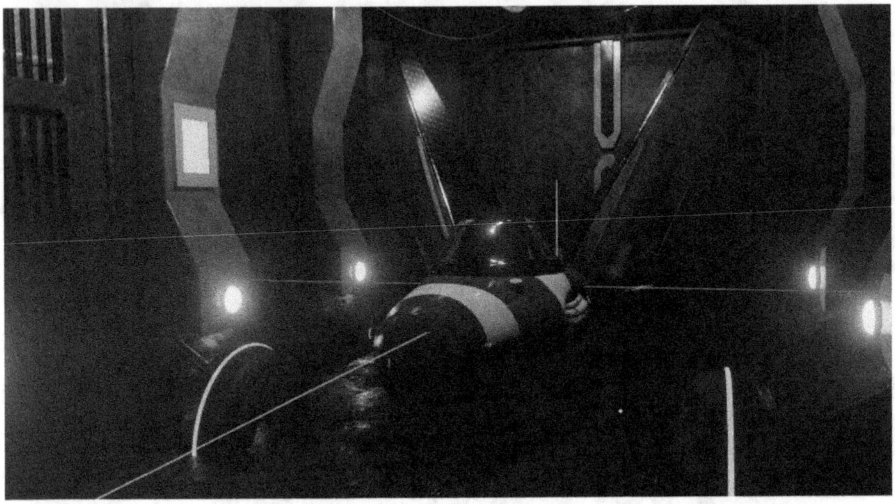

Figure 10.10: Before the Irradiance Volume

And this is the scene after adding the Irradiance Volume probe:

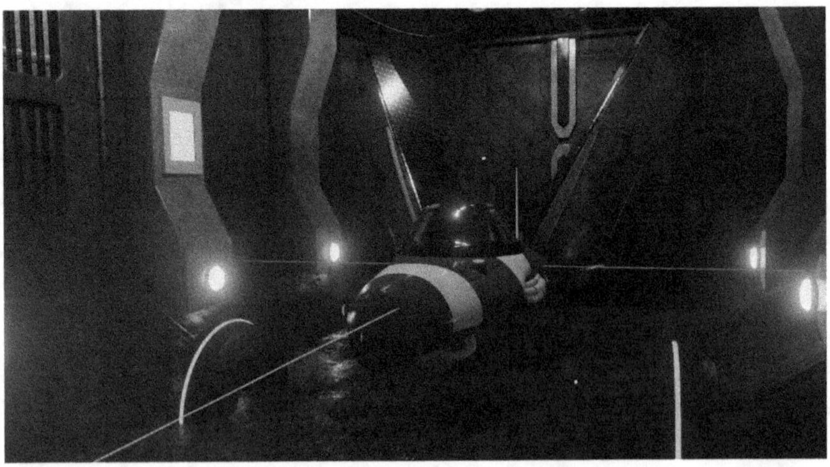

Figure 10.11: After the Irradiance Volume

You'll notice the differences are subtle, but very obvious if you look closely. The area under the spaceship is now more illuminated as light is bouncing from the underside of the ship to the floor. We can now see the thruster and pipe underneath. It's subtle but could make all the difference in adding realism to the render.

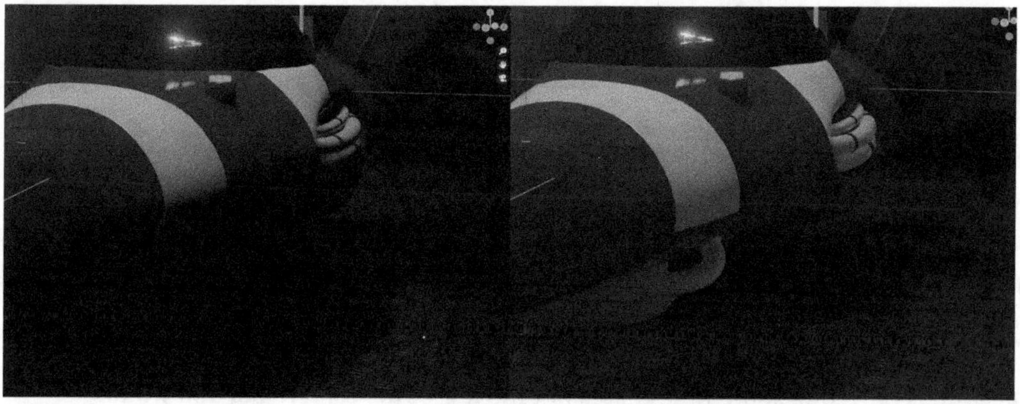

Figure 10.12: Close up of the Irradiance Volume before and after

As you can see, the underside of the ship is much more visible in the after (right-side) photo.

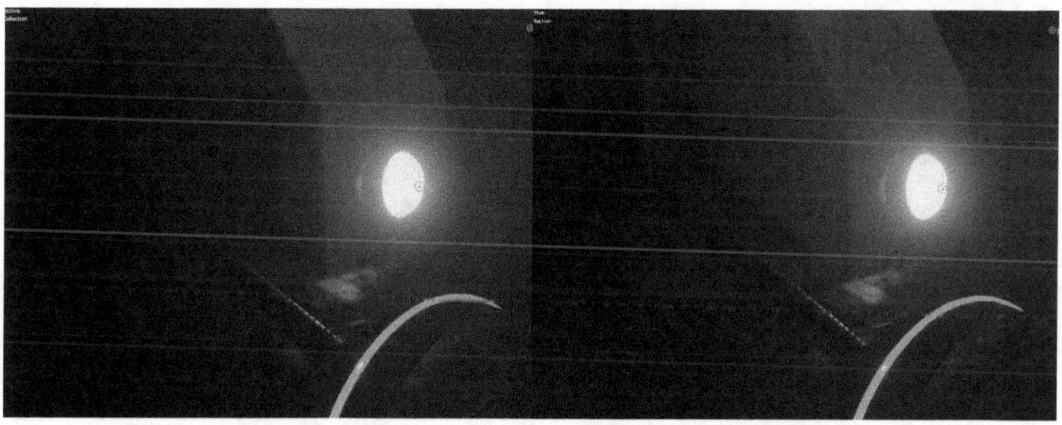

Figure 10.13: Close up of the Irradiance Volume before and after

Figure 10.12 and *Figure 10.13* both illustrate the differences before and after the Irradiance Volume has been baked.

Now that we have the indirect lighting baked using an Irradiance Volume, we can move on to the third type of light probe, which we haven't used yet – the Reflection Cubemap.

Implementing a Reflection Cubemap

We've talked through the two most important light probes that are included with EEVEE. The third is the Reflection Cubemap probe. Reflection Cubemap probes create general reflectivity in the area that the Reflection Cubemap occupies. This Reflection Cubemap probe cannot be used by itself; it can only be used in conjunction with Screen Space Reflections (in the EEVEE **Render** properties panel). It also functions similarly to the Irradiance Volume probe, in that the reflections must be baked in order to take effect. This means that reflections need to be calculated once, and then they are cached and don't need to be baked again unless the scene changes. A Reflection Cubemap is different from a Reflection Plane, in that a Reflection Plane only provides reflections for a flat surface or localized plane, with reflections only being created on one axis. The Reflection Cubemap can provide reflections for an entire area. You might be asking though, why should I use a Reflection Cubemap probe instead of just Screen Space Reflections? There is one situation where you might use a Reflection Cubemap instead of just Screen Space Reflections. Screen Space Reflections only provide reflections that are oriented to the camera. So if a reflection is reflecting something that is not in view of the camera but still would be reflected on something that is not oriented to the camera, we can get reflections from the orientation of the Reflection Cubemap probe, as well as the orientation of the camera. The following figure illustrates this concept. Notice how we can't see most of the interior red walls of the green cube until the reflection map is baked, even though Screen Space Reflections is enabled:

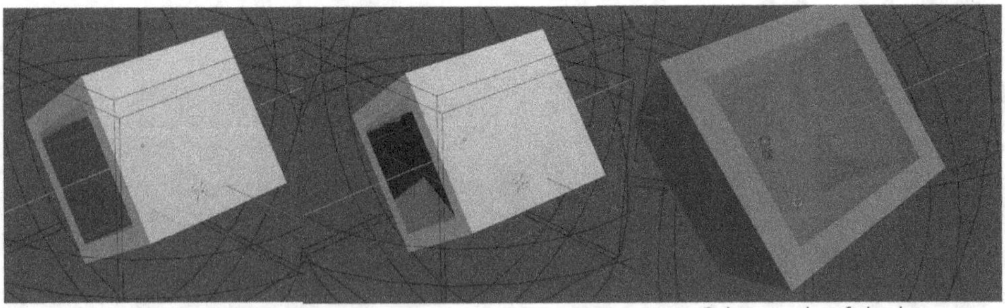

Without Reflection Cubemap *With Reflection Cubemap* *Other angle of the box showing Red Interior Walls*

Figure 10.14: Reflection Cubemap demonstration

Now that we've explored why we might use a Reflection Cubemap, let's add one to our scene. Reflection Cubemaps are designed to be used with Irradiance Volumes, so let's add the Reflection Cubemap to the area that the Irradiance Volume covers. We'll also add it to an area that might need more reflective fidelity. Let's get started with the Reflection Cubemap:

1. Add a Reflection Cubemap to the scene using *Shift* + *A* and then navigate to **Light Probe** and select the **Reflection Cubemap** option.

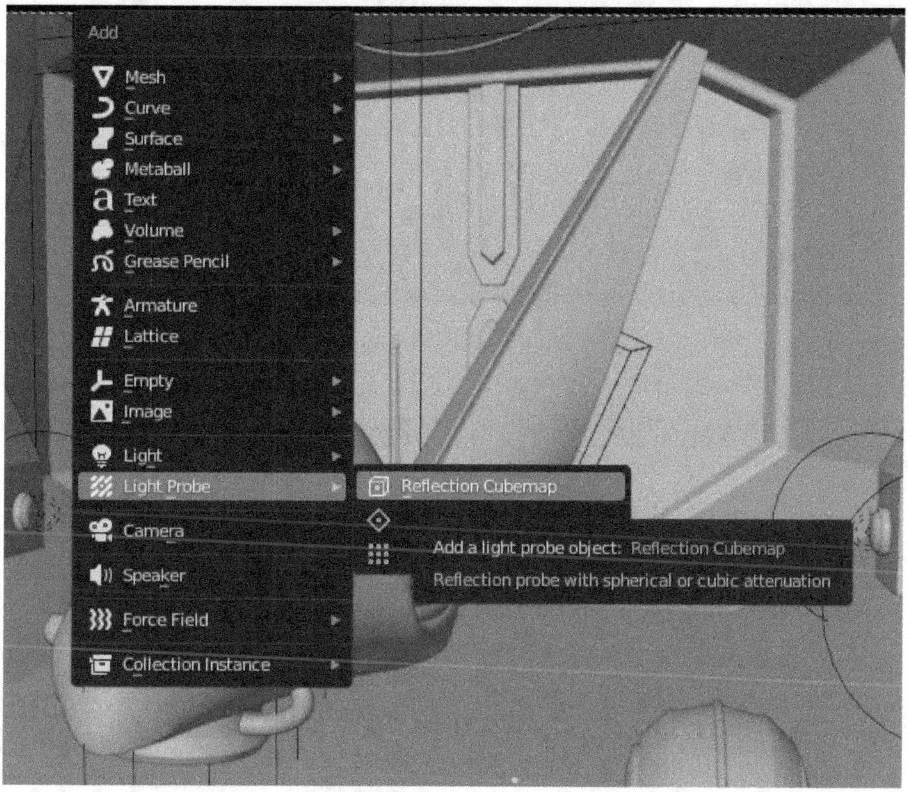

Figure 10.15: Adding a Reflection Cubemap

2. Use the *G* shortcut to move the Reflection Cubemap around the spaceship, so we'll get reflections from that area.

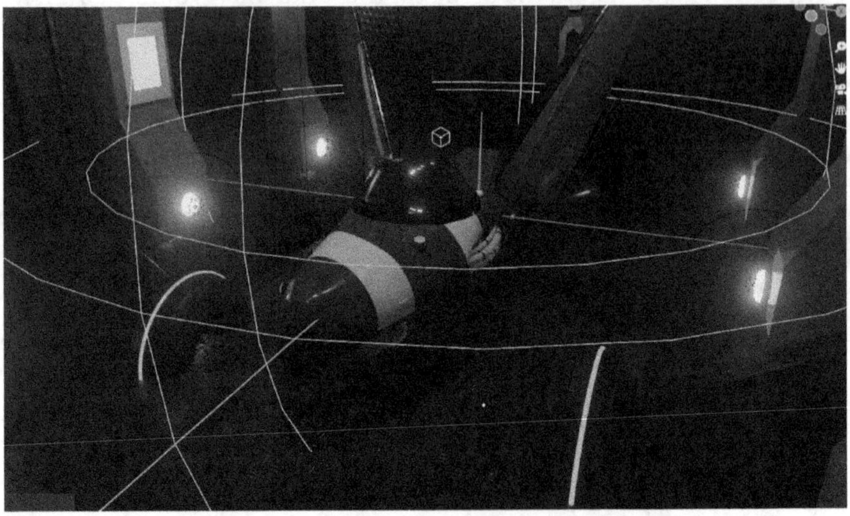

Figure 10.16: Sizing up the Reflection Cubemap

3. If we make sure the Reflection Cubemap is still selected and then open the **Light Probe** properties in the right-side menu, we can change some of the parameters of the Reflection Cubemap:

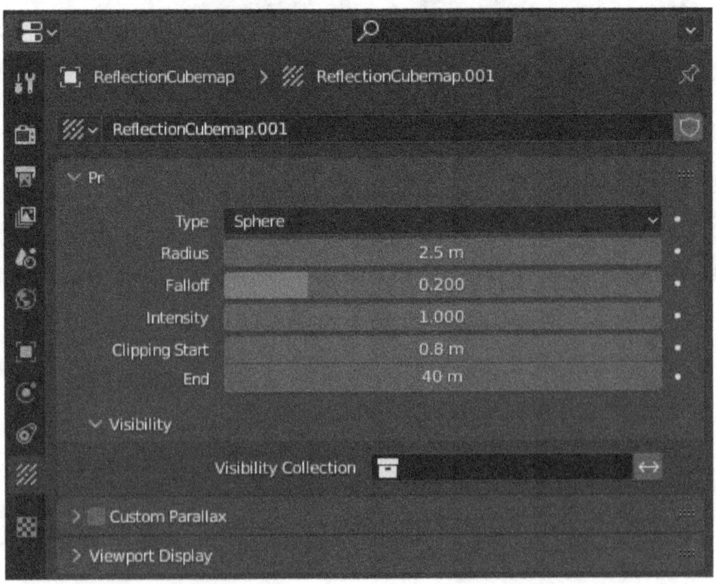

Figure 10.17: Reflection Cubemap parameters

- **Radius** dictates the size of the affected area. The larger the size, the more reflections will be baked, but the longer the bake is going to take.
- **Falloff** here is the same as **Falloff** for the Irradiance Volume. It indicates the size of the area that the effect decays from 100% to 0.
- **Clipping** can be used to limit what objects are being reflected by the probe.
- **Visibility Collection** can also be used to limit what objects are being reflected by the probe.

4. It's really important to try different settings on each subject we go through, to see how different aspects change the result. I used the values in *Figure 10.14*.
5. Once we've tweaked the settings we need to tweak, we can then go to the Render settings. Go to the **Indirect Lighting** section. Since we've already baked our Irradiance Volume, we can select the **Bake Cubemap Only** option. If you had not already baked the Irradiance Volume, you could bake both light probes at the same time by selecting the **Bake Indirect Lighting** option.

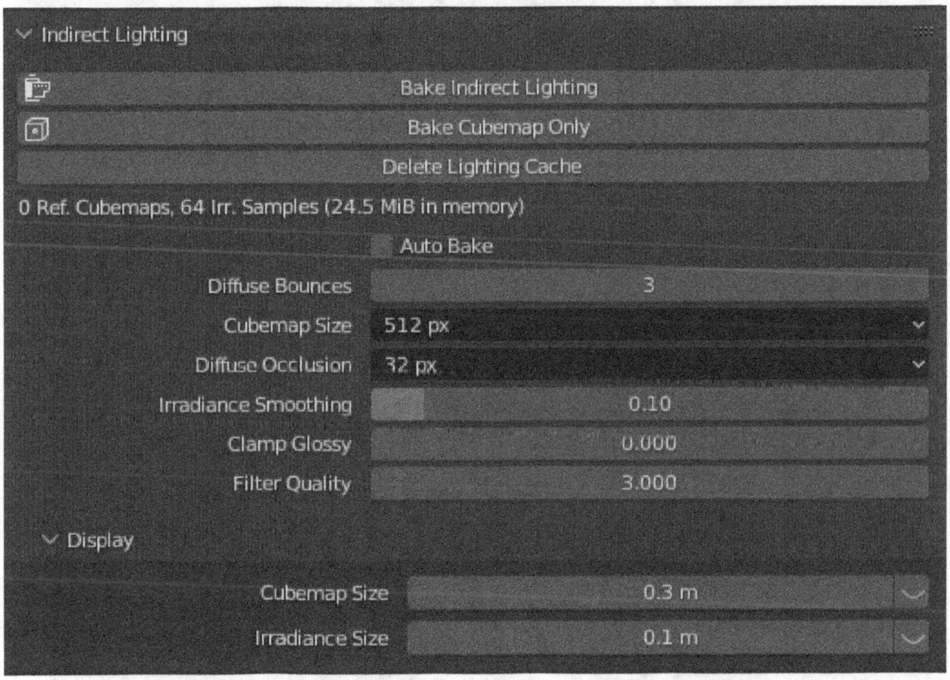

Figure 10.18: Indirection Lighting parameters after baking

And we'll take a look at the results!

We have the *before* Reflection Cubemap scene:

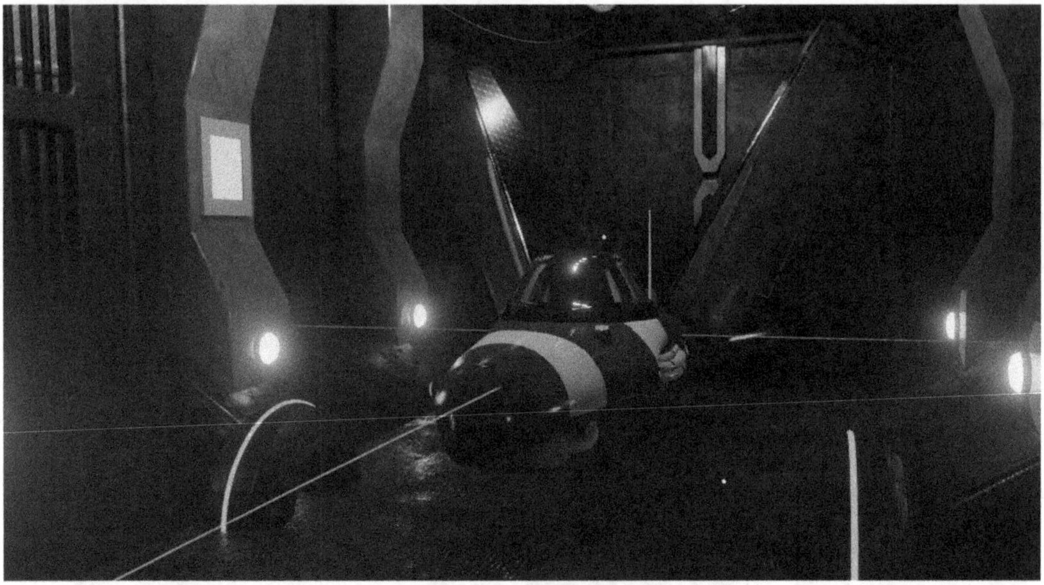

Figure 10.19: Before baking the Cubemap

And then the *after* scene (see *Figure 10.19*):

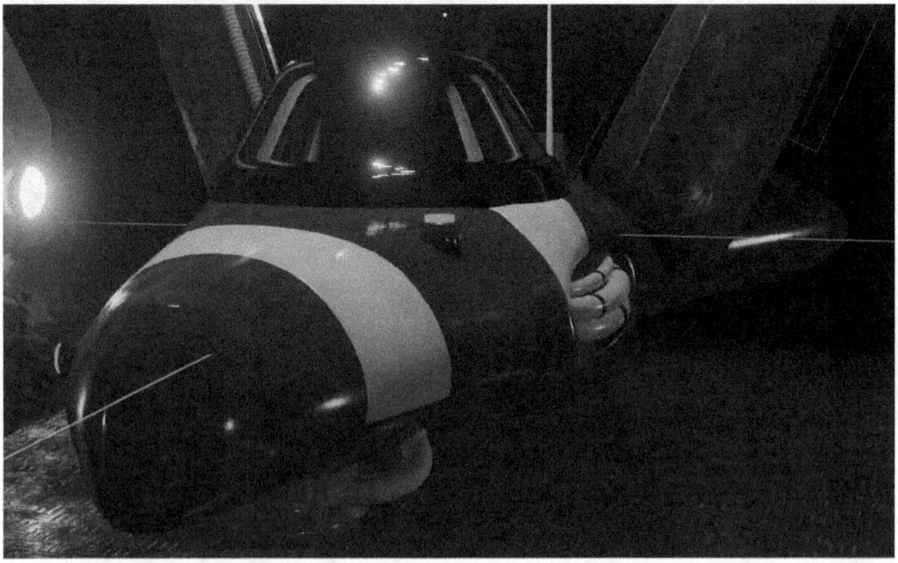

Figure 10.20: After baking the Reflection Cubemap

If we zoom in even further on the spaceship reflections, notice how in *Figure 10.21*, the before (left) picture's reflections on the nose and thruster are not even visible, whereas in the after (right) picture, the reflections of the blue lights on the spaceship are very sleek and realistic.

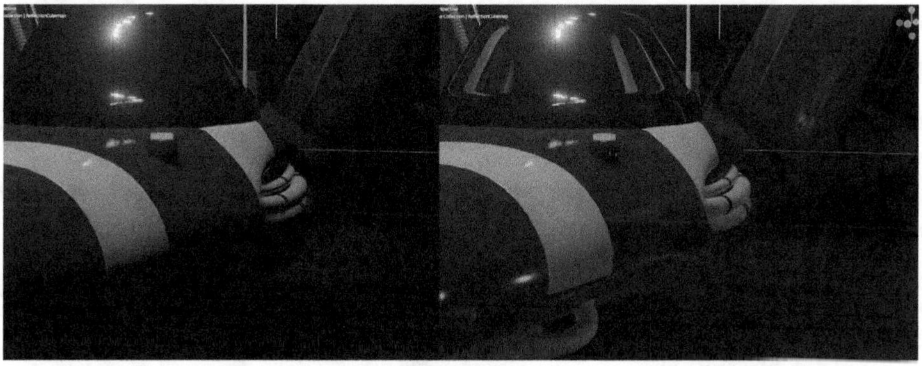

Figure 10.21: After baking the Reflection Cubemap

Once the Reflection Cubemap is baked, you could also select the **Delete Lighting Cache** option to get rid of the previous bake and start again. You can also view the size of the cache in MiBs. If your reflection results are less than satisfactory, try increasing the **Cubemap size** in the **Indirect Lighting** section of the Render panel, or increasing **Diffuse Bounces**. The gains will be subtle but may be very useful as you progress in your Blender career.

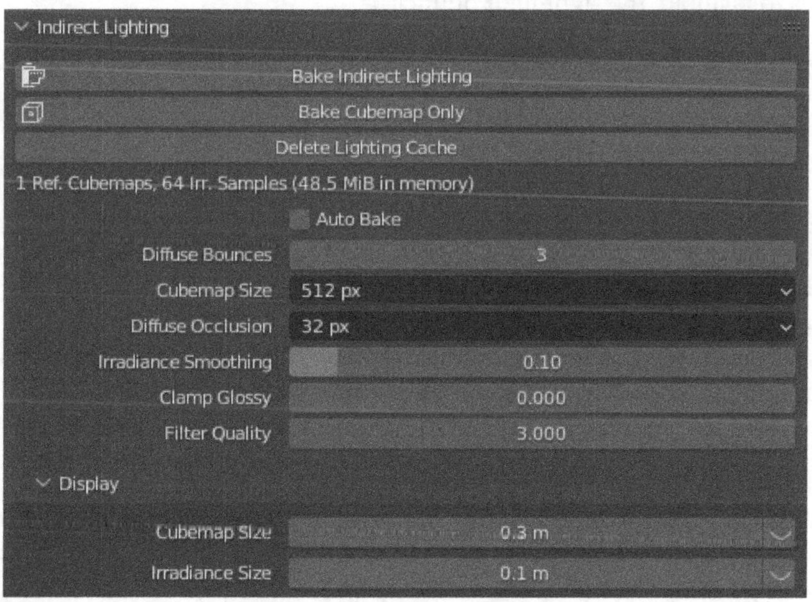

Figure 10.22: Indirect Lighting options

Now that we know how to use all the different types of probes, you should have a good grasp of how lighting works in EEVEE and how we can use different techniques to fake different types of ray tracing effects. Have fun trying different combinations of these effects to hone your ability to diagnose and fix problems with lighting in EEVEE.

Summary

In this chapter, we worked through using two different types of probes. First, we talked about Irradiance Volumes to increase the accuracy of the bounced light in the scene. Then, we discovered how Reflection Cubemaps can be used to reflect aspects of a scene that can be overlooked by Screen Space Reflections.

The number one problem that I see with a lot of renders in EEVEE is problems with lighting and reflectivity. It can be really hard to dial those in to make people think they're looking at a real image. Light probes are there to help you create something fast and flexible without sacrificing style and realism. It is important to use light probes sparingly, as they can increase the computing time and increase the size of the file. Knowing when to use a light probe is something that will come with practice and experience, but being able to implement them can be the difference between a mediocre render and a great render. I would recommend that any scene with reflections or that relies on indirect lighting should use an Irradiance Volume or a Reflection Plane, as long as you need realistic lighting. It can be completely impossible to capture realism without one of the three kinds of light probes to facilitate the right light bounces.

After this chapter and *Chapter 6, Screen Space Reflections – Adding Reflection to the Water,* hopefully you feel comfortable using light probes in a number of situations, and know when to use a probe and when they're not applicable. I would recommend trying out the three different types of probes in a new `.blend` file, trying different configurations, and then baking each to see how different lighting or parameters affect the end result.

At this point, we have a really well-lit scene with baked lighting and reflectivity that has been meticulously planned and executed. Now, you could call the scene done, but I want to take it up a notch. We're going to spend the next chapter adding more detail to the hangar and spaceship. You may realize that I tend to emphasize details a lot. Details are a really important part of creating something that seems real. Having multiple methods of adding detail quickly and flexibly is just one aspect of creating concepts that really resonate with the viewer.

In this next chapter, we're going to cover a technique called **Kitbashing**, which we will use with Geometry Nodes to add more detail to our scene. Don't worry if you've never heard of Kitbashing before – by the end of the next chapter, you'll be a professional.

11 Kitbashing – Adding Details Fast

As I hope you've noticed over the course of this book, it's not just about EEVEE. It's about making renders look great and look great fast. The bulk of the workflows and tips and tricks are about EEVEE, but there's also so much value in feeling like you can use EEVEE to make something that won't require you to sit in front of your computer for months and agonize over every single detail. The idea is to give you the tools to create something amazing, not just provide rote knowledge about the technical details of EEVEE. That's why I want to give you knowledge of Geometry Nodes, alphas, the Asset Browser, and more because EEVEE can't reach its full potential without further knowledge. So, in that spirit, in this chapter, we're going to learn about **kitbashing**, which is a way to add more visual interest by recycling smaller pieces of geometry to give life to an otherwise boring model. This way, it's easy to build a library of parts to mix and match for each scene that you work on.

In this chapter, we'll look at kitbashing and then look at some other ways to increase the overall quality of this project, without sacrificing a lot of time. We will cover the following topics:

- Kitbashing with small objects
- Using Geometry Nodes to create sci-fi panels

Technical requirements

As usual, either download the `Chapter 11-Start.blend` file from the GitHub repository for the book, or take your previous `Chapter 10-End.blend` file and keep working on what you had. If you choose to work on the file you previously created while working through *Chapter 10, Working with Irradiance Volumes and CubeMaps for Accurate Rendering*, download the `extra_objects.blend` file and import the `Details` collection and `SquareDetails` subcollection into your file. We're going to be using these extra objects as details to add to the main objects, so make sure they're in your scene.

The supporting files for this chapter can be found here:

`https://github.com/PacktPublishing/Shading-Lighting-and-Rendering-with-Blenders-EEVEE/tree/main/Chapter11`

Kitbashing with small objects

When working through a scene, I often like to work from the big details down to the small. After sorting the camera composition, adding the large objects to the scene, and setting up the lighting, it's now time to add little aspects that really make the scene realistic. We've done this before in the previous mini-project where we added alphas to the environment. In this section, we're going to take small, basic objects and add them to the main objects we've already defined. Let's get to work:

1. Grab one of the **detail** objects to work on first. I'm going to use this one called `Circle002` to demonstrate the technique.

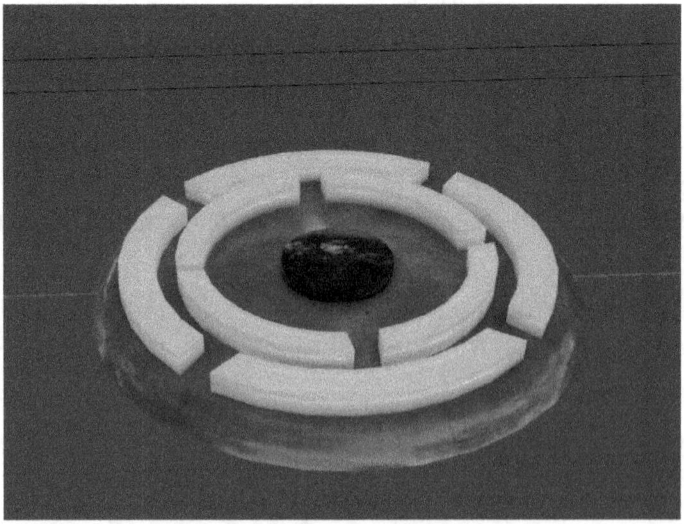

Figure 11.1: The Circle002 detail object

2. Select the object and press *Tab* to go into **Edit Mode**.
3. Holding down the *Alt* button while in the **Edge select** mode, select the outermost edge of the object by right-clicking on it.

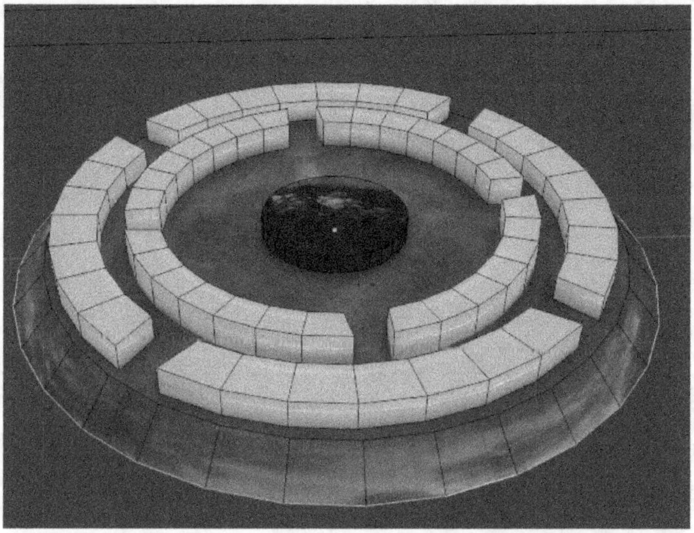

Figure 11.2: Tabbing into Edit Mode and selecting the outer edge

4. Then extrude this outer edge by pressing *E*, then using *S* to scale that new edge out.

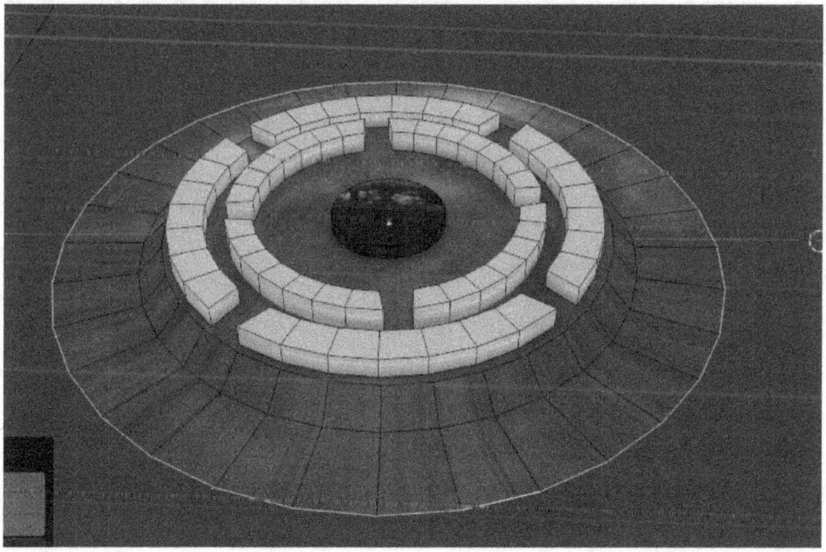

Figure 11.3: Extruding the outer edge

5. Now we want to make multiple loop cuts in the new extruded face we just made. Do that by using the *Ctrl* + *R* shortcut and then using the middle mouse button to scroll up and add multiple loop cuts all in one go:

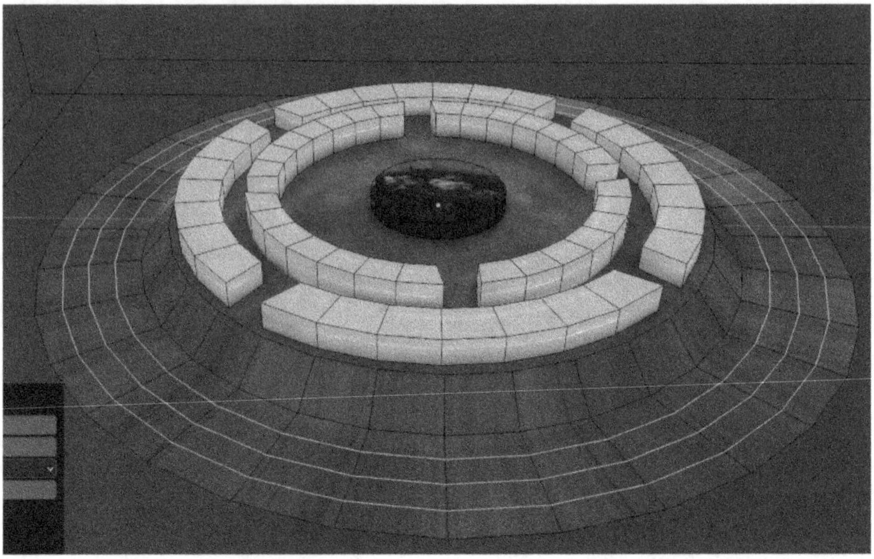

Figure 11.4: Adding loops around the extruded edge

Now we're going to add a Vertex Weight map, just like we did in *Chapter 5, Setting Up an Environment with Geometry Nodes*, where we used it to specify where the plants and rocks would be scattered on the landscape. For this object, we're going to use the Vertex Weight map to tell Blender how we want the object to be interpolated with others. Let's start by going to the **Object Data Properties** panel in the right-hand **Properties** panel.

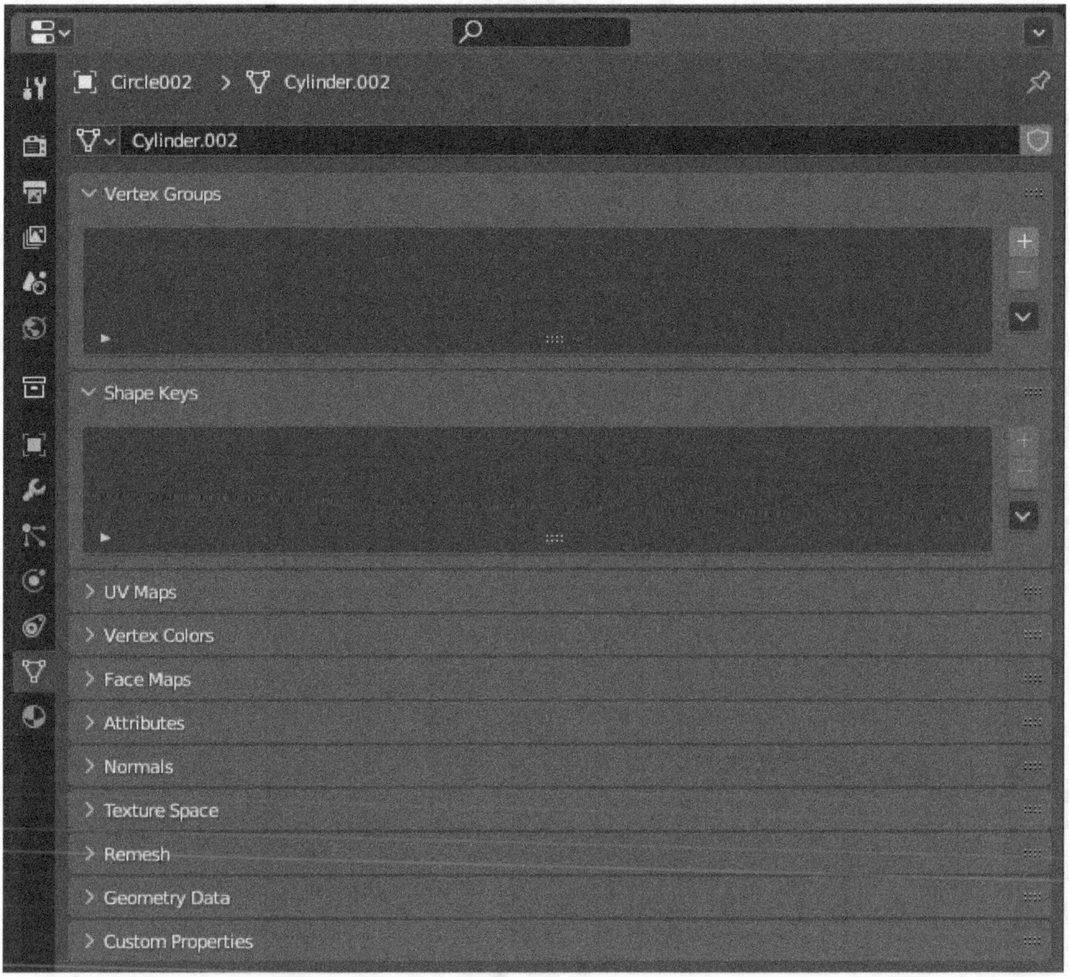

Figure 11.5: The Object Data Properties panel

6. Hit the plus sign to the right of the **Vertex Groups** section to add a new **Vertex Group** to this object.

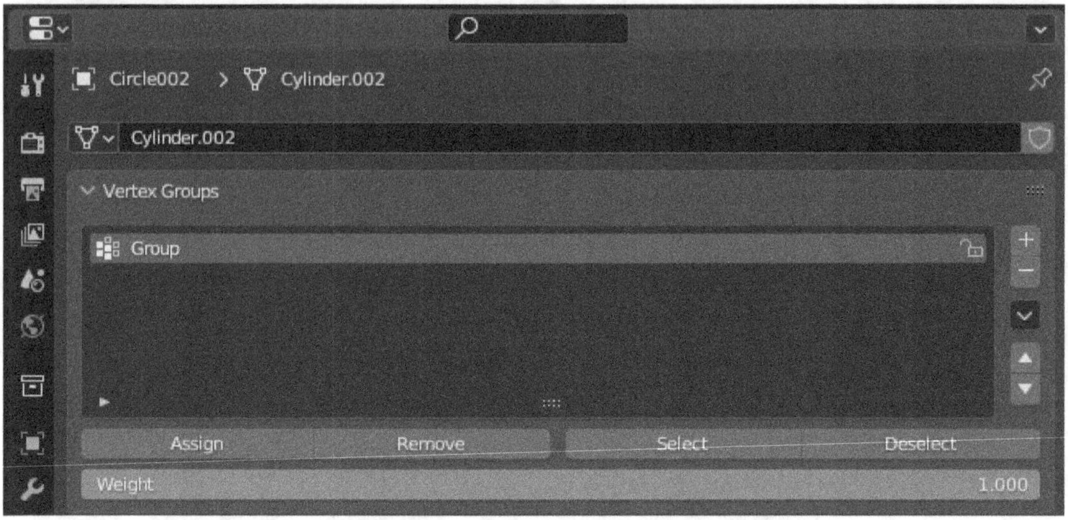

Figure 11.6: Adding a Vertex Group

7. Still in **Edit Mode**, select the entire object, and with the **Weight** slider set at **1**, hit the **Assign** button in the **Vertex Groups** section:

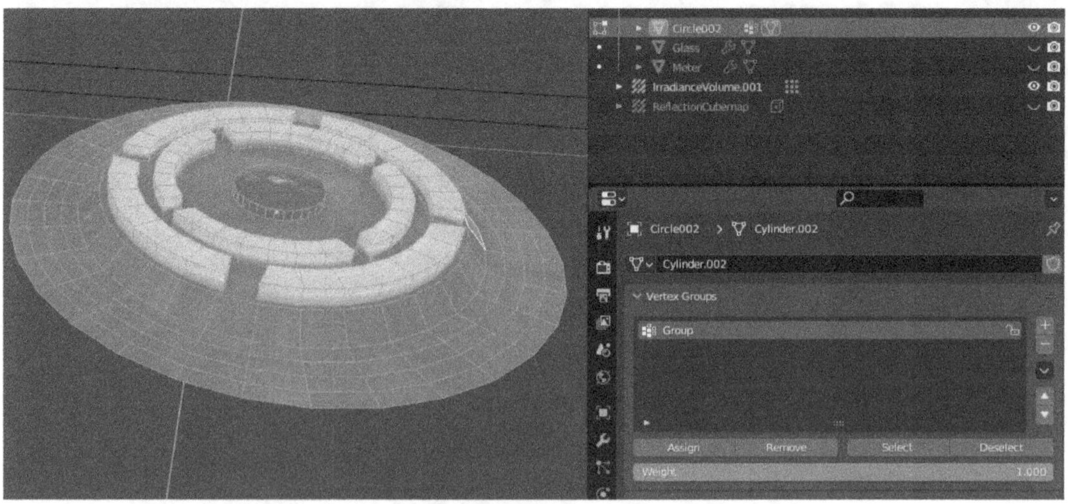

Figure 11.7: Applying a weight of 1 to the whole object

Now, when we move to **Weight Paint** mode, the object should be entirely red, which signifies that the whole object is set to a weight of 1. What we want is for the edges of our object to be red, but the inside of our object to be blue, with a gradient in between those two extremes. Luckily, Blender gives us a gradient tool to achieve this, so we don't have to try painting this effect by hand.

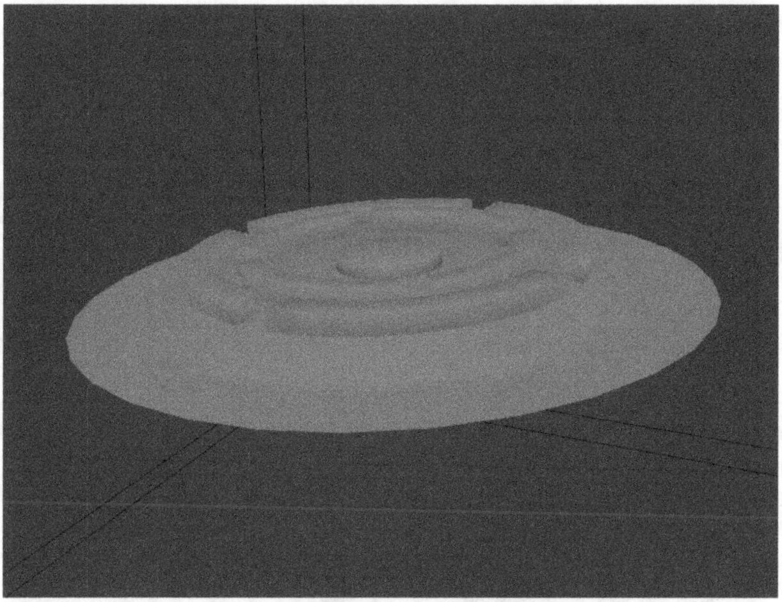

Figure 11.8: The weight map at present

8. When in **Weight Paint** mode, we can change our painting type to **Gradient** by selecting it from the options in the top left corner.

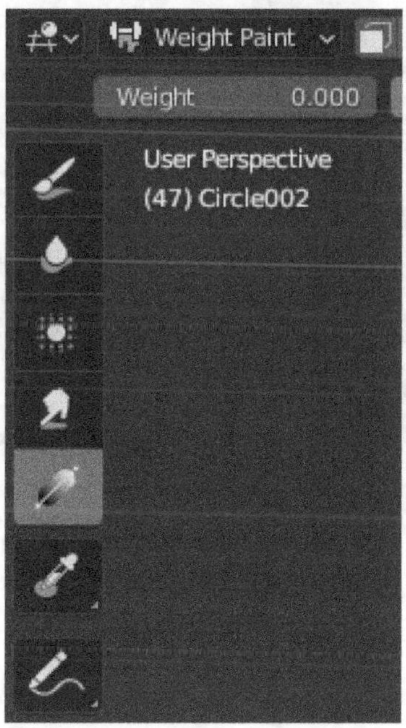

Figure 11.9: Changing the Weight Paint Mode to Gradient

Then, change the Gradient type from **Linear** to **Radial**, **Radial** being a circular gradient, which is exactly what we need. Make sure **Weight** is set to **0.000** as well. We want to start painting in the center of the circle with a weight of 0, and increase the weight as we get closer to the edges of the circle.

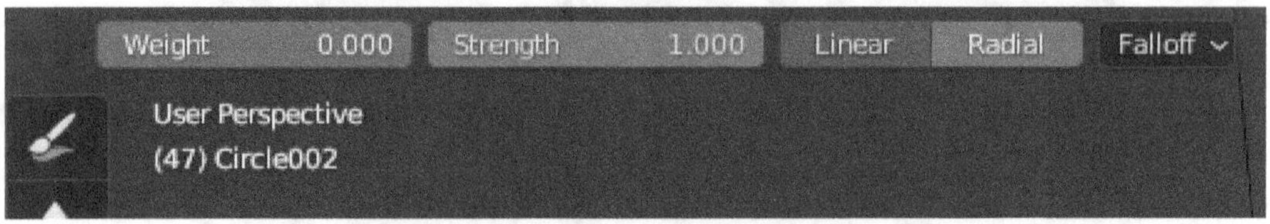

Figure 11.10: Changing the Gradient type to Radial

9. Since we will be painting in the **Viewport**, we also want to make sure we're seeing the object from directly above when we start to paint, so everything is even. Do this by hitting *7* on the Numpad, or by going to **View**, then **Viewport**, then selecting **Top**.

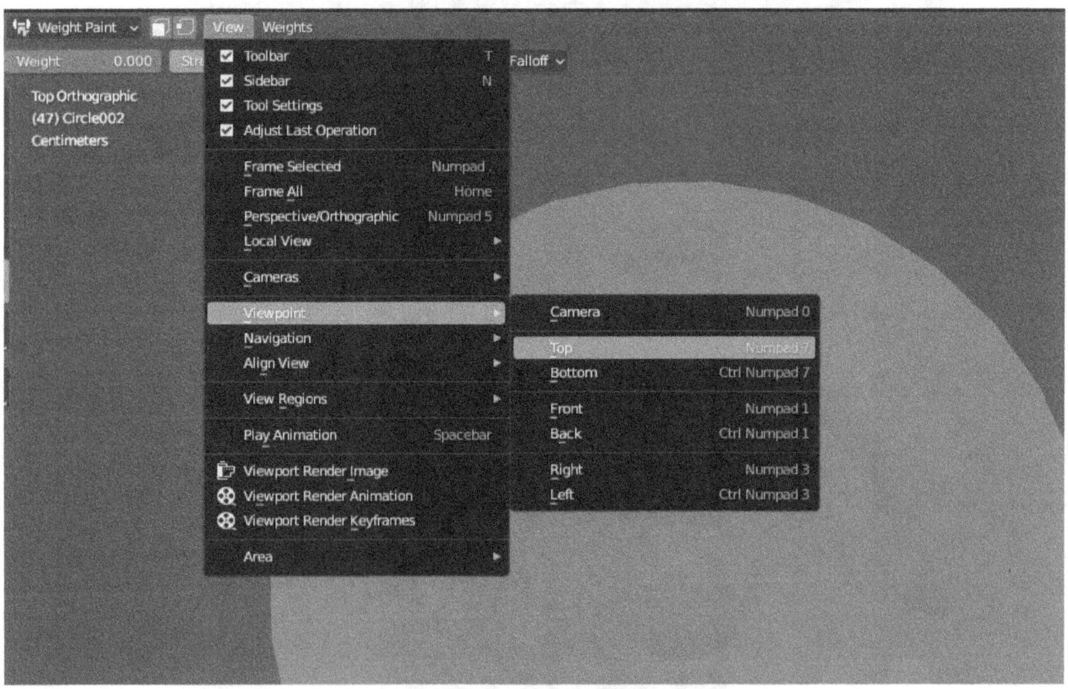

Figure 11.11: Changing the Viewport to a top-down view

10. Now we can start to paint. Click once in the very center of the circle, then drag outward until you are near the edge. You don't want to go all the way to the edge of the circle, as we still want some red at the edges.

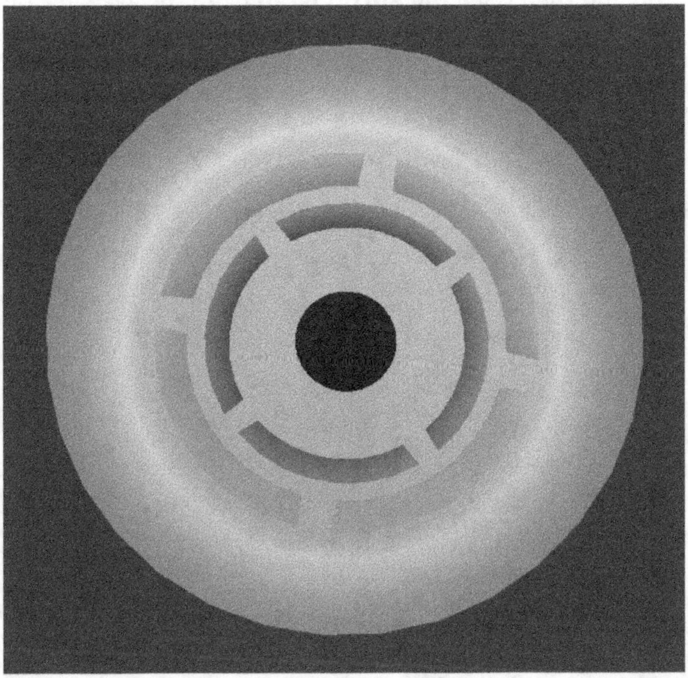

Figure 11.12: The finished weight map

With the gradient smoothly transitioning from blue to red, it's now easy to take this **Weight Paint** map and use it to influence the **Shrinkwrap** modifier we'll add to the object. The **Shrinkwrap** modifier takes one object and, exactly as the name suggests, shrink-wraps it onto another object. We'll add this modifier to the `Circle002` object and then tweak the outcome so we get the best possible result.

If you're still in Weight Paint mode, change back to Object mode. You should still have the `Circle002` object selected. If we go to the **Properties** panel, and then to the **Modifier Stack**, we can add a **Shrinkwrap** modifier by clicking on the **Add Modifier** button and then selecting **Shrinkwrap** from the available options.

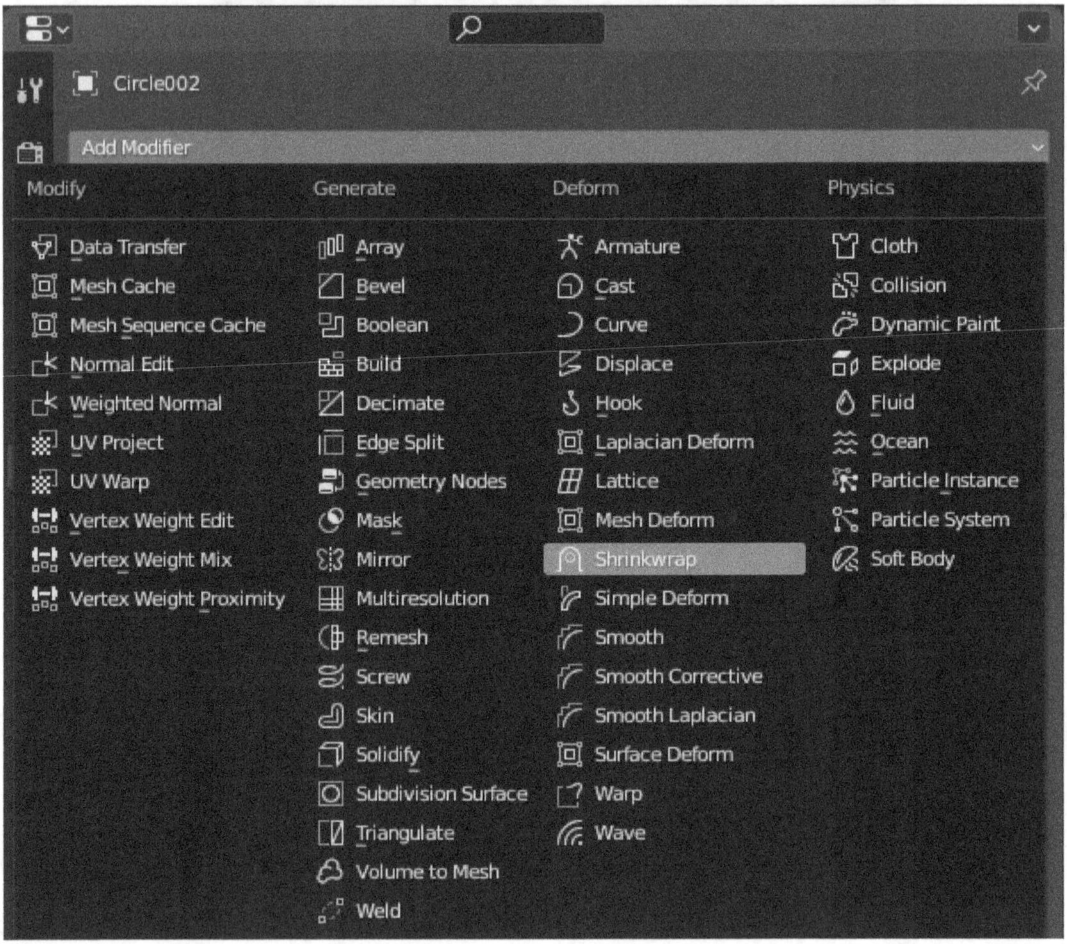

Figure 11.13: Adding the Shrinkwrap modifier

11. Next, we want to add the **Vertex Group** we just created. Click on the **Vertex Group** box and select the **Group** we made from the dropdown list:

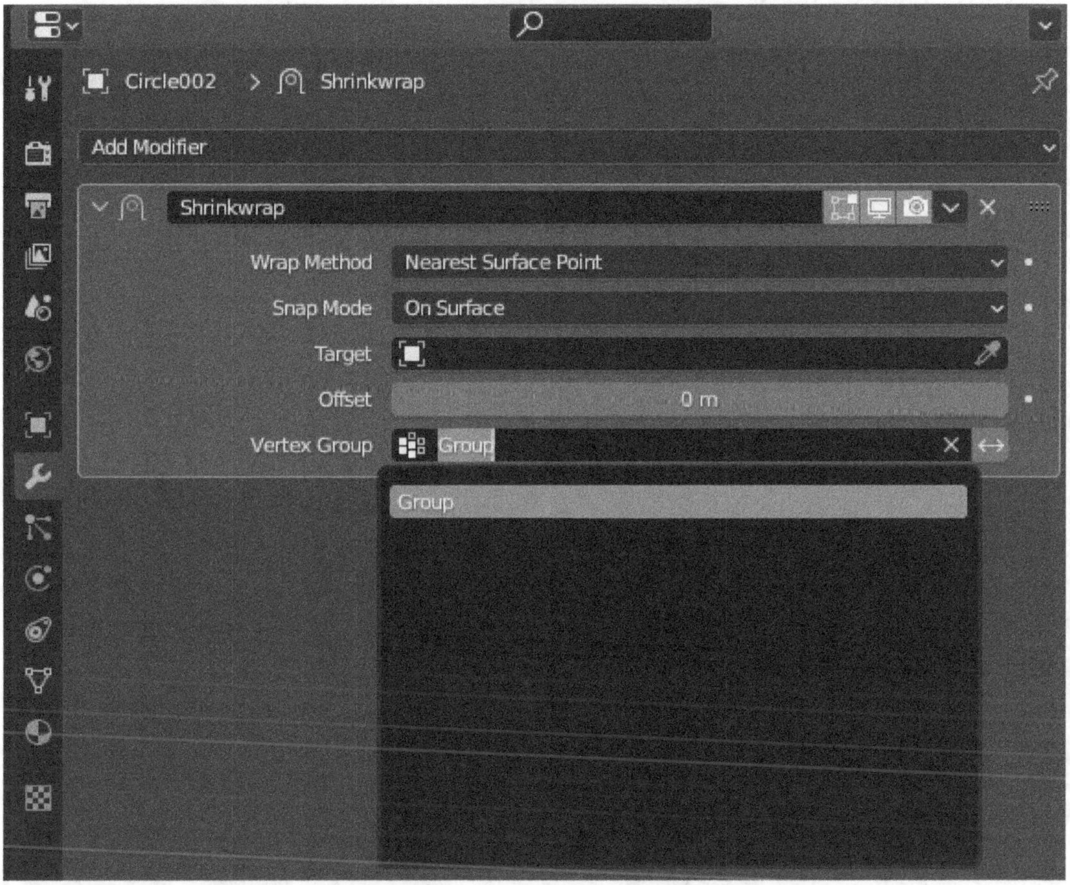

Figure 11.14: Adding the weight map to the Shrinkwrap modifier

12. The next step is designating what object we want to shrinkwrap the `Circle002` object to. Using the eyedropper tool next to the **Target** option, we can select the object in the viewport.

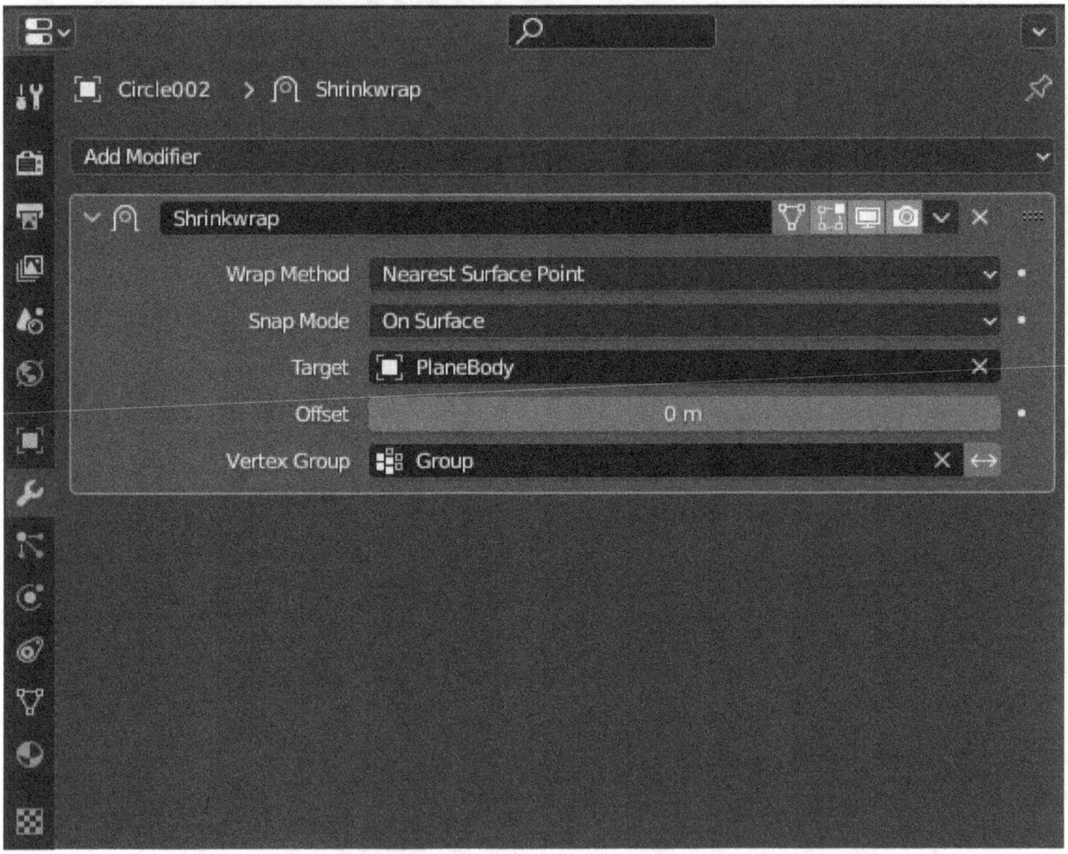

Figure 11.15: Adding the targeted mesh to the Shrinkwrap modifier

If you look at our object now, it looks pretty terrible... The **Shrinkwrap** Modifier is trying to move our geometry to the spaceship object, but it's a little too far away to look realistic.

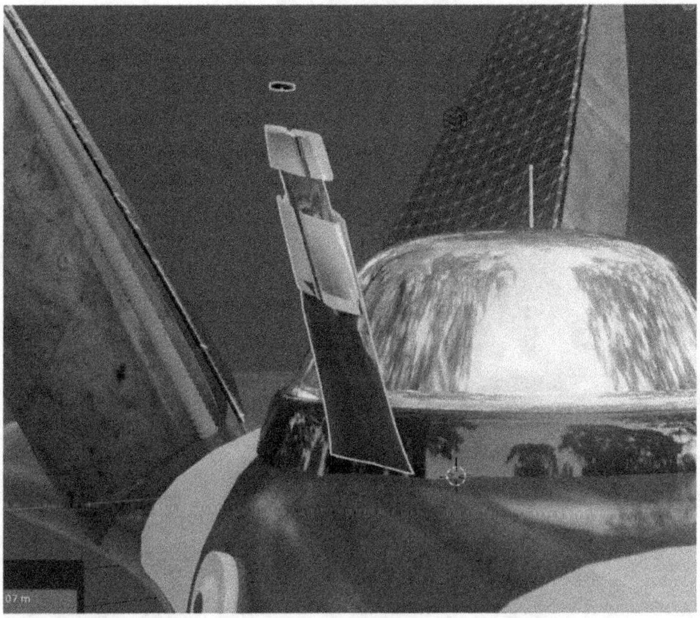

Figure 11.16: The Circle002 object stretched by the Shrinkwrap modifier

13. All we have to do to change that is move the `Circle002` object closer to the spaceship.

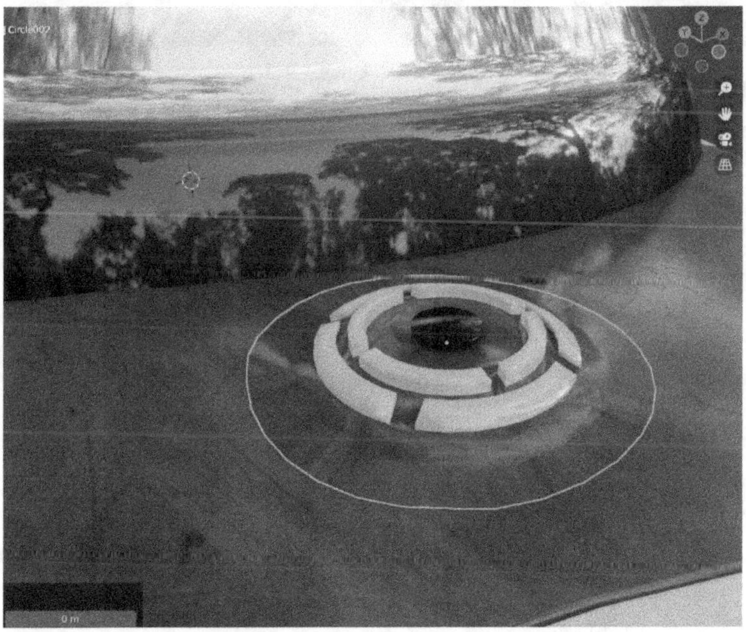

Figure 11.17: Moving the object closer to the spaceship to avoid stretching

14. The `Circle002` object becomes stuck to the surface of the spaceship. We can now move this detail anywhere on the surface of the mesh, rotating it to account for the orientation of the surface of the spaceship object.

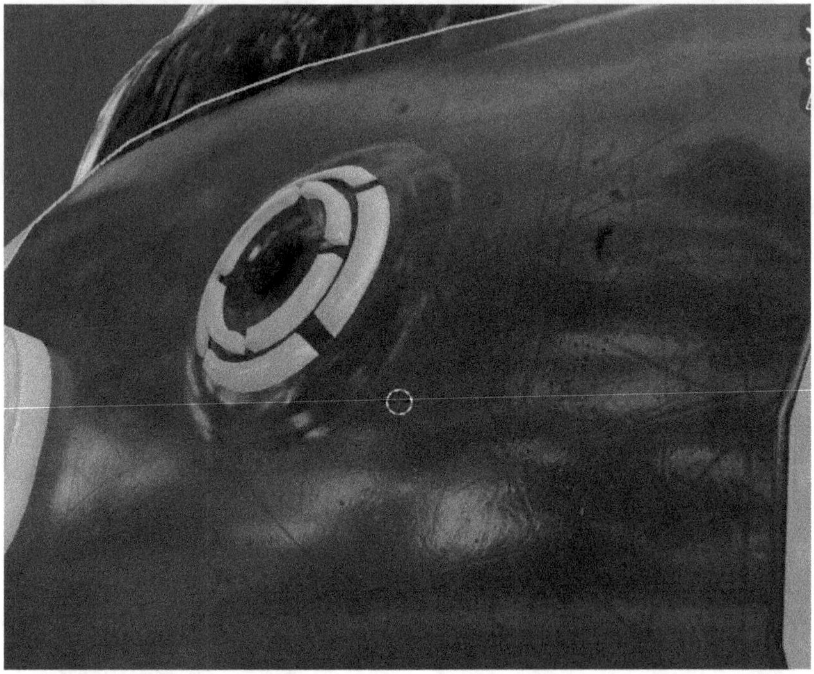

Figure 11.18: Rotating the detail object to align with the position of the larger object

The overall result is a very flexible piece of geometry that we can use again and again to create lots of detail in the span of a couple of minutes.

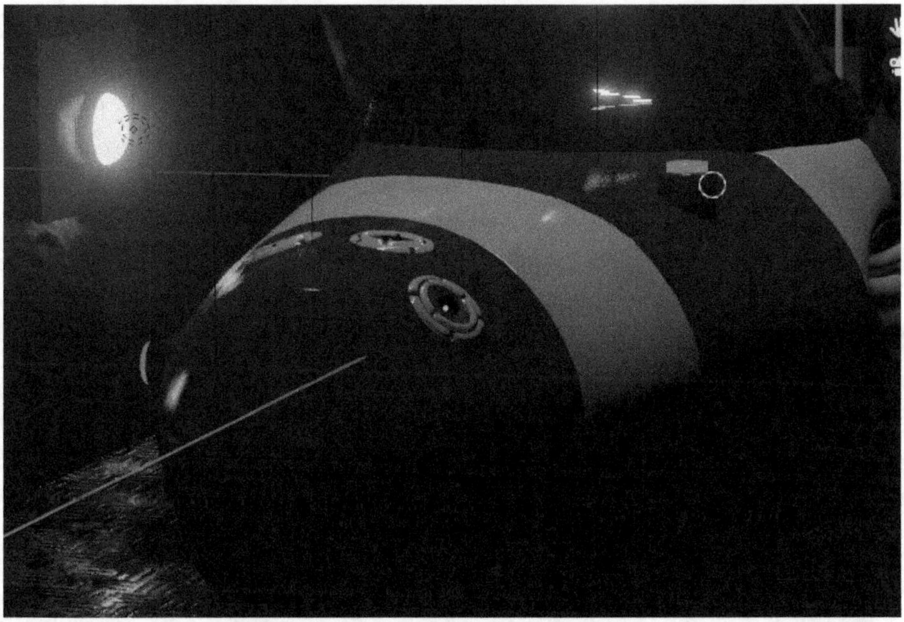

Figure 11.19: Duplicating the details and adding them to the spaceship

Copying the `Circle002` object and adding it to the nose of the spaceship adds detail to a ship that might look a little simple otherwise, avoiding the pain of trying to add the details directly to our original geometry. This is also a very flexible technique – if your director doesn't like a certain detail, you don't need to remodel the spaceship or try and break pieces off of the mesh, as the details are separate from the spaceship and can be changed or deleted easily. And the beauty of mechanical parts is that they are often reused over and over again, so it makes sense to do this in our scene.

Try taking the other parts that I modeled and preparing them with the correct **Vertex Maps**. Then, using the **Asset Browser** methodology that we covered in *Chapter 5, Setting Up an Environment with Geometry Nodes*, mark them as assets and add them to your `Blender_Assets` folder that we set up to store our Asset library. Now, you can import any detail into your scene and add it to any object anywhere in no time at all. Now that we've gone through this first method, let's move on to another method for adding detail quickly using small objects. We'll be using Geometry Nodes to achieve a similar purpose as before, but for larger areas.

Using Geometry Nodes to create sci-fi panels

To finish up this chapter, we'll create a sci-fi panel to put on the blank wall to the left of the spaceship. I've taken the simple geometry that I've prepared and placed in the **Square Details** collection, but feel free to model some of your own. My rule of thumb for designing larger panels is that the details need to fit together, so squares are obviously the simplest shape that fit together readily into larger panels. We'll take these pieces and create a random configuration out of them so that we get the illusion of a meticulously modeled panel. So, let's move on to the instructions:

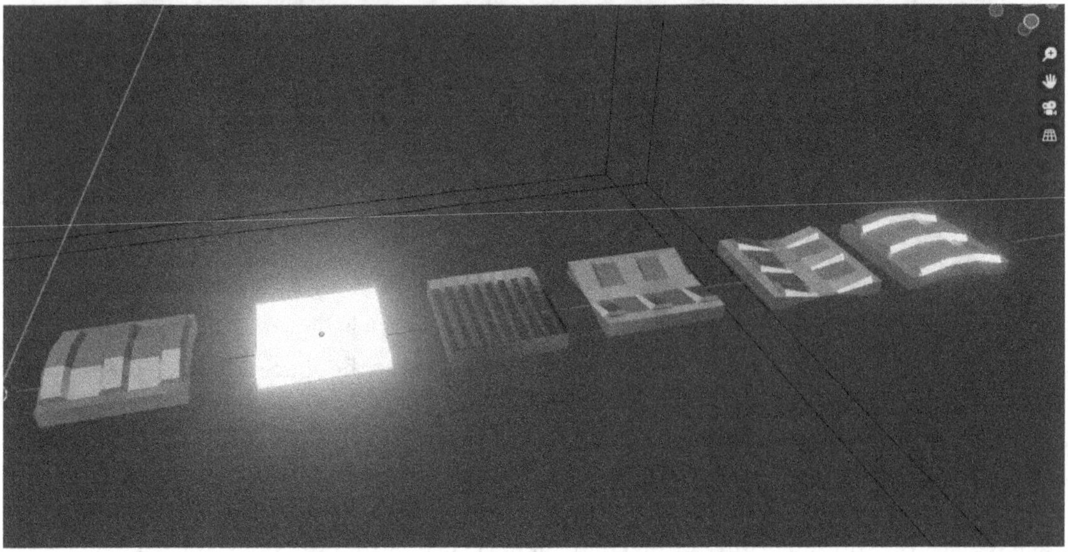

Figure 11.20: Assortment of pieces for the panel

1. Let's start out by creating a **Geometry Node** modifier for the object and call it `SciFiPanel`. Select the object, go to the **Modifier** panel in the **Properties** panel and use the dropdown to add a new **Geometry Nodes** modifier.

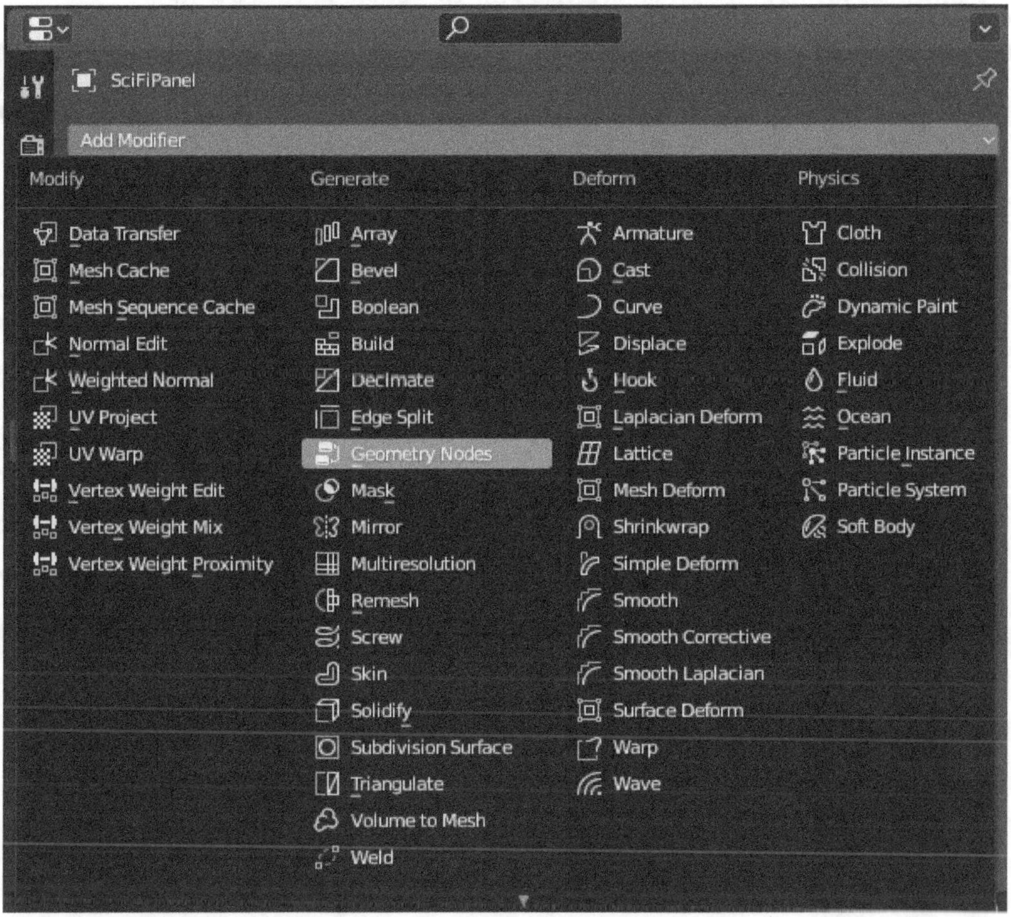

Figure 11.21: Geometry Nodes modifier

2. The first node we want to add is the **Instance on Points** node, and then check the **Pick Instance** option in the node's settings. This means we want the node to randomly pick one of the objects in the Square Detail collection and put it on a point, instead of putting all objects from the collection on each point.

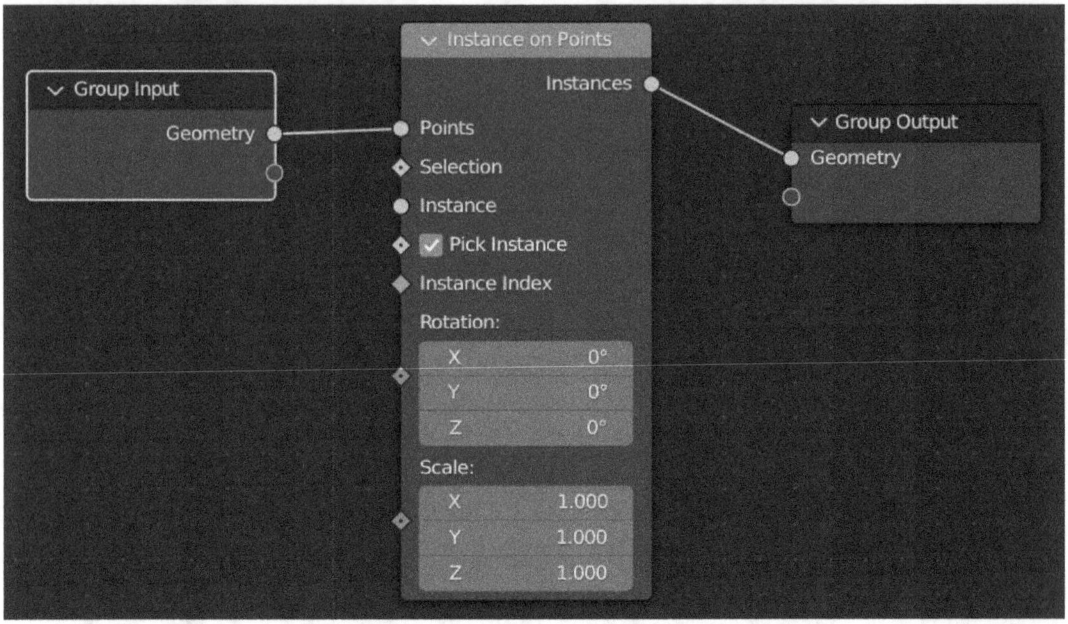

Figure 11.22: Adding an Instance on Points node

3. The next node we need is one to define which collection we want to instance. Add a **Collection Info** node and input the `SquareDetail` collection into the selection box. Then check both **Separate Children** and **Reset Children**. This indicates we want each separate object to be scattered, and it clears any transforms we have on the objects in the **SquareDetail** collection that might cause problems.

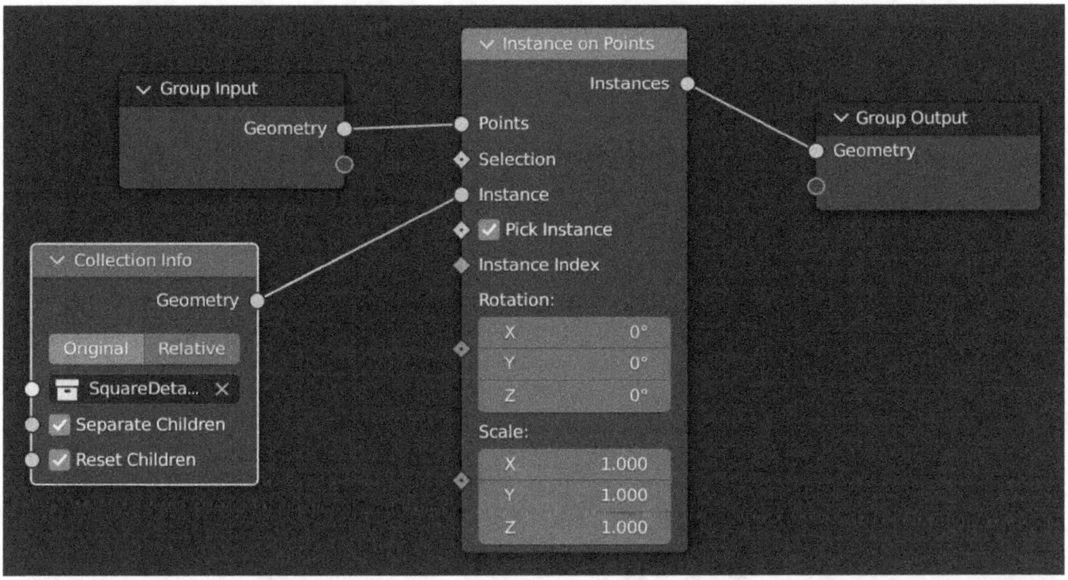

Figure 11.23: Adding the Collection Info settings

4. Alright, we have now created a really interesting pattern just by combining some simple shapes in a random pattern. But this isn't really flexible at this point. We can't try different configurations. Let's fix that by adding a **Random Value** node:

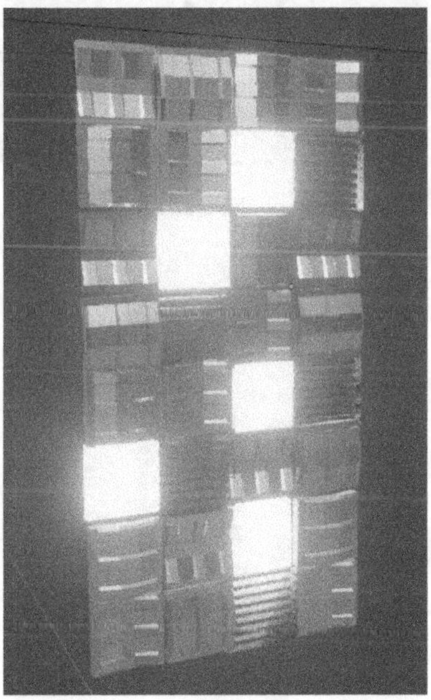

Figure 11.24: The random configuration of objects for our panel

5. After adding the **Random Value** node, connect it to the **Instance Index** input on the **Instance on Points** node.

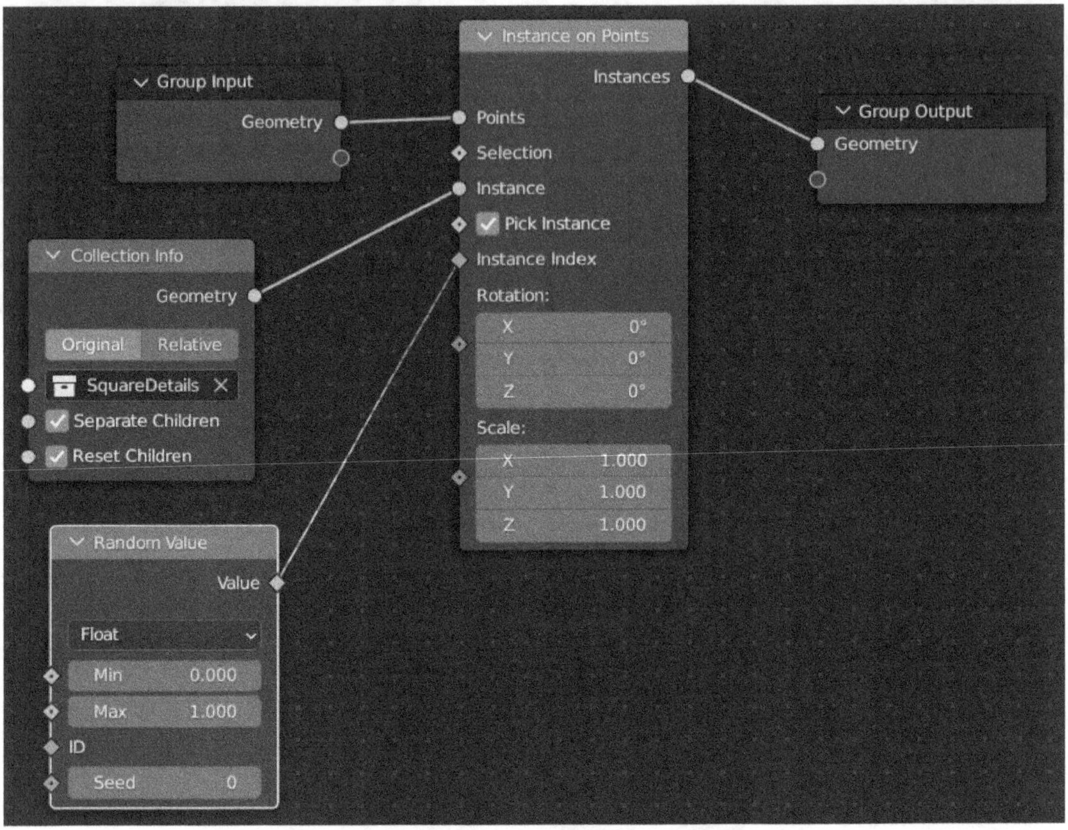

Figure 11.25: Adding the Random Value node

6. You may notice that now we don't have a random pattern or random scattering. We just have one object being repeated across the sci-fi panel.

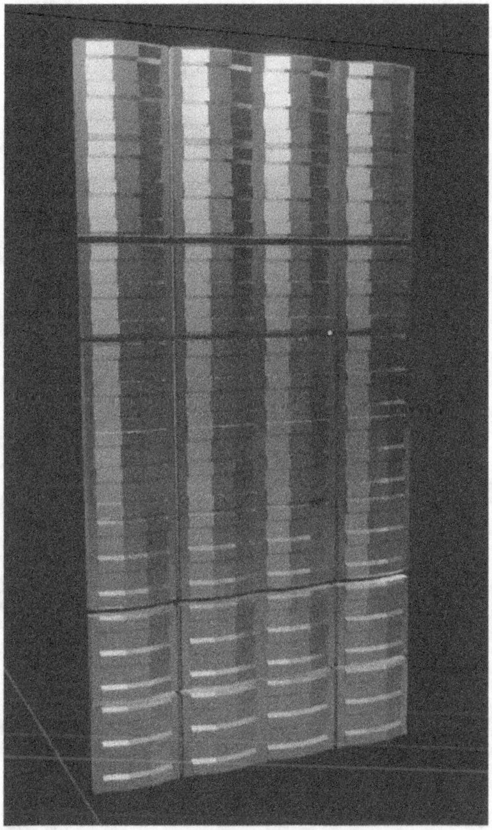

Figure 11.26: The panel with a Max value of 1.000

7. This might be the result we want. But, to get our other objects back, all that is needed is to increase the **Max** value for the **Random Value** node. This way, each point in the sci-fi panel is given a random number between `0` and `5`, each value standing for an object. We can then seed the different values to change our results by increasing the value in the **Seed** box of the **Random Value** node.

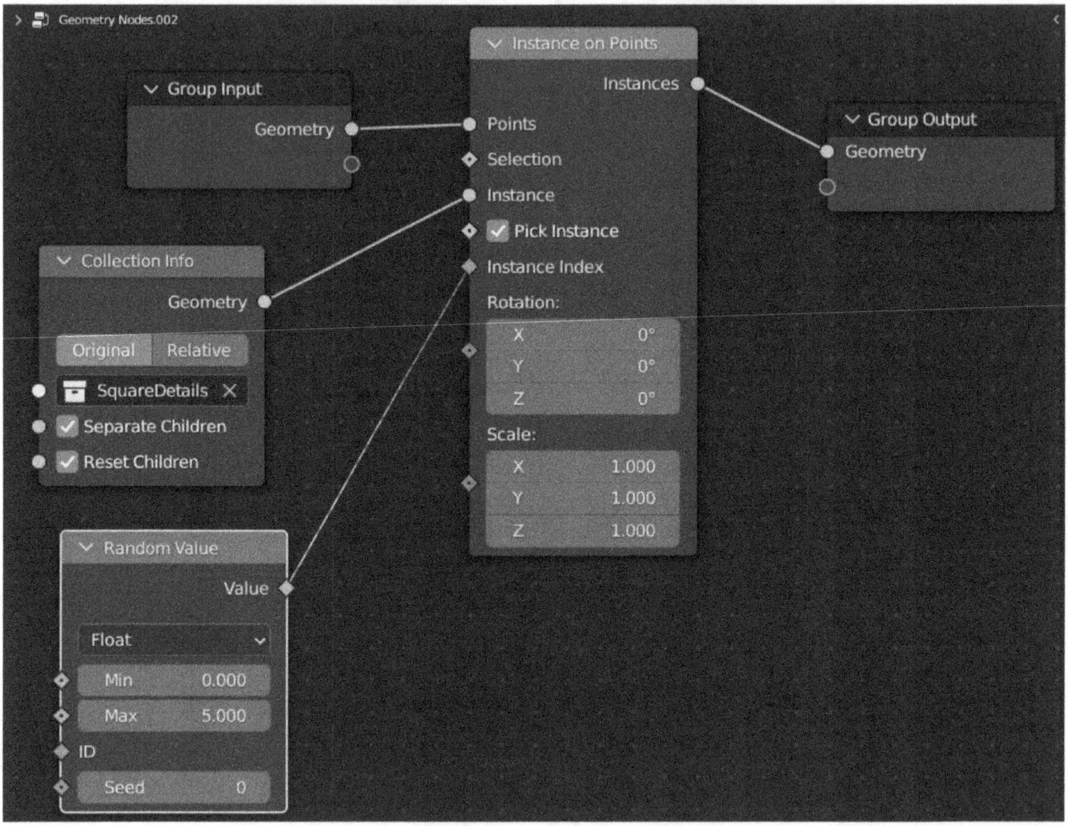

Figure 11.27: Changing the Max value to 5.000

8. This results in all of our objects being randomly scattered, just like before. But now we can change the **Max** value in the **Random Value** node to tell Blender to use more or less of our objects or increase the **Seed** value to see different configurations.

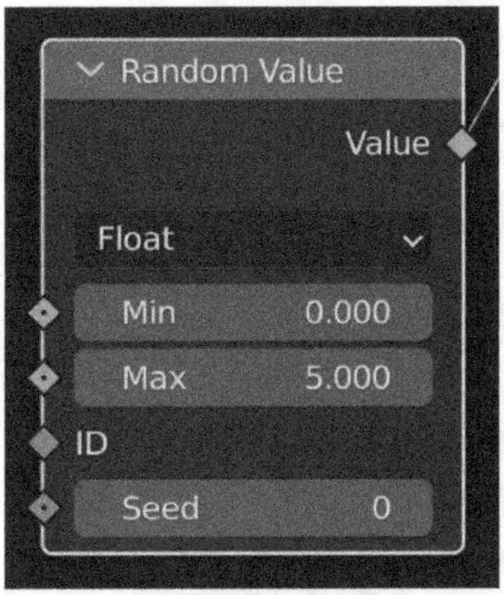

Figure 11.28: The Random Value node

9. If we decrease the **Max** value to `3.000`, we only get a few of the objects appearing on the grid:

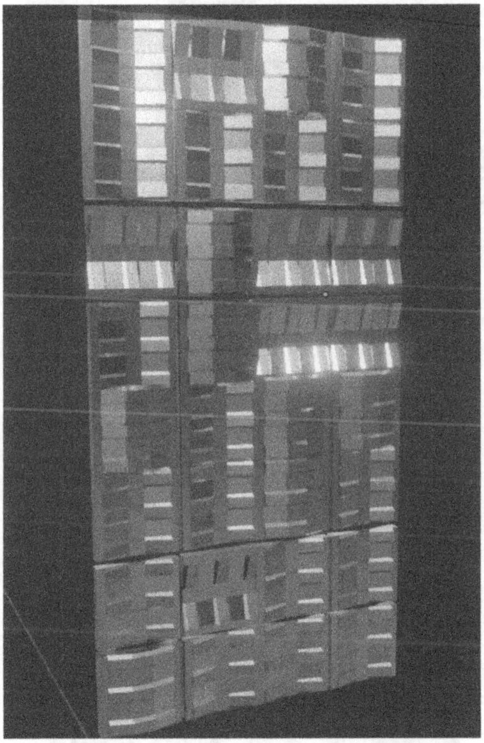

Figure 11.29: Changing the Max value to 3.000

10. Or alternatively, keep the **Max** value at `5.000` to have all of the panels used in the grid.

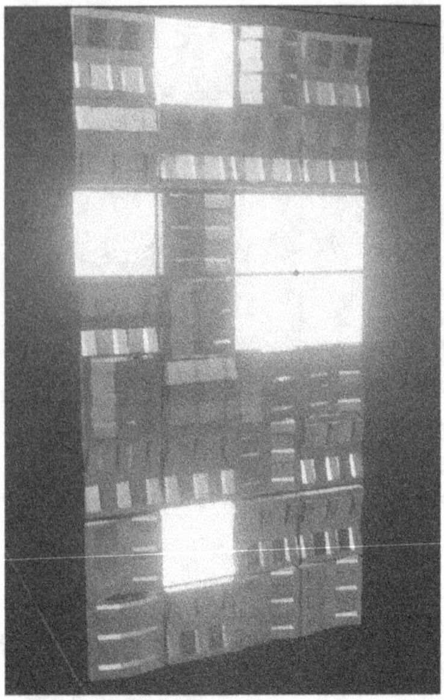

Figure 11.30: The results with a Max value of 5.000

11. Try increasing the **Seed** value to `2` and see how the different panels change their position and randomize.

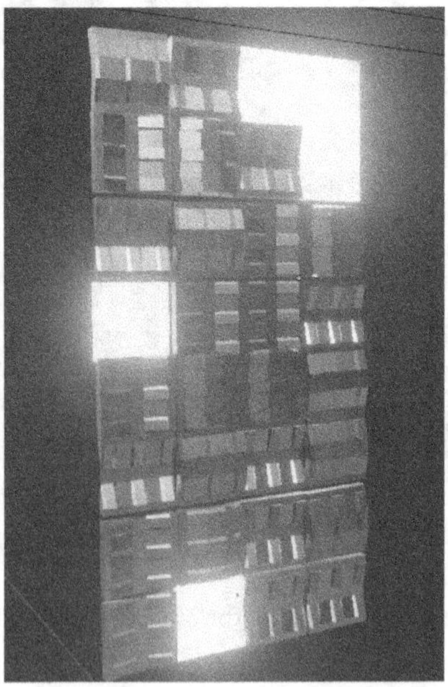

Figure 11.31: Changing the Seed value to change the configuration

And we now have a really simple, but complex-looking, sci-fi panel that we can tweak using the **Geometry Nodes** modifier to get the exact formation we want.

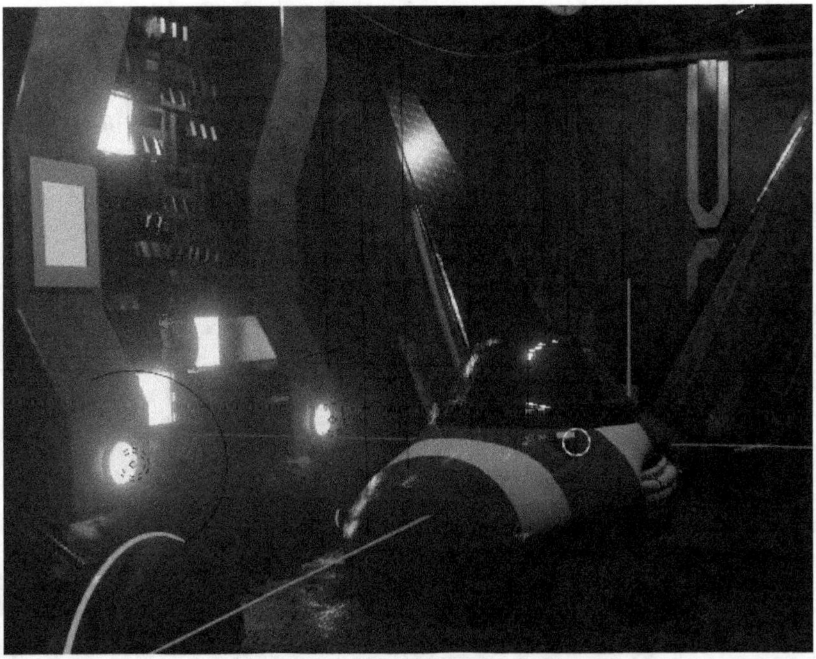

Figure 11.32: The panel in the scene

In this section, we worked through another application of Geometry Nodes, this time to create a machine panel incorporating some randomization but constraining the scattering to a more ordered grid formation. You can now see how truly amazing Geometry Nodes are, and should feel compelled to further your knowledge so you can create even more complicated procedural structures in Blender.

Summary

In this chapter, we took two different approaches to add small details to the spaceship and its hangar to make the scene look much more detailed and effective than what we would get by modeling and placing every single detail manually. First, we created small details that can be applied to different sections of the spaceship with a Shrinkwrap modifier. The other technique involved using Geometry Nodes to create a grid-based patterned panel that we can randomize at will. The scene I ended up with looks like this:

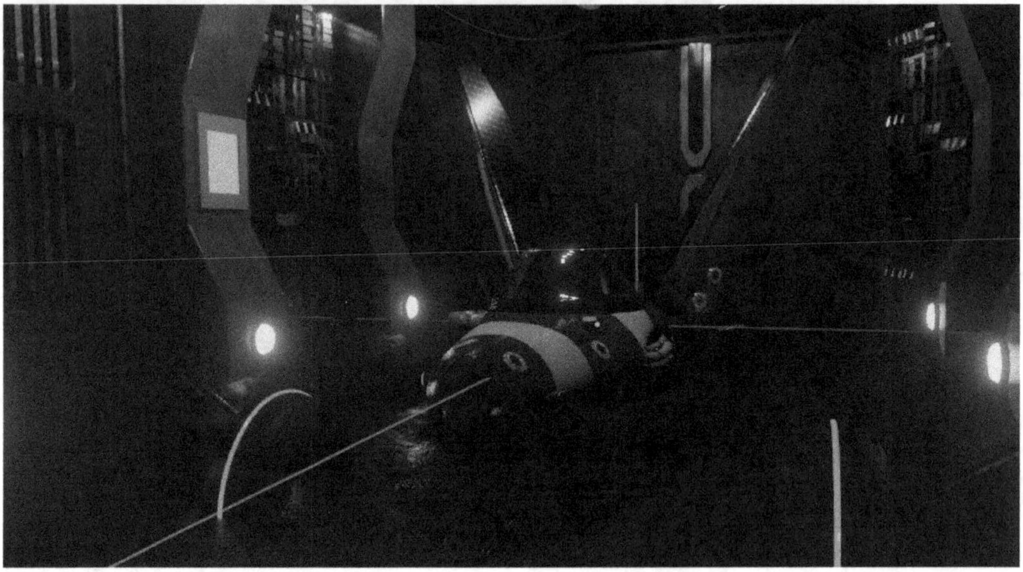

Figure 11.33: The sci-fi panels on the walls, with details added to the spaceship

Of course, you can spend as much or as little time as you want on adding more details, modeling your own additions to the scene, and taking it as far as you want to. Adding signs or pieces of text could be really cool for this scene, and you could also consider adding more complicated pieces of detail to the sci-fi panel. I just wanted to show you what is possible and give you the tools to take it further and make your artwork better, faster.

After working through this chapter, you should understand the importance of using small mechanical-style objects and being able to duplicate and scatter them for a really intricate visual effect. The next chapter is one of the most fun chapters in this book: *How to create fire with EEVEE*!

12 Special Effects with EEVEE – Fire and Smoke

In *Chapter 2*, *Creating Materials Fast with EEVEE*, we created an animated material that involved smoke. In this chapter, we're going to spend time creating a physical simulation of fire and then compositing it into our spaceship scene. The fire we make is part of the physics simulation suite that comes built into Blender. **Physics simulations** can cover anything, from fluid to smoke to dropping objects and having them shatter. The workflow for physics simulations is a little different than other workflows in Blender. First, the simulation is created using the parameters that we input, but we don't get to directly create the fire like we would when modeling. We can add or subtract forces from the simulation, change gravity, and add effects, but ultimately it's the computer that calculates each frame for us and then caches it so that we can play it again. This leads to more experimentation when creating physics simulations. It's prudent to change a value in the simulation and then test the simulation to see if it reached the desired outcome, and then try again and again until you get something that looks good. With more practice, you'll start to get a better feel for how each factor affects the simulation and need to do less testing, but I recommend experimenting with every step that we take in this chapter to really get the fundamentals of fire physics.

We're going to go over how to utilize the Quick Smoke function for faster results, the important aspects of a fire simulation, how to create a better shader using volumetrics, how to clear the **cache** of the simulation to keep working on the scene, and finally an example of how to use Cycles and EEVEE together.

The main topics we will cover are as follows:

- Creating fire with Quick Smoke
- Tweaking the shader for fire and smoke in EEVEE
- Optimal EEVEE render settings for the smoke and fire
- How to combine renders in Cycles and EEVEE

Technical requirements

As usual, you can download `Chapter12-Start.blend` from GitHub, or keep working from the file you created in *Chapter 11, Kitbashing – Adding Details Fast*. In this chapter, we will need some room on our drive for the fire cache, so make sure you save your files somewhere with a little bit of room to store the cache files.

The supporting files for this chapter can be found here: `https://github.com/PacktPublishing/Shading-Lighting-and-Rendering-with-Blender-s-EEVEE-/tree/main/Chapter12`.

Creating fire with Quick Smoke

Creating fire inside of Blender has never been so easy. While it can be immensely gratifying to create your own simulation from scratch, the Blender developers have done all the work for you with the **Quick Effects** menu options. With these options, you can really quickly create a smoke or liquid simulation, an explosion, or fur. As our recurring theme is how to do things quickly, we're going to use the **Quick Smoke** option to create our fire. While on the surface, **Quick Smoke** doesn't initially seem very logical as a way to create fire. But you know what they say, where there's smoke, there's fire. So let's jump into creating some fire with the **Quick Smoke** menu options:

1. In `Chapter 12-Start.blend`, I have hidden our hangar from view so that we can create the fire without Blender having to render the entire scene plus the fire at once. You'll notice the only object visible in the scene is the FireObject. This object is the exact size of one of the thrusters of our spaceship. We're going to use its geometry as the basis for the size of the fire. Select that FireObject by left-clicking on it.

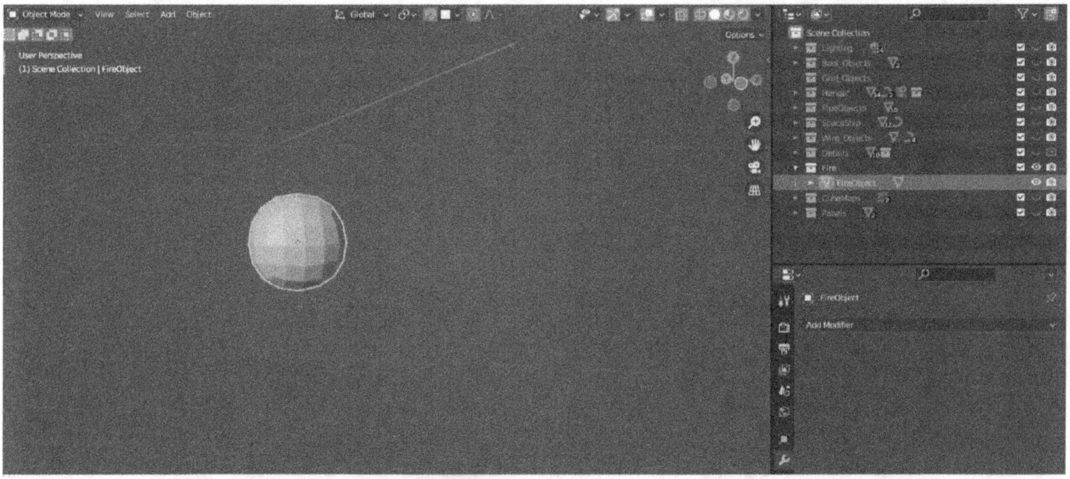

Figure 12.1: The FireObject

2. Next, go to the **Object** menu located in the top left corner (next to the **Add** menu) and click on it. Find **Quick Effects** on the list of menu options, then choose **Quick Smoke** from the **Quick Effects** menu.

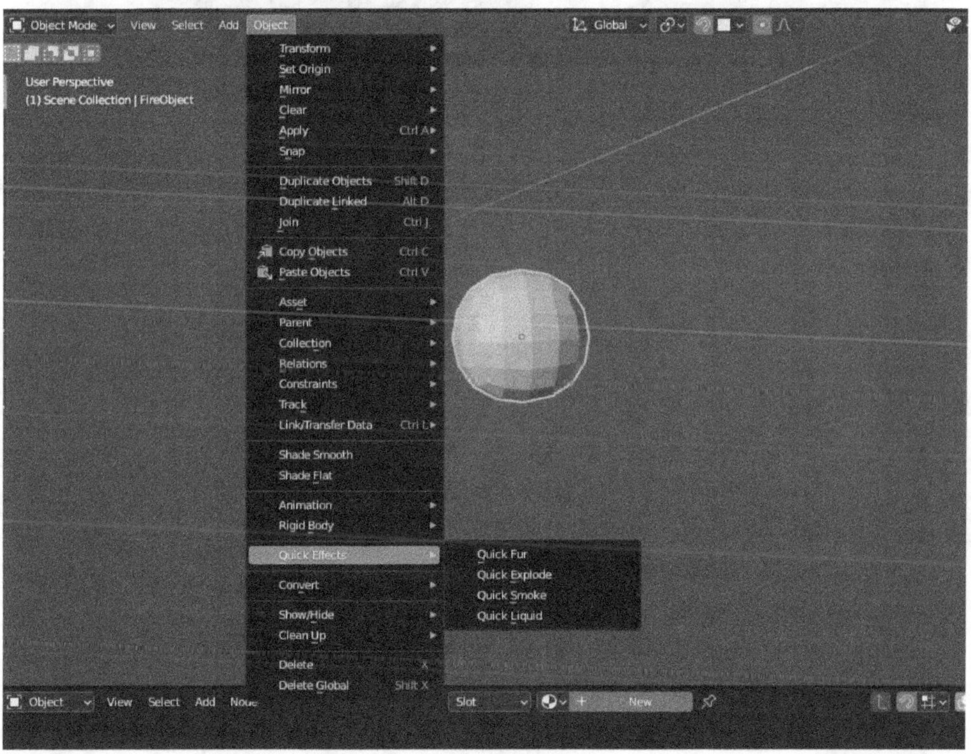

Figure 12.2: The Quick Effects menu

3. Blender will automatically add a new object called **Smoke Domain**.

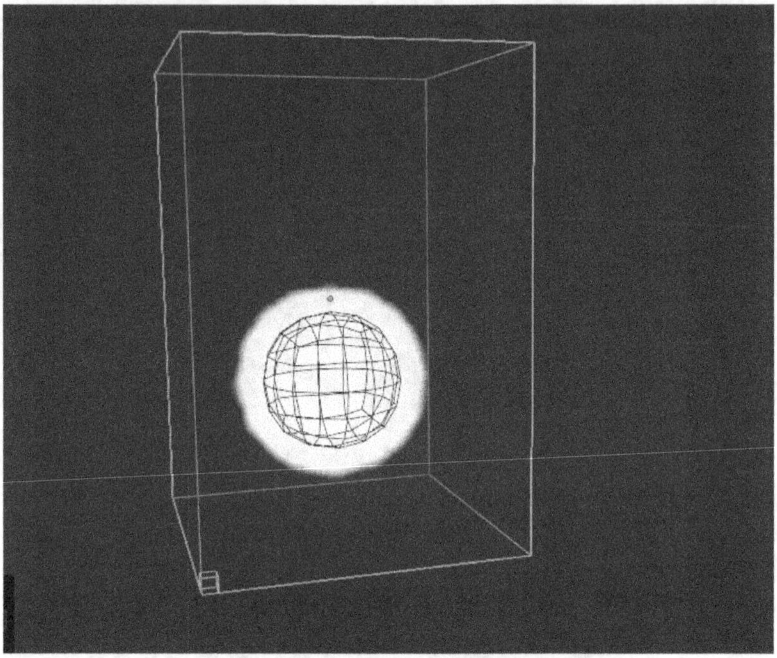

Figure 12.3: Smoke Domain added

4. Before clicking on anything else, there should be an **Add** menu that popped up in the bottom left corner of the screen – this is called the **last operator menu**. It can be recalled with *F9*. This menu should have **Smoke Style** as an option. Click the drop-down menu and change that option to **Fire**.

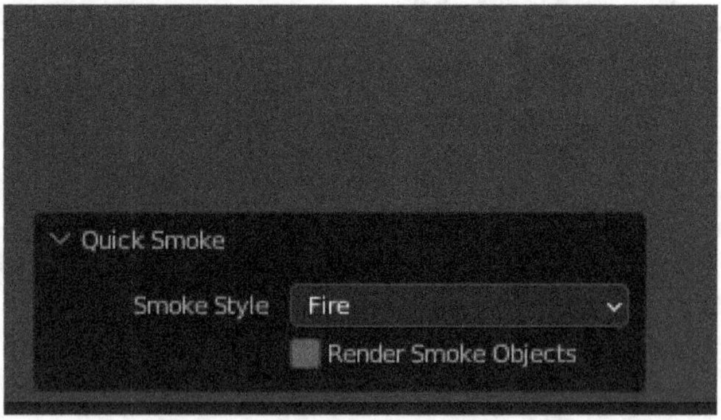

Figure 12.4: Changing from Smoke to Fire

And that's all you need to make fire! Let's prove that the fire is actually working by previewing it in the viewport.

5. Go to **Render** mode, then go to the Timeline (you may need to open your Timeline by using the **Editor Type** button, or by changing to the **Animation** workspace). Set your Timeline to the starting frame by dragging the playhead to the first frame of the animation.

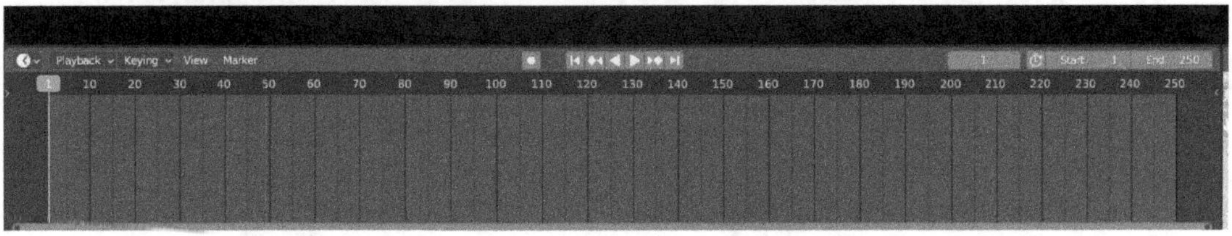

Figure 12.5: The Timeline

6. Next press the play button or *spacebar* on the Timeline and see how the fire looks.

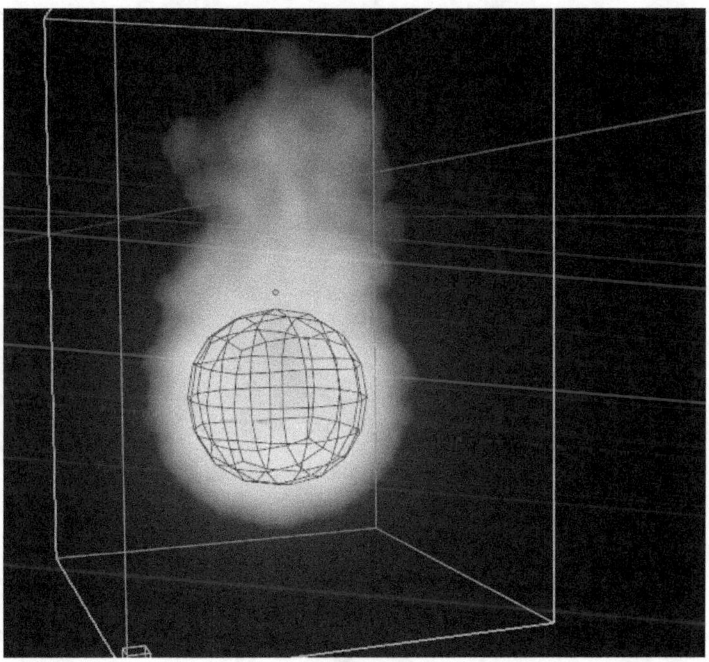

Figure 12.6: The default fire simulation

Using the default options, we already have something that looks like fire. Now we'll make some changes to the default and get our fire looking a little more like the controlled flame that we can imagine coming out of the thrusters of the spaceship.

There are two parts to a fire simulation:

- The first part is the **Domain**. The **Domain** is the box that Blender added when we opted for **Quick Smoke**. It describes the area where the fire simulation is taking place. Fire can only be simulated inside of the Domain box, simply so Blender isn't trying to calculate the fire over an infinite area. The bigger the Domain box, the harder the computer will have to work to run the simulation.
- The other part of the fire simulation is the **Inflow** object. This object is the FireObject that we created and that we had selected when we hit the **Quick Smoke** button. This **Inflow** object is where the simulation will flow from. It uses the geometry of the object to decide the size and shape of the simulation.

So, we have two visual representations of how the simulation is being simulated in the viewport. The other place we can change the properties of our simulation is in the physics properties when we have either the **Domain** or **Inflow** objects selected. We'll start with the Inflow object:

1. Select the **FireObject** we had originally. Go to the Properties menu and select the Physics (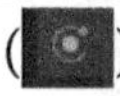) menu.

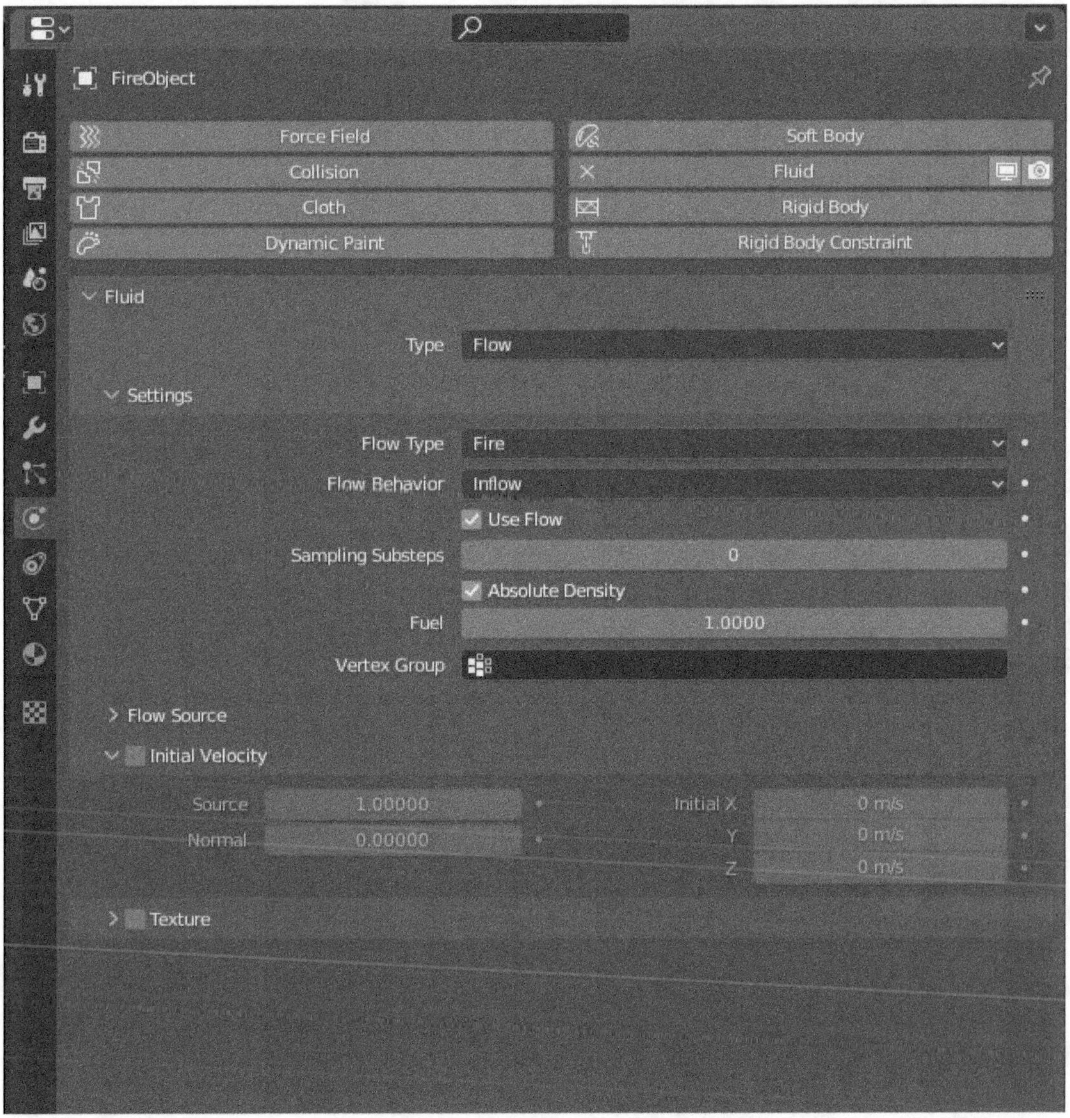

Figure 12.7: The Inflow options

2. These values are much less important than the values for the Domain of the simulation, but it still can be useful to tweak these if you need a certain effect. Here you'll find the **Flow Type** option, where you can change **Fire** back to **Fire + Smoke** or to just **Smoke** by clicking the drop-down menu in *Figure 12.7*.
3. Another interesting aspect to tweak is **Fuel**. This denotes the amount of computer-generated fuel that is added to the fire, so a higher fuel number will make the fire a lot bigger and more out of control (exactly like adding real-world fuel to a real-world fire). I'm going to leave my **Fuel** number at `1.000`, but you can experiment with different numbers.

Now that we've changed some settings for the **Inflow** object, let's try some different values in the Domain object. You may have noticed at this point that sometimes when you change values for the fire simulation, nothing actually happens. This happens because of the **cache** of the simulation. We've come across caching in *Chapter 10, Working with Irradiance Volumes and Cubemaps for More Accurate Rendering*, where we baked the **Irradiance Cube Probes**. The baked information is called a cache. This cache is Blender saving the simulation so it plays faster next time you press play on the timeline. Sometimes this caching is really useful, but sometimes it can get in the way of trying out different values in the simulation. Let's delete the cache for the simulation we've created so far so we can tweak some numbers in the Domain to get a different result than what we have:

1. Move the play head back to frame 1.
2. Select the **Smoke Domain** object.
3. Press the *F3* button on your keyboard. This brings up the search menu.
4. In the search menu, type `free`.

5. Select **fluid.free_all | Free All**. This tells Blender to dump all the cache data that we have stored so far. Unless we dump this data, Blender will not re-simulate the fire with our new parameters.

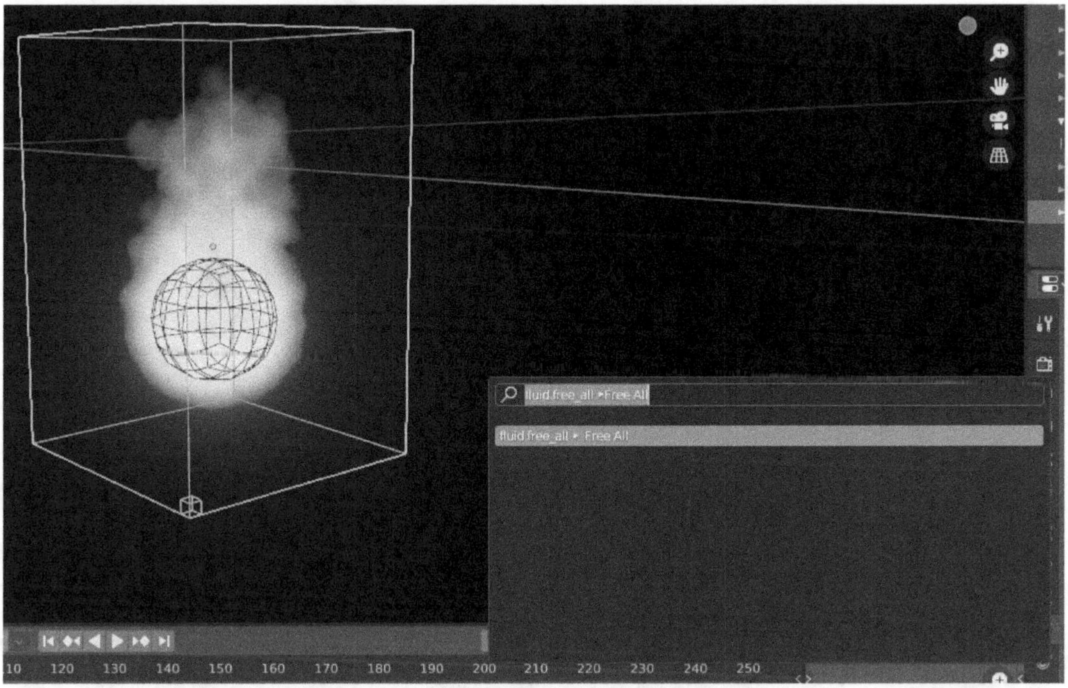

Figure 12.8: Freeing the cache

6. Now make a change to the options and see how it affects the fire simulation.

Now that we know how to reset our cache, it should be a lot easier to change our options and then test the fire simulation. Let's move on to changing the values for the Domain object:

1. Select the **Smoke Domain** and then navigate to the **Physics** menu, inside the Properties menu.

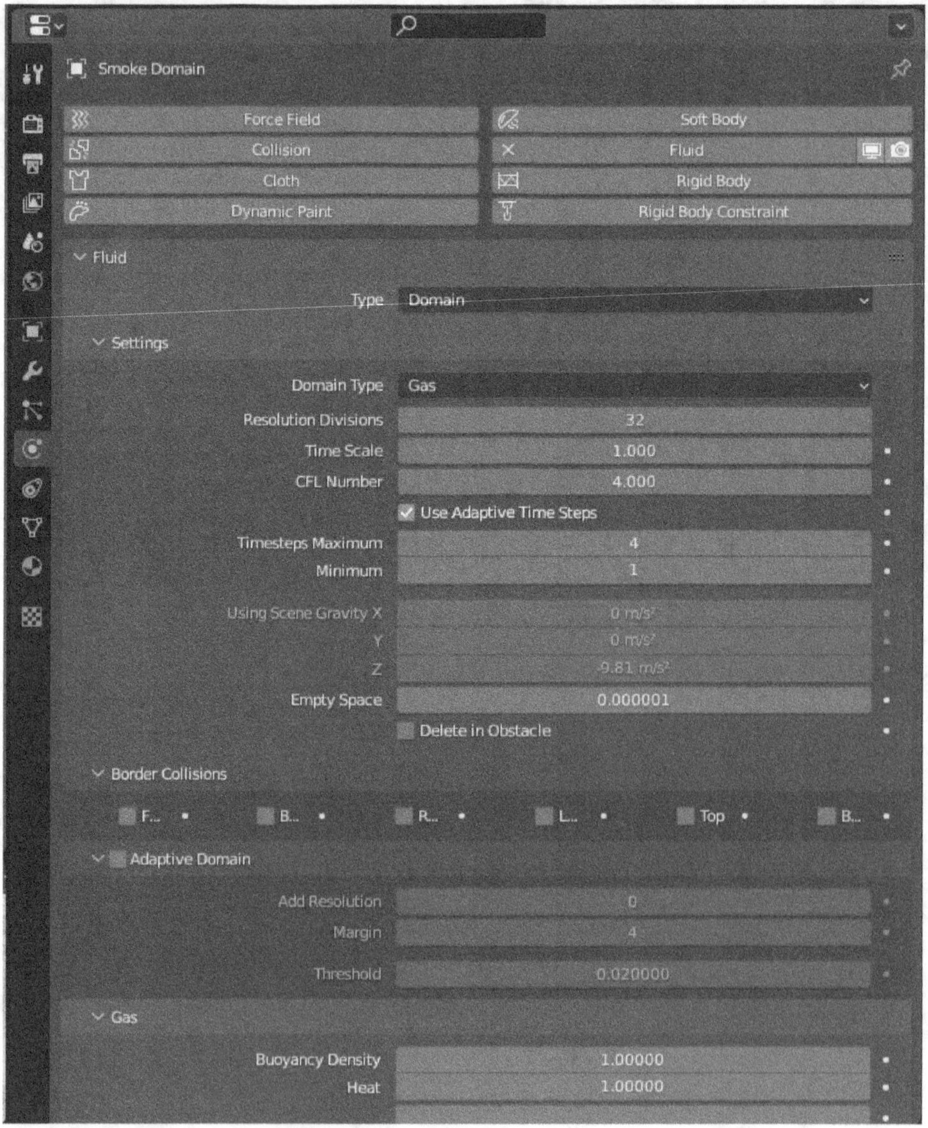

Figure 12.9: Smoke Domain options

2. The first change we'll make is to check the **Adaptive Domain** checkbox.

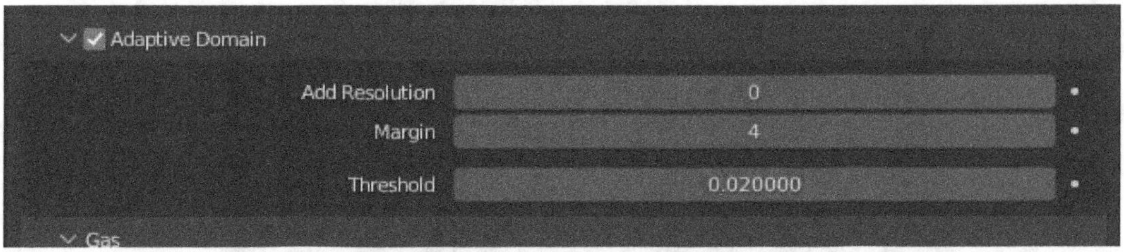

Figure 12.10: Adaptive Domain options

Adaptive Domain means that the Domain will get bigger as the fire simulation grows, so it will start small, and then move with the fire. This makes the simulation easier to render for Blender, as it maximizes the efficiency of the Domain. You can see in *Figure 12.11* the way the Domain has shrunk to only cover the area the fire is currently being simulated inside.

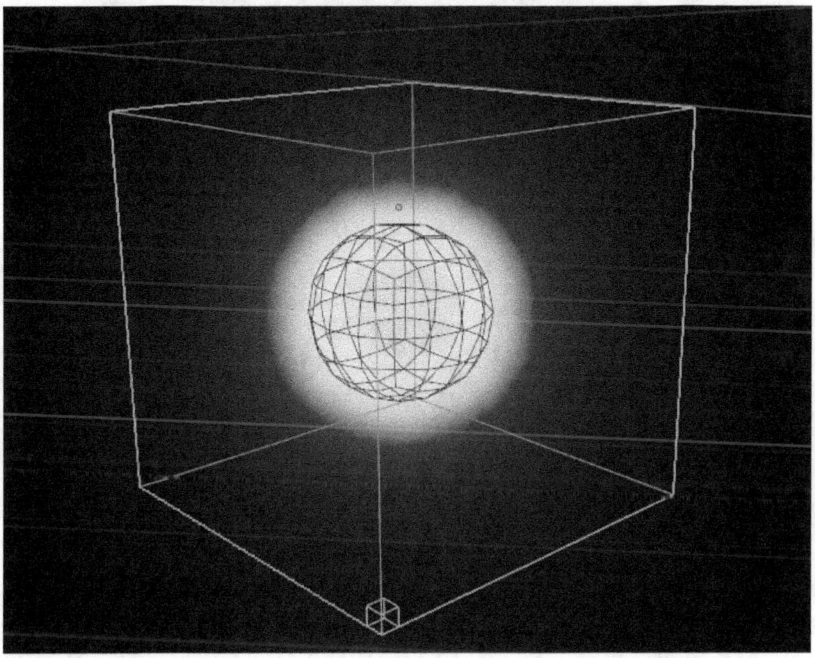

Figure 12.11: The Domain shrinking to only contain the Inflow object

And then as our simulation runs, the Domain grows so the fire is still contained:

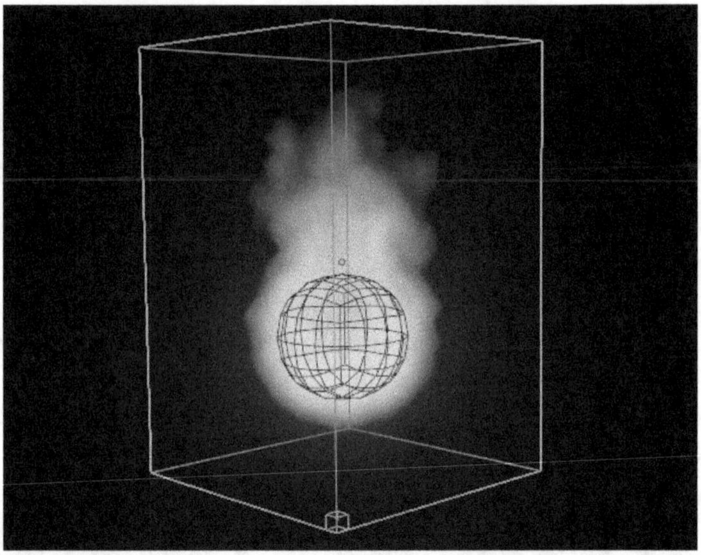

Figure 12.12: Domain size changes as the simulation grows

3. Next we need to scroll down to the **Fire** menu in the **Physics Properties** for our simulation.

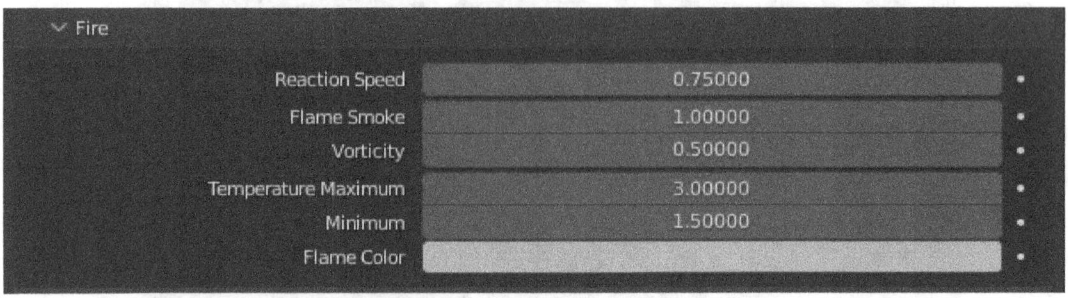

Figure 12.13: The Fire options

The **Fire** menu is the main factor that controls the fire simulation. The first value to change is **Reaction Speed**. This dictates the speed of the burning. A larger number will result in a smaller flame. *Figure 12.14* shows a simulation with a **Reaction Speed** value of `0.2`.

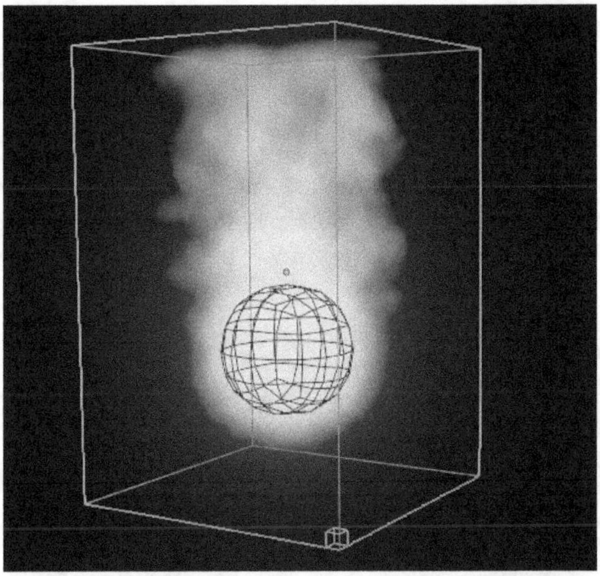

Figure 12.14: Fire simulation with Reaction Speed set to 0.2

Figure 12.15 shows a simulation with **Reaction Speed** set to `0.9`:

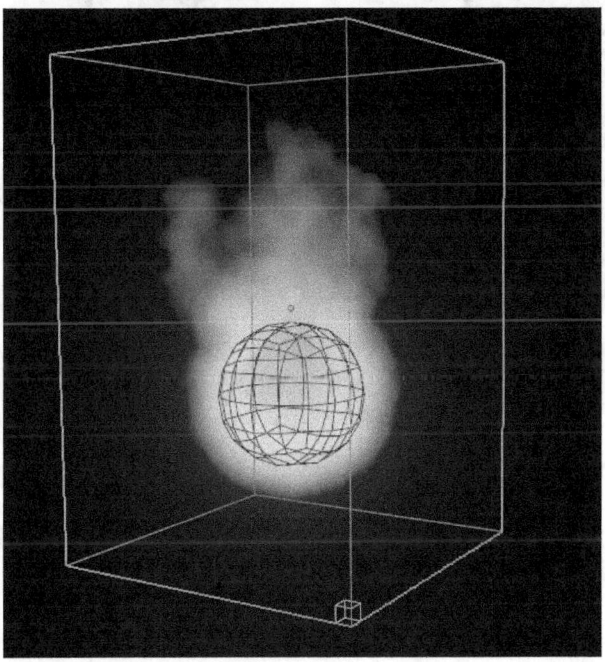

Figure 12.15: Flame simulation with a Reaction Speed value of 0.9

The lower **Reaction Speed** is so tall that it gets cut off by the Domain. The higher **Reaction Speed** results in a much shorter flame. Since we're trying to make a small and **controlled "thruster" type** flame, we probably want a lower **Reaction Speed** value, but feel free to experiment and make your own mind up.

4. We'll change the values for **Flame Smoke** next. This value determines how much smoke comes off the fire. I'm going to set my **Flame Smoke** option to `0`, as I think my thruster probably doesn't emit any smoke, but again, it's up to your own creative sensibilities to decide what to do.

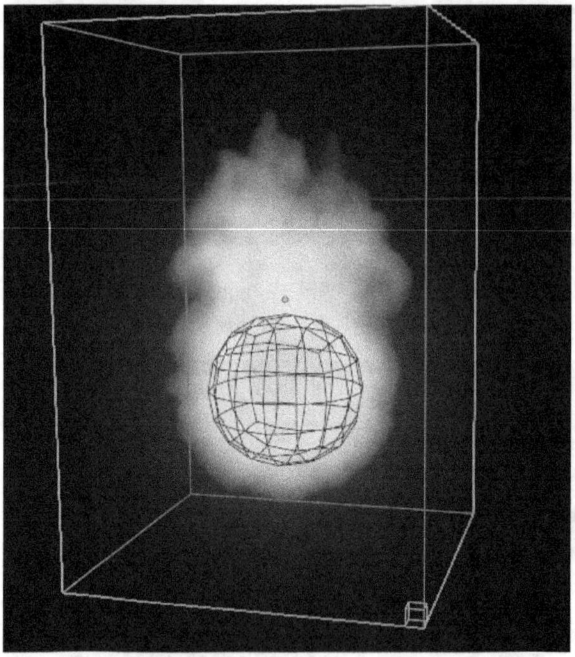

Figure 12.16: The fire with a Flame Smoke value of 0

5. There are a few other options in the **Fire** menu, but I don't often touch those. **Vorticity** is the rotational force of the flames, so you'll get slightly more flickery, broken-up flames with a higher **Vorticity** value. The **Temperature Maximum** and **Minimum** can help you tweak the animation of the fire, where higher values for both or either will make the flames rise faster, but since we're just going to render a single frame of the fire, we don't need to use those values.

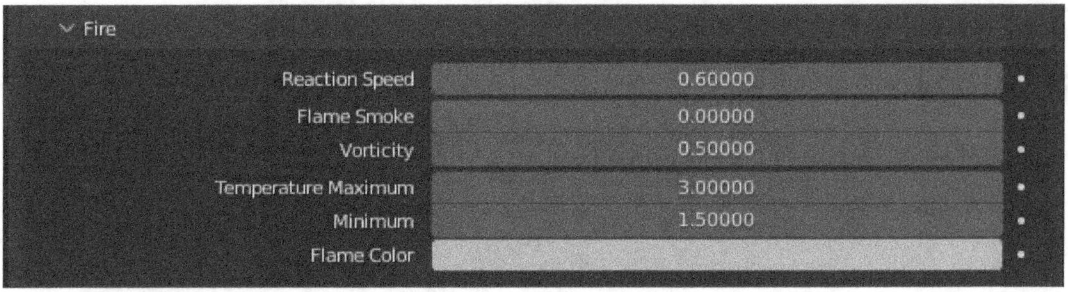

Figure 12.17: My final Fire values

6. The last value we want to change is back up in the **Settings** section of the **Domain** menu (*Figure 12.18*). Let's double the overall **Resolution** of the fire simulation. The higher the **Resolution** value, the more detailed the final simulation will be. If your computer has trouble simulating a fire at a **Resolution** value of `64`, drop back down to `32` for now, and then we can come back and raise the **Resolution** setting even higher than `64` right before we render, so we only have to cache that high-resolution simulation once.

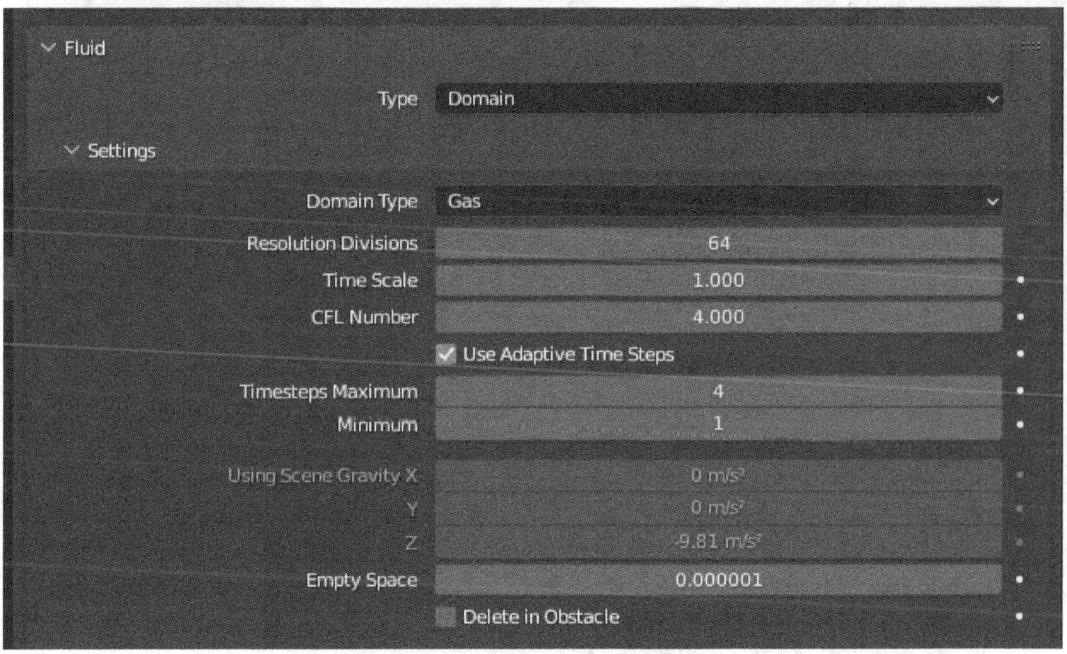

Figure 12.18: Domain settings

That will be it for the fire simulation for now. Let's move on to creating a better shader for the fire that will reduce the overall blurriness of the simulation and add more realism to the fire.

Tweaking the shader for fire and smoke in EEVEE

When using the **Quick Smoke** option, a shader is already created for us, which is why we can already see shades of red, yellow, and orange on our fire. In this section, we are going to create a much more complicated shader that gives a little more life to the fire:

1. Open the Shading workspace using the workspace editor that we talked about in *Chapter 3, Lights, Camera....*
2. The shader should look something like that shown in *Figure 12.19*. This is the default fire shader, but it doesn't give the ability to tweak any of the values or really change the color of the fire.

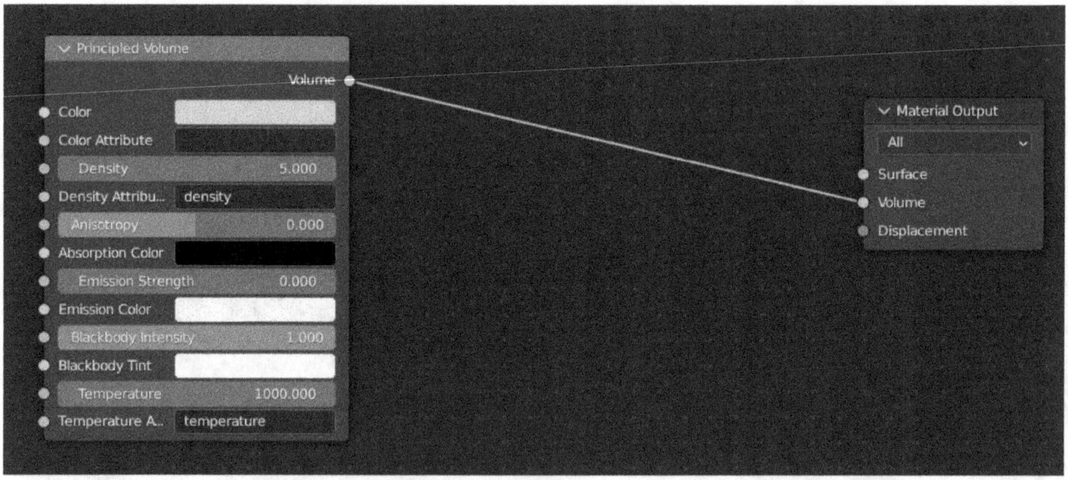

Figure 12.19: Principled Volume shader defaults for the fire simulation

3. To give some more variability, we'll add an **Attribute** node to this shader. We haven't used the **Attribute** node yet, but it isn't so different than other nodes. It just allows us to input an attribute into the node network. An attribute is a piece of data that Blender calculates for us. They are also used in the **Geometry Nodes** system. We can already see an attribute that Blender is using automatically in the **Temperature Attribute** box. You can see that `temperature` (the attribute we typed in) is driving the **Temperature Attribute**, which makes the fire different colors depending on the heat of the fire.

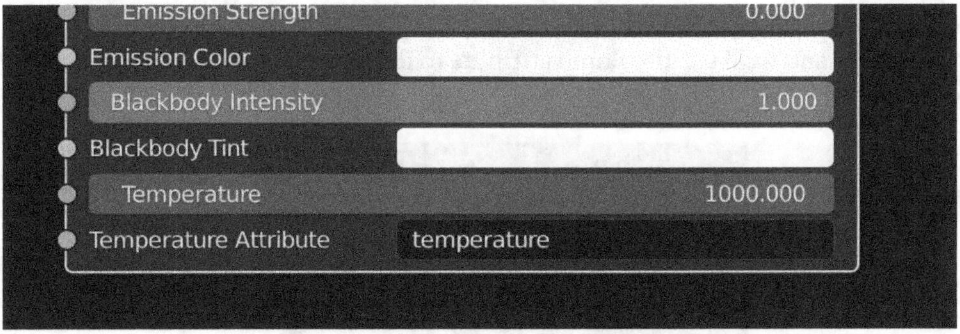

Figure 12.20: The Temperature Attribute

4. Let's add the **Attribute** node to our shader using *Shift* + *A* and searching for `Attribute`.

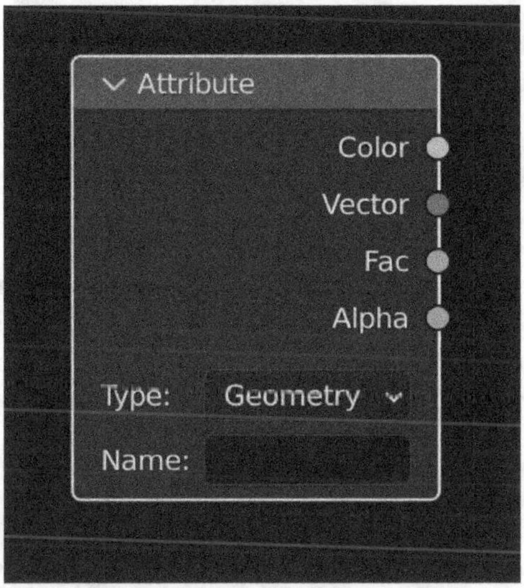

Figure 12.21: Attribute node

5. Now, we need to type `flame` in the **Name** box. This adds the **flame** attribute to the shader, and we'll use the **flame** attribute to drive the colors and emission in our shader.

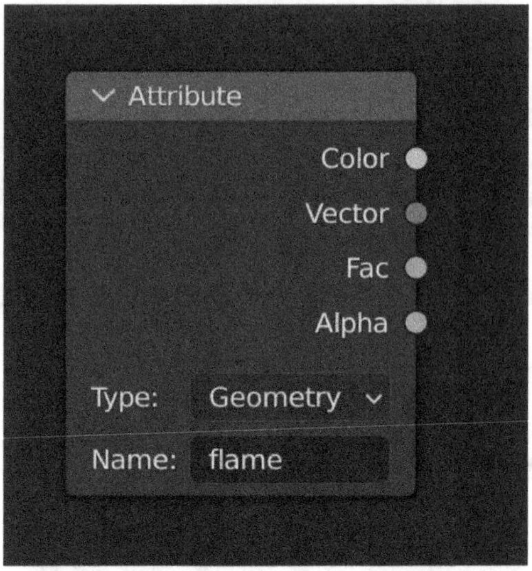

Figure 12.22: Adding the flame attribute

6. Next, we'll add a **Mix Shader** to combine the **Principled Volume** with an **Emission Shader**. Take the **Mix Shader** and drop it on the connection between the **Principled Volume** and the **Material Output** nodes. This should automatically add it to the connectors between those two nodes.

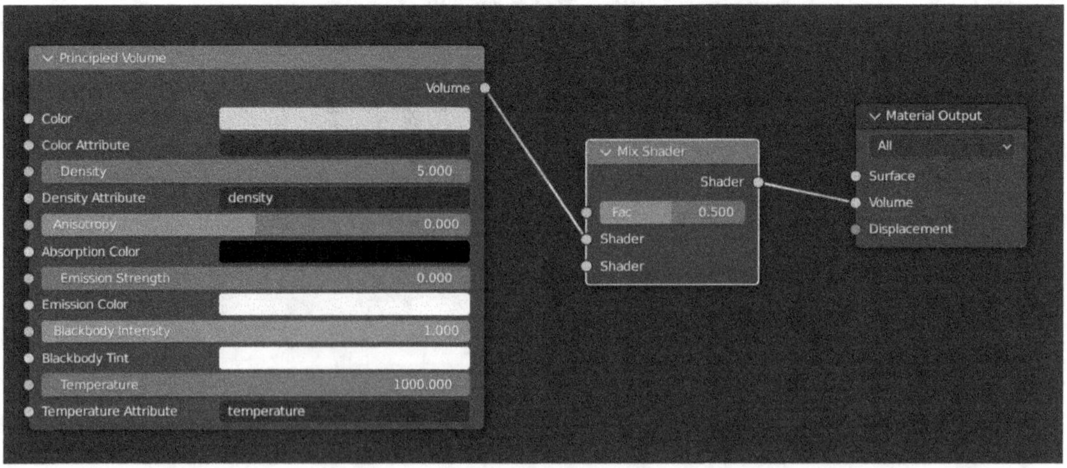

Figure 12.23: Adding the Mix Shader

7. Then, let's add the **Emission** shader and connect it to the bottom input of the **Mix Shader**.

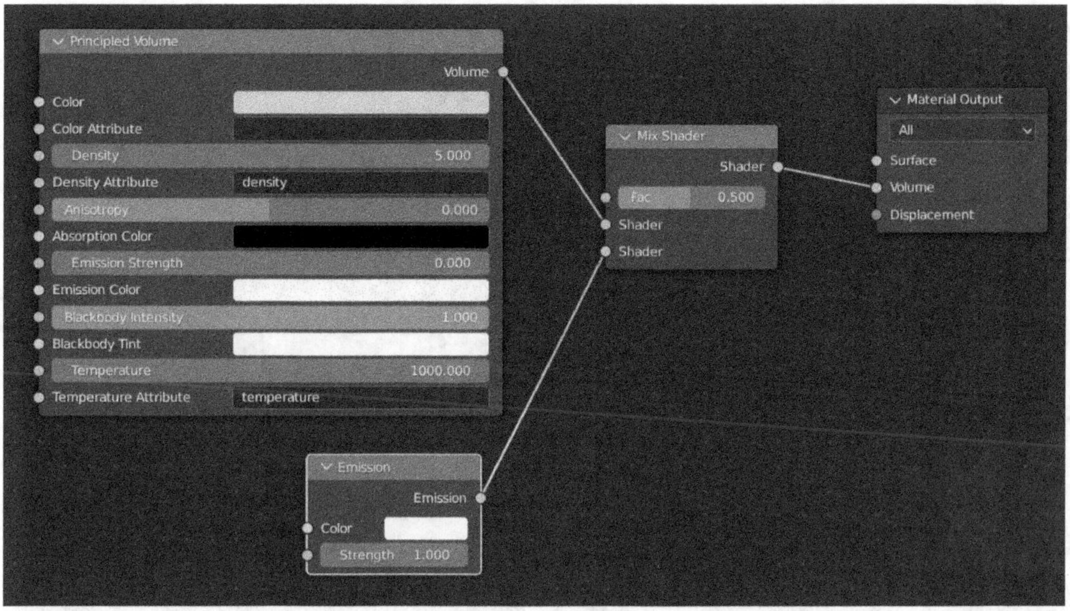

Figure 12.24: Adding the Emission shader to the Mix Shader node

Adding this **Emission** shader has completely changed how the fire looks in the viewport. And not for the better...but this is where our attribute comes in.

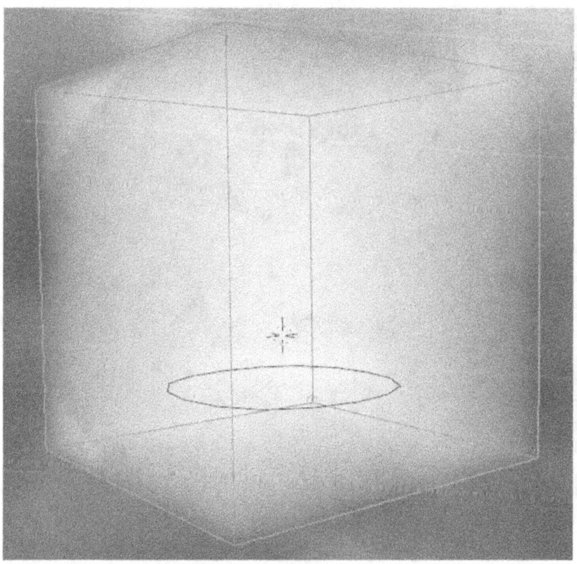

Figure 12.25: Result with Emission shader added

8. Take the output of the **Color** option from the **Attribute** node and attach it to the **Fac** input of the **Mix Shader** node, as follows:

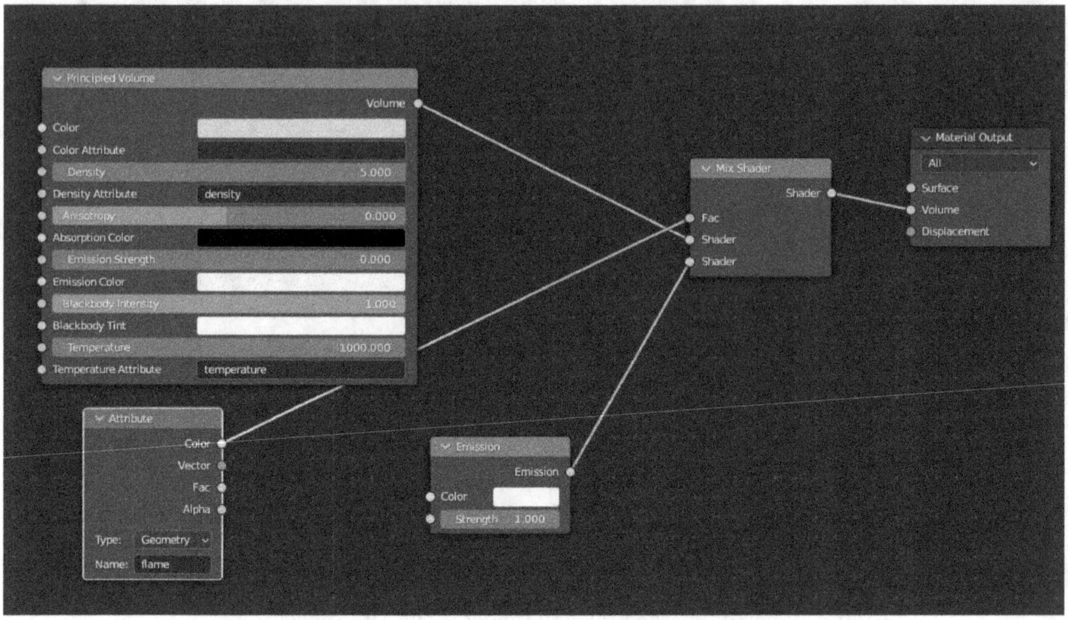

Figure 12.26: Adding the flame Attribute node as the Mix Shader node's factor

The fire is now at least looking like the correct shape again:

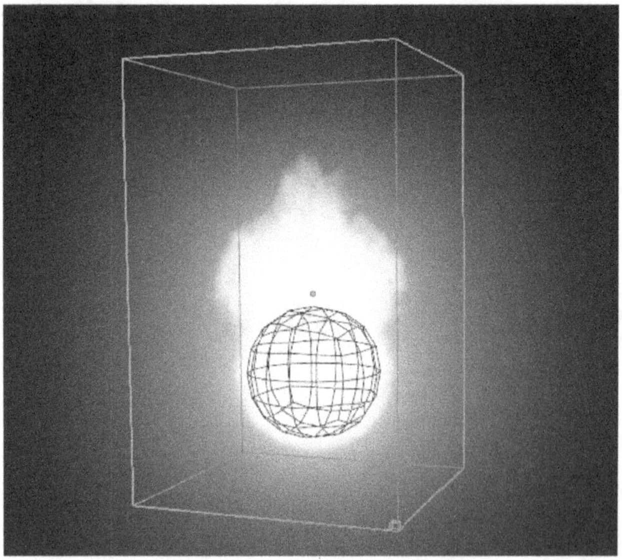

Figure 12.27: Result with the flame attribute added

9. Now, we'll add a **ColorRamp** node between the **Attribute** and **Mix Shader** nodes. ColorRamps are very versatile, allowing us to tweak colors, masks, and values, as we're already seen in *Chapter 2, Creating Materials Fast with EEVEE*. Change the **Interpolation** type on the **ColorRamp** node to **Ease** using the right-hand drop-down menu on the node.

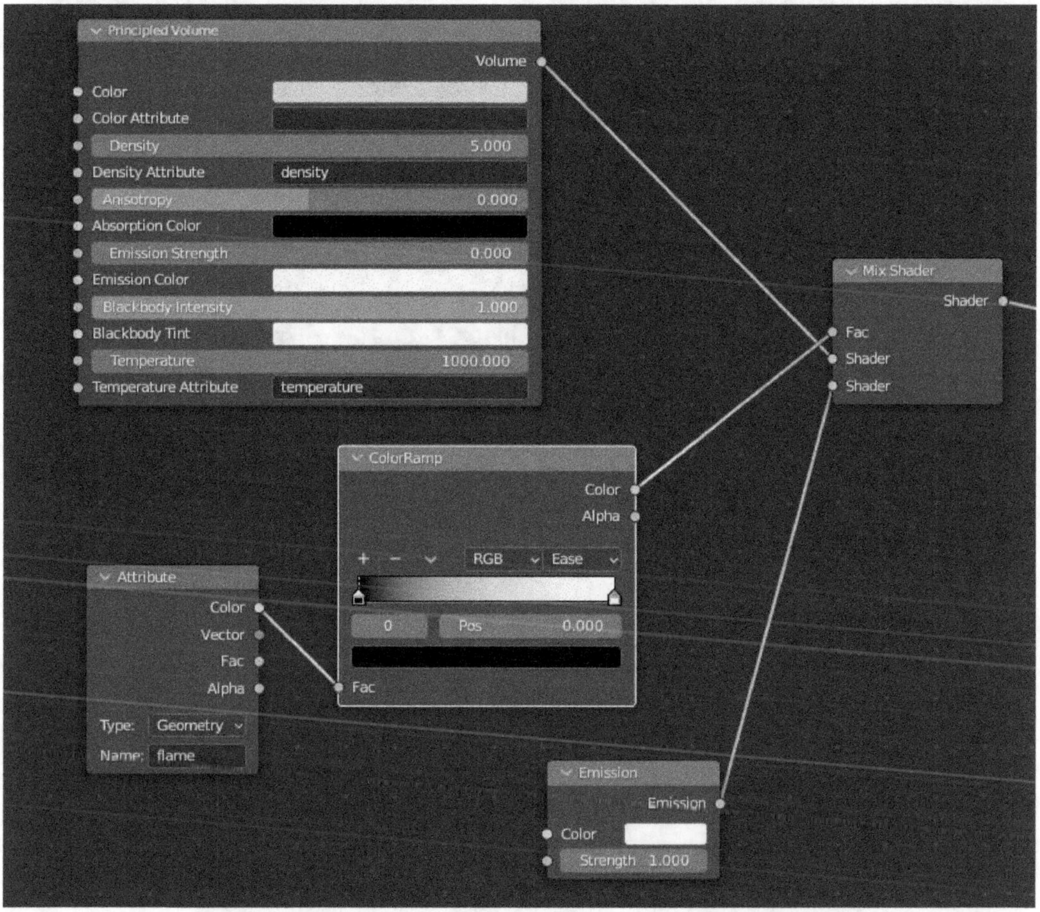

Figure 12.28: Adding a ColorRamp node to control the result

10. Copy the **ColorRamp** node and then hook it up between the **Color** output on the **Attribute** node and the **Color** input on the **Emission** node. Now we have controls for how we want to mix the nodes together and change the overall color of the fire.

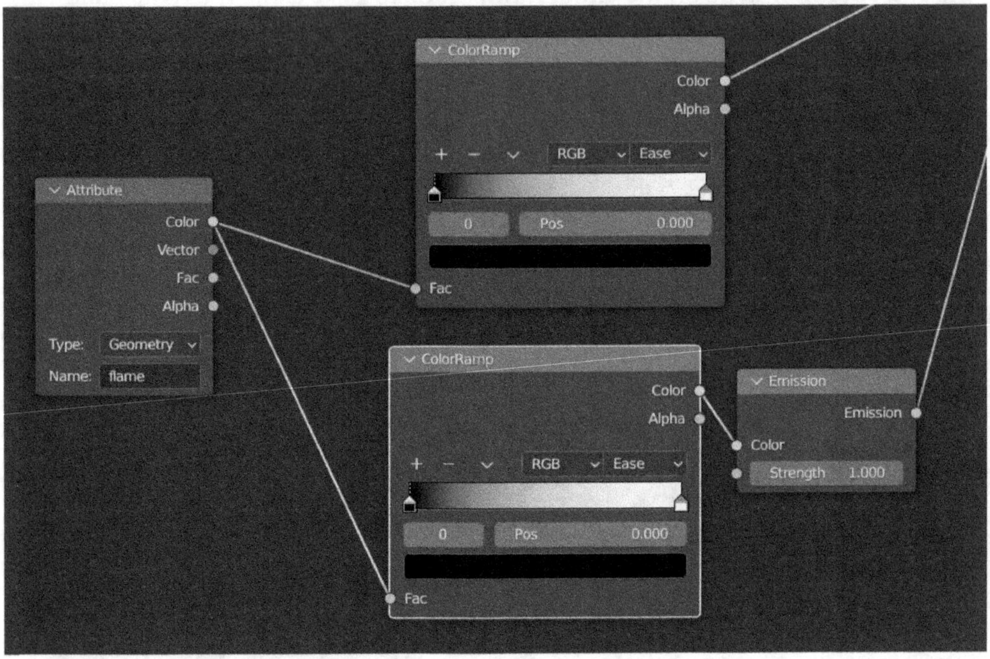

Figure 12.29: Adding another ColorRamp node for the Emission node

11. Change the **Emission** node's **Strength** value to `10`. This should add a lot of light to the scene, and we may want to dial it down later, but for now, this helps us see how the ColorRamps affect the scene:

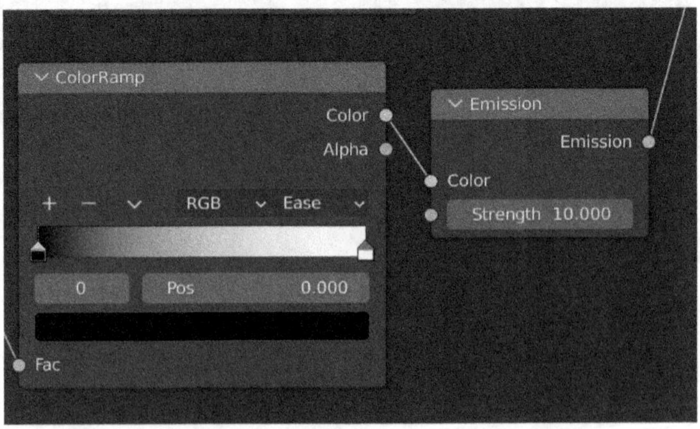

Figure 12.30: Increasing the Emission Strength to 10

12. Right now the colors of our new Emission shader are only black and white. Let's add two more colors to the **ColorRamp** node by clicking the plus button (+) on the left side of the node twice.

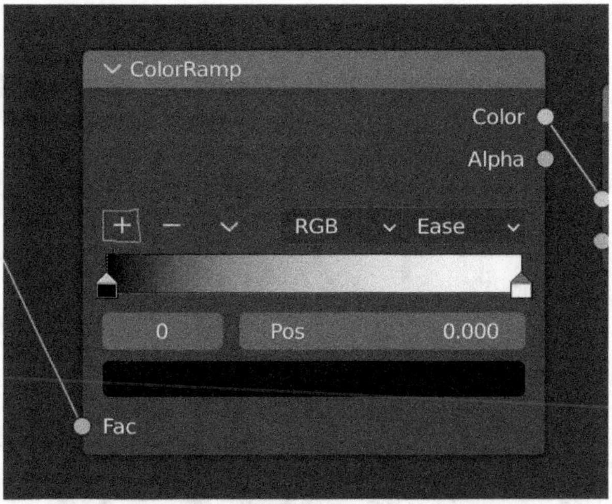

Figure 12.31: Adding Color inputs to the ColorRamp node

13. Now, click on each marker on the color gradient in turn, clicking on the bottom solid-color bar to change the color of each marker each time.

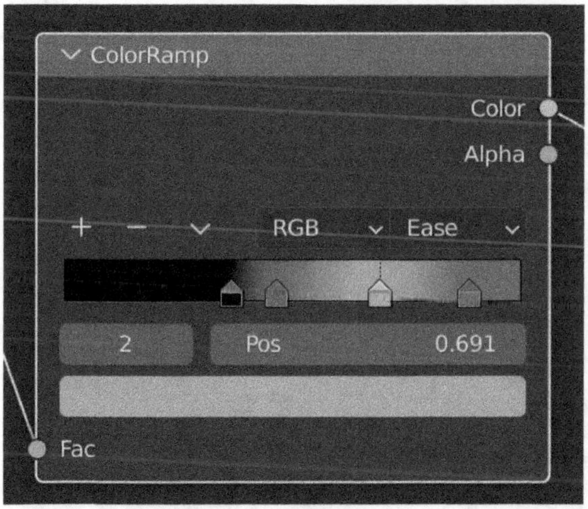

Figure 12.32: Mapping colors onto our fire

14. I created something like *Figure 12.32*, where blue is the middle of the fire, which is burning the hottest, which then turns to red and then orange as it gets closer to the edge of the fire. The blue color happens in really, really hot fires, and I think a thruster on a spaceship would probably have some blue flames at the core of the fire.

15. You can also use the **ColorRamp** node connected to the **Mix Shader** factor input to change how much of the **Volume** shader is being used as opposed to the **Emission** shader.

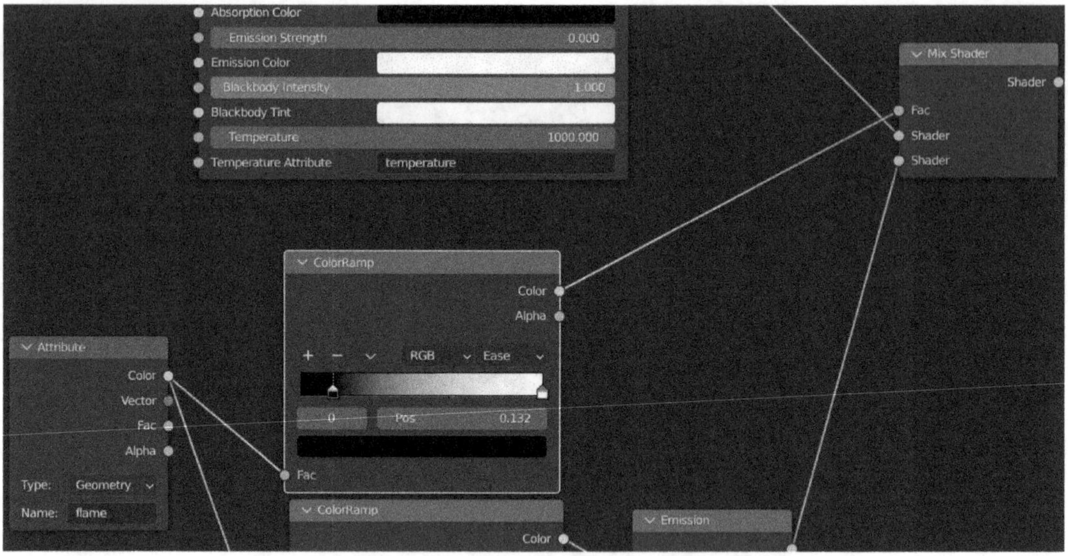

Figure 12.33: Changing the Volume Shader versus Emission Shader mix

After some careful tweaking, my fire shader looks something like this in **Render** mode:

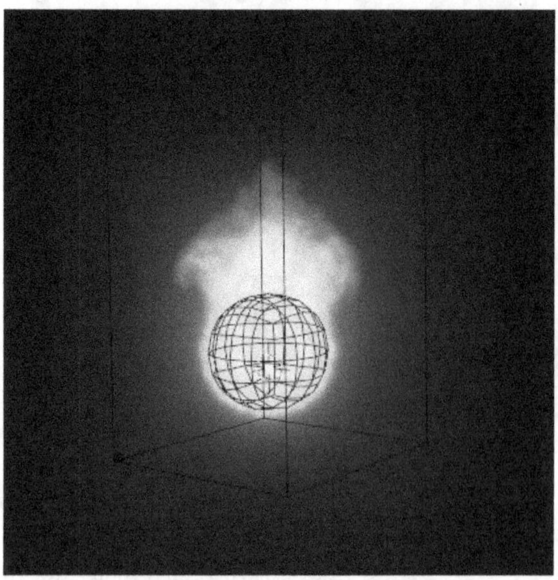

Figure 12.34: The fire shader

We're starting to get some more detail into the flame, but as you can see, it's still kind of blurry and amorphous compared to a real fire. We're going to do some work in the EEVEE rendering options to get a little closer to realism in the next section.

Optimal EEVEE render settings for the smoke and fire

Now that we have the overall settings and the shader done for the fire, we'll move into the EEVEE render settings to add more resolution to the fire. Let's get started:

1. The most basic things to do are turn on **Bloom** and **Screen Space Reflections**. They should already be turned on in this scene, but it never hurts to make sure. Go to **Render Properties** to check and turn these on if needed.

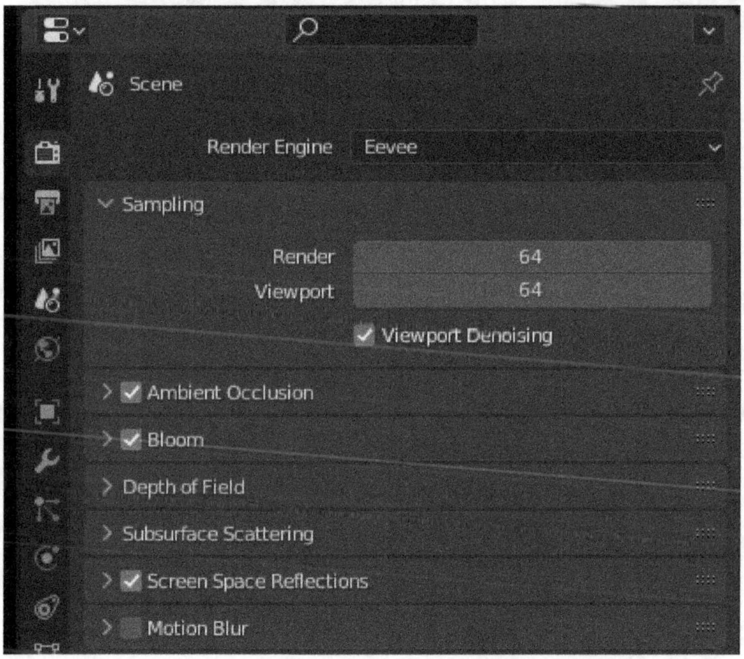

Figure 12.35: Turning on Bloom and Screen Space Reflections

2. The most important properties for the fire simulation are the volumetrics. Scroll down the **Render Properties** settings and you should see **Volumetrics** as a twirl-down menu.

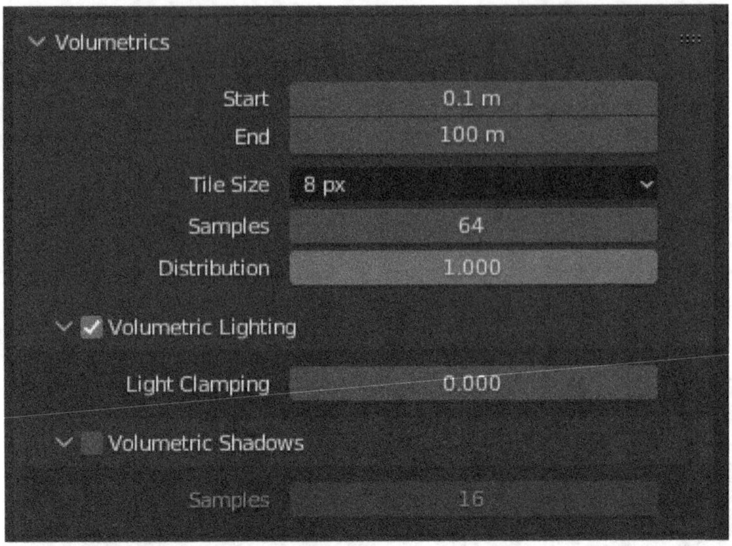

Figure 12.36: Volumetrics defaults

3. Let's change **Tile Size** first. **Tile Size** denotes how many pixels each tile of the simulation has. Therefore a smaller **Tile Size** value equals a higher resolution. We should change our **Tile Size** option to `2 px` for best results.
4. Check **Volumetric Shadows** on so that our fire will cast a shadow on itself, which should add to the realism.
5. I'm also going to change the **Samples** to `128`, doubling it from `64`. This increases the number of times the computer will sample the simulation. The greater the **Samples** value, the higher the resolution. Increasing the **Samples** value might cause your fire to disappear from view, but don't worry, we'll fix that in the next few steps.
6. It's very important that you do this next step from **Camera** view. Press *0* on the numpad to toggle **Camera** view or go to **View | Camera | Active Camera**. This is important because we're about to change the **Start** and **End** point for the volumetrics. This is calculated from the view used, and considering we're going to want to see the fire from the camera, we want to be in **Camera** view to ensure we set the relevant values correctly.

7. Change the **Distribution** value to `1`. This tells Blender we want more samples closer to the camera, and therefore we get better resolution closer to the camera.
8. Now, start lowering the **End** value. Keep lowering it until the flame starts to disappear, then go back up a little to get the whole flame in view with the smallest possible number. I found `24 m` was a good value that keeps the flame intact without clipping. This **End** value dictates the area in which the **Volumetrics** settings will apply. By decreasing the **End** value, we're telling Blender to only sample the fire in the area we want, and therefore although we get a smaller range of sampling, the sampling is more compact. More compact means a higher resolution, which increases the quality of the fire render.
9. Now change your **Start** value using the same principles that we applied to the **End** value. I found `7 m` was good for my fire.

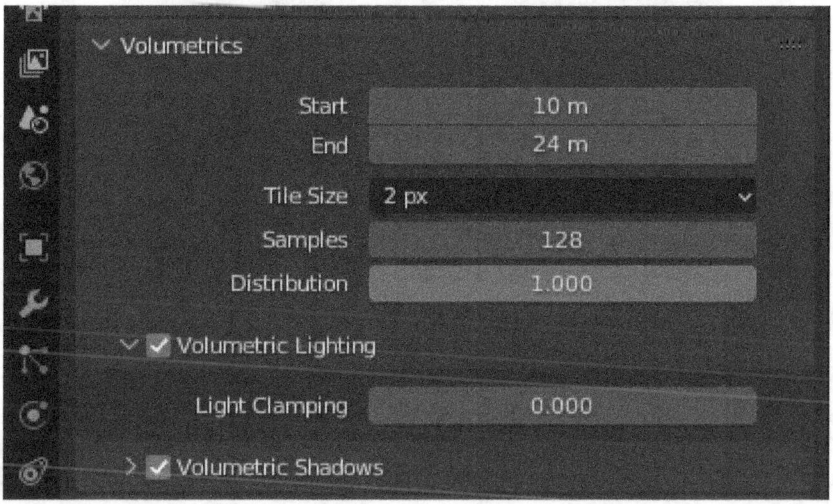

Figure 12.37: Final Volumetrics values

Figure 12.38 was what I ended up with. Try different settings depending on the strength of your computer and how you want the fire to look:

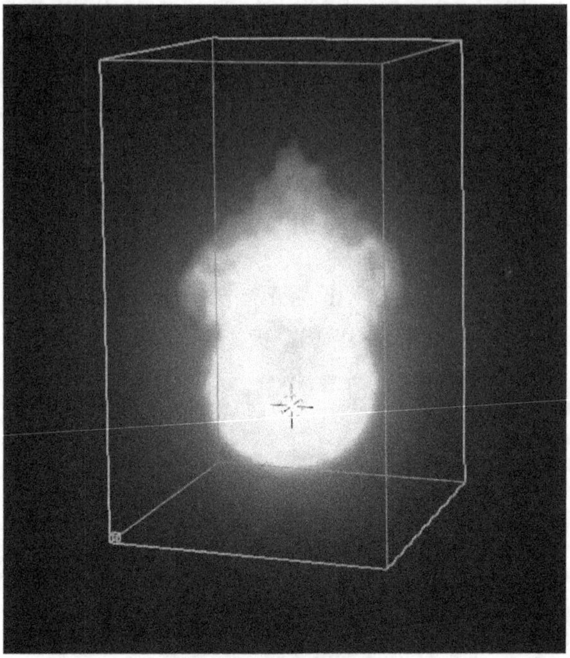

Figure 12.38: The fire

The last thing we're going to do in this section is rotate the fire so it simulates downward, instead of up, due to the fact that our thrusters are facing downwards. To do this, we need to grab the Domain and use *F3* to open our menu, then select **Free.all** to reset our cache. Then, take the Domain and rotate it 180 degrees. This will take the simulation we just created and run it upside down. There are many other ways to make the fire simulate downward, such as using force fields, changing the **Initial Velocity**, and others. But they all require tweaking and can be difficult to control without a lot of work. So, we're taking a shortcut and just turning our fire simulation upside down, which tricks Blender into making the fire shoot downward instead of up. Feel free to look up other ways of doing this, but we will now move on, as more complicated fire simulations are outside the scope of this book.

As you can see, the fire we created is starting to become clearer with more detail. This fire still probably needs a higher resolution, so if you have the time, set the **Domain Resolution** to `128` or `256` and let the animation run for a while. It might take 10-15 minutes for the fire to be simulated, but after the simulation is cached, you'll have a much more detailed-looking fire that can be rendered in EEVEE.

Putting everything together, I have something that looks like this. As you can see, while the fire looks very cool, it also doesn't look like it's coming from inside the thruster, but rather is bleeding over the top of the thruster:

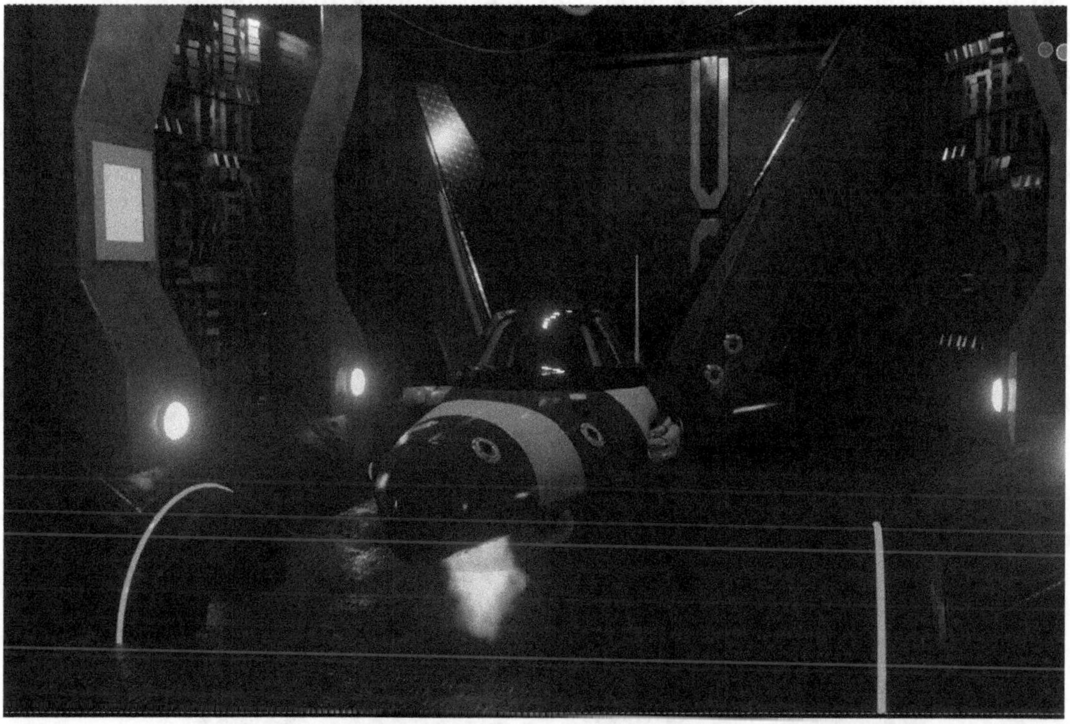

Figure 12.39: The render so far

It's okay, we don't need to spend more time tweaking the fire. Rather, we're going to use some rendering tricks to composite the fire into the scene.

How to combine renders in Cycles and EEVEE

In *Chapter 4*, *Non-Physical Rendering*, we went through a workflow to render different layers of a scene and then combine them later, with full creative control. Since we've already gone through that procedure, we're going to do something different here. I spoke a little bit in the introduction about how EEVEE can be used with Cycles, so in this chapter, we're going to render the fire we just created with Cycles, then composite it into a scene with EEVEE. Just know, it is still completely valid to separate the fire, spaceship, and hangar, render each of them in EEVEE, and then composite them together exactly as we did in *Chapter 4*, *Non-Physical Rendering*. But it's also worth learning how you can utilize Cycles while still letting EEVEE do all the heavy lifting. Let's start by rendering the fire:

1. First, we'll do something we haven't done in this entire book: switch to **Cycles**. This option is in **Render Properties**, at the very top of the available options.

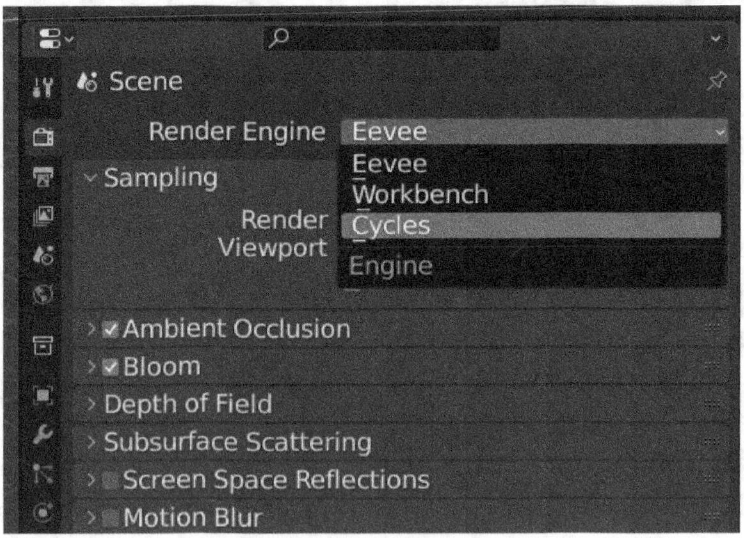

Figure 12.40: Changing to Cycles

Our viewport is immediately different. But, the fire is now contained inside the Thruster object, which is an improvement!

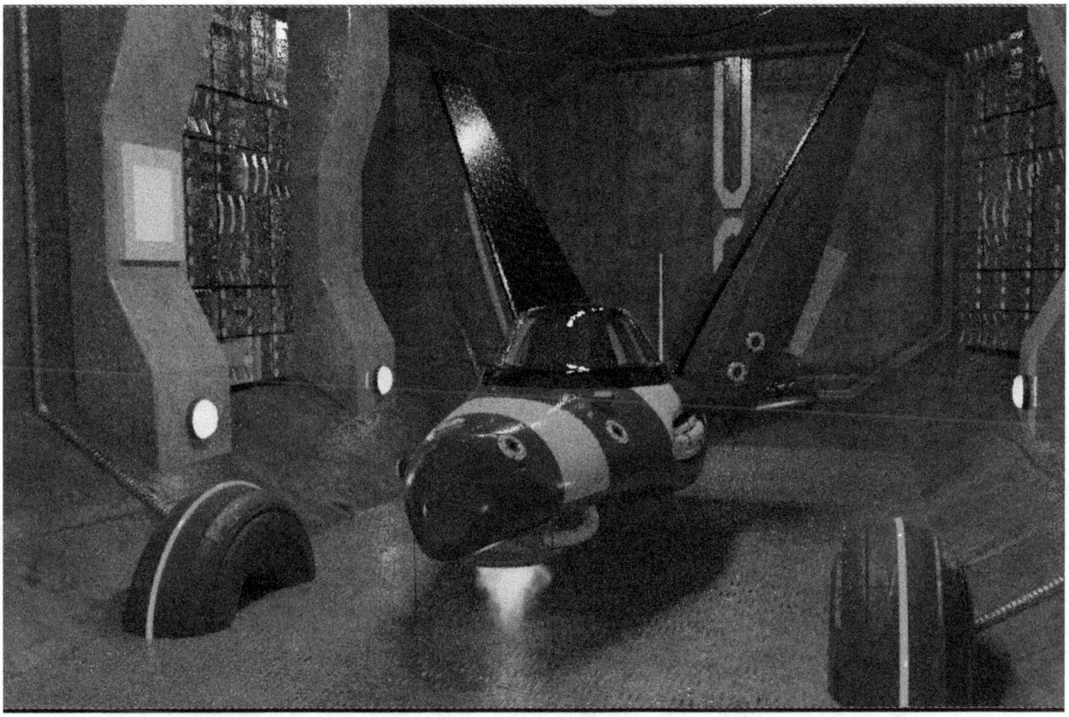

Figure 12.41: The viewport in Cycles

2. In the top right of the Blender window are the **Scene** and **View Layer** options. I renamed my **ViewLayer** to `Cycles` by double-clicking on it to edit.

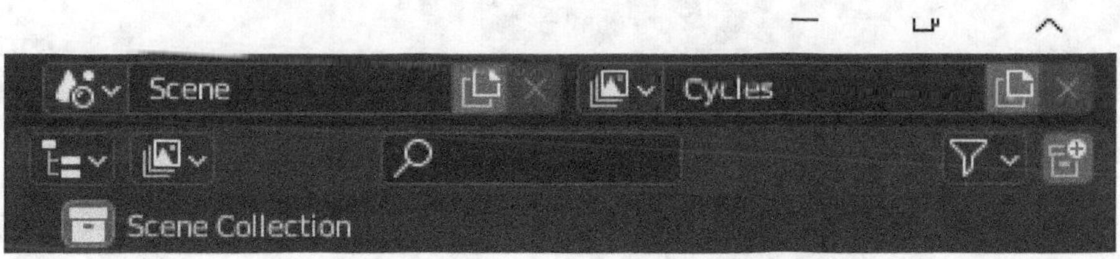

Figure 12.42: The Scene and ViewLayer options

3. Now we're going to exclude everything from the **ViewLayer** except the **Fire**, **SpaceShip**, and **Lighting** collections. We do that by unchecking the checkbox next to each collection:

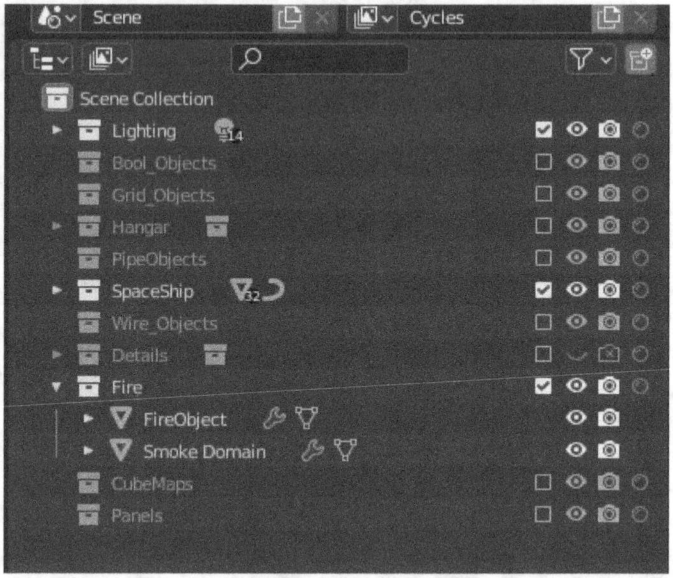

Figure 12.43: Deactivating the collections we don't need for the render

The viewport should look something like this now:

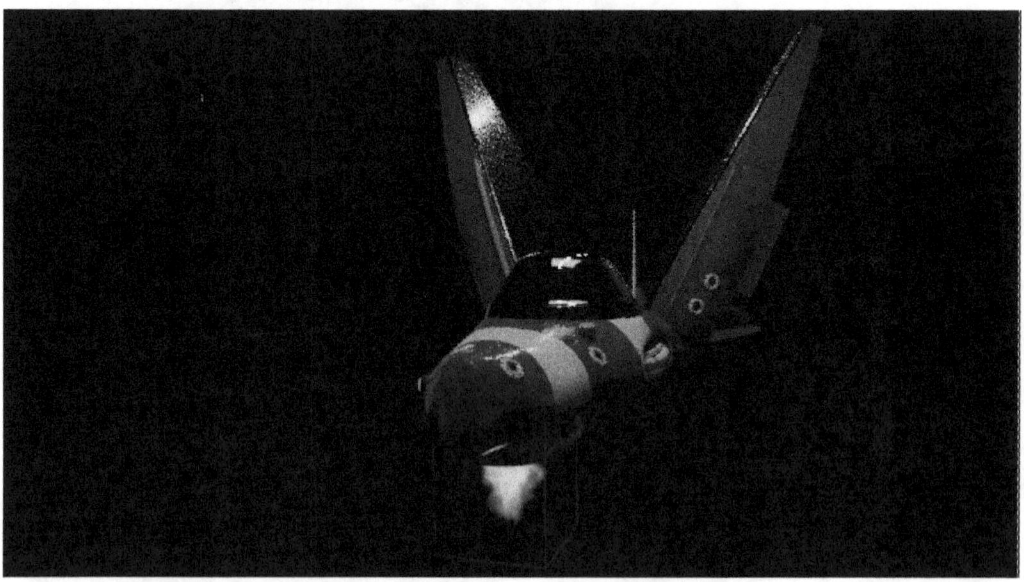

Figure 12.44: The viewport with only three collections activated

4. We need to do something special to the spaceship now since if we just unchecked it, we'd be able to see the entirety of the fire, rather than just the part coming out of the thruster as we want. We want to set the spaceship as a **holdout**, meaning that it still blocks other objects behind it, but these blocked objects will render transparently. If we click the **Restriction Toggles** filter in the top right of the Outliner, we can activate the ability to set the **SpaceShip** object as a holdout.

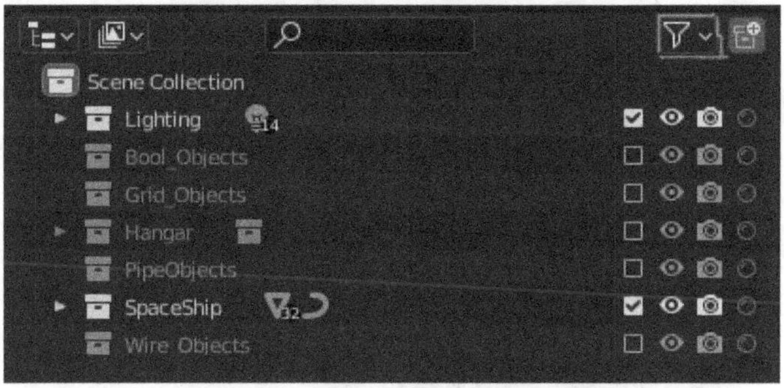

Figure 12.45: The Restriction Toggles filter

5. Once we click the **Restriction Toggles** filter, a menu should open. Click the button that looks like a square with a circle cut out of it, shown in *Figure 12.46*:

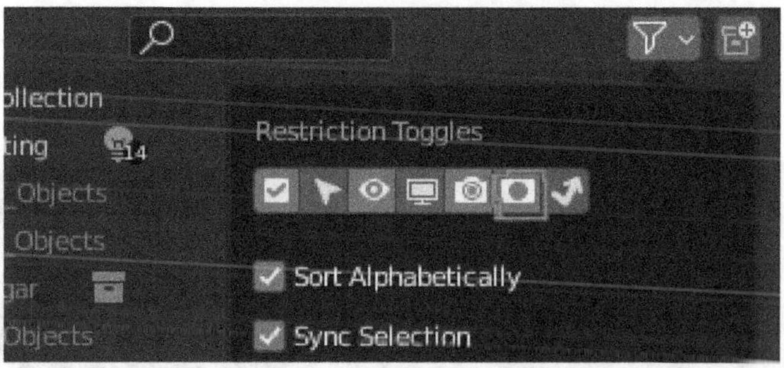

Figure 12.46: The Restriction Toggles menu

6. You'll notice that this creates a new column in the options for each collection, a little circle. Click on the bubble that corresponds to the SpaceShip object:

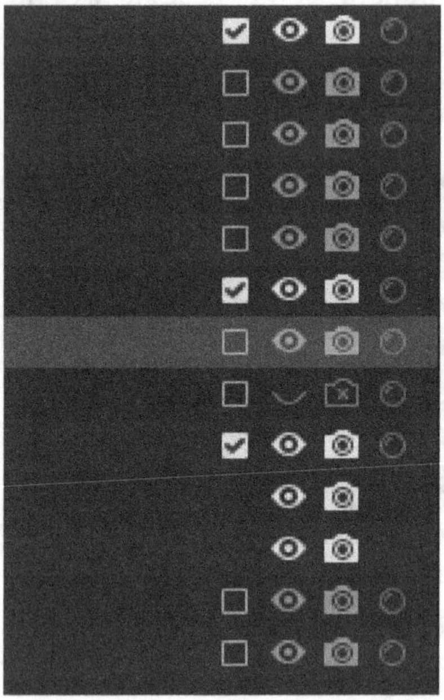

Figure 12.47: The added column for holdout toggles

You'll notice that the spaceship is no longer visible, but is also still blocking out parts of the fire.

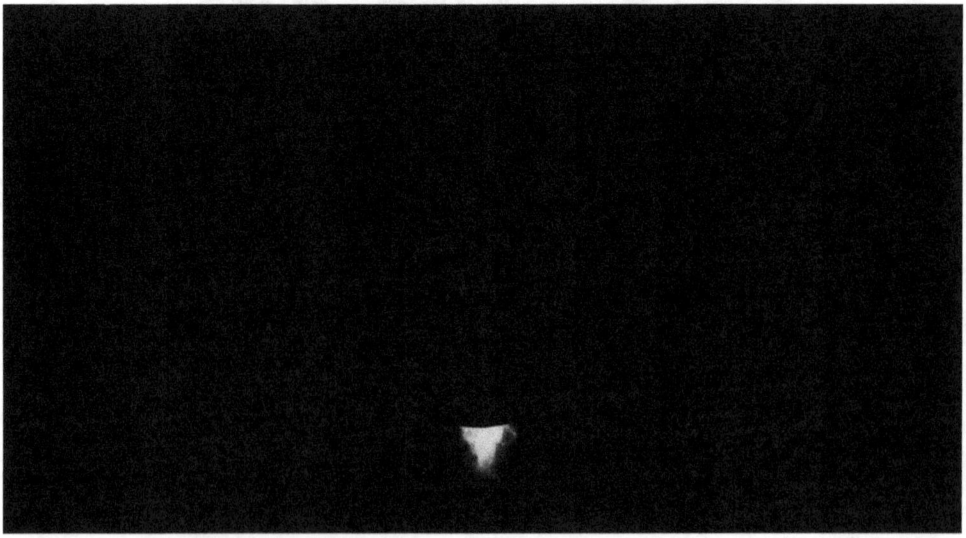

Figure 12.48: The flame is partially obscured by the thruster

7. The last thing to do is go back to the **Render** menu and make the background transparent. This option is under the **Film** twirl-down menu in the **Render Properties**. Check the box next to **Transparent**.

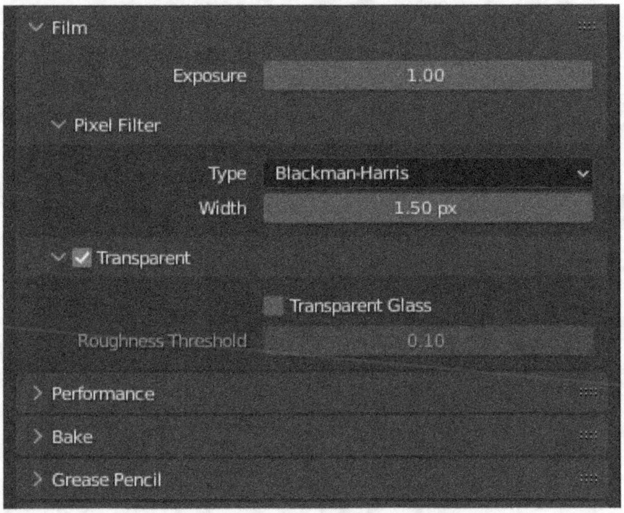

Figure 12.49: Turning transparency on

8. Our scene is now ready to render in Cycles, so hit *F12* or the **Render** button in the **Render Properties** panel. Once the render is done, go to the **Image** menu in the top left of the **Render** window and choose **Save As**.

   You can save this image in **OpenEXR Multilayer** format. This is the best format for most compositing in Blender.

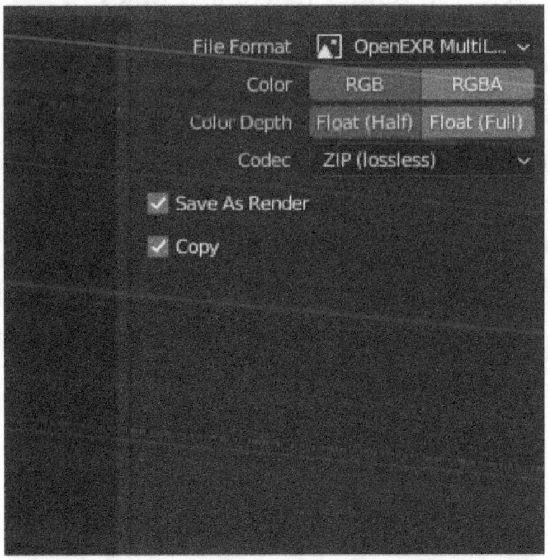

Figure 12.50: Saving the image in OpenEXR MultiLayer format

My render looks like this:

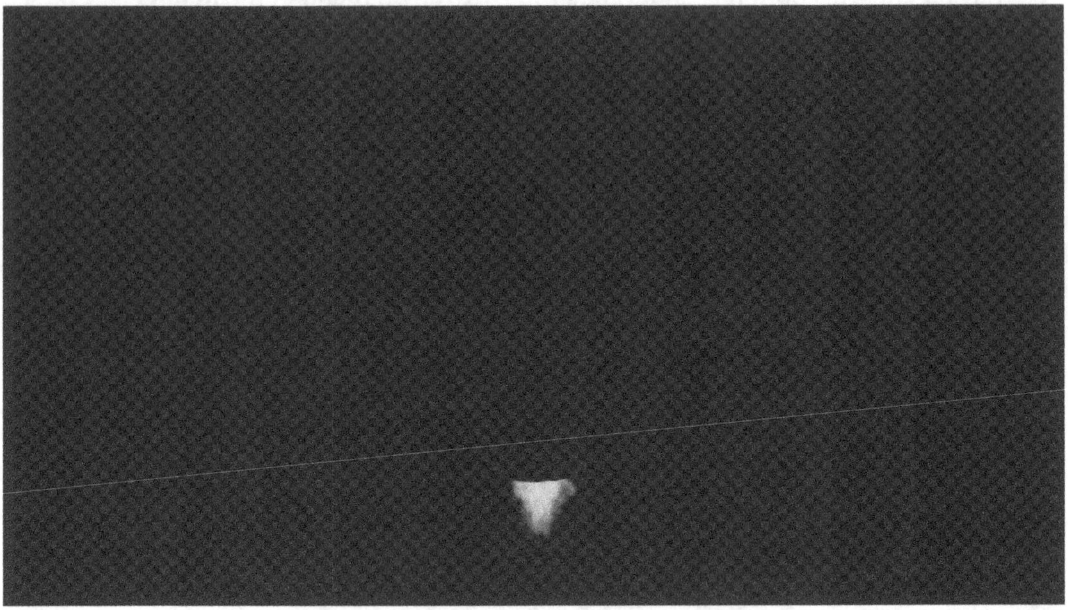

Figure 12.51: Fire render in Cycles

Now that we've successfully rendered the fire in Cycles, let's move back to EEVEE, render our other layer, and then composite it all together. I'll be doing this in a little less detail than I did in *Chapter 4, Non-Physical Rendering*, so check out that chapter again if you need a more granular explanation of this process. We now have the fire rendered and it's time to switch back to our preferred rendering engine, EEVEE:

1. Switch back to **EEVEE**!
2. Re-activate all the layers in the scene that we turned off to isolate the fire.
3. I don't really like how little light the fire is casting on the ground, but if we turn up the **Emission Strength** in the fire shader, we'll just wash out the color of the fire. As a solution, I'm going to add a **Point** light right under the thruster, change its color to something orangey, and increase its **Power** to `100 W`.

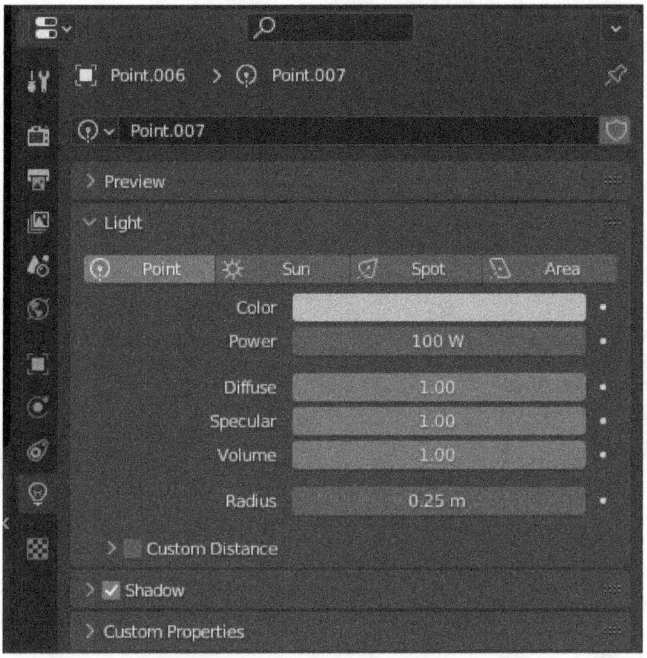

Figure 12.52: Values for the Point light

4. Then copy it and put another Point light closer to the back of the spaceship to show that there's another Thruster back there; we just can't see it because of the camera angle. This is a little bit of artistic license on my part, so take it with a pinch of salt.

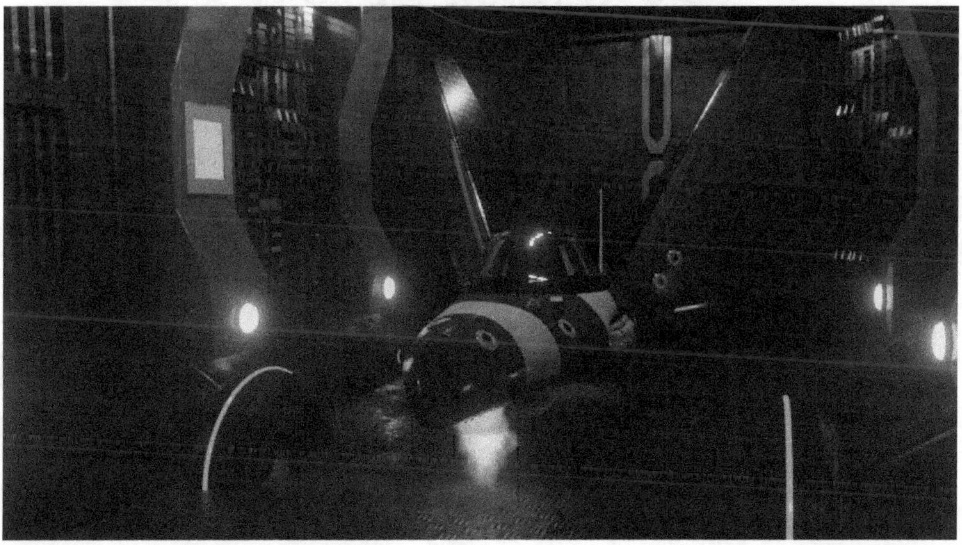

Figure 12.53: The Render in EEVEE with Point lights

5. Now let's bake our lighting again in the Render panel, as we learned in *Chapter 10, Working with Irradiance Volumes and Cubemaps for More Accurate Rendering*, to make sure our lighting is up to date.
6. Deactivate the **Fire** collection in the **ViewLayer**.
7. Render again, this time with EEVEE.
8. Once the render is done, switch to the **Compositing** workspace.
9. Activate the **Use Nodes** checkbox in the menu bar.

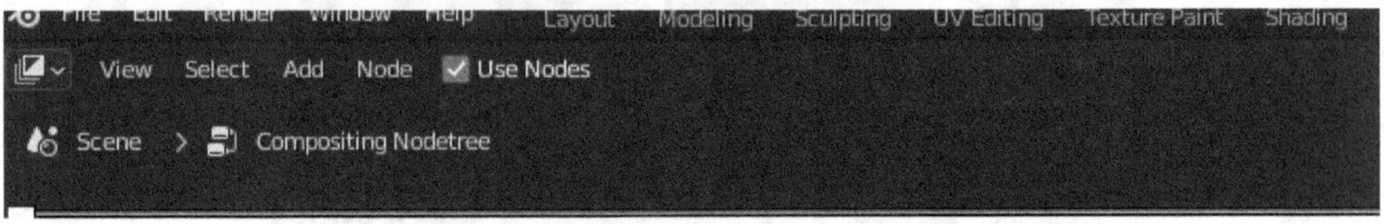

Figure 12.54: The Use Nodes checkbox

10. Also make sure to check the **Backdrop** checkbox in the **Node** menu. If you can't see the **Node** menu, open it using the *N* keyboard shortcut, and it's in the **View** submenu section.

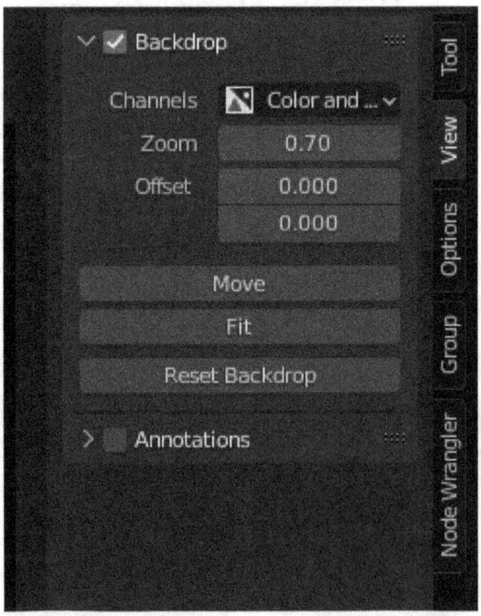

Figure 12.55: Backdrop checkbox

Our node tree is simple at the moment, and luckily we just need to add two nodes to incorporate the fire render from Cycles.

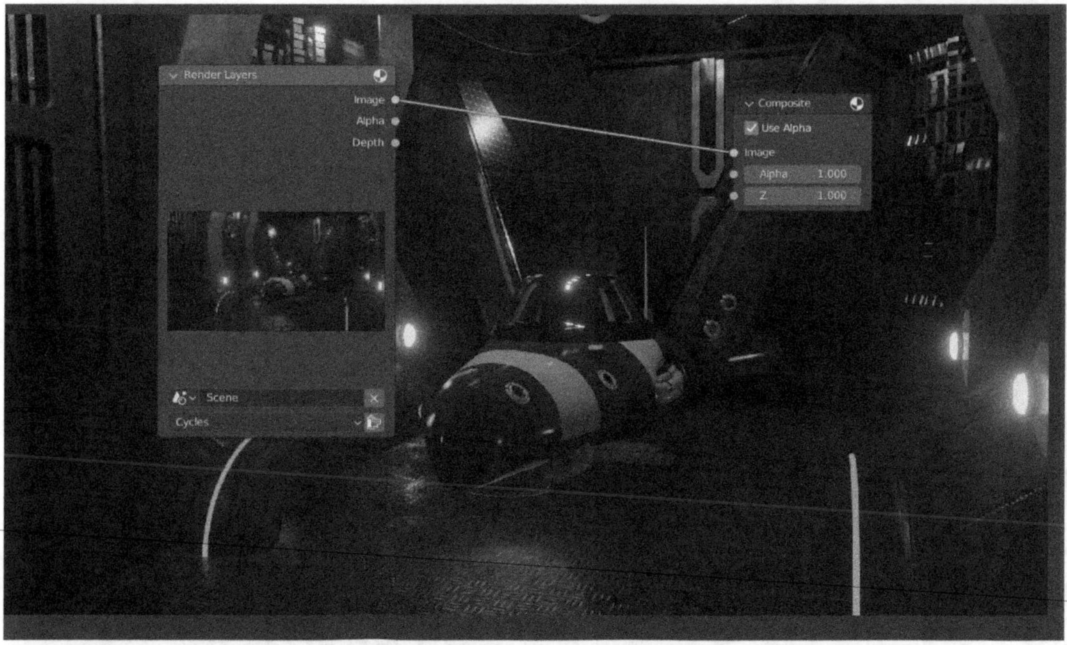

Figure 12.56: Compositing the backdrop

11. Add an **Alpha Over** node and put it between **Render Layers** and **Composite**.

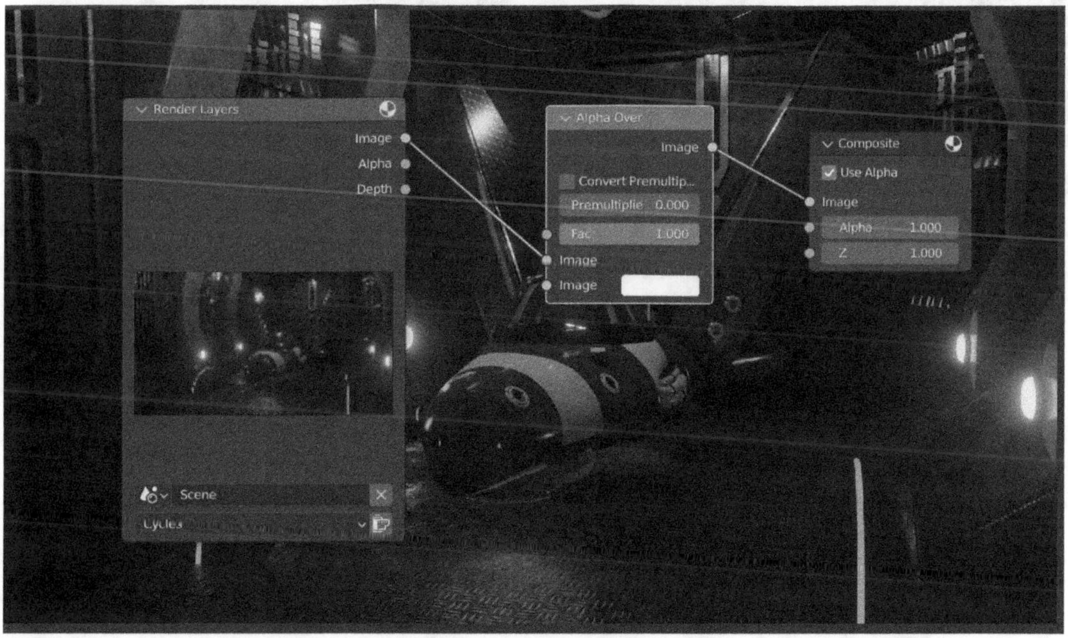

Figure 12.57: Alpha Over node added

12. And then import the `Fire.exr` we made in Cycles. You can just drag and drop the image from a folder into the Blender window. Take the **Combined** output and hook it up to the bottom **Alpha Over** input.

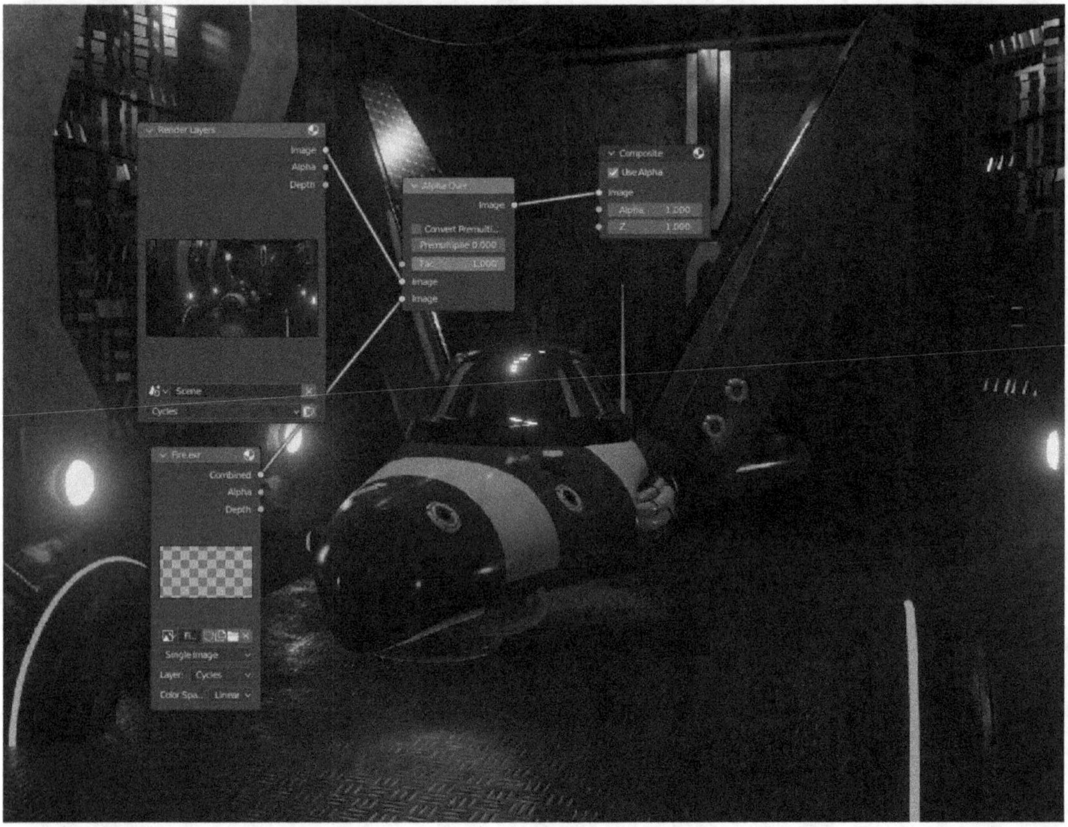

Figure 12.58: Adding the Fire render from Cycles

13. Hold down *Control* + *Shift* and click on the **Alpha Over** node. A **Viewer** node is now enabled and we can see how the final product looks.

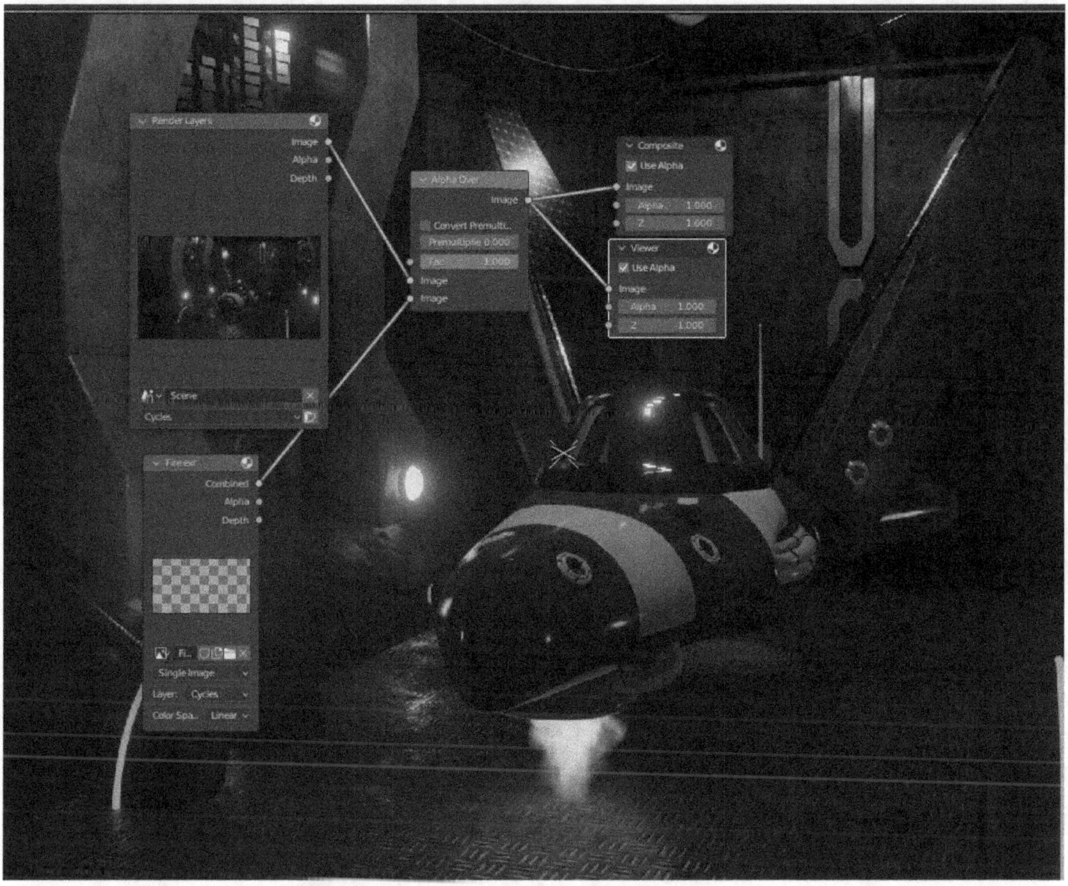

Figure 12.59: The viewport with added flame

14. Now we just render again using *F12* and we have a final product we can save in our preferred file format.

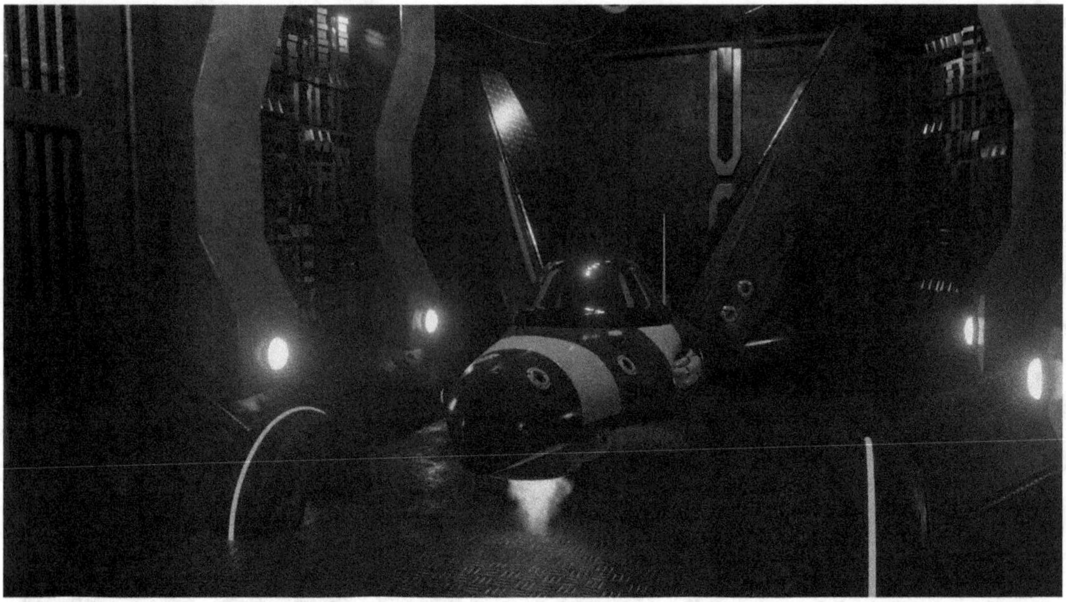

Figure 12.60: Final product

Hopefully you have enjoyed incorporating Cycles into our workflow – I really like the versatility that using both render engines together can bring. There are a myriad of ways you could use Cycles and EEVEE together, not just when rendering special effects, so go out and try a few.

That is the end of this mini-project. I hope that you got a chance to exercise your creativity in this sci-fi scene and made it your own.

Summary

We have officially come to the end of this last mini-project! Thanks for sticking with it to the end, I think it's worth it with the outcome we have. In this chapter, we talked about how to create a fairly realistic fire simulation inside EEVEE, and then how to incorporate Cycles into our EEVEE workflow. It is really important to remain flexible when creating your scenes, so don't discount using both Cycles and EEVEE when the need arises.

I hope you really enjoyed all three of the projects we worked on and I hope you feel more confident about your Blender abilities and now have the skills to create the things you can imagine. The next chapter is a conclusion of sorts, where I'll talk about the next steps you could take in your Blender career. I'll cover learning materials, other software you should learn, and further projects that you can work on.

13
Exploring the Wide World of Blender

Now that we've made three different renders, explored the depths of the EEVEE rendering engine, and learned some of the amazing new aspects that have been added in Blender 3.0, I hope that you feel like you can use Blender for all your creative needs. In this last chapter of the book, I want to take some time to review some of the main points that we covered in the previous chapters. Then, I am going to take some time to outline the next steps in Blender and what you can do to keep learning and growing your 3D skills. I'll talk about some of my favorite add-ons, learning materials, and equipment to purchase. Then, I'll talk about projects that you could tackle next or ideas to further develop. I hope that you've enjoyed the past 12 chapters and feel like you're ready to keep exploring the wide world of Blender.

In this chapter, we'll cover the following:

- Review of the main concepts covered in this book
- Further reading (or watching)
- Add-ons for further improving your workflow
- Further projects to tackle

Technical requirements

In this chapter, you really only need a computer or phone and access to the internet. I'll be talking about some video tutorials that you can watch, so having headphones might be helpful if you're accessing these videos in a public area.

There are no files to download for this chapter, but I have added a text file with links to all the resources outlined in the GitHub repository, in case you are accessing this book physically and don't want to have to type out the web addresses of the resources: `https://github.com/PacktPublishing/Shading-Lighting-and-Rendering-with-Blenders-EEVEE/tree/main/Chapter13`.

Review of the main concepts covered in this book

Taking up several pages trying to reiterate the entirety of this book is not what I will be doing in this section. Instead, I am going to cover some of the main topics, with a few sentences of explanation for each aspect. I want you to be able to remember any new words or technical concepts we discovered and to have this section as a reference for the future if you want to come back to it to brush up on terms. It can also be really good for your memory to review concepts again after you finish learning them, just to cement them in your brain. So, let's get started:

- **Geometry Nodes** (covered in *Chapter 5, Setting Up an Environment with Geometry Nodes*): Geometry Nodes are a system of small pieces of code (inside of nodes) that can be put together to create a series of instructions for Blender to enact an outcome. Geometry Nodes can be used to create systems to scatter rocks on an island, create houses with infinite custom dimensions, express mathematical concepts visually, or, really, anything you can imagine. This system was updated in Blender 3.0.
- **EEVEE**: EEVEE is a **real-time rendering engine** that rasterizes lights in order to speed up the rendering time of a scene. Many game engines use real-time rendering. EEVEE is an engine included with Blender that facilitates a truly fantastic breadth of 3D applications.
- **Volumetrics** (covered in multiple chapters, including *Chapter 4, Non-Physical Rendering, Chapter 8, Using Alphas for Details*, and *Chapter 12, Special Effects with EEVEE – Fire and Smoke*): Volumetrics is a technique that involves using the volume of an object and rendering that volume as smoke, clouds, mist, or other types of semi-transparent materials.

- **Asset Browser** (covered in *Chapter 5, Setting Up an Environment with Geometry Nodes*): The Asset Browser is a new feature in Blender 3.0 that allows us to create a library of assets that can be dragged and dropped into any Blender file. This way, we can cut down on rework and increase our iteration speed.
- **Kitbashing** (covered in *Chapter 11, Kitbashing – Adding Details Fast*): A technique that takes simple geometry and reuses it in patterns to create complicated machines, decorations, or embellishments.
- **Light Probes** (covered in multiple chapters, including *Chapter 6, Screen Space Reflections – Adding Reflection to the Water,* and *Chapter 10, Working with Irradiance Volumes and CubeMaps for Accurate Rendering*): Light Probes are an essential part of EEVEE, and if you've never used a real-time rendering engine, you may not have experience with these. **Light Probes** are scene objects that we place to tell Blender where we want to calculate lighting more accurately. We can use Light Probes to calculate **reflections**, **ambient occlusion**, and **indirect lighting** with greater accuracy.
- **Materials** (covered in *Chapter 2, Creating Materials Fast with EEVEE*): Materials are how we define the reflective and color properties of geometry. These reflective and color properties are how we see the difference between metal, dirt, and grass. In Blender, there are many ways to create materials; we used the two main ways, using **Image Textures** and **Procedural Textures.**
- **Lights** (covered in multiple chapters, including *Chapter 3, Lights, Camera...* and *Chapter 9, Lighting an Interior Scene*): Lights are exactly what they seem – they provide light to a scene. Lighting can be the most important part of look development, after modeling. Lights in EEVEE can work differently than in **Cycles**. We went over some of the aspects of lighting that can be difficult to understand when moving from Cycles to EEVEE, using point, area, and sun lights in our different projects. We also went over ways to use HDRIs without losing the ability to have shadows in the scene.
- **Cameras** (covered in *Chapter 3, Lights, Camera...*, configuring settings for your render): Cameras work exactly as they do in real life. We use them to make renders of the scenes we have created. Cameras need some tweaking in EEVEE, though they do work almost exactly the same in **Cycles**. We used some different settings that can make Cameras a little easier to work with.
- **Physics simulations** (covered in *Chapter 12, Special Effects with EEVEE – Fire and Smoke*): Physics simulations are useful for creating fire, smoke, water, destruction, and more. You can use physics simulations for natural phenomena, as well as unnatural phenomena, such as explosions. Mastering the use of these simulations can be a lifelong pursuit, as they can take a lot of trial, error, and intuition built over time.

- **Render panel**: The Render panel is the right-side panel we used in most of our chapters. In EEVEE, it is essential to know where to find the Render options we learned about over the course of this book, such as **Bloom**, **Ambient Occlusion**, and **Screen Space Reflections**.

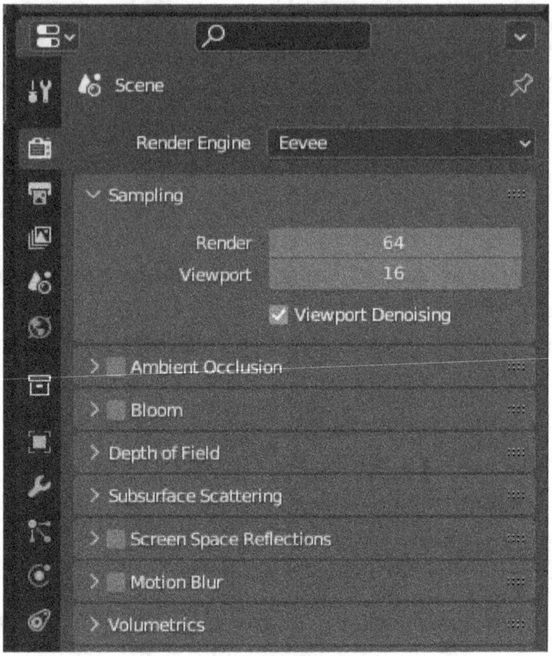

Figure 13.1: The Render panel

- **Grease Pencil** (covered in *Chapter 5, Setting Up an Environment with Geometry Nodes*): The Grease Pencil is a tool that allows you to draw with a 2D pencil in 3D space. This can be useful for creating cartoons and other non-realistic animations. Previous iterations of the Grease Pencil have been lacking in features, but with the 3.0 update, Grease Pencil has really been fleshed out into a full-featured animation tool.

Now that we've reviewed some of the main concepts that were covered in this book, let's look to the future and outline some places to learn more about each topic.

Further reading (or watching)

One of the things I love about Blender is that there's always more to learn. It truly has infinite depths and I never stop being surprised when I learn about new shortcuts or different ways of doing things that I had previously never even contemplated. In this section, we're going to talk about other learning resources. These will include books as well as video tutorials.

Learning more about: Geometry Nodes

If you feel compelled to jump deeper into **Geometry Nodes**, the best resource for Geometry Nodes information and tutorials is *Erindale*, located on YouTube at `https://www.youtube.com/channel/UCGMyyn2FdEFcDfP1wQRh51Q`.

Erindale has a great Geometry Nodes 101 series, as well as regular live streams where he walks through his thought process and creates cool systems, such as rope bridges and trains, all with Geometry Nodes. I am never disappointed with his work or his way of simplifying the math that can be involved in creating such complicated objects. If you like to read instead of watch, *Silverjb* has put together a really useful PDF on Geometry Nodes, detailing some workflows and nodes you may be interested in. It can be found here: `https://www.tamarindcreativegraphics.com/GN_Compiled.pdf`.

Learning more about: The Asset Browser

The **Asset Browser** is also one of the best new features of Blender 3.0. It allows for so much possibility, as long as you keep organized and save your materials to the appropriate folder. A really great way to get familiar with both the Asset Browser and the **Pose Library** (which is another version of the Asset Browser that can store character deformation poses) is to download the Asset Demo Bundle on *blender.org*. These files can be found at `https://www.blender.org/download/demo-files/`.

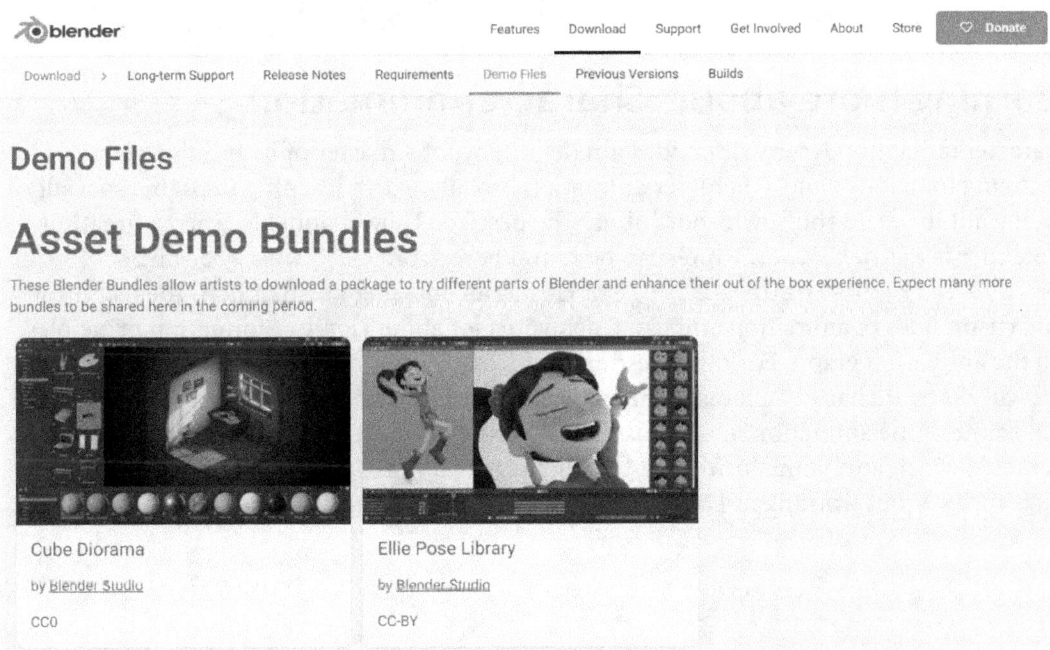

Figure 13.2: Blender Demo Files

Cube Diorama is a great demo of the Asset Browser and *Ellie Pose Library* shows a character from a recent Blender short film with which you can practice deforming and then saving poses. If you have trouble just opening these files and getting them to work, there's a great tutorial by *CG Essentials* at `https://www.youtube.com/watch?v=NMpjb7kl94s` that takes you through using *Cube Diorama* and how to use the Asset Browser as a whole.

Learning more about: Physics simulations

In this book, we really only used one type of simulation, fire. There are several different types of physical simulations that you can run in Blender that can be really useful to understand in greater detail. We can use simulations to create rain, snow, wind, objects crumbling, sand, oceans, hair, cloth, and much more. A great resource to learn more about physics simulations is simply searching on YouTube for the type of simulation you want to do. There are a myriad of tutorials out there; it's really impossible to choose just one to highlight here. Make sure you are selecting a video to learn from that uses Blender 2.9 or above, as videos that use Blender versions before 2.9 can be very different and not have the same functionality. Another resource that I love is *Two Minute Papers*, which can be found here: `https://www.youtube.com/c/K%C3%A1rolyZsolnai`. This YouTube channel recaps research into a variety of computational engineering topics, including simulations and AI. It is really awesome to see how many cool new ideas people are exploring for 3D animation.

Learning more about: Character animation

Character animation is very difficult! I am definitely not a master of it, and I've been practicing for a long time. Character animation is really worth learning though, especially if you want to create your own short films. The best YouTube channel to learn animation in Blender is *Pierrick Picaut*, which can be found here: `https://www.youtube.com/c/PierrickPicaut_P2DESIGN`. He has an amazing grasp of both the technical and artistic sides of animation and can teach you a lot about rigging, animation principles, and the animation graph. For other resources, I would recommend *The Animator's Survival Kit* by Richard Williams. While it was written for 2D animators who are drawing each frame of the animation, it still has so many different lessons to teach about creating characters when animating, using the 12 principles of animation, and as a bonus has some great stories about working at Disney Animation when it was just a little studio.

Learning more about: Modeling

We didn't really cover modeling, as I assume you already have some basis of modeling skills when you start this book. If you want to hone your modeling skills, I would recommend *Hard Surface Modeling in Blender* by Creative Shrimp, available on *Gumroad*: `https://creativeshrimp.gumroad.com/l/HardSurfaceModeling`. For 60 USD, you'll get a really concise and interesting course on creating robots, spaceships, and more, as well as learning more about Kitbashing and different techniques that can speed up your modeling. Of course, the most well-known Blender YouTuber is *Blender Guru*, who has a series of videos on beginner modeling for free, located here: `https://www.youtube.com/watch?v=Hf2esGA7vCc`.

Learning more about: Materials

Materials are usually really difficult for beginner and intermediate users to get the hang of. After you learn most of the basics, it can just be a matter of practice and looking closely at the materials around you. Try doing material studies on varied objects and see whether you can get them looking realistic.

Learning more about: The Grease Pencil

We didn't talk about the Grease Pencil a lot, even though it's a fantastic tool, especially in non-physically accurate rendering. The Grease Pencil can be a little bit difficult to use at first, especially if you don't have a tablet or other drawing device. A great tutorial to follow is *Kevandram's Blender 3.0 Grease Pencil Tutorial*, found on YouTube at `https://www.youtube.com/watch?v=nZyB30-xZFs`, or follow tutorials by *Dedouze*, a cool French artist whose art you may recognize from *Blender's splash-screen* a few versions back. Dedouze can be found at `https://www.youtube.com/channel/UC7VX1zRzqiA_Gc-bQglpXvw`.

Learning more about: Sculpting

Sculpting is another concept we didn't really touch on in this book. I think it can be really fun to learn to sculpt and it can lead to some amazing creations. The unparalleled master of sculpting in the Blender community is *Zach Reinhardt*. He works for *CG Boost*, which produce free tutorials such as *Full Advanced Creature Creation Workflow*, `https://www.youtube.com/watch?v=tQfFlzHJJ88`, or they have paid courses such as *Mastering Sculpting in Blender*: `https://academy.cgboost.com/p/master-3d-sculpting-in-blender`. Both will work if you want to learn sculpting, but obviously, the paid courses are much more extensive and provide a lot more support if you get stuck.

Learning more about: Scripting

Scripting is not something that I would suggest all artists learn. If you want to dive deeper into Blender and understand how to make your own add-ons and tools, it can be great to know some fundamentals. Blender uses a Python API, so that means you can execute any tool or command from inside the scripting window. The benefit to this is that you can string many commands together to execute them all in order, thus turning a 5-10 minute process into a 3-second process. *Curtis Holt* has a really interesting crash course for Blender Python on his YouTube channel, `https://www.youtube.com/watch?v=XqX5wh4YeRw`, but another way to learn scripting in Python is by reading the Blender Python API documentation: `https://docs.blender.org/api/current/index.html`. Note that as Blender is updated, the API moves to a new link, so if the link I have provided doesn't work, try using a search engine to find *Blender Python API*.

Add-ons for further improving your workflow

I know firsthand that it can be hard to justify spending money on something when you could just do it yourself. I resisted buying **add-ons** for the first 5 years of my Blender career, just because I could do anything an add-on could do myself! But at some point, you realize that time is money, and buying an add-on for a small fee could save you hundreds of hours of work. That's why I will say, don't be afraid to spend a little bit of money on Blender add-ons (if you have the money to spare, that is). Paying will save so much time and energy and leave you with the ability to spend more time on what is important, namely creativity and inspiration. That being said, some of the add-ons we're going to talk about are free, so make sure you download these and use them.

Before we get into add-on recommendations, I wanted to show a quick tutorial on adding add-ons to Blender that you might have bought or downloaded from GitHub. It's almost the same as activating an add-on that comes with Blender, but not quite. Let's learn how to add those add-ons:

1. Download whatever add-on you want to add to Blender as a `.zip` file.
2. Open Blender and go to the **Edit** menu (in the top-left corner) and select **Preferences...**.

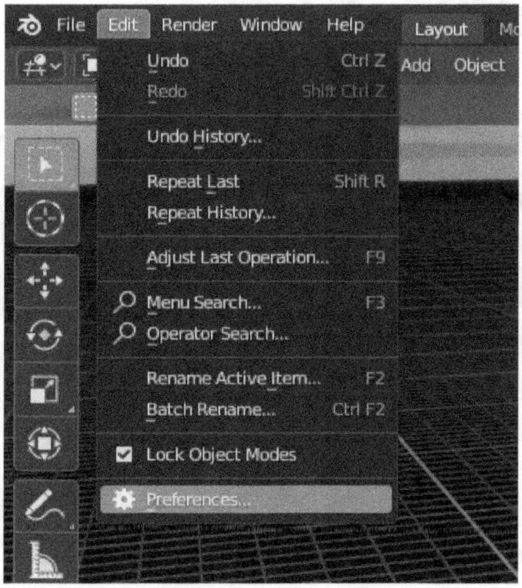

Figure 13.3: Opening the Preferences menu

3. Inside **Preferences**, navigate to the **Add-ons** menu.

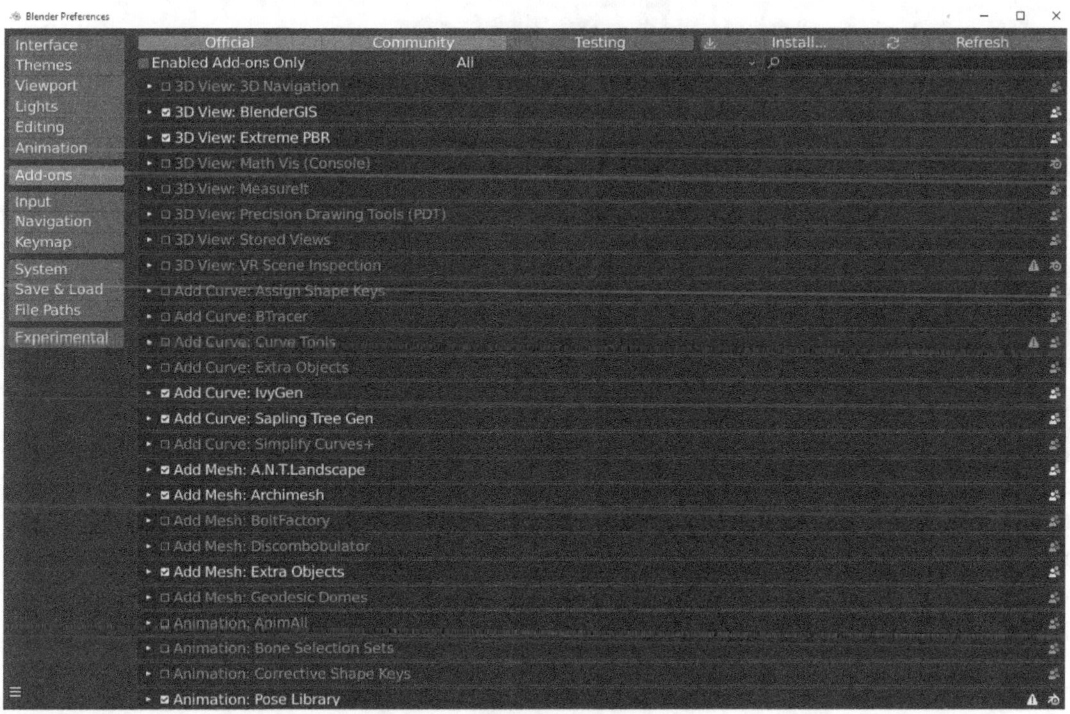

Figure 13.4: The Preferences menu

4. Click the **Install...** button in the top-right corner, next to **Refresh**.

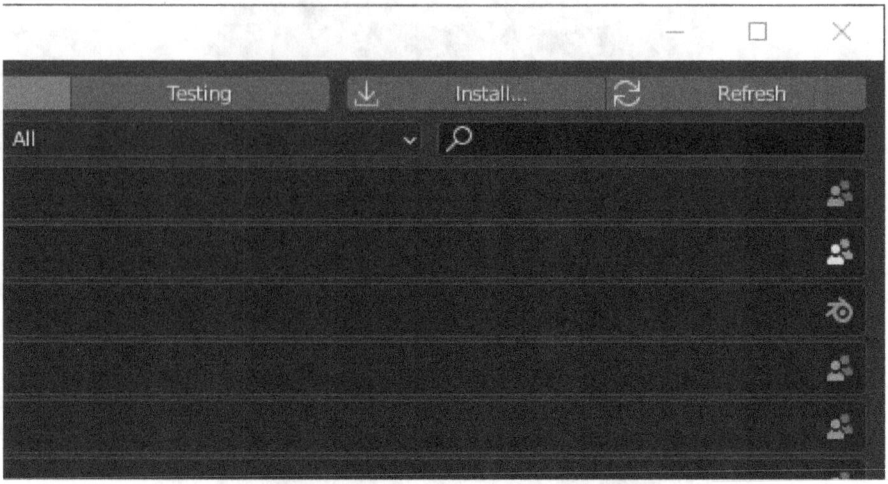

Figure 13.5: Install... button

5. This opens a file search window. Find the ZIP package you downloaded and click **Install** add-on.

   Your add-on should be ready to use!

Now let's talk about all the best add-ons out there that will make your time with Blender pain-free and smooth.

Free

Free add-ons can sometimes be almost as useful as paid add-ons. Try these add-ons that people have made available for free, so that users like you can get the most out of the Blender experience!

Node Wrangler

We talked about this one a lot in *Chapter 2, Creating Materials Fast with EEVEE*. This add-on comes free with Blender and allows you to use shortcuts to more efficiently preview materials. While simple, this add-on has saved me probably 20 hours of work at this point, just because of how useful those simple shortcuts are. Get familiar with Node Wrangler and you will save yourself so much time and avoid the headache of trying to work with **Materials** nodes.

Images as Planes

We used this in *Chapter 8*, *Using Alphas for Details*, as a method of adding bird alphas to the scene. This add-on comes free with Blender and can be used as a method of creating flowers from pictures of flowers, cutouts of landscapes to stage in the background of scenes, and more. It is incredibly versatile and I would recommend you use it as often as you find yourself needing transparent backgrounds.

IvyGen

IvyGen also comes free with Blender. It's an incredibly focused tool, in that it only does one thing: create ivy. But it does that one thing very well. It allows you to grow vines over any object and then add leaves to the vines to create ivy in a simple, straightforward way.

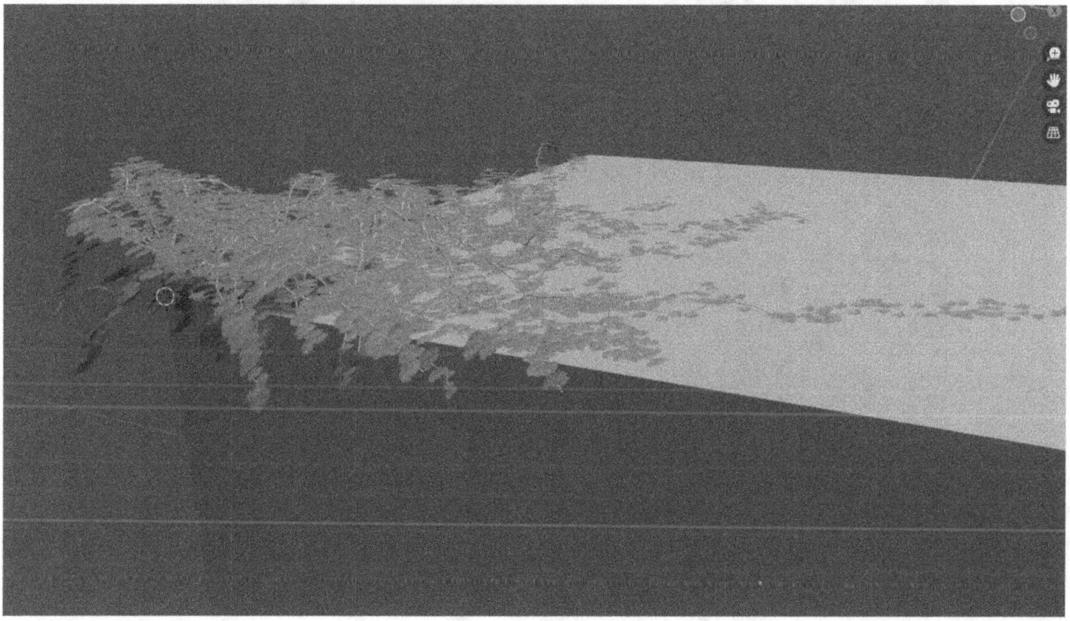

Figure 13.6: IvyGen

Rigify

Rigify is a free add-on that facilitates adding an **armature** to a character, a process that is called **rigging**. This armature is a series of controls that can be used to move a character in a lifelike way. Rigging can be very difficult, so using this add-on can be a lifesaver when creating both human and animal characters.

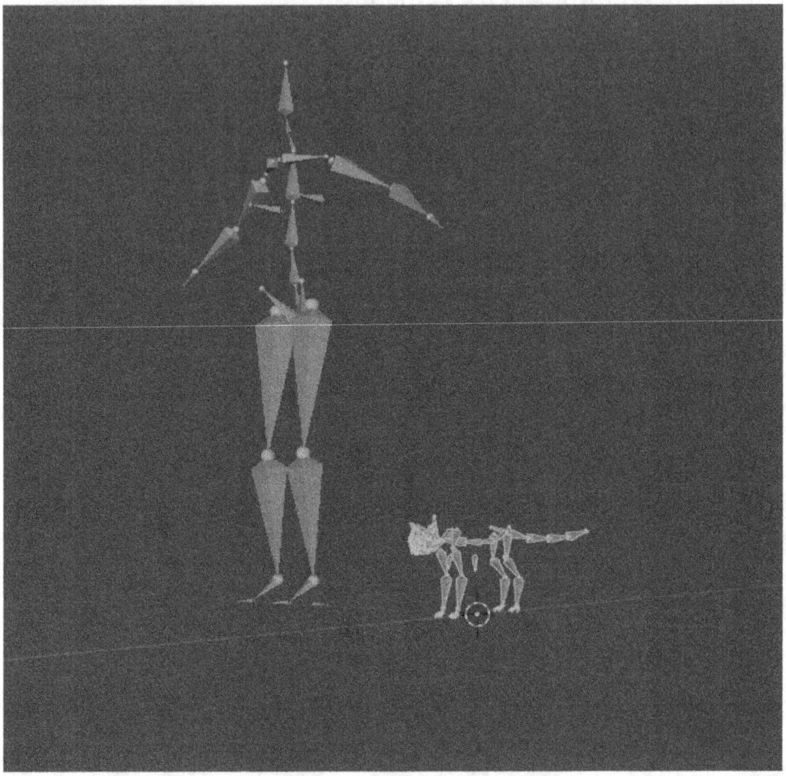

Figure 13.7: The Rigify add-on

BlenderGIS

This add-on does not come already installed in Blender. You can find the latest build of this add-on at GitHub: `https://github.com/domlysz/BlenderGIS`. *BlenderGIS* imports satellite images into Blender with a few clicks. It can be extremely useful as a base to start a landscape scene. You can also import building vectors and other data, so you can quickly create cities or towns based on real data.

A.N.T. Landscape Generator

In a similar vein to BlenderGIS, A.N.T. Landscape Generator creates landscapes based on procedural noise displacement. While you don't get real data from this add-on, it can be good to create custom landscapes quickly. It comes with a long list of default terrains that you can use to quickly populate a mountain range, lake, or any landscape on earth.

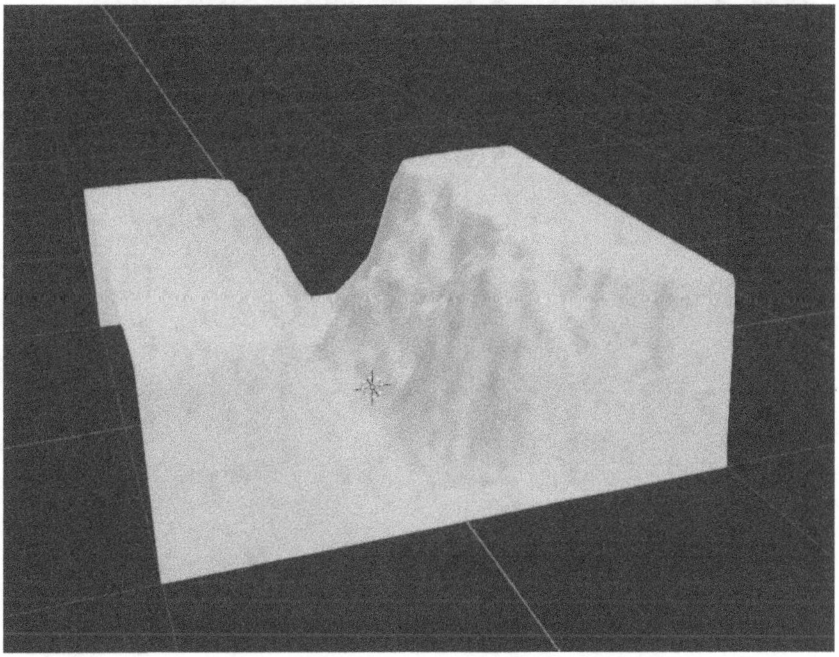

Figure 13.8: A.N.T Landscape

Paid

The number-one place to buy add-ons is *BlenderMarket* (`https://blendermarket.com/`). They have a great range of add-ons that have been developed just for Blender, and as an added bonus, some add-ons that you purchase give money directly to the Blender Development Fund. This means that you can support future Blender development while making your own life easier.

Botaniq

Botaniq is a really cool vegetation library that I have been using for years now. Instead of spending hours of time creating different grasses, plants, and trees, I found it a huge saving of time to just buy a library of all the vegetation I could ever need. The add-on allows you to select plants by season and type and then spawn them directly into the file. This takes several hours of work and condenses it down to 30 seconds. There are several other vegetation packs available on BlenderMarket. Graswald is another excellent vegetation add-on, along with many others.

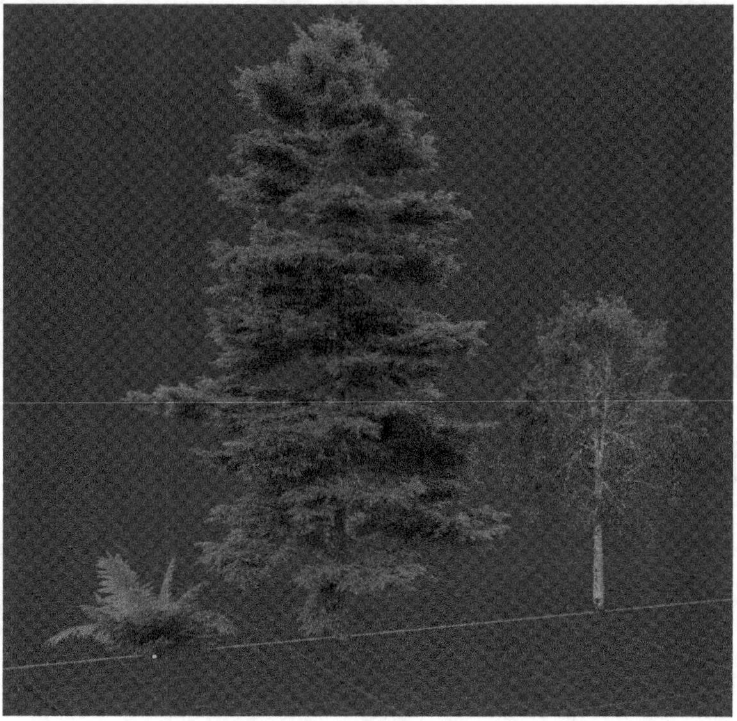

Figure 13.9: Botaniq vegetation add-on

Retopoflow

Retopoflow is the best add-on (at the time of writing) for **retopologizing** meshes. When sculpting, it makes more sense to disregard the topology of the mesh while you're dealing with more artistic details, but to rig and animate a sculpt, you need to redo the mesh of the object to give yourself a regular topology so the rig will work correctly. To redo this mesh or retopologize by hand would take a long and painstaking amount of time. Retopoflow gives you the tools to speed up the retopologizing process and get you to the rigging and animation stage faster.

BoxCutter

BoxCutter is a fantastic little add-on that speeds up **hard-surface modeling**. If you want to be designing robots or other mechanical objects, BoxCutter is a must-have. It can be quite complicated and relies heavily on shortcuts, so there is a little bit of a learning curve.

Physical Starlight and Atmosphere

Physical Starlight and Atmosphere is an add-on that directly simulates a real outdoor environment; no HDRIs are needed. This can speed up the time it takes for you to create environments or landscapes. There are a number of controls that allow you to set the time of day, the brightness of the stars, and the size of the sun. And, best of all, you can create cool binary sunsets.

Figure 13.10: Binary sunset in Physical Starlight and Atmosphere

Extreme PBR

Extreme PBR is a real time saver. It stores over 2,000 materials within it, also making it easy to find those materials and then add them to whatever object you wish. It really is that easy and the materials are great! Sometimes, creating materials for a scene with hundreds or thousands of objects can be really daunting, but Extreme PBR saves a ton of time by giving you the materials already made. There are many other material add-ons, such as Materialiq, Definitely EEVEE Material System, and many, many others. And, of course, if you're willing to spend the time on making your own Material Library, you can easily replicate what each of these assets is offering with the Asset Browser. But setting up a library can take a lot of time and just depends on your own process.

Other free sites to use

There is a myriad of free assets available to work with online. It can be difficult enough to learn Blender without feeling like you have the resources to make truly imaginative works, so here is a short list of places to start looking at free assets, or to get feedback on your work:

- `https://polyhaven.com` has free textures, HDRIs, and models to use.
- `https://ambientcg.com` is a great place to source free textures.
- `https://freepbr.com/` has a lot of high-quality free PBR textures.
- `Blendernation.com` has a lot of great tutorials and news to do with Blender.
- `https://blenderartists.org/` has message boards where you can ask for critique and advice.
- `Artstation.com` is more for the wider CG community, instead of just Blender-focused, but it's a great place to ask for critique and ways to improve your art.

Further projects to tackle

I know that sometimes it can be daunting to open Blender, look at the blank file with only the default cube, and be completely overwhelmed by the possibilities of what could be accomplished. That's why I thought I would end this chapter with a section on further projects you could tackle, now that you have mastered EEVEE. If none of these appeal to you, don't worry, I find going on `Artstation.com` or searching the `#b3d` Twitter hashtag to be an endless source of inspiration, so go out and figure out what you'd like to do.

Environments

Environments are really great to practice lighting and trying to create the illusion of randomness. As humans, we don't really do "random" very well, but nature is exceptionally random! Try creating environments with a variety of trees, rocks, leaves, and water; creating a truly random environment can be really difficult and full of surprises. I would recommend that you always include a focal point, something that the audience will look at first, such as a castle, a character, or an animal. Close-up environments can especially be a really good test of your ability to create, so try something using techniques that stretch yourself beyond this book.

Characters

We didn't cover characters at all in this book. Characters do require some modeling, but creating a character and then creating materials, lighting, and rendering can be a great way to learn more about how to light a scene and create believable materials. We didn't cover subsurface scattering in this book, but looking deeper into creating people and other mythical creatures is a great way to do small projects that have a big impact on your skills.

Grease Pencil

The Grease Pencil is a wonderful tool to create fantastic illustrations. I would recommend anyone who likes to draw to find an illustration from your favorite children's book and try to recreate it in 3D with **Grease Pencil**. You'll gain a lot of understanding of perspective, camera placement, and more.

Studies

The cornerstone of any art practice is the study. A study is where you spend time studying an object or group of objects in preparation for a more refined piece later. This is kind of a chance to practice specific pieces of your skill set in preparation for a larger work. If you're planning on working on a huge piece that involves a lot of animal hair, try doing a smaller piece where the focus is on the hair so you can really nail down how to create the look and style you're hoping to recreate.

Summary

In this chapter, we went through a review of previous concepts, hoping to cement them in your mind. We then talked about how to further hone your skills in specific areas that this book touched on, and then talked about some of the amazing add-ons that can increase the speed of your workflow. Then, we talked about further projects you could tackle, in the hopes that you are inspired to continue on the road to Blender mastery. I hope that you really enjoyed the journey through EEVEE that we have undertaken together. I started this book with the intention of teaching you about EEVEE, but also about new aspects of Blender 3.0 that will increase your ability to create. When you think about it, what is important is the end result, not the tool you use, but I do hope that you now consider EEVEE to be a formidable tool in your toolbelt. Blender will never cease to amaze me and I hope that you are similarly excited about the present and future of Blender. If you have a few dollars, please give them to the Blender Foundation, so that they can continue to do the fantastic work they do!

Index

A

B

C

D

E

F

G

H

I

K

L

M

N

O

P

Q

R

S

T

V

W

Other Books You May Enjoy

If you enjoyed this book, you may be interested in these other books by Packt:

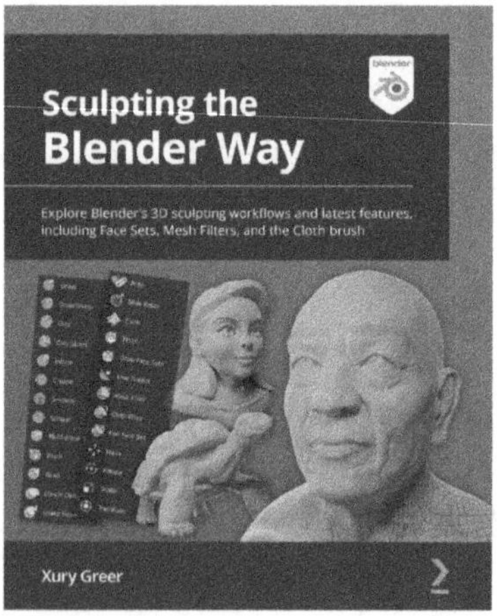

Sculpting the Blender Way

Xury Greer

ISBN: 978-1-80107-387-5

- Configure your graphics tablet for use in 3D sculpting
- Set up Blender's user interface for sculpting
- Understand the core sculpting workflows
- Get the hang of using Blender's basic sculpting brushes
- Customize brushes for more advanced workflows
- Explore high-resolution details with brush alphas and Multiresolution
- Try out the all-new Cloth brush
- Render your finished artwork for your portfolio

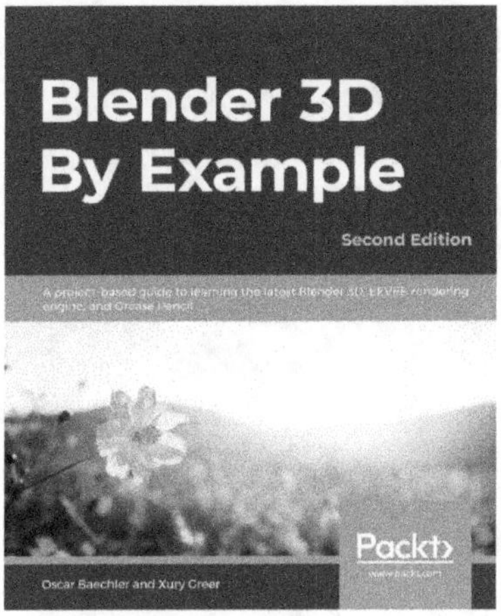

Blender 3D By Example – Second Edition

Oscar Baechler, Xury Greer

ISBN: 978-1-78961-256-1

- Explore core 3D modeling tools in Blender such as extrude, bevel, and loop cut
- Understand Blender's Outliner hierarchy, collections, and modifiers
- Find solutions to common problems in modeling 3D characters and designs
- Implement lighting and probes to liven up an architectural scene using EEVEE
- Produce a final rendered image complete with lighting and post-processing effects
- Learn character concept art workflows and how to use the basics of Grease Pencil
- Learn how to use Blender's built-in texture painting tools

Packt is searching for authors like you

Hi!

I am Sammie Crowder, author of *Shading, Lighting, and Rendering with Blender's EEVEE.* I really hope you enjoyed reading this book and found it useful for increasing your productivity and efficiency in Blender.

It would really help me (and other potential readers!) if you could leave a review on Amazon sharing your thoughts on *Shading, Lighting, and Rendering with Blender's EEVEE.*

Go to the link below or scan the QR code to leave your review:

`https://packt.link/r/1803230967`

Your review will help me to understand what's worked well in this book, and what could be improved upon for future editions, so it really is appreciated.

Best Wishes,

Sammie Crowder

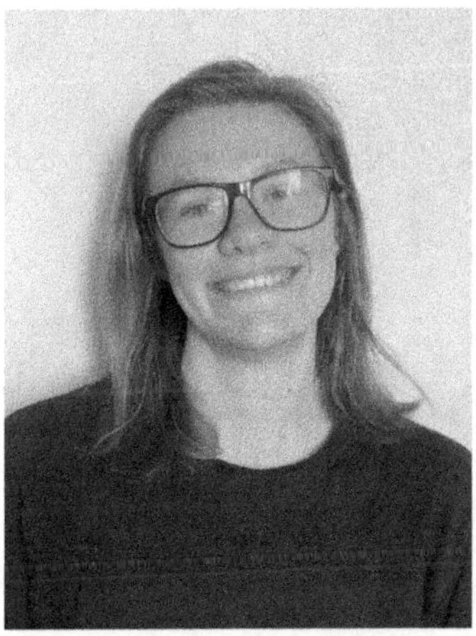

www.ingramcontent.com/pod-product-compliance
Lightning Source LLC
LaVergne TN
LVHW080017210926
848481LV00011B/3047
* 9 7 8 1 8 0 3 2 3 0 9 6 2 *